**Studia Fennica**
Historica 23

The Finnish Literature Society (SKS) was founded in 1831 and has, from the very beginning, engaged in publishing operations. It nowadays publishes literature in the fields of ethnology and folkloristics, linguistics, literary research and cultural history.

The first volume of the Studia Fennica series appeared in 1933. Since 1992, the series has been divided into three thematic subseries: Ethnologica, Folkloristica and Linguistica. Two additional subseries were formed in 2002, Historica and Litteraria. The subseries Anthropologica was formed in 2007.

In addition to its publishing activities, the Finnish Literature Society maintains research activities and infrastructures, an archive containing folklore and literary collections, a research library and promotes Finnish literature abroad.

Studia Fennica Editorial Board

Editors-in-chief
Pasi Ihalainen, Professor, University of Jyväskylä, Finland
Timo Kallinen, University Lecturer, University of Helsinki, Finland
Taru Nordlund, Professor, University of Helsinki, Finland
Riikka Rossi, Title of Docent, University Researcher, University of Helsinki, Finland
Katriina Siivonen, Title of Docent, University Teacher, University of Turku, Finland
Lotte Tarkka, Professor, University of Helsinki, Finland

Deputy editors-in-chief
Anne Heimo, Title of Docent, University of Turku, Finland
Saija Isomaa, Professor, University of Tampere, Finland
Sari Katajala-Peltomaa, Title of Docent, Researcher, University of Tampere, Finland
Eerika Koskinen-Koivisto, Postdoctoral Researcher, Dr. Phil., University of Helsinki, Finland
Laura Visapää, Title of Docent, University Lecturer, University of Helsinki, Finland

Tuomas M. S. Lehtonen, Secretary General, Dr. Phil., Finnish Literature Society, Finland
Tero Norkola, Publishing Director, Finnish Literature Society, Finland
Virve Mertanen, Secretary of the Board, Finnish Literature Society, Finland

oa.finlit.fi

Editorial Office
SKS
P.O. Box 259
FI-00171 Helsinki
www.finlit.fi

# Personal Agency
at the Swedish Age of
Greatness 1560–1720

Edited by Petri Karonen and Marko Hakanen

Finnish Literature Society • SKS • Helsinki • 2017

**STUDIA FENNICA HISTORICA 23**

The publication has undergone a peer review.

VERTAISARVIOITU
KOLLEGIALT GRANSKAD
PEER-REVIEWED
www.tsv.fi/tunnus

The open access publication of this volume has received part funding via a Jane and Aatos Erkko Foundation grant.

© 2017 Petri Karonen, Marko Hakanen and SKS
License CC-BY-NC-ND 4.0 International

A digital edition of a printed book first published in 2017 by the Finnish Literature Society.
Cover Design: Timo Numminen
EPUB: Tero Salmén

ISBN 978-952-222-882-6 (Print)
ISBN 978-952-222-954-0 (PDF)
ISBN 978-952-222-953-3 (EPUB)

ISSN 0085-6835 (Studia Fennica)
ISSN 1458-526X (Studia Fennica Historica)

DOI: http://dx.doi.org/10.21435/sfh.23

This work is licensed under a Creative Commons CC-BY-NC-ND 4.0 International License.
To view a copy of the license, please visit http://creativecommons.org/licenses/by-nc-nd/4.0/

 A free open access version of the book is available at http://dx.doi.org/10.21435/sfh.23 or by scanning this QR code with your mobile device.

BoD – Books on Demand, Norderstedt, Germany 2017

# Contents

Acknowledgements 7

Chronology of Swedish History 8

## I Approaches and Perspectives

PETRI KARONEN & MARKO HAKANEN
Personal Agency and State Building in Sweden (1560–1720) 13

## II Councillors of the Realm

MARKO HAKANEN & ULLA KOSKINEN
The Gentle Art of Counselling Monarchs (1560–1655) 47

## III Royal Secretaries

MARKO HAKANEN & ULLA KOSKINEN
Secretaries as Agents in the Middle of Power Structures (1560–1680) 83

## IV Governors

MIRKKA LAPPALAINEN
Loyal Servants of the King and the Crown (1620–1680): Stewards and Governors in Sweden before the Age of Absolutism 113

## V Judges

OLLI MATIKAINEN
Judges, Law-Readers and Malpractice (1560–1680) 143

## VI Bailiffs

Janne Haikari
The Bailiff: Between a Rock and a Hard Place (1600–1690)? 165

## VII Clergy

Mikko Hiljanen
Servants of the Crown or Trustees of the People? Personal Agency Among the Local Clergy (1550–1610) 193

## VIII Royal Mayors

Petri Karonen
Royal Mayors (1620–1700): The Bane of the Burghers, the Crown's Scourge, Effective Developers of Urban Government? 219

## IX Burgomasters

Piia Einonen
Burgomasters of Stockholm as Agents of the Crown and Self-Interest (1590–1640) 247

## X Students

Kustaa H. J. Vilkuna
Study Abroad, The State and Personal Agency (1640–1700) 275

List of Contributors 297

Abstract 298

Index of Names 299

Index of Subjects 303

# Acknowledgements

The origin of this volume lies in the discussions inside the research project *"Personal Agency in the Age of State Building, Sweden c. 1550–1650"*, funded by the Academy of Finland (2011–2015). The aim of the project was to provide fresh insight into the state building process in Sweden in the transitional period c. 1550–1650. During those years, many far-reaching administrative reforms were carried out, and the Swedish state developed into a prime example of the early modern "power-state". The project approached state building in early modern Sweden from the point of view of personal agency. This has long remained in the shadow of the study of structures and institutions. We believe that with this novel approach we will shed light on numerous important questions about the nature of administration and the possibilities of state formation. The emphasis on individuals also corresponds well with the the sixteenth-century reality. The powerful, all-pervasive centrally controlled structures that characterized the Swedish power state of the following century were simply not a reality in the sixteenth century. This anthology is result of those many fruitful discussions attached to the project, but also all the colleagues who were part of the projects network and those who participated the international *Agency and State Building in the 16th and 17th centuries* Conference held at University of Jyväskylä in November 2013. The editors wish to thank all the contributors for their insightful chapters, but also the diligence and forgiveness they have expressed during this long writing and editing process. It has been great privilege to work with all of you. The assembling this collected volume has also required linguistic support and we warmly thank all involved parties. The Finnish Literature Society deserves our acknowledgements for the easy and engaging cooperation. Finally, the editors would like to thank the anonymous evaluators whose remarks and suggestions have been very valuable.

# Chronology of Swedish History

1397 Kalmar Union was established
1442 The Country Law of Christopher
1477 Uppsala University founded
1520 Stockholm Bloodbath
1521 Gustavus Vasa to the Protector of the Realm (*Riksföreståndare*)
1523 Gustavus Vasa declared as the King of Sweden (to 1560)
1523 Sweden's declaration of independence from Kalmar Union
1527 The Diet at Västerås opened the door to the Reformation
1527 The church comes under the authority of monarchy
1542 Dacke War (uprising) (to 1543)
1544 Hereditary kingship
1554 Russo-Swedish War (to 1557)
1557 Treaty of Novgorod
1560 Eric XIV of Sweden (to 1568)
1561 Eric XIV introduce new noble titles: Count (*Greve*) and Baron (*Friherre*)
1563 Northern Seven Years' War (to 1570)
1567 Sture murders
1568 John III of Sweden (to 1592)
1569 The nobility becomes hereditary
1570 Treaty of Stettin
1571 The Church Ordinance (*Kyrkoording*) confirms Protestant organization
1592 Sigismund of Poland as King of Sweden (to 1599, dethroned)
1592 Duke Charles to the protector of the Realm (to 1604)
1595 Treaty of Teusina
1596 Cudgel War (uprising) (to 1597)
1597 Duke Charles rebels against the King
1599 King Sigismund is declared deposed
1600 Polish War (to 1629)
1607 Charles IX (to 1611)
1610 Ingrian War (to 1617)
1611 Gustavus Adolphus (to 1632) gives a charter of guarantees

|  |  |
|---|---|
| 1612 | Axel Oxenstierna appointed as Lord High Chancellor of Sweden (*rikskanslern*) (to 1654) |
| 1611 | All of the high posts in civil administration guaranteed to the nobility by privileges |
| 1614 | The Svea Court of Appeal (*Svea hovrätt*) founded |
| 1617 | Treaty of Stolbovo |
| 1617 | Swedish Diet Act (*riksdagsordningen*) was given to regulate the Diet (the Riksdag) |
| 1618 | Thirty Years' War (to 1648) |
| 1623 | The Turku Court of Appeal (Åbo *hovrätt*) founded |
| 1626 | The House of Nobility ordinance |
| 1629 | Armistice of Altmark |
| 1632 | Gustavus Adolphus dies at battle of Lützen |
| 1632 | Regency (*Förmyndarregering*) (to 1644) |
| 1634 | The Instrument of Government, The Göta Court of Appeal (*Göta hovrätt*) founded |
| 1635 | The instruction for county governors (*Landshövdingeinstruktionen*) |
| 1640 | Academy of Turku is founded |
| 1644 | Christina of Sweden is proclaimed of age on her 18th birthday and becomes Queen of Sweden |
| 1648 | Peace of Westphalia |
| 1654 | Queen Christina abdicate the throne |
| 1654 | Charles X Gustav (to 1660) |
| 1655 | Second Northern War (to 1661) |
| 1658 | Treaty of Roskilde |
| 1660 | Treaty of Oliva |
| 1660 | Treaty of Copenhagen |
| 1660 | Regency (*Förmyndarregering*) (to 1672) |
| 1661 | Treaty of Kardis |
| 1668 | Riksbank, first national bank in the world |
| 1672 | Charles XI (to 1697) is declared of age |
| 1674 | Scanian War (to 1679) |
| 1680 | The Great Reduction |
| 1681 | The Council of the Realm (*Riksrådet*) becomes Royal Council (*Kungligt råd*) |
| 1696 | The Great Famine in Finland, Norrland and in the Baltic Region |
| 1697 | Charles XII (to 1718) declared of age |
| 1700 | The Great Northern War (to 1721) |
| 1709 | Swedish army is defeated in Poltava |
| 1720 | Treaty of Frederiksborg |
| 1721 | Treaty of Nystad |

# Approaches and Perspectives I

Petri Karonen
ⓘ http://orcid.org/0000-0001-6090-5504

Marko Hakanen
ⓘ http://orcid.org/0000-0002-4214-960X

# Personal Agency and State Building in Sweden (1560–1720)

*Structures, institutions and personal agency*

Who took care of the civil administration and ecclesiastical tasks in the kingdom of Sweden in the sixteenth and seventeenth centuries? What kind of agency they performed in their official duties? What was the significance of the personal agency of officials in their usually unrewarding position between the government and local communities? In this book, early modern state building in Sweden is studied particularly from the point of view of personal agency and collective biography. This brings a new personal level to the much debated state building process, which has so far been mainly studied from a structural perspective. Macro-level studies have forgotten the practical significance of persons as agents, a factor which offers the opportunity to see the sixteenth- and seventeenth-century reality from a new point of view.

In this period, the realm of Sweden saw significant progress in various areas of social activity. The major reason for this was simply the demands of wartime, which had forced the country into developing its activities. Practically speaking, Sweden was on a continuous war footing from 1560 to 1721, which in a country with poor resources and a small population caused a significant need for development. The whole of Swedish society had been harnessed to support the preparation for war and engagement in it and to a lesser extent the transition from war to peace. War, together with its after- and side-effects, was a significant factor in the formation of society and political life right up to the mid-eighteenth century.

Our study deals with an era when centralized states of a new kind began to emerge in Europe. Internationally, the case of early modern Sweden is especially interesting as the state building process at the beginning of the seventeenth century transformed a locally dispersed and sparsely populated area into a strongly centralized absolute monarchy that possessed an overseas empire in Europe.[1] The Swedish state building process began in the sixteenth century, although the major structural changes were not implemented until the next century. The administrative system was mostly in place by the beginning of eighteenth century, when Sweden's position as a great European power collapsed as a result of the Great Northern War (1700–1721).

From the point of view of state building, the sixteenth century was indeed chronologically a long one, and consequently the studies in this collection analyze the so-called "long great power period", which in the case of this work embraces approximately the years 1560–1721. Many of the events connected with the development of Sweden's external position took place in this period, but most importantly it was then that the central organizations and their individual actors that were crucial for the development of the state assumed their forms and functionalities. Concomitantly, many far-reaching administrative reforms were carried out during those years, and the Swedish state developed into a prime example of the early modern "power-state". The time period chosen here does not follow the usual timelines, which have generally emphasized the sovereignty of the Swedish Crown and Gustavus Vasa's (1496–1560) rise to power in the 1520s.[2]

The chosen period does not, however, undermine the important steps taken by Gustavus Vasa. Among other things, he recruited several experts from Germany who were crucial in the formation period of the administration in the 1530s. However, radical changes were not implemented until after 1560, which is also the starting point for this study. Thorough-going reforms in central and local government, state finances, the Church and everyday life likewise took place only in the latter half of the sixteenth century. This era of change continued into the seventeenth century.

This book's emphasis on individuals also corresponds well with the early modern reality. The powerful, all-pervasive centrally controlled structures that characterized the Swedish power state of the following century simply did not exist in the sixteenth century. The administration of the state lay in the execution of various tasks that the king delegated to his followers, and the most important posts, such as the lordship of castles and the government of territories were reserved for members of the nobility.

During its time as a great power, Sweden was internally relatively peaceful, which gave it a competitive advantage over its neighbors with their greater resources. It was important for the unity of the Swedish realm that the position of the monarch was strong and that there were only a few truly powerful noble families in the country. Thus the ruler was able control the activities of the nobles and to regulate the successful development of the small towns by granting special rights (privileges). Noble privileges were important for many of those groups of office-holders who occupy a central place in this volume. Common (non-noble) servants of the Crown also received strong backing for their activities through authorizations and directions issued by the ruler, although no group could base its actions on such normative texts alone.

Significant changes took place in the administrative system of the Swedish realm during the period studied in this work. Figure 1 shows the main features of these organizational changes: local and intermediary administration was mainly developed in the sixteenth century, while in the first decades of the seventeenth century the focus shifted to reinforcing the central administration.[3] The centralized system was also preserved in the period known as the Age of Liberty (1718–1772) that followed the Age of Absolutism (1680–1718), although in practice the focus of power and political activity shifted significantly to the ruling estates and the Diet (which was composed of the representatives of the four estates: the Nobles, the Clergy, the Burghers and the Peasants). Even so, the organizations and practices in the central administration that had prevailed in the Age of Absolutism survived in the Age of Liberty. An illustrative example with regard to the distribution of resources is the Office of State (*Statskontoret*), which from the very outset was a monocratic agency, i.e. one in which the decisions were made by one state official. Previously the collegial system of governance had been adhered to according to the principle that no-one should be able to take decisions alone.[4]

In the latter half of the sixteenth century and the early decades of the seventeenth, an administrative organization that worked well considering the conditions of the time was created in the capital, Stockholm. It was based on a system of collegiums (central agencies). The system was specifically designed to operate in wartime and to serve the needs of war. Sweden was forced by the continual wars to transform itself into a new kind of state, one that could exploit its scarce material resources. In practice, the state extended its strict control throughout the whole of society. This intensification of administration and control considerably increased the number of offices and administrative units. A concentrated, relatively simple and clear structure ensured what was for the period an effective communication of information and orders from the summit of government down to the remote regions and back. Taken as a whole, the system was in its time the most efficient in Europe. Later the Swedish model was copied in both Denmark and Russia. In the mid-seventeenth century there were about 700 civil service posts (including those of officials serving in castles), while around 1730 the number of posts was about one thousand.[5]

The reorganization of the position of the Church had occupied a central position in the foundations of Gustavus Vasa's state structure. In Sweden, the ecclesiastical administration had been established according to the Roman Catholic model as an independent concentration of power that enjoyed special rights in the secular sphere as well: for example, the bishops held a strong position in the Council of the Realm (*Riksrådet*). The heavy debts of the Swedish Crown and the huge property of the Church enticed Gustavus Vasa first into reforming the organizational and economic structure of the Church and subsequently into extending these reforms into a full-scale reformation. The Diet of 1527 opened the door to the Reformation, and a large part of the Church's property was transferred to the Crown and the nobles who supported the King. The political power of the Church was crushed, and there was a swift shift to a Lutheran people's church with the King at its head. Naturally, ties with the Vatican were broken. The bishops were ejected from the Council of the Realm, which became mainly the seat of the King's noble advisers.[6]

In the period studied here, the bishops were appointed by the ruler. However, the bishops who were in charge of dioceses still possessed considerable power, for example in choosing their direct subordinates. The cathedral chapter (*consistorium ecclesiasticum*) was the highest administrative organ in the diocese and it possessed judicial power all in cases that came under the jurisdiction of the Church. In the early part of the period under investigation here, the cathedral chapters were for the most part mainly stooges of the bishops, but the situation changed before the mid-seventeenth century, when the collegial system that prevailed in the state administration was adopted by the Church as well. The cathedral chapters had considerable power in the appointment of clergymen for the parishes, especially if the diocese was a consistorial one, when the choice of a clergyman was jointly made by the chapter and the parishioners. In patronage parishes, on the other hand, the appointment was entrusted to a leading local noble, and in royal parishes to the ruler alone. In any case, the Church continued, despite the Reformation, to hold a significant position in the local community and also to wield some administrative and judicial power.[7]

In the short run, the Reformation weakened the educational system, which had been administered by the Church, but by the seventeenth century it had become necessary to develop education at all levels and to provide resources for it. The ever-expanding realm, the continuous warring, the growing bureaucratic machinery and the concomitantly intensifying control at all levels of society required a constant supply of educated new clergymen to communicate the official message and political education of the Crown to all subjects in every corner of the realm. The pressure gradually pushed the educational system throughout the country into reform and expansion with the aim of producing professional officials in both ecclesiastical and secular administration.

In Sweden and Finland, we cannot speak of the profession of civil servant until the nineteenth century, when the criteria pertaining to the qualifications for a civil servant were defined.[8] Even so, many of the groups and persons studied in this work are called civil servants, functionaries or officials because the functions and limits of their work were defined in official guidelines.[9]

The administrative changes that began in earnest in Sweden in the early seventeenth century meant an increase in bureaucracy and a change in the position of functionaries. Their activities started to be governed by official rules, and attention began to be paid to their qualifications. However, through the awarding of privileges accorded to the nobility, the highest posts passed over to that estate, whose members had previously sought above all to pursue a military career. Thus in 1569 John III (1537–1592) awarded considerable advantages to the higher nobility in particular, but at the same time the members of this estate were required not only to engage in military service but also to take a greater part in administration both in the royal court and in the provinces. Subsequently, in 1611, 1612 and 1617, Gustavus Adolphus (1594–1632) promised that all the "high posts" (*höga ämbeten*) would remain in the hands of the nobility and that many other duties should also preferably (*hälst af*) be entrusted to nobles. The Instrument of Government 1634 (*regeringsform*), which was of central importance in the administrative reorganization of the realm, marked off a large number of posts in central and local government and in the judiciary for members of the nobility, although there are very few direct mentions of this in this important document.[10]

Appointments to official posts were linked to expertise and education, although the reality was to some extent different as a result of clientage networks. The higher estates kept a strong hold over the hubs of power, and thanks to the status they enjoyed the civil service professions continued to maintain close contact with the ruling class. However, the privileges that went with official posts were no longer the sole preserve of a single estate, but were now rather reserved within the family and the clan.[11]

In terms of numbers, there might have been enough members of the nobility to man the civil service, but the army took the vast majority of the potential candidates, and for the rest of the available nobles a general inability to handle the posts was an impediment. As the administrative machinery swelled, the situation soon became difficult.[12] The development and growth of university education took place alongside the increase in the number of official posts, and the ruler was forced to elevate university-educated lower functionaries with ecclesiastical or bourgeois backgrounds to the nobility so that higher posts in central and local government might be open to them.[13]

The increased significance of education did not, however, lead directly to the creation of a civil service profession, in which expertise gained through education constituted the qualification for functioning as an office-holder. Formal competence requirements only became common in the Nordic countries, and indeed elsewhere, from the eighteenth century on.[14] The application of merits as a qualification for official posts was to some extent impossible in the seventeenth century because no criteria for the necessary competences had been established. The regulations mainly concerned times and ways of working. For example, the qualifications for lawyers working in the courts of appeal did not require a university education. All in all, then, suitably trained men were needed for many judicial and administrative posts and for the collection and registration of taxes: indeed, in many cases, sound experience alone was qualification enough.[15]

## Interaction, conflict and agency

State building has been studied from numerous points of view in both the European and the Swedish contexts. The traditional approach, concentrating on the actions of kings and other rulers, has broadened to encompass conditions at the local level, which largely determined the extent of the central government's power. The relationship between kings and their subjects has been described as a form of bargaining. Depending on the point of view adopted, researchers have emphasized either the "top-down" model, represented, in the Swedish context, in a strong-power state in the seventeenth century, or the "bottom-up" model, in which the subjects are the decisive factor behind all state organization.[16]

In an agrarian state like Sweden, the Crown had to have an efficient machinery of taxation and control in order to carry out its ambitious plans. In many states, like the Dutch Republic, with a largely monetary economy, funds could be collected through quickly improvised temporary arrangements, but this was not possible in Sweden. According to Charles Tilly, war and preparation for it were in a key position in the actual process of state building. He asserts that states that based their activities mainly on coercion and the use of armed force had to create massive administrative machineries in order to efficiently gather the taxes and men needed to wage war. Such states were, according to Tilly, often agrarian and little urbanized. At the general level, this categorization would seem to describe Sweden in the era studied here, although the typology is too strict. Sweden at that time certainly lacked capital, the cities were weak, the land was centrally governed and Swedish society was militarized. Even so, it is difficult to regard the state of Sweden as being based on "coercion" since there was also an undeniable need for negotiation and compromise. The chapters in this volume for their part bring new perspectives on these phenomena and processes.[17]

From the 1970s on, there has been extensive discussion on the nature of the relationship of subordination between the rulers (élites) and the ruled in the Nordic countries during the early modern period. Put simply, the interpretations are mainly divided between the "interaction model" and the "military state model": the former approach stresses the importance of negotiation and interaction, while the latter underlines coercion and a general focus on the military sphere. However, both of these major characteristics were present in Swedish society during the early modern period, and consequently the 'truth' lies somewhere between these two extremes. Since the beginning of the 21st century, intermediate views have also appeared, but research has not yet reached any final conclusion on this issue.[18]

In general, the ruler-ruled relationship seems to have been a quite viable one, especially during the Great Power period. For instance, there were few major violent conflicts in the Kingdom of Sweden during the period under investigation.[19] Most of the people were represented at the four-estate Diet, in whose meetings representatives of all the four estates in society from all corners of the realm participated and could decide on matters freely, at least in theory. The relationship between the Crown and the Diet was normally based exclusively either on positive interaction and negotiation or the imposition of the king's authority. In practice, the relationship was a combination of both and varied according to the circumstances. During the period of intense conquest (approx. 1600–1660), the rulers were constantly obliged to turn to the estates with requests to levy new taxes and draft new men into the army. It was during the heaviest periods of warfare that the interaction between the monarch, or a regency acting for him or her, and the people was most intense.

The role of individuals in state building has been mostly overlooked in previous research. A widely accepted idea is that the scope for action of the central power was circumscribed because it had to legitimate its power and integrate the subjects into the decision-making processes. The approaches taken by earlier research have not permitted a synthesis between agents and institutions. We believe that studying persons and their actions can reveal new mechanisms of the distribution of power in practice and the dynamics of networks of influence.[20]

The much discussed subject of state building needs new basic research at the micro-level that focuses on the concrete manifestations of the phenomenon. The broad outlines and structural development have already been well researched at the macro level especially with regard to political events and war history. The basic problem of the current picture is that state building is usually seen as an institutional process that develops inexorably, following its own internal logic. The role of persons at different levels of society in initiating and realizing the process of state building has largely remained uninvestigated.

The point of view of personal agency has long remained in the shadow of the study of structures and institutions. We believe that by adopting this novel perspective we can shed light on numerous important questions about the nature of administration and the conditions of state-formation. The emphasis on individuals also corresponds well with the sixteenth-century reality. The powerful, all-pervasive, centrally controlled structures that characterized the Swedish power state of the following century simply did not exist in the sixteenth century. Administration consisted in the execution of various tasks that the king delegated to his followers.

The concept "agency" has been widely used, especially in sociology, economics and political science,[21] and indeed it is the perspectives of sociology that are most closely akin to the approaches adopted in this volume. In sociology, the concept has a long history, going back to the studies of Max Weber.[22] Edgar Kiser has reviewed the varieties of agency theory in different disciplines and found that the approaches differ considerably. According to Kiser, "Agency theory is a general model of social relations involving the delegation of authority, and generally resulting in problems of control, which has been applied to a broad range of substantive contexts."[23]

However, even in sociology, there are differing conceptions of how "the relationship between 'the individual' and 'society', or 'social structure'" is to be seen and valued. For example, according to S. Barry Barnes, "The central problems of sociology are actually problems of collective agency." For Barnes, it is a question particularly of collective agency since his approach is an "anti-individualist" one,[24] Likewise, Stephan Fuchs is suspicious of personal agency "at least when it comes to explaining society and culture." However, he notes, clearly with justification, "Agency and structure, and micro/macro, are not opposite natural kinds but variations along a continuum." He also interestingly suggests: "As a variable, 'agency' increases when the numbers are small, the distance is short, the relations are intimate, and the observer takes an intentional stance [... while] 'structure' increases when the numbers get larger, the distance between observer and referent becomes longer, and the observer employs more mechanical and deterministic explanatory frames."[25]

Rational choice theory actually consists of a set of theories, some of which have been imported from economics. The governing principle of rational choice theory is utility maximization: an individual makes choices based on reasoning, weighing costs against benefits. This controversial theory has also been accused of over-simplifying human behavior.[26] Aware of the criticism, we use rational choice theory merely as a tool and in a modified form to emphasize the role of private agency in administrative structures. We take into account the fact that choices are culturally bound to values, ideals, norms and emotions, which causes humans often to act in a seemingly irrational way. "Rational" does not have to mean adherence to some traditional, often economically understood logic. What is important is that the theory regards human action as rational as opposed to random. Costs and benefits can vary from economic to symbolic or social. We use the theory as a hypothetical implement to evaluate the real choices that individuals made against the ideal, rational ones. In this way, we can analyze their actions at a deeper level and get fuller answers about the functioning of society.

We believe that, applied in a modified form to early modern history, rational choice theory can help conceptualize different forms of individual agency. Taking the basic concept of rational choice to a deeper level, rational reasoning can here include cultural factors like honor and life style as determined by status. The concept of rational choice provides a tool to analyze individual actions and, knowing the outcome, to estimate how successful they were. It helps us to understand the choices early modern individuals made and to analyze their reasons for making them. We also use this theory to create unity between our separate studies of biographies that highlight different aspects of the state-building process. We want to explore whether the theory can help to reveal patterns of individual agency: individuals in similar positions in similar situations make similar choices because the costs and benefits are similar. Agency theory in economics treats information as a commodity that can be purchased and exchanged. In this respect, it is analogous to the patron-client networks in the early modern period.[27]

"Agency" is one of the key concepts in this anthology, even when it is not directly mentioned, because when we analyze personal (conscious or unconscious) actions within the state-building process it is always a direct result of human actions, even when it is unintended. Agency connected to the "self" opens up people's decision making and actions to closer analysis, and through social interaction, intervention or influence it is possible to map out individual agency in the state building process. Moreover, when we combine personal agency with a collective approach dealing with particular groups, we can understand much better how the state structures were built.[28]

State building was a more diversified and personalized process than has previously been assumed. In the case of Sweden, the state formation process has often been presented as an ongoing evolution directed by the ruler and his closest counselors or institutions, However, numerous individuals – noblemen, office-holders, etc. – were also crucially important actors in the process, and the development itself was not a straightforward progression but fundamentally intertwined with the ability and activeness of these "lower-level" actors. Consequently, this research re-evaluates the process of state building by focusing on actors and individuals rather than macro-level institutions.

Our approach to state-building thus concentrates on individuals within structures. It could be best described as a "sideways" approach in contrast to the better known "top-down" and "bottom-up" models, without however forgetting the broader picture formed by the macro-level context. In addition, our approach makes it possible to study how personal power and institutional power were interwoven. Patron-client networks and informal relations within "public" institutions have so far received little attention in research dealing with Sweden.[29]

The structure of societies, especially in the field of state-building studies, has been a central theme in a number of scholarly fields like cultural anthropology, sociology and history. Most of the time, these studies have concentrated on the role of social structure in searching for the reasons behind human actions.[30] However, if we turned that order around, could we better understand how the individuals within the structures knowingly or unconsciously shape existing structures or create totally new ones? In other words, the question is: Should we devote more study to the agency of particular individuals or groups of professionals whose actions played a key role in the state-building process?[31] At that time, Swedish society was based on a strict system of estates, in which every person's formal rank was defined at birth. That, at least, is how the system should have functioned in theory, but since humans are social animals who are capable of achieving goals by cooperation,[32] purposive agents who have reasons for their activities and are able to elaborate discursively upon those reasons,[33] in reality the people of the time had ways of influencing their situation and could move between estates. Thus individuals clearly had the possibility to alter or influence their surroundings and the structures of society.

It is clear that if we want to understand the motives for human activities, we must also understand the context in which human action takes place. In social theory, the notions of action and structure presuppose one another, even though it is possible to study these different factors separately. From a functionalist point of view, social systems are reproductions of relations between actors and collectivities, organized in the form of regular social practices. These systems are structured, and the totality of systems of social interaction constitutes the structure of society. In these interactive social systems, an important role is played by social practices and the social actors who produce and reproduce the systems and who at same time know a great deal about the institutions and the practices that comprise them.[34]

In writing about the structure of society and the social systems within it, Anthony Giddens emphasizes the significance of tradition.[35] It is important to note that new systems are always linked to the past, particularly when social systems are changing. On the other hand, we cannot regard social systems as progressing in a linear manner through time and space. Much of the time, new systems simply adopt parts of older ones and adjust them to the new values and practices of contemporary society. For this reason, an examination of how people advanced their interests within the context of seventeenth-century institutions provides an unusually lucid window onto the ways in which individuals strategized and exercised their personal agency within networks that nonetheless arose within a fairly rigid social hierarchy.

Each of the writers in this volume has had to address the question of biographical research. In many studies it has been claimed that the position of structuralism has declined over the last few decades, generally after the end of the Cold War.[36] Barbara Caine has noted the advent of "a biographical turn" in international research around the year 2000. However, scholars have varied considerably in their views about the ability of biographies to provide more general information about the life and ways of thinking of particular periods.[37] From the end of the nineteenth century on, Finnish and Swedish researchers produced a wealth of biographies dealing with people of that period: rulers, officials, military commanders, members of the nobility, scholars, clergymen and even influential peasants. There is, therefore, a need to exploit this enormous repertory of available basic information in order to produce an overall picture based on modern methodological approaches.

Particularly in Sweden, numerous biographical works and historical studies dealing with individuals in this period have been published. At the beginning of 2014, the Swedish National Union Catalogue of Libraries (LIBRIS), which is the joint catalogue of Swedish academic and research libraries, contained nearly 750 biographical research works dealing with the period extending approximately from 1500 to 1799. At a rough estimate, only about five percent dealt with the sixteenth century, and less than a third with the seventeenth, while about two thirds concerned the eighteenth century.[38] In Finland, there were rather fewer biographical studies and historical works dealing with individuals in this period, but their distribution over the centuries is considerably more even.[39]

Thus the last few decades have seen a revaluation of biographical studies, especially in Sweden. One focus has been on the sixteenth- and seventeenth-century Swedish rulers, almost all of whom have been the subjects of new biographies: Gustavus Vasa, Eric XIV (1533–1577), John III, Charles IX (1550–1611), Gustavus Adolphus, Christina (1626–1689), Charles X Gustav (1622–1660) and Charles XI (1655–1697).[40] There have also been biographical studies of important individuals and their actions in history outside the royal families: Chancellor of the Kingdom of Sweden (*kanslern*) Axel Oxenstierna (1583–1654), Lord High Chancellor (*drots*) Per Brahe the elder (1520–1590) and Lord High Chancellor Per Brahe the younger (1602–1680). In addition to individual biographies, influential dynasties like the Creutz, Fleming, Kurck, Tawast and Tott families (and therefore individual members of these families) have been the subjects of biographical studies.[41]

Many of the afore-mentioned research works have been of a high quality in their own genre, but apart from those that were originally approved as doctoral dissertations, they almost all lack a proper scientific definition of research questions since most of them were written for the general public. Consequently, the observations made in them very rarely differ from previous findings, as their lack of precise source references and a failure to address the results of earlier research emphasize.[42] Moreover, only rarely have these studies moved outside the so-called ruling groups. That is one important justification why this work takes precisely groups below the top echelons of society as the object of its examination.[43]

There still remain a number of controversies concerning the role of individuals in our current picture of state-building. As Simone Lässig says, "The fundamental question of biographical research is thus [...] the individual *in* society;" and "... a good biography rises once again above the individual; it is neither structure nor agency, but always *both*."[44]

## Methods and source materials

Our researchers' varied methods, which include the use of public and private sources, mixed quantitative and qualitative approaches and a comprehensive comparative approach, make it possible to exploit sources that have formerly remained little utilized and also to re-interpret already used source material from a fresh point of view.

Our source material focuses in many ways on persons and their agency, but mostly it is not personal, nor does it deal with individuals as such. Sources like personal correspondence, diaries and personal accounts involve both the public and the private spheres, thus reflecting the reality in which their writers lived; the public and the private were inseparably intertwined and were not perceived as separate spheres of life. That is why our sources are very well suited to approaches that combine the two; in other words, sources that deal with the diverse aspects of personal agency within administrative structures.

The authors of the chapters in this volume exploit the "national biographies" that have been written and published by scholars ever since the latter half of the nineteenth century in practically all European countries. Barbara Caine considers these often extensive series dealing with "national heroes" to be collective biographies.[45] The concept 'collective biography' is often understood very broadly: it can include comparative biographical research, which goes back to ancient times, prosopography and group biography. For Caine, prosopography is above all the classified and systematic examination of people's activities: "Prosopography is heavily dependent on the huge quantities of biographical data contained within national dictionaries of biography, but in my view it is impossible to accept it as a biographical enterprise." She further states: "Its aim is not in any way to create or establish a better understanding of individuals and their motives or their life experiences."[46]

By combining agency theories and the methods of prosopography and collective biography, this book seeks to develop within historical studies a new interpretive approach that is more focused on personal agency.[47] Prosopography is used as the data-collection method by which the same biographical information (concerning positions, activities and marital and blood relations) is systematically collected for a selected group of individuals. Collective biography refers to the method by which these data are then systematically analyzed, comparing the life histories of individuals within the selected group so as to discern strategic alliances within it (marriage and patronage ties, for instance) and examining overlaps in the activities of its members (when they served together in official capacities, for instance).

23

Several of the researchers in this work have systematically utilized previous biographical research. We want to give the individuals and their actions under discussion backgrounds that reflect the contemporary structures of their individual life cycles. There exist several national biographical collections and publication series that include hundreds of persons who lived in the early modern period: for example, *Kansallisbiografia* (the National Biography of Finland) and *Svenskt biografiskt lexikon* and its predecessor *Svenskt biografiskt handlexikon*. In addition, there are many more or less biographically orientated studies which describe various social groups from the time period under discussion: noblemen, officers and local state officials and judges. Although their approach is descriptive, they still contain a vast amount of information that can be used to provide a solid background for our own approach. *Turun hiippakunnan paimenmuisto* (the Pastoral register of the Diocese of Turku) and *Ylioppilasmatrikkeli* (Matriculations register of the University of Helsinki) are also crucial sources for this purpose.[48]

With the existing biographical research, it has been possible to create a comprehensive set of databases that provide the general outlines of individual lives or the career tracks of various estates or social groups, and even to construct collective biographies of certain groups. Individuals can be compared with the groups' 'average' figures. Comparative methods are also applied in outlining temporal changes and geographical differences.

The research carried out here is not biographical in the traditional sense, and thus the source material consists mainly of documents that describe the activities of individuals. While there are plenty of personal and biographical sources available, such as the correspondence of noble families, in previous research they have not been regarded as source material that is relevant beyond the private spheres of their authors' lives. However, correspondence is not the only source we utilize: local court records, in particular, often provide a continuous fount of source material, revealing the activities of individuals in both civil and criminal cases, and particularly in their office-holding functions. The material offered by sixteenth-century local administrative records such as bailiffs' accounts (*landskapshandlingar*) has been sparsely exploited in recent decades, although these accounts furnish not only quantitative but also qualitative data. These records have also been used in this work. Thus various types of sources are combined here in order to construct a cohesive picture of state-building and its implementation both at the micro level and more generally.

The methods employed by the sub-areas of research in this publication are partially different depending on the source material and the subject, but an eclectic approach is also characteristic of this project as a whole. This means that both qualitative and quantitative material is combined, different ways of making sense of it (i.e. research traditions) are brought together, and a multi-method design is used in analyzing the source materials. The aim of using mixed methods is to enable us to pose different kinds of questions, to use different ways of analyzing sources, and to prove our general hypothesis by combining different kinds of source material and methods. The project thus uses mixed methods both within the sub-areas of research and at the overall level.

## This volume

In this volume, state-building in the Swedish Age of Greatness (1560–1720) is analyzed from the perspective of personal agency. The ten chapters of this volume will provide concrete examples of how personal agency enabled, limited or influenced activity at the personal level of office-holders or special groups inside the civil administration. The authors in this volume argue that even while the administrative machinery expanded significantly over the course of the seventeenth century, space remained for personal agency. As seen in figure 1, there are several levels of administration during the research period which needs to be studied. Starting from the top, the councillors of the realm and the secretaries of the royal chancellery are included to the analysis. The role of the stewards and governors are crucial at the county level. For the local rural communities there are three especially important functionary groups which affected a great deal to the subjects of the Swedish King: the judges, bailiffs and the clergymen. Even though the urbanization rate of Sweden was during this period extremely low, the burgomasters and mayors of the towns were the most heavy-weighted officials in the urban environments. Thus, this anthology analyses, including the students of the Academy of Turku (Åbo akademi), the actions and agency of the most important office-holders of the civil society in the sixteenth and seventeenth-century Sweden Sweden.[49]

The development of the nation state had peaked by the end of the seventeenth century, at which time the bureaucratic administrative machinery was already in place and merely gained strength in later centuries. In this volume, authors concentrate on elucidating the construction and maintenance of individual office-holders' agency within the context of state building in the early modern Swedish empire. In order to gain a holistic perspective, certain groups of office-holders at every level of the civil administration in Sweden c. 1550–1720 have been selected for scrutiny. By concentrating on individual volition and action rather than normative administrative structures, it is possible to examine the process of state building from the inside out.

Approaching state-building processes from a primarily structural point of view, without looking at the actors involved, can create a misleading impression given that the number of actors working within early modern state institutions was often small. In this volume, the focus is on the actors inside the state-building process and the chapters reveal that these individuals and their actions had significant influence on the direction taken by the state-building process. In many administrational offices, the loose structure of civil administration provided plenty of room to maneuverer. In some cases the agency exercised by the office-holder was more the result of his personal character and social network connections than of strict job descriptions or regulations. But the further the state building process proceeded, the less room there was for individual choice of action. The Swedish Age of Greatness can be seen as a lengthy period of transformation in which individual office-holders created piece by piece an administrational machine which gradually took away their possibilities to influence matters and gave more power to collective action.

In two separate chapters, Marko Hakanen and Ulla Koskinen study changes in the central administration of the kingdom of Sweden during the sixteenth and seventeeth centuries. They concentrate on two groups, councillors of the realm (*riksråd*) and the secretaries (*sekreterare*) working at the royal chancellery (*kansli, kanslikollegium*). The position of the councillors of the realm was well recognized by the whole society. They were an elite group which enjoyed formal position in the power structure. Their job was to help the monarch reach decisions. The secretary's job was also to help the monarch, but the points of departure of the two were totally different. Their position was not based on noble birth and almost all of them came from a lower status background. Even their position was informal, but they possessed significant power through social networks, which increased in importance over the course of the seventeenth century. In practice, the internal crisis taking place in the central administration at the turn of the seventeenth century meant that the type of power wielded by secretaries and councillors of the realm changed places: the formal power of secretaries shifted from the limelight to behind the scenes, while the councillors of the realm were brought out from the shadows of the palace back rooms to be seated at the same table as the monarch. The research in both chapters is based on biographical source materials collected by using prosopographic methods. By using the resulting database as a foundation and incorporating analysis of additional narrative source materials, the chapters offer important insights into the personal agency of councillors of the realm and royal secretaries.

Stewards (*ståthållare*) and later governors (*landshövding*) play a central role in the chapter written by Mirkka Lappalainen. These were high local office-holders who formed the backbone of the administration at the local level and played a pivotal role in centralizing power in seventeenth-century Sweden. Lappalainen's point of departure has been to analyze how the system of stewards and governors was constructed. It is crucial to first understand the administrational system before we can understand how these officials exercised personal agency and begin asking: how did these officers carry out their duties? What were the boundaries they had to deal with? Although their job was to extend the centralized system into the local level, they were also subordinate to the monarch and thus themselves objects of centralizing processes. Lappalainen argues that despite this, the personal agency possessed by stewards and governors personal loyalties were based on personal loyalties.

In many cases, an individual's personal agency was defined by his personal skills or personality, but sometimes the duties of an office were so demanding and significant for the whole community that it limited the amount of personal agency possible within his position. Olli Matikainen studies how the role and status of judges (*häradshövding, lagläsare*) developed prior to the important reform of 1680, when Swedish judges were granted lifelong tenure. Lord High Chancellor Per Brahe stressed the important role of judges in society, because "the welfare of the fatherland was dependent on their calling". Matikainen states that most existing studies have focused on the social background, education and careers of judges, and there has been surprisingly little interest in historical studies of the judge's position as an actor in the society. Matikainen shows that over the course of the seventeenth century, judges became educated juridical experts, but more importantly the judge's office meant the birth of a profession.

It can be argued that the bailiffs (*fogde, häradsfogde*) were the most important individuals in the early modern Swedish countryside. In the early stages of state building in the sixteenth century, bailiffs were the key group acting as a bridge between the king and local resources. In the following century, bailiffs remained an important part of the expanding administration at the local level. The chapter by Janne Haikari raises interesting questions about the personal agency of these bailiffs as well as their personalities, when they faced the all-too-common situation of having to answer various demands made by people who did not always want to pay taxes or disputed the amount to be paid. The job of these bailiffs was extremely demanding and to succeed in it, they needed to cultivate their interaction skills and maintain good personal relationships in the local community. Haikari studies which factors shaped the limits of bailiffs' agency and how the community viewed the bailiffs' actions within the community.

The Reformation in sixteenth-century Sweden was one of the major issues which dictated the direction of the state-building process, and at the local level the clergy (*präst, kyrkoherre*) played a central role in transferring Reformation ideology to the common people. In his chapter, Mikko Hiljanen draws upon his sizeable clerical database in which he has collected information from various sources including official documents but also informal biographical information. He asks: if the position of the clergy at the center of the local community was important for connecting local and central levels of power, who was appointed to the clergy and why? Who had the right to make appointments and who was consulted during the process? The answers reveal not just clergymen's personal agency, but also shed light on the boundaries of that agency.

In his chapter, Petri Karonen takes a closer look at the so-called royal mayors (*kungliga borgmästare*). These civil officials, appointed by the King and other state authorities, had to deal with problems in their local communities that were often serious. Karonen analyses the reasons why the King appointed these men to their posts, their duties and activities in their towns and what kinds of obstacles and problems these mayors faced – and sometimes caused. He argues that conflicts were exceptional, since the interaction between state authorities, royal mayors and members of local communities tended to function smoothly.

Political circumstances have always influenced urban administration and therefore personal agency. This was especially true for Swedish administration in the late sixteenthcentury and first decades of the seventeenth century. Traditionally Stockholm's burgomasters (*borgmästare*) and magistrates (*borgmästare och råd, magistrat*) had worked mainly to guard the interests of their own group, but that changed in the 1620s when royal burgomasters began to act as guardians of the common good for all town subjects. In her chapter, Piia Einonen looks at social and organizational structures as constituting the functional limits of agency, and studies the changes that took place when burgomasters and magistrates became more educated and the agency of office-holders was gradually formalized.

A sizeable database[50] providing information on the young men who studied at the Academy of Turku is the core around which Kustaa H. J. Vilkuna builds his chapter. Using this source material, he addresses one of the key problems faced by seventeenth -century state builders: how to recruit a sufficient number of well-educated officers to work in local administration. The founding of more universities was too slow a solution, and many young men were told that getting educated abroad would be of greater benefit to them personally, but was such education a solution to the problem of administrative recruitment? By studying the ideology that influenced students' life choices and combining this with biographical information on students' social origin, Vilkuna illuminates the role of personal agency in the early careers of crown officials.

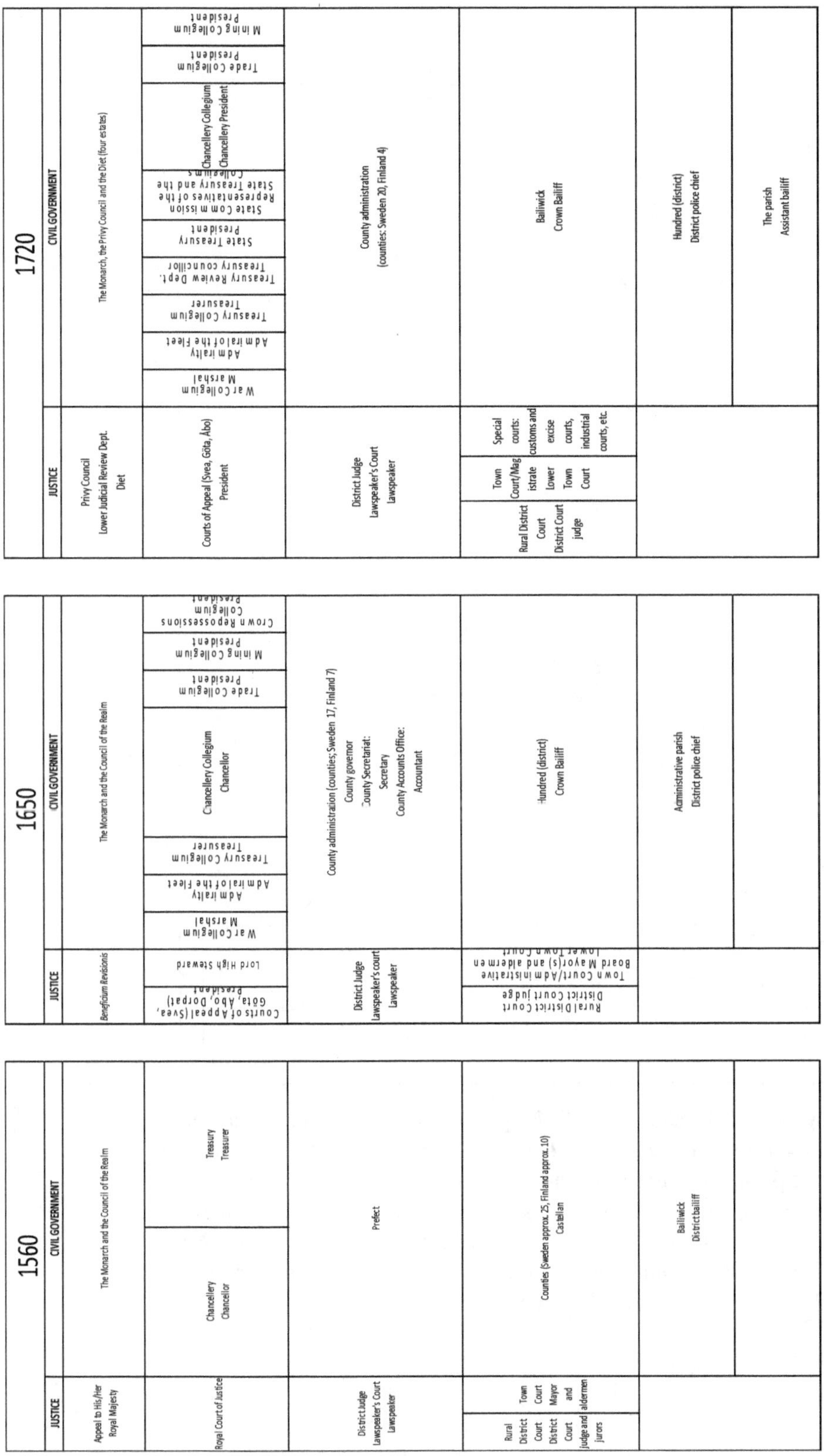

*Figure 1: The Administration and Legislature of Sweden 1560–1720.*

Map 1. Kingdom of Sweden c. 1560. Map compiled from Jukka Paarma, *Hiippakuntahallinto Suomessa 1554–1604*. Suomen kirkkohistoriallisen seuran Toimituksia 116 (Helsinki: The Finnish Society of Church History, 1980), 163; Montgomery, "Enhetskyrkans tid", p. 136; Marko Lamberg, Marko Hakanen, Janne Haikari (eds), *Physical and Cultural Space in Pre-Industrial Europe: Methodological Approaches to Spatiality* (Lund: Nordic Academic Press, 2011). Map: Jari Järvinen.

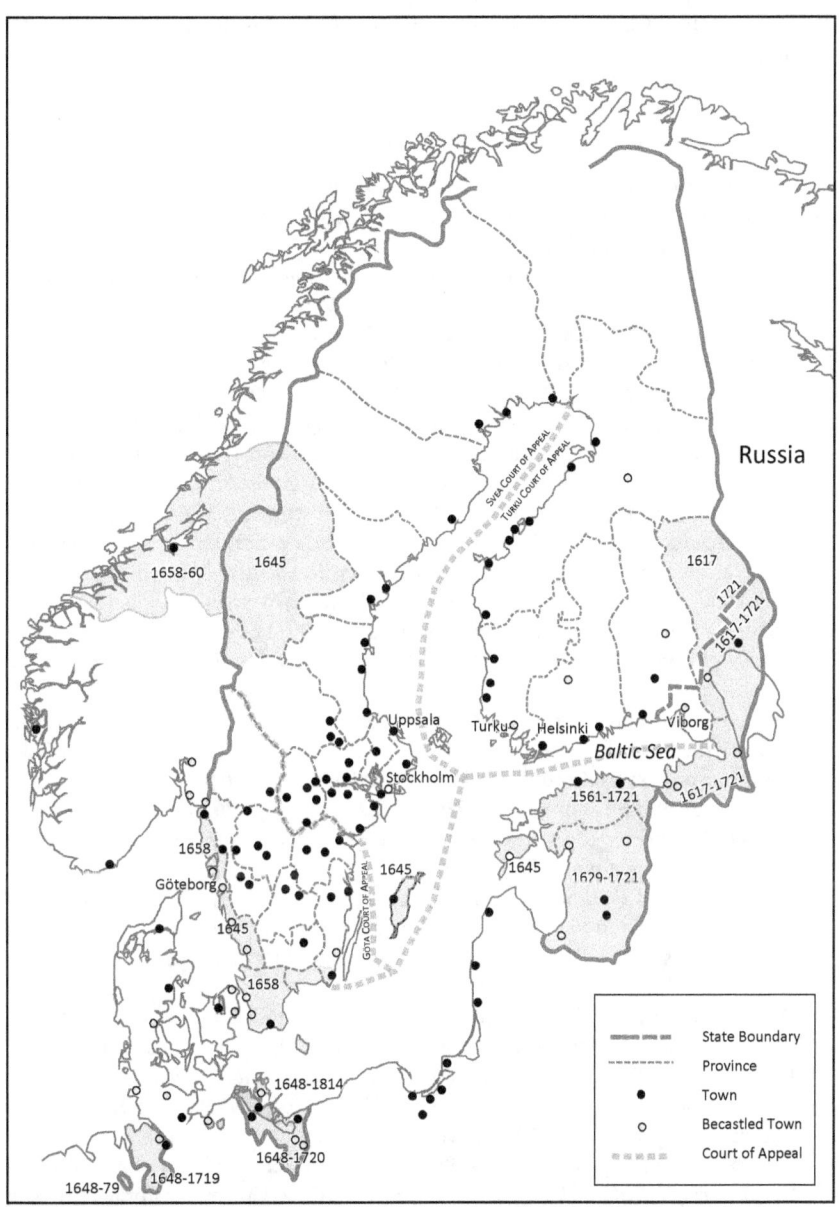

Map 2. Changes in the boundaries of the Kingdom of Sweden 1660–1721: Provinces, Court of Appeal districts, and Towns. Map compiled from Petri Karonen, "The Worst Offenders in the Provincial Towns. Serious Urban Crime and its Perpetrators in the Early Years of Sweden's Period as a Great Power", *Scandinavian Journal of History* (23, 1998), p. 23; Villstrand, Sveriges historia, p. 425; Lamberg, Hakanen & Haikari (eds), *Physical and Cultural Space*. Map: Jari Järvinen.

The research on which this publication is based was funded by the Academy of Finland (grant no. 137741).

## NOTES

1  Jan Glete has noted that the Swedish state building process was not a unique one as such, but that the speed and earliness of its implementation was exceptional among European "fiscal-military" states. Jan Glete, *Swedish naval administration, 1521-1721. Resource flows and organisational capabilities.* The Northern World. North Europe and the Baltic, c. 400–1700 A. D. Peoples, Economies and Cultures. Volume 46 (Leiden: Brill, 2010), pp. 652–653.

2  On the grounds for periodization, see for instance Michael Roberts (ed.), *Sweden's Age of Greatness 1632-1718* (Aylesbury: Macmillan, 1973); Michael Roberts, *The Swedish Imperial Experience 1560-1718* (Cambridge: Cambridge University Press, 1979); Stellan Dahlgren, Anders Florén, Åsa Karlsson (red.), *Makt & vardag. Hur man styrde, levde och tänkte under svensk stormaktstid. Femton uppsatser* (Trelleborg: Atlantis, 1993), pp. 8–9; Nils Erik Villstrand, *Riksdelen. Stormakt och rikssprängning 1560-1812.* Finlands svenska historia 2. Skrifter utgivna av Svenska litteratursällskapet i Finland 702: 2 (Helsingfors: The Society of Swedish Literature in Finland, 2009), pp. 342, 344; Nils Erik Villstrand, *Sveriges historia 1600-1721.* Norstedts Sveriges historia (Stockholm: Nordstedt, 2011); Petri Karonen, *Pohjoinen suurvalta. Ruotsi ja Suomi 1521-1809* (Helsinki: The Finnish Literature Society, 2014).

3  Figure 1 is based on the following sources: Per Frohnert, "Administration i Sverige under frihetstiden". In: *Adminstrasjon i Norden på 1700-talet. Det nordiska forskningsprojekt Centralmakt och lokalsamhälle – beslutsprocess på 1700-talet 4* (Karlsham, 1985); Björn Asker, *Hur riket styrdes. Förvaltning, politik och arkiv 1520-1920.* Skrifter utgivna av Riksarkivet 27 (Stockholm: Riksarkivet, 2007); Karonen, *Pohjoinen suurvalta*, pp. 488–492.

4  See for instance Pasi Ihalainen, Michael Brengsbo, Karin Sennefelt, Patrik Winton (eds), *Scandinavia in the Age of Revolutions. Nordic Political Cultures, 1740-1820* (Cornwall: Ashgate, 2011); Nils Herlitz, *Grunddragen av det svenska statsskickets historia* (Stockholm: Nordstedt, 1967).

5  David Gaunt, *Utbildning till statens tjänst. En kollektivbiografi av stormaktstidens hovrättsauskultanter.* Studia Historica Upsaliensia 63 (Uppsala: Uppsala universitet, 1975), p. 86; Ingvar Elmroth, *För kung och fosterland. Studier i den svenska adelns demografi och offentliga funktioner 1600-1900.* Bibliotheca Historica Lundensis L (Lund: Lunds universitet, 1981), p. 208.

6  Herlitz, *Grunddragen*, pp. 57–59; Ingmar Brohed (red.), *Reformationens konsolidering i de nordiska länderna 1540-1610* (Otta: Universitetsförlaget, 1990); Karonen, *Pohjoinen suurvalta*, pp. 72–77.

7  See for instance Kauko Pirinen (toim.), *Turun tuomiokapituli 1276-1976* (Loimaa: Turun Arkkihiippakunnan Tuomiokapituli, 1976); Pentti Laasonen, *Papinvirkojen täyttö Suomessa myöhäiskaroliinisena aikana 1690-1713.* SKHST 124 (Saarijärvi: The Finnish Society of Church History, 1983); Kauko Pirinen, "Keskiaika ja uskonpuhdistuksen aika." In: *Suomen kirkon historia 1* (Porvoo: WSOY, 1991); Pentti Laasonen, "Vuodet 1593-1808." In: *Suomen kirkon historia 2* (Porvoo: WSOY, 1991); Åke Andrén, "Reformationstid". In: *Sveriges kyrkohistoria 3* (Stockholm: Verbum,1999); Ingun Montgomery, "Enhetskyrkans tid", In: *Sveriges kyrkohistoria 4* (Stockholm: Verbum, 2002).

8  Even in the nineteenth century, the highest administrative posts were still mainly filled through family networks. Esa Konttinen, *Perinteisesti moderniin. Professioiden yhteiskunnallinen synty Suomessa* (Tampere: Vastapaino, 1991); Raimo Savolainen, *Suosikkisenaattorit. Venäjän keisarin suosio suomalaisten senaattoreiden*

*menestyksen perustana 1809-1892*. Hallintohistoriallisia tutkimuksia 14 (Helsinki: Valtioneuvosto, 1994), pp. 229-232; Kristiina Kalleinen, *"Isänmaani onni on kuulua Venäjälle": vapaaherra Lars Gabriel von Haartmanin elämä*. Suomalaisen Kirjallisuuden Seuran toimituksia 815 (Helsinki: The Finnish Literature Society, 2001), pp. 12, 35-36; Rolf Torstendahl, Michael Burrage (eds), *The formation of professions: knowledge, state and strategy* (London: Sage, 1990). The present-day qualifications for a profession are regarded as including at least the following components: a member of a profession should possess theoretical knowledge of his or her special field and be able to demonstrate through particular job descriptions (and symbols) a specialized mastery of the field. In addition, he or she should be capable of functioning independently in his or her field of activity and be (officially) responsible for his or her decisions. See for example Hilde de Ridder-Symoens, "Training and Professionalization" In: Wolfgang Reinhard (ed.), *Power Elites and State Building*. European Science Foundation, The Origins of the Modern State in Europe, 13th-18th Centuries, Theme D. General Editors: Wim Blockmans & Jean-Philippe Genet (Oxford: Clarendon Press, 1996), p. 149.

9   However, for a person of the time studied here, the Swedish word *profession* meant above all a university professorship. See *SAOB* (http://g3.spraakdata.gu.se/saob/), "profession".

10  See for example Konungaförsäkran 1611, 5§, 1634 års regeringsform, 12 §. In: *Sveriges regeringsformer 1634-1809 samt konungaförsäkringar 1611-1800*. Utg. av Emil Hildebrand (Stockholm, 1891); Herlitz, *Grunddragen*, pp. 63, 95-96, 104, 107-108, 134; Elmroth, *För kung och fosterland*, pp. 218-221; Svante Norrhem, *Uppkomlingarna. Kanslitjänstemännen i 1600-talets Sverige och Europa*. Umeå Studies in the Humanities 117 (Stockholm: Umeå universitet, 1993), p. 153.

11  Konttinen, *Perinteisesti moderniin*, pp. 24, 90; Petri Karonen, "Kuninkaan luottomiehiä, siniverisiä puoluejunkkareita, päteviä byrokraatteja ja säätyläisten parhaimmistoa: virkamiehet ja yhteiskunnan muutos uuden ajan alussa (noin 1520-1810)". In: Heikki Roiko-Jokela (toim.), *Siperiasta siirtoväkeen. Murrosaikoja ja käännekohtia Suomen historiassa* (Jyväskylä: Kopi-Jyvä, 1996), pp. 60-61.

12  See for example Herlitz, *Grunddragen*, passim.; Elmroth, *För kung och fosterland*, pp. 10-11, 206-207; Gunnar Wetterberg, *Kanslern Axel Oxenstierna i sin tid I-II* (Stockholm: Atlantis, 2002), p. 253.

13  Norrhem, *Uppkomlingarna*, pp. 36, 39-40.

14  Konttinen, *Perinteisesti moderniin*; Karonen, "Kuninkaan luottomiehiä"; Jay M. Smith, *The Culture of Merit: Nobility, Royal Service, and the Making of Absolute Monarchy in France, 1600-1789* (Ann Arbor: The University of Michigan Press, 1996), pp. 2-5, 15-17.

15  Gaunt, *Utbildning till statens tjänst*, pp. 34-38; Pia Letto-Vanamo, *Suomalaisen asianajolaitoksen synty ja varhaiskehitys. Oikeushistoriallinen tutkimus*. Suomen Lakimiesyhdistyksen julkaisuja. A: 181 (Vammala: Suomen lakimiesyhdistys, 1989), pp. 10-12, 41-43; Heikki Kulla, "Valtion virkamiehistön kehitys". In: Pia Letto-Vanamo (toim.), *Suomen oikeushistorian pääpiirteet: sukuvallasta moderniin oikeuteen* (Helsinki: Gaudeamus, 1991), pp. 168-170, 172-174; Ridder-Symoens, "Training and Professionalization", pp. 149-151; Liisa Lagerstam, Jessica Parland-von Essen, "Aatelin kasvatus". In: Hanska, Jussi, Vainio-Korhonen, Kirsi (toim.), *Huoneentaulun maailma: kasvatus ja koulutus Suomessa keskiajalta 1860-luvulle* (Helsinki: The Finnish Literature Society, 2010), p. 204; Mia Korpiola (ed.), *The Svea Court of Appeal in the Early Modern Period: Historical Reinterpretations and New Perspectives*. Rättshistoriska studier 26. Stockholm: Institutet för rättshistorisk forskning, 2014).

16  See Jan Lindegren, "The Swedish "Military State", 1560-1720", *Scandinavian Journal of History* 10, 1985, pp. 305-336; Charles Tilly, *Coercion, Capital, and European States AD 990-1990* (Oxford: Blackwell, 1990); Giorgio Chittolini, "The "Private",

the "Public", the "State"". In: Julius Kirshner (ed.), *The Origins of the State in Italy, 1300–1600* (Chicago: University of Chicago Press, 1996); Reinhard (ed.), *Power Elites*; Peter Blickle (Hrsg.), *Gemeinde und Staat im Alten Europa* (München: Oldenbourg, 1998); Harald Gustafsson, "The Conglomerate State: A Perspective on State Formation in Early Modern Europe", *Scandinavian Journal of History* (1998), pp. [189]–213; Michael J. Braddick, *State Formation in Early Modern England, c. 1550–1700* (Cambridge: Cambridge University Press, 2000); Mirkka Lappalainen, "Regional Elite Group and the Problem of Territorial Integration: The Finnish Nobility and the Formation of the Swedish "Power State", c. 1570–1620," *Scandinavian Journal of History* 26, 2001, pp. 1–24; Jan Glete, *War and the State in Early Modern Europe. Spain, the Dutch Republic and Sweden as Fiscal-Military States, 1500–1660* (London: Routledge, 2002); André Holenstein, *"Gute Policey" und lokale Gesellschaft im Staat des Ancien Régime. Das Fallbeispiel der Markgrafschaft Baden(-Durlach)* (Epfendorf: Bibliotheca-Academica-Verlag, 2003); Mats Hallenberg, *Kungen, fogdarna och riket. Lokalförvaltning och statsbyggande under tidig Vasatid* (Stockholm: Symposion, 2001); Mats Hallenberg, Johan Holm, Dan Johansson, "Organization, Legitimation, Participation. State Formation as a Dynamic Process – the Swedish Example, c. 1523–1680", *Scandinavian Journal of History* 33, 2008, pp. 247–268; Mats Hallenberg, *Statsmakt till salu. Arrendesystemet och privatiseringen av skatteuppbörden i det svenska riket 1618–1635* (Lund: Nordic Academic Press, 2008); Wim Blockmans, André Holenstein and Jon Mathieu (eds) in collaboration with Daniel Schläppi, *Empowering Interactions. Political Cultures and the Emergence of the State in Europe 1300–1900* (Aldershot: Ashgate, 2009); Villstrand, *Riksdelen*.

17 See for instance Tilly, *Coercion, Capital, and European States*; Petri Karonen (ed.), *Hopes and Fears for the Future in Early Modern Sweden, 1500–1800*. Studia Historica 79 (Helsinki: The Finnish Literature Society, 2009); Karonen, *Pohjoinen suurvalta*, pp. 183, 329–331. Jan Glete (for example *War and the State*) has also noted Charles Tilly's difficulties in locating Sweden within the European system of state organization.

18 On the interaction model, see esp. the studies of Eva Österberg (*Gränsbygd under krig. Ekonomiska, demografiska och administrativa förhållanden i sydvästra Sverige under och efter nordiska sjuårskriget*. BHL XXVI (Lund: Lund universitet, 1971); "Svenska lokalsamhällen i förändring ca 1550–1850. Participation, representation och politisk kultur i den svenska självstyrelsen. Ett angeläget forskningsområde", *Historisk Tidskrift* 1987; "Bönder och centralmakt i det tidigmoderna Sverige. Konflikt – kompromiss – politisk kultur", *Scandia* 1989; "Folklig mentalitet och statlig makt. Perspektiv på 1500- och 1600-talets Sverige", *Scandia* 1992: 1; "Vardagens sträva samförstånd. Bondepolitik i den svenska modellen från vasatid till frihetstid". In: Gunnar Broberg, Ulla Wikander, Klas Åmark (red.), *Tänka, tycka, tro. Svensk historia underifrån* (Stockholm: Ordfront, 1993). The military state model in Sweden has been discussed by Sven A. Nilsson in "Den karolinska militärstaten. Fredens problem och krigets". In: Gudrun Ekstrand (ed.), *Tre Karlar: Karl X Gustav, Karl XI, Karl XII* (Livrustkammaren: Stockholm, 1984); *De stora krigens tid. Om Sverige som militärstat och bondesamhälle*. Studia Historica Upsaliensia 161 (Uppsala: Uppsala universitet 1990) and Jan Lindegren (for instance *Utskrivning och utsugning. Produktion och reproduktion i Bygdeå 1620–1640*. Studia Historica Upsaliensia 117 (Uppsala: Uppsala universitet, 1980); "The Swedish 'Military State'"; see also Sören Klingnéus, *Bönder blir vapensmeder. Protoindustriell tillverkning i Närke under 1600- och 1700-talen*. Studia Historica Upsaliensia 181 (Uppsala: Uppsala universitet, 1997); Peter Ericsson, *Stora nordiska kriget förklarat. Karl XII och det ideologiska tilltalet*. Studia Historica Upsaliensia 202 (Uppsala: Uppsala universitet, 2002); Martin Linde, *Statsmakt och bondemotstånd. Allmoge och överhet under stora nordiska kriget*. Studia Historica Upsaliensia 194 (Uppsala:

Uppsala universitet, 2000); Martin Linde, *I fädrens spår? Bönder och överhet i Dalarna under 1700-talet* (Hedemora: Gidlund, 2009). A synthesis of work in this field can be found in Leon Jespersen (ed.), *A Revolution from Above? The Power State of 16th and 17th Century Scandinavia* (Odense: Odense University Press, 2000). On the "third interpretation model", see for instance Johan Holm, "Att välja sin fiende. Allmogens konflikter och allianser i riksdagen 1595-1635" (*Historisk Tidskrift 123*, 2003: 1); Johan Holm, *Konstruktionen av en stormakt. Kungamakt, skattebönder och statsbildning 1595-1640*. AUS – SH 90 (Stockholm: Stockholm universitet, 2007); Joakim Scherp, *De ofrälse och makten. En institutionell studie av riksdagen och de ofrälse ståndens politik i maktdelningsfrågor 1660-1682*. Stockholm Studies in History 96 (Stockholm: Stockholm universitet, 2013). For a general discussion of the field, see also Karonen. *Pohjoinen suurvalta*, p. 22, note 15. See Börje Harnesk's critical views of the so-called interactive point of view in Swedish research in "Den svenska modellens tidigmoderna rötter?", *Historisk tidskrift*, 122, 2002; "Konsten att klaga, konsten att kräva. Kronan och bönderna på 1500- och 1600-talen". In: Harnesk, Börje (red.), *Maktens skiftande skepnader. Studier i makt, legitimitet och inflytande i det tidigmoderna Sverige* (Umeå: Umeå universitet, 2003).

19 One extreme exception to this rule was the so-called War of the Cudgels (*klubbekriget, nuijasota*) in Finland at the turn of 1596 and 1597, in which as many as 3000 peasants were slain, a considerable figure in terms of the population of the country. On the debate on the Cudgels War, see esp. Eric Anthoni, *Konflikten mellan hertig Carl och Finland. Konfliktens uppkomst och hertigens seger* (Helsingfors, 1935); Eric Anthoni, *Konflikten mellan hertig Carl och Finland. Avvecklingen och försoningen*, Skrifter utgivna av svenska litteratursällskapet i Finland (Helsingfors: The Society of Swedish Literature in Finland, 1937); Pentti Renvall, *Kuninkaanmiehiä ja kapinoitsijoita Vaasakauden Suomessa* (Helsinki: Tammi, 1949); Pentti Renvall, "Ruotsin vallan aika". In: *Suomen kansanedustuslaitoksen historia*, Vol. 1: *Suomen kansanedustuslaitoksen vaiheet 1850-luvun puoliväliin* (Helsinki: Eduskunnan historiakomitea, 1962); Heikki Ylikangas, *Nuijasota*, 3rd edition (Helsinki: Otava, 1996); Karonen, *Pohjoinen suurvalta*, pp. 106-21, and note 42; Kimmo Katajala (ed.), *Northern Revolts. Medieval and Early Modern Peasant Unrest in the Nordic Countries* (Helsinki: The Finnish Literature Society, 2004); Mirkka Lappalainen, *Susimessu. 1590-luvun sisällissota Ruotsissa ja Suomessa* (Helsinki: WSOY, 2009); see also Geoffrey Parker and Lesley M. Smith (eds), *The General Crisis of the Seventeenth Century*, 2nd edition (London: Routlegde, 1997).

20 The situation has not changed a lot since Björn Asker's comment over two decades ago, when he remarked that there was not much research on seventeenth century civil servants or military personnel in Sweden: Björn Asker, "Från godsägarstat till ämbetsmannastat. Byråkraterna, officerarna och enväldets införande". In: Stellan Dahlgren, Anders Florén, Åsa Karlsson (red.), *Makt & vardag. Hur man styrde, levde och tänkte under svensk stormaktstid. Femton uppsatser* (Trelleborg: Atlantis, 1993), pp. 68-69.

21 On philosophical definitions of agency see for example Michael E. Bratman, *Structures of Agency: Essays* (Cary: Oxford University Press, 2006).

22 See Edgar Kiser, "Comparing Varieties of Agency Theory in Economics, Political Science, and Sociology: An Illustration from State Policy Implementation", *Sociological Theory*, Vol. 17, No. 2 (Jul. 1999), for instance p. 162. Kiser remarks that especially in economics few references to Weber have been made. For sociological approaches, see also Susan P. Shapiro, "Agency Theory". *Annual Review of Sociology*, Vol. 31 (2005), pp. 263-284.

23 Kiser, "Comparing Varieties", p. 146.

24 Barry S. Barnes, *Understanding Agency: Social Theory and Responsible Action* (London: Sage, 2000), Preface x-xi (quotation), pp. 1-2, Chapter 4.

25 Stephan Fuchs, "Beyond Agency", *Sociological Theory*, Vol. 19, No. 1 (Mar. 2001), pp. 26, 29 (quotation), 39–40 (quotations).
26 Pioneers of the idea of rational behavior have included Max Weber, Bronislaw Malinowski, Marcel Mauss and later Talcott Parsons. The actual theory of rational choice in sociology has been developed by G. Homans, P. Blau, M. Olson, J. Coleman, J. Elster and R. Boudon, among others. Key literature regarding rational choice theory includes: Gary S. Becker, *The Economic Approach to Human Behavior* (Chicago: Chicago University Press, 1978); James Coleman, *The Mathematics of Collective Action* (Chicago: Transaction Publishers, 1973); Peter Hedström, *Dissecting the Social. On the Principles of Analytical Sociology* (Cambridge: Cambridge University Press, 2005). On the use of rational choice theory and criticism of it in historical research, see for instance Juha-Antti Lamberg, *Taloudelliset eturyhmät neuvotteluprosesseissa. Suomen kauppasopimuspolitiikka 1920–1930-luvulla* (Saarijärvi: Suomen Tiedeseura, 1999); Petri Karonen, *Patruunat ja poliitikot. Yritysjohtajien taloudellinen ja yhteiskunnallinen toiminta Suomessa 1600–1920*. Historiallisia Tutkimuksia 217 (Tampere: The Finnish Literature Society, 2004). For a critical assessment of rational choice, see for instance Barnes, *Understanding Agency*, ch. 2. For perspectives in economics, see also Ilana Gershon, "Neoliberal Agency", *Current Anthropology*, Vol. 52, No. 4 (August 2011), pp. 537–547. On agency theory with regard to organization theory (principal – agent relationships in firms), see also for instance Kathleen M. Eisenhardt, "Agency Theory: An Assessment and Review", *The Academy of Management Review* 14, 1989, pp. 57–74; for a critical approach, see Kiser, "Comparing Varieties", pp. 150–151.
27 Eisenhardt, "Agency Theory", p. 64.
28 Ellen Messer-Davidow, "Acting Otherwise". In: Judith Kegan Gardiner (ed.), *Provoking Agents. Gender and Agency in Theory and Practise* (Urbana and Chicago, University of Illinois Press, 1995), p. 25.
29 Marko Hakanen, *Vallan verkostoissa. Per Brahe ja hänen klienttinsä 1600-luvun Ruotsin valtakunnassa*. Jyväskylä Studies in Humanities 157 (Jyväskylä: Jyväskylän yliopisto, 2011).
30 For a good overview of different views of agency theories, see Messer-Davidov, "Acting Otherwise", pp. 23–51.
31 Ivar Svalenius, *Rikskansliet i Sverige 1560–1592*. Skrifter utgivna av Svenska Riksarkivet 7 (Stockholm: Riksarkivet, 1991), pp. 4–6.
32 Michael Mann, *The sources of social power. Volume 1. A history of power from the beginning to A.D. 1760* (Cambridge: Cambridge University Press, 1987), p. 5.
33 Anthony Giddens, *Central Problems in Social Theory: Action, Structure and Contradiction in Social Analysis* (Berkeley: University of California, 1984), p. 3.
34 Anthony Giddens, *Central Problems in Social Theory. Action, Structure and Contradiction in Social Analysis* (Haundmills and London, Palgrave MacMillan, 1979), pp. 53–59, 66, 71.
35 Anthony Giddens, *Central Problems*, pp. 198–201, 236–243. See also Barnes, *Understanding Agency*, p. 27: "In Giddens´ well-known formulation, structure may both constrain and facilitate action, but not determine it, just because individuals have agency."
36 See for instance Simone Lässig, "Introduction: Biography in Modern History – Modern Historiography in Biography". In: Volker R. Berghahn, Simone Lässig (eds), *Biography between Structure and Agency. Central European Lives in International Historiography*. Studies in German History 9 (S. l.: Berghahn Books, 2008), pp. 3–4; Ian Kershaw, "Biography and the Historian. Opportunities and Constraints". In: Berghahn, Lässig (eds), *Biography*, p. 31; Volker R. Berghahn, "Structuralism and Biography. Some Concluding Thoughts on the Uncertainties of a Historiographical Genre", Berghahn, Lässig (eds), *Biography*, pp. 234–235.

37 Barbara Caine describes the relationship between biographical research and history in *Biography and History*. In: Donald MacRaild (ed.), *Theory and History Series* (S.l.: Palgrave Macmillan, 2010), pp. 1 and 23 (on "the biographical turn"), 24–25 (on different attitudes among researchers), and especially Chapter 2 (on historiography). Volker Berghahn and Simone Lässig ("Preface". In: Berghahn, Lässig (eds), *Biography*, p. vii) date the "return of biography" to the 1990s.

38 The search criteria were the general keywords "Sverige", "biografi", "1500-talet", "1600-talet", "1700-talet". The calculations do not take account of the matriculations registers or of articles that appear only sporadically in the database of *Svenskt biografiskt lexikon* (http://sok.riksarkivet.se/sbl/Start.aspx) . – http://libris.kb.se/ (accessed 27 January 2014).

39 Petri Karonen, "Ruotsin ajan tutkimuksen nykytila ja resurssit", *Historiallinen Aikakauskirja* 2010: 4.

40 Biographies on rulers and other important persons include Peter Englund, *Silvermasken. En kort biografi över drottning Kristina* (Stockholm: Bonnier, 2006); Marie-Louise Rodén, *Drottning Christina. En biografi* (Stockholm: Prisma, 2008); Svante Norrhem, *Ebba Brahe. Makt och kärlek under stormaktstiden* (Lund: Historiska Media 2007); Björn Asker, *Karl X Gustav. En biografi* (Lund: Historiska Media, 2009); Lars-Olof Larsson, *Gustav Vasa – landsfader eller tyrann?* (Stockholm: Prisma, 2002); Wetterberg, *Kanslern Axel Oxenstierna*; Lars-Olof Larsson, *Arvet efter Gustav Vasa* (Stockholm: Prisma, 2005); Lars Ericson, *Johan III. En biografi* (Lund: Historiska Media, 2006); Bo Eriksson, *I skuggan av tronen. En biografi over Per Brahe d.ä.* (Stockholm: Prisma, 2009); Erik Petersson, *Vicekungen. En biografi över Per Brahe den yngre* (Stockholm: Natur & Kultur, 2009); Göran Rystad, *Karl XI. En biografi* (Lund: Historiska Media, 2001); Erik Petersson, *Den skoningslöse. En biografi över Karl IX* (Stockholm: Natur och kultur, 2008; Lennart Hedberg, *Karl IX: företagare fursten och enväldshärskaren* (Stockholm: Prisma, 2009).

41 Biographies of noble families and individuals include Mirkka Lappalainen, *Suku – valta – suurvalta. Creutzit 1600-luvun Ruotsissa ja Suomessa* (Helsinki: WSOY, 2005); Alexander Jonsson, *De norrländska landshövdingarna och statsbildningen 1634–1769*. Skrifter från institutionen för historiska studier 10 (Umeå: Umeå universitet, 2005); Tuula Hockman, *Kolmen polven perilliset. Ingeborg Aakentytär (Tott) ja hänen sukunsa (n. 1460–1507)* (Helsinki: The Finnish Literature Society, 2006); Anu Lahtinen, *Sopeutuvat – neuvottelevat – kapinalliset. Naiset toimijoina Flemingin sukupiirissä 1470–1620* (Helsinki: The Finnish Literature Society, 2007); Liisa Lagerstam, *A Noble Life. The Cultural Biography of Gabriel Kurck (1630–1712)*. Suomalaisen tiedeakatemia toimituksia, Humaniora 349 (Helsinki: Finnish Academy of Science and Letters, 2007); Kirsi Vainio-Korhonen, *Sophie Creutzin aika. Aateliselämää 1700-luvun Suomessa*. Suomalaisen Kirjallisuuden Seuran toimituksia 1183 (Helsinki: The Finnish Literature Society, 2008); Svante Norrhem, *Kvinnor vid maktens sida 1632–1772* (Lund: Nordic Academic Press, 2010); Ulla Koskinen, *Hyvien miesten valtakunta. Arvid Henrikinpoika Tawast ja aatelin toimintakulttuuri 1500-luvun lopun Suomessa*. Bibliotheca Historica 132 (Helsinki: The Finnish Literature Society, 2011). For an overview, see Bo Eriksson, *Svenska adelns historia* (Stockholm: Norstedt, 2011). A biographical work that places the clergy in context is Simo Heininen, *Agricolan perintö. Paulus Juustenin elämä* (Helsinki: Edita, 2012). On the burgher elite and the manifestion of their power in various circumstances in towns in the seventeenth and eighteenth centuries, see Gudrun Andersson, *Stadens dignitärer. Den lokala elitens status- och maktmanifestation i Arboga 1650–1770* (Stockholm: Atlantis, 2009). On women and power in Sweden in the early modern age, also see Anu Lahtinen and Kirsi Vainio-Korhonen, "Valta ja naiset esimodernia koskevassa historiantutkimuksessa. Pohjoismaista keskustelua toimijoista ja rakenteista". In:

Ilana Aalto et al. (eds), *Vallan teoriat historiantutkimuksessa*. Historia mirabilis 7 (Turku: Turun historiallinen yhdistys, 2011), pp. 19–39.

42 An important exception is Asker's *Karl X Gustav*, which engages extensively with earlier research. Even so, the work does not set out from a basically theoretical or "strictly" scientific point of view. Jan Berggren for his part, presents the grim image of his main character given in historiography in *Rikets mest hatade man. Georg Heinrich von Görtz. En biografi* (Stockholm: Carlsson, 2010). A presentation that takes an interesting stand on the culture of history is Andreas Marklund, *Stenbock. Ära och ensamhet i Karl XII:s tid* (Lund: Historiska media, 2008).

43 Women have also received scant attention: cf. however endnote 41 above and the works mentioned therein. Svante Norrhem (*Kvinnor vid maktens sida*) investigates the use of power by the wives of privy counsellors, which was most evident in "arrangements" in the domestic and political spheres relating to such matters as the allocation of diplomatic posts and recommendations. Particularly in the seventeenth century, their opportunities for exerting influence were considerable since their spouses were often away at war or engaged on other state duties. Henrik Ågren, for his part, uses genealogical research among other methods to study the Höök dynasty of high-ranking office holders from the province of Uppland in "Herremän och bönder. En uppländsk ämbetsmannasläkts sociala rörlighet under 1600-talet och det tidiga 1700-talet", *Karolinska förbundets årsbok 2006*.

44 Lässig, "Introduction", pp. 11, 21.

45 Caine, *Biography and History*, Chapter 3, quotations p. 50.

46 Caine, *Biography and History*, 57–58. Lawrence Stone, "Prosopography", *Daedalus 100(1)* (1971); Gunner Lind, "Prosopografi med relationelle databaser". In: Peter Aronsson, Solveig Fagerlund, Jan Samuelsson (red.), *Nätverk i historisk forskning. Metafor, metod eller teori?* (Växjö: Växjö Universitet, 1999); Donald Broady, French prosopography: definition and suggested readings, *Poetics* 30, 2002. Cf. for instance Merja Uotila, *Käsityöläinen kyläyhteisönsä jäsenenä. Prosopografinen analyysi Hollolan käsityöläisistä 1810–1840*. Jyväskylä Studies in Humanities 237 (Jyväskylä: Jyväskylän yliopisto, 2014), pp. 31–43. For more on prosopographical studies, see http://prosopography.modhist.ox.ac.uk/bibliographyHand.pdf

47 William Bruneau, *Towards a new Collective Biography. The University of British Columbia Professoriate, 1915–1945*, Canadian Journal of Education 19, 1994, pp. 65–79; Diana K. Jones, Researching groups of lives: a collective biographical perspective on The Protestant ethic debate, *Qualitative Research 1(3)*, 2001; Krista Cowman, Collective Biography. In: Simon Gunn and Lucy Faire (ed.), *Research Methods for History* (Edinburgh University Press, Edinburgh, 2012).

48 http://www.kansallisbiografia.fi/; http://sok.riksarkivet.se/sbl/Start.aspx; http://www.lysator.liu.se/runeberg/sbh/; http://www.kansallisbiografia.fi/paimenmuisto/?p=search; http://www.helsinki.fi/ylioppilasmatrikkeli/.

49 The role of the army and the military functionaries are instead not included to the study; this huge entity deserves a study of its own.

50 Collected by Yrjö Kotivuori, located in university of Helsinki [http://www.helsinki.fi/ylioppilasmatrikkeli/].

# Sources

*Printed sources*

*Sveriges regeringsformer 1634–1809 samt konungaförsäkringar 1611–1800*. Utg. av Emil Hildebrand. Stockholm 1891.

## Electronic sources

*SAOB* (http://g3.spraakdata.gu.se/saob/), "profession".
*Svenskt biografiskt lexikon* (http://sok.riksarkivet.se/sbl/Start.aspx). – http://libris.
  kb.se/ (accessed 27.1.2014).
http://prosopography.modhist.ox.ac.uk/bibliographyHand.pdf
http://www.kansallisbiografia.fi/
http://sok.riksarkivet.se/sbl/Start.aspx
http://www.lysator.liu.se/runeberg/sbh/
http://www.kansallisbiografia.fi/paimenmuisto/?p=search
http://www.helsinki.fi/ylioppilasmatrikkeli/

## Literature

Andersson, Gudrun 2009: *Stadens dignitärer. Den lokala elitens status- och maktmanifestation i Arboga 1650–1770.* Stockholm: Atlantis.
Andrén, Åke 1999: "Reformationstid." In: *Sveriges kyrkohistoria* 3. Stockholm: Verbum.
Anthoni, Eric 1935: *Konflikten mellan hertig Carl och Finland. Konfliktens uppkomst och hertigens seger.* Helsingfors.
Anthoni, Eric 1937: *Konflikten mellan hertig Carl och Finland. Avvecklingen och försoningen*, Skrifter utgivna av svenska litteratursällskapet i Finland. Helsingfors: The Society of Swedish Literature in Finland.
Asker, Björn 1993: "Från godsägarstat till ämbetsmannastat. Byråkraterna, officerarna och enväldets införande". In: Stellan Dahlgren, Anders Florén, Åsa Karlsson (red.), *Makt & vardag. Hur man styrde, levde och tänkte under svensk stormaktstid. Femton uppsatser.* Trelleborg: Atlantis.
Asker, Björn 2007: *Hur riket styrdes. Förvaltning, politik och arkiv 1520–1920.* Skrifter utgivna av Riksarkivet 27. Stockholm: Riksarkivet.
Asker, Björn 2009: *Karl X Gustav. En biografi.* Lund: Historiska Media.
Barnes, Barry S. 2000: *Understanding Agency: Social Theory and Responsible Action.* London: Sage.
Becker, Gary S. 1978: *The Economic Approach to Human Behavior.* Chicago: Chicago University Press.
Berggren, Jan 2010: *Rikets mest hatade man. Georg Heinrich von Görtz. En biografi.* Stockholm: Carlsson.
Berghahn, Volker R. 2008: "Structuralism and Biography. Some Concluding Thoughts on the Uncertainties of a Historiographical Genre". In: Berghahn, Lässig (eds), *Biography*.
Blickle, Peter (Hrsg.) 1998: *Gemeinde und Staat im Alten Europa.* München: Oldenbourg.
Blockmans, Wim, Holenstein, André and Mathieu, Jon (eds) in collaboration with Daniel Schläppi 2009: *Empowering Interactions. Political Cultures and the Emergence of the State in Europe 1300–1900.* Aldershot: Ashgate.
Braddick, Michael J. 2000: *State Formation in Early Modern England, c. 1550–1700.* Cambridge: Cambridge University Press.
Bratman, Michael E. 2006: *Structures of Agency: Essays.* Cary: Oxford University Press.
Broady, Donald 2002: "French prosopography: definition and suggested readings", *Poetics* 30.
Brohed, Ingmar (red.) 1990: *Reformationens konsolidering i de nordiska länderna 1540–1610.* Otta: Universitetsförlaget.
Bruneau, William 1994: "Towards a new Collective Biography: the University of British Columbia Professoriate, 1915–1945", *Canadian Journal of Education* 19.

Caine, Barbara 2010: *Biography and History*. In: Donald MacRaild (ed.), *Theory and History Series*. S.l.: Palgrave Macmillan.
Chittolini, Giorgio 1996: "The 'Private', the 'Public', the 'State'". In: Julius Kirshner (ed.), *The Origins of the State in Italy, 1300–1600*. Chicago: University of Chicago Press.
Coleman, James 1973: *The Mathematics of Collective Action*. Chicago: Transaction Publishers.
Cowman, Krista 2012: "Collective Biography". In: Simon Gunn and Lucy Faire (ed.), *Research Methods for History*. Edinburgh: Edinburgh University Press.
Dahlgren, Stellan, Florén, Anders, Karlsson, Åsa (eds) 1993: *Makt & vardag. Hur man styrde, levde och tänkte under svensk stormaktstid. Femton uppsatser*. Trelleborg: Atlantis.
Eisenhardt, Kathleen M. 1989: "Agency Theory: An Assessment and Review", *The Academy of Management Review* 14.
Elmroth, Ingvar 1981: *För kung och fosterland. Studier i den svenska adelns demografi och offentliga funktioner 1600–1900*. Bibliotheca Historica Lundensis L. Lund: Lunds universitet.
Englund, Peter 2006: *Silvermasken. En kort biografi över drottning Kristina*. Stockholm: Bonnier.
Ericson Wolke, Lars 2006: *Johan III. En biografi*. Lund: Historiska Media.
Ericsson, Peter 2002: *Stora nordiska kriget förklarat. Karl XII och det ideologiska tilltalet*. Studia Historica Upsaliensia 202. Uppsala: Uppsala universitet.
Eriksson, Bo 2009: *I skuggan av tronen. En biografi over Per Brahe d.ä.* Stockholm: Prisma.
Eriksson, Bo 2011: *Svenska adelns historia*. Stockholm: Norstedt.
Frohnert, Per 1985: "Administration i Sverige under frihetstiden". In: *Adminstrasjon i Norden på 1700-talet*. Det nordiska forskningsprojekt Centralmakt och lokalsamhälle – beslutsprocess på 1700-talet 4. Karlsham.
Fuchs, Stephan 2001: "Beyond Agency", *Sociological Theory*.
Gaunt, David 1975: *Utbildning till statens tjänst. En kollektivbiografi av stormaktstidens hovrättsauskultanter*. Studia Historica Upsaliensia 63. Uppsala: Uppsala universitet.
Gershon, Ilana 2011: "Neoliberal Agency", *Current Anthropology*.
Giddens, Anthony 1979: *Central Problems in Social Theory. Action, Structure and Contradiction in Social Analysis*. Haundmills and London: Palgrave MacMillan.
Giddens, Anthony 1984: *Central Problems in Social Theory: Action, Structure and Contradiction in Social Analysis*. Berkeley: University of California.
Glete, Jan 2002: *War and the State in Early Modern Europe. Spain, the Dutch Republic and Sweden as Fiscal-Military States, 1500–1660*. London: Routledge.
Glete, Jan 2010: *Swedish naval administration, 1521–1721. Resource flows and organisational capabilities*. The Northern World. North Europe and the Baltic, c. 400–1700 A. D. Peoples, Economies and Cultures. Volume 46. Leiden: Brill.
Gustafsson, Harald 1998: "The Conglomerate State. A Perspective on State Formation in Early Modern Europe", *Scandinavian Journal of History*.
Hakanen, Marko 2011: *Vallan verkostoissa. Per Brahe ja hänen klienttinsä 1600-luvun Ruotsin valtakunnassa*. Jyväskylä Studies in Humanities 157. Jyväskylä: Jyväskylän yliopisto.
Hallenberg, Mats 2001: *Kungen, fogdarna och riket. Lokalförvaltning och statsbyggande under tidig Vasatid*. Stockholm: Brutus Östlings Bokförlag Symposion.
Hallenberg, Mats 2008: *Statsmakt till salu. Arrendesystemet och privatiseringen av skatteuppbörden i det svenska riket 1618–1635*. Lund: Nordic Academic Press.
Hallenberg, Mats, Holm, Johan, Johansson, Dan 2008: "Organization, Legitimation, Participation. State Formation as a Dynamic Process – the Swedish Example, c. 1523–1680", *Scandinavian Journal of History* 33.
Harnesk, Börje 2002: "Den svenska modellens tidigmoderna rötter?", *Historisk tidskrift* 122.

Harnesk, Börje 2003: "Konsten att klaga, konsten att kräva. Kronan och bönderna på 1500- och 1600-talen". In: Börje Harnesk (ed.), *Maktens skiftande skepnader. Studier i makt, legitimitet och inflytande i det tidigmoderna Sverige*. Umeå: Umeå universitet.

Hedberg, Lennart 2009: *Karl IX: företagare fursten och envåldshärskaren*. Stockholm: Prisma.

Hedström, Peter 2005: *Dissecting the Social. On the Principles of Analytical Sociology*. Cambridge: Cambridge University Press.

Heininen, Simo 2012: *Agricolan perintö. Paulus Juustenin elämä*. Helsinki: Edita.

Herlitz, Nils 1967: *Grunddragen av det svenska statsskickets historia*. Stockholm: Nordstedt.

Hockman, Tuula 2006: *Kolmen polven perilliset. Ingeborg Aakentytär (Tott) ja hänen sukunsa (n. 1460–1507)*. Helsinki: The Finnish Literature Society.

Holenstein, André 2003: *"Gute Policey" und lokale Gesellschaft im Staat des Ancien Régime. Das Fallbeispiel der Markgrafschaft Baden(-Durlach)*. Epfendorf: Bibliotheca-Academica-Verlag.

Holm, Johan 2003: "Att välja sin fiende. Allmogens konflikter och allianser i riksdagen 1595–1635", *Historisk tidskrift* 123.

Holm, Johan 2007: *Konstruktionen av en stormakt. Kungamakt, skattebönder och statsbildning 1595–1640*. Stockholm Studies in History 90. Stockholm: Stockholms universitet.

Ihalainen, Pasi, Brengsbo, Michael, Sennefelt, Karin, Winton, Patrik (eds) 2011: *Scandinavia in the Age of Revolutions. Nordic Political Cultures, 1740–1820*. Cornwall: Ashgate.

Jespersen, Leon (ed.) 2000: *A Revolution from Above? The Power State of 16th and 17th Century Scandinavia*. Odense: Odense University Press.

Jones, Diana K. 2001: "Researching groups of lives: a collective biographical perspective on The Protestant ethic debate", *Qualitative Research* 1 (3).

Jonsson, Alexander 2005: *De norrländska landshövdingarna och statsbildningen 1634–1769*. Skrifter från institutionen för historiska studier 10. Umeå: Umeå universitet.

Kalleinen, Kristiina 2001: *"Isänmaani onni on kuulua Venäjälle": vapaaherra Lars Gabriel von Haartmanin elämä*. Suomalaisen Kirjallisuuden Seuran toimituksia 815. Helsinki: The Finnish Literature Society.

Karonen, Petri 1996: "Kuninkaan luottomiehiä, siniverisiä puoluejunkkareita, päteviä byrokraatteja ja säätyläisten parhaimmistoa: virkamiehet ja yhteiskunnan muutos uuden ajan alussa (noin 1520–1810)". In: Heikki Roiko-Jokela (toim.), *Siperiasta siirtoväkeen. Murrosaikoja ja käännekohtia Suomen historiassa*. Jyväskylä: Kopi-Jyvä.

Karonen, Petri 1998: "The Worst Offenders in the Provincial Towns. Serious Urban Crime and its Perpetrators in the Early Years of Sweden's Period as a Great Power", *Scandinavian Journal of History* 23.

Karonen, Petri 2004: *Patruunat ja poliitikot. Yritysjohtajien taloudellinen ja yhteiskunnallinen toiminta Suomessa 1600–1920*. Historiallisia Tutkimuksia 217. Helsinki: The Finnish Literature Society.

Karonen, Petri (ed.) 2009: *Hopes and Fears for the Future in Early Modern Sweden, 1500–1800*. Studia Historica 79. Helsinki: The Finnish Literature Society.

Karonen, Petri 2010: "Ruotsin ajan tutkimuksen nykytila ja resurssit", *Historiallinen Aikakauskirja*.

Karonen, Petri 2014: *Pohjoinen suurvalta. Ruotsi ja Suomi 1521–1809*. Helsinki: The Finnish Literature Society.

Katajala, Kimmo (ed.) 2004: *Northern Revolts. Medieval and Early Modern Peasant Unrest in the Nordic Countries*. Helsinki: The Finnish Literature Society.

Kershaw, Ian 2008: "Biography and the Historian. Opportunities and Constraints". In: Berghahn, Lässig (eds), *Biography*.

Kiser, Edgar 1999: "Comparing Varieties of Agency Theory in Economics, Political Science, and Sociology: An Illustration from State Policy Implementation", *Sociological Theory*.

Klingnéus, Sören 1997: *Bönder blir vapensmeder. Protoindustriell tillverkning i Närke under 1600- och 1700-talen*. Studia Historica Upsaliensia 181. Uppsala: Uppsala universitet.

Konttinen, Esa 1991: *Perinteisesti moderniin. Professioiden yhteiskunnallinen synty Suomessa*. Tampere: Vastapaino.

Korpiola, Mia (ed.) 2014: *The Svea Court of Appeal in the Early Modern Period: Historical Reinterpretations and New Perspectives*. Rättshistoriska studier 26. Stockholm: Institutet för rättshistorisk forskning.

Koskinen, Ulla 2011: *Hyvien miesten valtakunta. Arvid Henrikinpoika Tawast ja aatelin toimintakulttuuri 1500-luvun lopun Suomessa*. Bibliotheca Historica 132. Helsinki: The Finnish Literature Society.

Kulla, Heikki 1991: "Valtion virkamiehistön kehitys". In: Pia Letto-Vanamo (toim.), *Suomen oikeushistorian pääpiirteet: sukuvallasta moderniin oikeuteen*. Helsinki: Gaudeamus.

Laasonen, Pentti 1983: *Papinvirkojen täyttö Suomessa myöhäiskaroliinisena aikana 1690–1713*. SKHST 124. Saarijärvi: The Finnish Society of Church History.

Laasonen, Pentti 1991: "Vuodet 1593–1808". In: *Suomen kirkon historia 2*. Porvoo: WSOY.

Lagerstam, Liisa 2007: *A Noble Life. The Cultural Biography of Gabriel Kurck (1630–1712)*. Suomalaisen tiedeakatemia toimituksia, Humaniora 349. Helsinki: Finnish Academy of Science and Letters.

Lagerstam, Liisa, Parland-von Essen, Jessica 2010: "Aatelin kasvatus". In: Hanska, Jussi, Vainio-Korhonen, Kirsi (toim.), *Huoneentaulun maailma: kasvatus ja koulutus Suomessa keskiajalta 1860-luvulle*. Helsinki: The Finnish Literature Society.

Lahtinen, Anu 2007: *Sopeutuvat – neuvottelevat – kapinalliset. Naiset toimijoina Flemingin sukupiirissä 1470–1620*. Bibliotheca Historica 108. Helsinki: The Finnish Literature Society.

Lahtinen, Anu, Vainio-Korhonen, Kirsi 2011: "Valta ja naiset esimodernia koskevassa historiantutkimuksessa. Pohjoismaista keskustelua toimijoista ja rakenteista". In: Aalto, Ilana et. al. (eds), *Vallan teoriat historiantutkimuksessa*. Historia mirabilis 7. Turku: Turun historiallinen yhdistys.

Lamberg, Juha-Antti 1999: *Taloudelliset eturyhmät neuvotteluprosesseissa. Suomen kauppasopimuspolitiikka 1920–1930-luvulla*. Saarijärvi: Suomen Tiedeseura.

Lamberg, Marko, Hakanen, Marko, Haikari, Janne (eds) 2011: *Physical and Cultural Space in Pre-Industrial Europe.Methodological Approaches to Spatiality*. Lund: Nordic Academic Press.

Lappalainen, Mirkka 2001: "Regional Elite Group and the Problem of Territorial Integration: The Finnish Nobility and the Formation of the Swedish 'Power State', c. 1570–1620", *Scandinavian Journal of History* 26.

Lappalainen, Mirkka 2005: *Suku – valta – suurvalta. Creutzit 1600-luvun Ruotsissa ja Suomessa*. Helsinki: WSOY.

Lappalainen, Mirkka 2009: *Susimessu. 1590-luvun sisällissota Ruotsissa ja Suomessa*. Helsinki: WSOY.

Larsson, Lars-Olof 2002: *Gustav Vasa – landsfader eller tyrann?* Stockholm: Prisma.

Larsson, Lars-Olof 2005: *Arvet efter Gustav Vasa*. Stockholm: Prisma.

Letto-Vanamo, Pia 1989: *Suomalaisen asianajolaitoksen synty ja varhaiskehitys. Oikeushistoriallinen tutkimus*. Suomen Lakimiesyhdistyksen julkaisuja. A: 181. Vammala: Suomen lakimiesyhdistys.

Lind, Gunner 1999: "Prosopografi med relationelle databaser". In: Peter Aronsson, Solveig Fagerlund, Jan Samuelsson (red.), *Nätverk I historisk forskning. Metafor, metod eller teori?* Växjö: Växjö Universitet.

Linde, Martin 2000: *Statsmakt och bondemotstånd. Allmoge och överhet under stora nordiska kriget.* Studia Historica Upsaliensia 194. Uppsala: Uppsala universitet.

Linde, Martin 2009: *I fädrens spår? Bönder och överhet i Dalarna under 1700-talet.* Hedemora: Gidlund.

Lindegren, Jan 1980: *Utskrivning och utsugning. Produktion och reproduktion i Bygdeå 1620–1640.* Studia Historica Upsaliensia 117. Uppsala: Uppsala universitet.

Lindegren, Jan 1985: "The Swedish "Military State", 1560–1720", *Scandinavian Journal of History* 10.

Lässig, Simone 2008: "Introduction: Biography in Modern History – Modern Historiography in Biography". In: Volker R. Berghahn, Simone Lässig (eds), *Biography between Structure and Agency. Central European Lives in International Historiography.* Studies in German History 9. S. l.: Berghahn Books.

Mann, Michael 1987: *The sources of social power. Volume 1. A history of power from the beginning to A.D. 1760.* Cambridge: Cambridge University Press.

Marklund, Andreas 2008: *Stenbock. Ära och ensamhet i Karl XII:s tid.* Lund: Historiska media.

Messer-Davidov, Ellen 1995: "Acting Otherwise". In: Judith Kegan Gardiner (ed.), *Provoking Agents. Gender and Agency in Theory and Practise.* Urbana and Chicago: University of Illinois Press.

Montgomery, Ingun 2002: "Enhetskyrkans tid". In: *Sveriges kyrkohistoria* 4. Stockholm: Verbum.

Nilsson, Sven A. 1984: "Den karolinska militärstaten. Fredens problem och krigets". In: Gudrun Ekstrand (ed.), *Tre Karlar: Karl X Gustav, Karl XI, Karl XII.* Livrustkammaren: Stockholm.

Nilsson, Sven A. 1990: *De stora krigens tid. Om Sverige som militärstat och bondesamhälle.* Studia Historica Upsaliensia 161. Uppsala: Uppsala universitet.

Norrhem, Svante 1993: *Uppkomlingarna. Kanslitjänstemännen i 1600-talets Sverige och Europa.* Umeå Studies in the Humanities 117. Stockholm: Umeå universitet.

Norrhem, Svante 2007: *Ebba Brahe. Makt och kärlek under stormaktstiden.* Lund: Historiska Media.

Norrhem, Svante 2010: *Kvinnor vid maktens sida 1632–1772.* Lund: Nordic Academic Press.

Paarma, Jukka 1980: *Hiippakuntahallinto Suomessa 1554–1604.* Suomen kirkkohistoriallisen seuran Toimituksia 116. Helsinki: The Finnish Society of Church History.

Parker, Geoffrey, Smith, Lesley M. (eds) 1997: *The General Crisis of the Seventeenth Century*, 2nd edition. London: Routlegde.

Petersson, Erik 2008: *Den skoningslöse. En biografi över Karl IX.* Stockholm: Natur och kultur.

Petersson, Erik 2009: *Vicekungen. En biografi över Per Brahe den yngre.* Stockholm: Natur & Kultur.

Pirinen, Kauko 1991: "Keskiaika ja uskonpuhdistuksen aika". In: *Suomen kirkon historia* 1. Porvoo: WSOY.

Pirinen, Kauko (ed.) 1976: *Turun tuomiokapituli 1276–1976.* Loimaa: Turun Arkkihiippakunnan Tuomiokapituli.

Renvall, Pentti 1949: *Kuninkaanmiehiä ja kapinoitsijoita Vaasakauden Suomessa.* Helsinki: Tammi.

Renvall, Pentti 1962: "Ruotsin vallan aika". In: *Suomen kansanedustuslaitoksen historia*, Vol. 1: *Suomen kansanedustuslaitoksen vaiheet 1850-luvun puoliväliin.* Helsinki: Eduskunnan historiakomitea.

Ridder-Symoens, Hilde de 1996: "Training and Professionalization". In: Wolfgang Reinhard (ed.), *Power Elites and State Building.* The Origins of the Modern State in Europe, 13th–18th Centuries, Theme D. General Editors: Wim Blockmans & Jean-Philippe Genet. Oxford: Clarendon Press.

Roberts, Michael (ed.) 1973: *Sweden's Age of Greatness 1632–1718*. Aylesbury: Macmillan.
Roberts, Michael 1979: *The Swedish Imperial Experience 1560–1718*. Cambridge: Cambridge University Press.
Rodén, Marie-Louise 2008: *Drottning Christina. En biografi*. Stockholm: Prisma.
Rystad, Göran 2001: *Karl XI. En biografi*. Lund: Historiska Media.
Savolainen, Raimo 1994: *Suosikkisenaattorit. Venäjän keisarin suosio suomalaisten senaattoreiden menestyksen perustana 1809–1892*. Hallintohistoriallisia tutkimuksia 14. Helsinki: Valtioneuvosto.
Shapiro, Susan P. 2005: "Agency Theory", *Annual Review of Sociology*.
Scherp, Joakim 2013: *De ofrälse och makten. En institutionell studie av riksdagen och de ofrälse ståndens politik i maktdelningsfrågor 1660–1682*. Stockholm Studies in History 96. Stockholm: Stockholm universitet.
Smith, Jay M. 1996: *The Culture of Merit: Nobility, Royal Service, and the Making of Absolute Monarchy in France, 1600–1789*. Ann Arbor: The University of Michigan Press.
Stone, Lawrence 1971: "Prosopography", *Daedalus 100 (1)*.
Strömberg-Back, Kerstin 1963: *Lagen rätten läran. Politisk och kyrklig idédebatt i Sverige under Johan III:s tid*. Lund: Lunds universitet.
Svalenius, Ivar 1991: *Rikskansliet i Sverige 1560–1592*. Skrifter utgivna av Svenska Riksarkivet 7. Stockholm: Riksarkivet.
Tilly, Charles 1990: *Coercion, Capital, and European States AD 990–1990*. Oxford: Blackwell.
Torstendahl, Rolf, Burrage, Michael (eds) 1990: *The formation of professions: knowledge, state and strategy*. London: Sage.
Uotila, Merja 2014: *Käsityöläinen kyläyhteisönsä jäsenenä. Prosopografinen analyysi Hollolan käsityöläisistä 1810–1840*. Jyväskylä Studies in Humanities 237. Jyväskylä: Jyväskylän yliopisto.
Vainio-Korhonen, Kirsi 2008: *Sophie Creutzin aika. Aateliselämää 1700-luvun Suomessa*. Suomalaisen Kirjallisuuden Seuran toimituksia 1183. Helsinki: The Finnish Literature Society.
Wetterberg, Gunnar 2002: *Kanslern Axel Oxenstierna i sin tid I–II*. Stockholm: Atlantis 2002.
Villstrand, Nils Erik 2009: *Riksdelen. Stormakt och rikssprängning 1560–1812*. Finlands svenska historia 2. Skrifter utgivna av Svenska litteratursällskapet i Finland 702: 2. Helsingfors: The Society of Swedish Literature in Finland.
Villstrand, Nils Erik 2011: *Sveriges historia 1600–1721*. Norstedts Sveriges historia. Stockholm: Nordstedt.
Ylikangas, Heikki 1996: *Nuijasota*, 3rd edition. Helsinki: Otava.
Ågren, Henrik 2006: "Herremän och bönder. En uppländsk ämbetsmannasläkts sociala rörlighet under 1600-talet och det tidiga 1700-talet", *Karolinska förbundets årsbok*.
Österberg, Eva 1971: *Gränsbygd under krig. Ekonomiska, demografiska och administrativa förhållanden i sydvästra Sverige under och efter nordiska sjuårskriget*. Bibliotheca Historica Lundensis XXVI. Lund: Lund universitet.
Österberg, Eva 1987: "Svenska lokalsamhällen i förändring ca 1550–1850. Participation, representation och politisk kultur i den svenska självstyrelsen. Ett angeläget forskningsområde", *Historisk tidskrift*.
Österberg, Eva 1989: "Bönder och centralmakt i det tidigmoderna Sverige. Konflikt – kompromiss – politisk kultur", *Scandia*.
Österberg, Eva 1992: "Folklig mentalitet och statlig makt. Perspektiv på 1500- och 1600-talets Sverige", *Scandia*.
Österberg, Eva 1993: "Vardagens sträva samförstånd. Bondepolitik i den svenska modellen från vasatid till frihetstid". In: Gunnar Broberg, Ulla Wikander, Klas Åmark (red.), *Tänka, tycka, tro. Svensk historia underifrån*. Stockholm: Ordfront.

# Councillors of the Realm  II

Marko Hakanen
http://orcid.org/0000-0002-4214-960X

Ulla Koskinen
http://orcid.org/0000-0002-3430-9810

# The Gentle Art of Counselling Monarchs (1560–1655)

The Council of the Realm (*riksrådet*) was an aristocratic institution positioned at the heart of the centralized power structure in Sweden along with the king and the Diet. Consequently, political structures and events related to it have been well studied in historical research. Nevertheless, contrary to what many might believe, the personal political agency of those on the Council had not always been so extensive. We examine how the agency of these councillors (*riksråd*) was shaped in Sweden between 1560 and 1655. It was a twofold period: the first part after Gustavus Vasa's death was marked by an ongoing shaping and testing of forms of agency, and the latter by the establishment of clear regulations for the councillors' work. After Queen Christina came to the throne, the role of the Council of the Realm stabilized. As the political chronology of this period is already quite well-known from extensive historical research, we are able to concentrate more precisely on the factors that both contributed to and constrained councillors' agency as a collective entity, and as individuals; and how these factors changed during this epoch. To be able to get a more detailed view of this, we have thus created a database for all the councillors of this period.

In early modern Sweden, the king's councillors had the traditional right to give counsel to the ruler in important matters. Gustavus Vasa pushed through the law that allowed for inherited kingship in 1540, ending the tradition of elected kingship. However, legislation did not stop Eric XIV, John III and Charles IX (1550–1611) all having to gradually increase the power of the nobility to continue to receive support for their kingship. The nobility thus gained privileges and large fiefdoms for supporting the Vasa kings throughout the sixteenth century. The latter part of the century was marked by a balancing act between aristocratic demands and the rulers' efforts to control them.

The wars in Europe pushed Sweden into a rapid state-building process at the turn of the sixteenth century and the civil administration was completely restructured. This also meant that the notion of an ideal aristocrat changed from that of a military official to that of a civil servant. It became useful to serve the king in his administration, and at the same time, the power of the king's council increased because it was in charge of the whole administrative system, naturally reporting to the king.[1]

The continuous institutionalised power of the most distinguished aristocratic families in Sweden contrasts with the rest of Western Europe, where generally the upper nobility had lost much of its political predominance by this time. As Richard Bonney has pointed out, in France and Spain, where university education was readily at hand, trained professionals of lesser nobility and commoners came to replace aristocrats in the administrative councils; whereas in Sweden, Poland, and Russia, it was still the inherited aristocracy that prevailed.[2]

Through privilege, all the high offices belonged to the aristocratic nobility, but the problem was finding those of them who were educated, capable, and willing enough to work in the lower administrative offices.[3] This meant a growing demand for civil servants at this level, and eventually the lower nobility began to infiltrate the power structure. Although the Ordinance for the House of Nobility restricted appointments in 1626, and the higher nobility took up all the places in the Council, a new administrative nobility was born.

Even though the Councillors of the Realm held a significant position in the Swedish administration, they have been mainly studied in either short articles or as parts of a larger study, without a comprehensive database or register for the whole period to hand.[4] The database that forms the basis of this chapter of the book covers the 257 acting councillors who were in office for the period 1523–1680, of which 185 councillors were active between 1560 and 1655. The information has been collected from various sources: biographical registers and databases, biography collections, lineage databases, and research literature. It consists of data on births, deaths and marriages; dates of appointments; age at appointment; spouses and their parents; information on family relations inside the Council; and the number of acting councillors per year. All persons appear in the database with their names. The data has been collected using *collective group biography*[5] and *new prosopography*[6] methods. Prosopographic analysis enables the councillors to be studied collectively, while still taking into account their individual agency and personal life stories.[7] It is a method that has been used in medieval and early modern studies since the 1960s[8], but in this chapter we seek to develop a new interpretive historical approach which focuses more on personal agency by combining agency theories with the group's biographical information database (on status, activities, marriage details, and blood relations).

In this chapter, we examine how the personal agency of councillors changed from the sixteenth century to the seventeeth century. The database used throughout this article is compiled from biographical registers based on primary sources, examined with strict source criticism. The database is the foundation of our interpretation, but to gain a deeper analysis of the councillors' personal agency, we have added more qualitative information to support the quantitative material. This biographical information is based on previous research from primary source materials (for example *Svenska biografiskal lexikon*, *Kansallisbiografia*, and biographies when available).

## *The source of agency – a tradition of giving counsel*

The Council of the Realm was an institution dating back to early medieval times. According to the Law of the Realm (1442), it was to consist of 12 lay councillors (*riksråd*) representing the Swedish aristocracy and an undetermined number of bishops and other clerics.[9] It was the Council's task to give advice, help the king in important administrative matters, and stand together as representatives of the realm. The members were chosen from the most prominent aristocratic families or, exceptionally, from among other persons especially trusted by the current ruler. Councillors also took care of numerous other prominent tasks in central and regional administration, the armed forces and the judicial system. In this respect they formed the general administrative elite of the realm.

In the sixteenth-century, giving counsel (*rådgivning*) was an emblematic feature of the administration in Sweden. It was at the same time a right and a duty. Righteousness (*rättrådighet*) was among the virtues of a decent subject. It is mentioned in vows of loyalty by office-holders to the king.[10] Indeed, a culture of negotiation not only permeated the aristocracy but also society as a whole. Friendly counsel from a trustworthy person was expected before major decisions. This communal practice can also be seen in juridical documents, such as contracts of sale, which typically mention that the decision has been made with the counsel and agreement of family and friends.[11] Giving counsel was also part of an educated and courtly identity, as it was central to the classical ideal of friendship. It can be found in the influential writings of Cicero as well as medieval Scandinavian chronicles. In the latter, the king appears as a lord among others and it was important that he listened to the counsel of righteous persons.[12]

The Council of the Realm exemplified this tradition by giving reciprocal advice in an institutionalized form. In medieval Europe, it had been customary that princes ruled with councils consisting of both spiritual and lay aristocrats. Typically, the councils did not have the formal power to make decisions, but only offered advice to the ruler; and this left room for negotiation. The exercise of actual power depended on the current relations between king, aristocracy and representatives of the church. In Sweden, these foreign models were utilized as the early medieval gatherings of aristocracy around the king developed into a more established institution by the late thirteenth century. The institution was called in Latin *consilium*, and later this became *rikets råd* in Swedish.[13]

The Swedish Council held an ambiguous position with regards to an elective kingship. The king was elected at the Council's consent, and yet the Council was subject to the king at the same time. As far back as King Magnus Eriksson's Law of the Realm (circa 1350), the king had nominated the Council, but before long the Council was also asked to help in the appointment of new councillors. In effect, the king and the Council were both needed to represent the realm.[14] The fifteenth century became the century in which the Council consolidated itself as the centre of power in Sweden. Late medieval Sweden has been described as an "aristocratic republic" or "aristocratic power system".[15] A hundred years later a less powerful and humbler Council started to look back on those days with nostalgia.

According to the Law of King Christopher from 1442 (the so-called *landslag*), the councillors took an oath confirming that they "shall advise the king, of what they know in front of God to be for his and his kingdom's gain and benefit, and not leave it aside because of partiality, kinship, affinity or friendship". The law also stated that a councillor must keep all confidential information secret and support the king to uphold the laws and keep his oaths.[16] In practice, the Council's task was to give advice to the king and help him in decision-making with regard to foreign affairs, the armed forces, state finances, legislation, and taxation. They also took care of the highest judicial matters, although they had no right to award fiefs (*förläningar*).[17] It is worth noticing the somewhat vague definition in the law mentioning that the king rules with the help of counsel from the Council (*med råds råde*). This was to become a key point of dispute between Crown and Council later.[18]

During the last decades of the Union of Kalmar 1470–1520, Sweden was ruled by a regent and the Council. Councillors were active in developing the idea of state in opposition to the king. The end of the Union was, however, marked by the notorious Stockholm Bloodbath in November 1520. An influential number of the Swedish high aristocracy, including ten councillors, were executed after the accession of King Christian II of Denmark (1481–1559) to the throne of the Kalmar Union. The purpose seems to have been to break the aristocratic opposition to his rule in Sweden, led by Sten Sture the younger (1493–1520), but the final result was in fact the end of the Union, and the accession of Gustavus Vasa (1496–1560) to the Swedish throne.[19]

For most of the sixteenth century, Diet and the Council of the Realm were not the only official representative bodies in Sweden that gave counsel to the king. There still existed other means of counsel that only came to an end at around the turn of the century. Gatherings of nobility (*herredag*), for example, aimed at making a unanimous suggestion to the king, and regional meetings (*landsdag*) gathered representatives of other societal groups for the same purpose too.[20]

The Council worked within a central administration that was rather simple in structure. In practice, Gustavus Vasa took care of the realm personally, even to the point of being in touch with local bailiffs. He organized the state according to German models. The Chancellery and the Chamber, which were occupied by non-aristocratic secretaries, were permanent institutions which took care of the king's correspondence and the state finances. They officially played no part in making decisions; but unofficially the royal secretaries wielded significant power, as we will see later in this book.[21]

## Setting the rules – vaguely defined limits to agency

The agency of individual councillors becomes more visible with the emergence of Council Protocols from the 1620s onwards. Before that, there are mostly only sporadic documents covering negotiations within the Council. This is due to the fact that the Council was not yet either an administrative organ or a continuous assembly with responsibilities to keep tabs on everyday administrative matters. As it was only called into being by the king as and when he needed the Council's pronouncements on separately defined matters, it was sufficient to give a joint statement to the king. A collection of these *rådslag* survive from the early sixteenth century onwards, but shed no light on the role of individual councillors.[22]

Generally the position of councillors vis-à-vis administration and the limits of their agency remained vague throughout the Vasa dynasty, even if Gustavus Vasa did make some attempt to shape the Council into a supreme administrative and legal power that met on a regular basis. The experiment of a Governing Council (*regementsråd*) was conducted by his trusted German Chancellor, Conrad von Pyhy (d. 1553), in line with Habsburgian principles, but it came to an end in 1542.[23] After that, it was not until the 1620s that an effective reorganisation of the central administration took place.

In the sixteenth century, the king and Council represented the realm together, but the Council had no independent role in the administration. Relations between the king and councillors remained flexible and personal rather than defined by written orders. This purely supportive role of the Council was particularly prevalent in the reign of Gustavus Vasa. The king appointed all the members, many of them from among his own kin; and the frequency of Council meetings (*rådsmöten*) varied greatly, but was usually low. As late as 1593 Duke Charles suggested there should be three meetings of the Council every year.[24]

Meetings of the Council received the king's written proposition and gave a written counsel that was signed and sealed by the councillors who were present. However, the king was not tied to their verdict. In fact, if anything, the Council was customarily utilized as a tool by the king to consolidate and legitimize his ordinances, or to sign important documents alongside him and thus add emphasis to a matter.[25]

This lack of definition in the Council's role can also be seen in the councillor's oath (*rådsed*) which, in the late fifteenth century consisted of four articles: to be loyal to the realm, to only counsel in the realm's best interests, to act in confidentiality, and to avoid arbitrariness. At the coronation of John III, the oath was changed to stipulate that councillors had to take part in the meetings, to have freedom of speech, to be in agreement with each other, and to stick to the decisions taken.[26]

John III also doubled the official number of councillors to 24 in 1569. This effectively confirmed what had already become an established practice of exceeding the regulated number.[27] In this respect the Council resembled the *duma* of Muscovy, which varied considerably in size. This has been seen as reflecting the instability and inconsistency of the Muscovite state and its policy.[28] The same easily applies to the political situation in Sweden in the times of Gustavus Vasa's sons.

New members to the Council were nominated at meetings of either the Council or Diet, and at coronations. Under the Kalmar Union it was ordered that councillors had to be Swedish men born in Sweden. Some exceptions were made along the way, but it was also customary that councillors came from the most prominent aristocratic families of the kingdom, many with a long line of predecessors in the Council. Emil Hildebrand calls them "the finest or most splendid flower of nobility". So when the clerical members of the Council were removed in 1527, as a consequence of the Reformation, virtually all the Council's members came from the ranks of the highest aristocracy.[29]

Whereas the agency of a councillor was vaguely defined, his post was permanent. Among the councillors who served between 1560 and 1655, the majority stayed in office until their death. Those who did not were related to the crisis of the 1590s, when Charles IX acceded to the throne and the remaining cases were related to personal conditions, like health matters. This said, the deaths of councillors were not always natural (i.e., falling into royal disgrace could lead to execution), and this will be dealt with more later.[30]

Most of the councillors appointed in the mid-sixteenth century were provincial magnates and they remained in their residences, scattered around the kingdom for the duration of their appointments. The councillors that lived closest to the king, in the vicinity of Stockholm, may have had a greater degree of personal agency, but most seemed reluctant at the idea of permanent service in the heart of the realm. A hundred years later however, the aristocracy were only too keen to flock to Stockholm for a place in the centralized state administration. Gustavus Vasa tried to make the Council more permanent, so it could help the king in everyday administration, and for a while the Council agreed that two of its members should take turns to accompany the king for one month at a time; but it seems that this was more the exception than the rule.[31]

Jan Samuelson has noted that the key regions of recruitment were, in the sixteenth century, Västergötland, Uppland and Södermanland. The Finnish part of the realm was generally represented by one or two councillors at a time, equating roughly to Swedish provinces Småland and Östergötland. In the next century, the number of councillors of Finnish origin gradually increased and even exceeded 10 in the 1660s.[32]

The individual political agency of councillors was more visible in their numerous other offices in central and regional administration. The kings gave them permanent and temporary tasks that were, among others, military, judicial, and financial, or related to steward (*ståthållare*). The most distinguished councillors took part in foreign policy negotiations and were used in diplomatic missions, but at all times they remained instruments for the king's decision-making, with no agency of their own.[33]

Some councillors were at times referred to as Secret Councillor or Highest Secret Councillor (*sekrete råd, överste sekrete råd*), which was reminiscent of the *regementsråd* experiment in the 1530s and 1540s, when the highest department was referred to in this way. It can be regarded as an honorary title, as the concrete significance remained undefined and there were no special tasks or status as a permanent minister attached to it.[34]

## The Council gains new confidence but is bound by old constraints

All over Europe, the trend of sixteenth century was that administrative and military power became ever more concentrated in the hands of monarchs as a consequence of the gradual process of state formation. Aristocratic groups could not efficiently compete with this monopoly of power.[35] Even in Sweden, the agency of aristocratic councillors remained subordinate to the king throughout the reign of Gustavus Vasa's sons 1560–1611. Their status varied according to political fluctuations.

The break from the Kalmar Union under the strong leadership of Gustavus Vasa meant that the Council relented from asking the king to delegate more of his power. Even his sons did not want to risk passing power to their aristocratic rivals, as they perceived them. Instead, they relied on the practical but unofficial help of non-noble secretaries in the royal Chancellery. The Council of the Realm thus remained a temporary meeting to be summoned as and when needed. The period was marked by an active foreign policy, inner power struggles, and dire state finances. The tense relations between king and aristocrats, and the councillors' lack of political agency and reliance on the king's grace eventually culminated in massive tribunals and executions of councillors in the 1560s and 1599–1600.[36]

As he had lost his father in a similar fashion, Gustavus Vasa trusted the sons of councillors executed in 1520 and managed to make Sten Eriksson (Leijonhufvud) (1518–1568) and Per Brahe the elder (1520–1590) his sturdiest supporters.[37] However, Eric XIV was paranoid of aristocratic plots against his rule. One of his main targets was the Sture family of councillors, that before Gustavus' reign had provided the last Regents of Sweden (*riksföreståndare*). They had so far successfully preserved their agency in the new Vasa dynasty by not arousing mistrust, but this came to an end when Eric XIV eliminated three of its most prominent members in the Sture Murders of 1567.[38]

Secret Councillors[39] Per Brahe and Sten Eriksson (who had barely escaped with his life) became the central figures of the Council that took care of the administration during the king's subsequent mental breakdown. This was the first time since the Kalmar Union that the Council had a role independent of the king. The Council suggested that if King Eric could now no longer take responsibility of the government personally, he should delegate authority, organize the central administration on a clearly defined basis, and give members of the Council the mandate to take care of matters. As the king recovered, this brief period was soon forgotten about, but it remains the first occasion that councillors requested a defined structure to their agency.[40]

Although the councillors continued to have no formal power over the sovereign, they sought other ways to balance the king's power. Secret Councillor Sten Eriksson (Leijonhufvud) figures as one of the leading men of the aristocracy. He not only negotiated the nobility's responsibilities for cavalry service in early 1560s, but when Dukes John and Charles staged an uprising against King Eric in 1568, Sten Eriksson became the leader of their aristocratic allies. He was the one who led the troops into Stockholm and got killed in doing so.⁴¹ The 66-year old Secret Councillor Gustav Olofsson (Stenbock) (1502–1571), who had been Gustavus Vasa's brother-in-law, trusted ally, and promotor of princely power also joined this uprising, as Erik had previously condemned his two sons to death for treacherous speech.⁴²

Statements about the need to delegate supreme power between the king and the Council reappeared after John III seized power in 1568. This is an important turning point. Traditionally, the councillors had been rather defensive towards the kings' suggestions about a permanent organization for their work, but now they took on a more active political role, initiating propositions and demanding that their counsels be carried out. The councillors felt confident once again that they could criticise the king's actions. One of their main concerns was "the rule of secretaries". In the years 1573–1575 the Council, led by the king's brother Duke Charles, made several suggestions about reorganizing the central administrative institutions.⁴³

The upsurge of interest in central government among the leading councillors has been interpreted in different ways. The most obvious explanation seems to be they were interested in more power at the expense of the king. But for a deeper evaluation, one needs to take into account the changes that had occurred in the international military, political and economic situation and called for an overhaul of Sweden's central government. The vague principles of personal cooperation between the royal family and aristocracy were now no longer suitable as they served instead as a constant source of rivalry and unrest. Although both Gustavus Vasa and John III could always rely on kungafränder (members of royal kin) in the Council, in John III's case they were already more distant relatives, forming such a tight social structure in itself that rather than creating an atmosphere of loyalty to the king, gave them confidence to disagree with him.⁴⁴

The remarkable thing is that the councillors did not demand a weakening of central administration, which would have been the traditional aristocratic position. Instead, they wanted the central organs of power to remain strong but with the aristocracy given a prominent position within them. Although they were asking that royal power be restricted by law, the central role of a monarch remained unquestioned. This reflects the general European trend at the time to see royal power as emanating from God.⁴⁵

Nils Edén (1899) and Michael Roberts (1968) have stressed how, at this point, the aristocracy had become more conscious of the need to cooperate with the king and to secure their position by taking part in courtly life and the central administration in Stockholm.⁴⁶ Meanwhile, Richard Bonney (1991) has referred to the nobility's attempts to reclaim their 'lost freedoms' from the lowborn secretaries who were effectively wielding more power than them at the time.⁴⁷ Aristocratic demands for more extensive privileges and less dependence on the inconsistent grace of the monarch have been most profoundly addressed by Sven A. Nilsson (1952).⁴⁸ In such a state, which was under the personal rule of Vasa monarchs, personal factors were more important than they perhaps should have been. According to Lars Ericson Wolke's biography of John III (2006), the king's mood swings made his governance volatile rather than well-considered. In order to control the monarch's ad hoc decision-making process, the councillors thus had to be physically present and find a secure place within the central administration.[49]

Finnish historians Pentti Renvall and John E. Roos (1934) have highlighted the importance of specific rewards called *beställningar*, introduced in John III's reign. These became a common form of payment for the highest office-holders. Only then did councillors become willing to take on duties that required absence from their landed properties.[50] Another factor that gradually led towards a paid office-holding nobility was the simultaneous reduction in the number of fiefs awarded. Sven A. Nilsson has pointed out that this was especially relevant to the leading group of councillors (Bielke, Banér, and Sparre), who held the highest state offices, earned *beställningar*, and who also voiced the hardest criticism over John III's reductions.[51] According to Jan Glete, the aristocrats shifted their support quickly toward a more centralized administration, because their position as regional magnates had been comparatively modest in Sweden and they perceived a strong Vasa state as the best form of administrative and military organisation, provided that they had a share in it.[52]

However sophisticated their views on the delegation of power, the councillors could not form a united aristocratic front that would have been necessary to take on John III. The leading group consisted of Hogenskild (1538–1605) and Ture Bielke (1548–1600), Gustaf (1547–1600) and Sten Axelsson Banér (1546–1600), Per Brahe the elder, and his son-in-law Erik Larsson Sparre (1550–1600).[53] But instead of determined action, their agency was wasted on power struggles and voicing their powerless critique over the way Sweden was ruled. In this situation, the only means of having a greater agency in state matters depended on the councillors' personal relations to the king.

Pontus De la Gardie (1520–1585) serves as an example of this. He came to the realm as an outsider to the councillor families, a foreigner with no connection to existing domestic power struggles and with capabilities that were rare among the Swedish aristocracy at the time. He had international political expertise, knowledge of military tactics, and linguistic skills that made him a useful diplomat. De la Gardie came to Sweden in Eric XIV's service, but quickly changed sides. The French diplomat, Danzay, reported that he was one of those to whom John III felt most indebted, upon becoming king. De la Gardie's rise to become the most powerful man in the realm was quick after that. In the beginning, he was not a steady royalist, as he plotted with foreign powers and may have even had some part in a conspiracy against John III. However, John was able to tie him to the royal throne so that De la Gardie found he was in the best position as a strong supporter of the Swedish king. With royal grace, his authorizations and agency was strong and his family was permanently blended in with the other councillors, although in the beginning their relationship was not quite so harmonious.[54]

The widowed John III married Gunilla Bielke (1568–1597), the daughter of Councillor Johan Axelsson Bielke (d. 1576), in 1585. Despite this symbolic diminishing of distance between the aristocracy and royalty, the councillors clashed with the king over foreign policy. The meeting at Reval in 1589 served as the next turning point for their agency. Briefly they returned to the independent role they had once had within the Kalmar Union, as a strong representative body between king and the people, as they formulated it.⁵⁵ John III wanted to take his son Sigismund (1566–1632), King of Poland, to Sweden, but had to give this up because of the strict opposition of the Council and other nobility. A king having been scandalously forced to bend before his Council was too humiliating for John III however, and in retaliation he punished councillors by disgracing them and stripping six of their titles before the Estates. They were the aforementioned Bielke and Banér brothers, Erik Sparre, and Claes Åkesson (Tott) (c. 1525–1590).⁵⁶

Meanwhile, councillors Claes (Eriksson) Fleming (1535–1597) and Nils (Göransson) Gyllenstierna (1526–1601), basked in royal grace and were awarded additional offices. These men had, however, used two quite different strategies to achieve greater agency. Gyllenstierna had enjoyed a long career as a councillor by being a mediator, or "caution personified", throughout;⁵⁷ while the Finnish "Iron Marshal" Claes Fleming had been the only councillor who stood on John III's side in Reval, confident that with the backing of his army in Finland, he could defeat the rest of the Council and Duke Charles. Fleming became a favourite of John III in the same way that Pontus De la Gardie had done earlier. Both were competent military leaders and outsiders with respect to the Swedish aristocracy. After the death of Claes Åkesson (Tott) in 1590, Fleming was the only councillor from Finland for the years 1591–1597.⁵⁸ Like De la Gardie, he was also tied to the throne through marriage to the sister-in-law of Gustavus Vasa.⁵⁹

Fleming's relations with the rest of the councillors, especially the Sparre-Bielke-Banér network, were tense. He was not particularly interested in their constitutional ideas about delegating power, being more content with the traditional autocratic role of the king and the possibilities this afforded to those who showed loyal service. In this respect, he allied himself quite clearly with the Vasa dynasty's ideas of ruling Sweden, which explains the enormously powerful position he eventually gained, controlling the whole of Finland as a separate entity as Governor, Marshal and Admiral. Ironic as it may seem, his strategy of subordinating himself to the monarch had led to a greater agency that bypassed the rest of the councillors. If he had, however, joined the aristocratic front, they would have gained the strong leading figure they were lacking.⁶⁰

As John III died in 1592, the Crown passed to his son Sigismund, who resided in his other kingdom, Poland. Duke Charles thus took over the reins of government alongside the Council. The Council's propositions for central rule included a systematic organization of central government, dividing it into different sections led by high-ranking office-holders, and with defined hierarchical links to the lower offices. Although these propositions were rejected, they bear a striking resemblance to the reorganization that eventually occurred thirty years later, in the 1620s. The leading councillors had evidently internalized the idea that supporting a centralized state controlled by themselves was the best way to attain greater agency. This was now quite the opposite of the traditional aristocratic ideals that prevailed in Denmark, Germany and Poland.⁶¹

Hogenskild Bielke and Erik Sparre were perhaps the most politically aware councillors of this period. Both were well-educated political theorists, doing their utmost via research and writing to restore the privileges and political power that they argued the nobility had held in earlier centuries. Their basic thesis was that the realm should be governed by "rule of the law" and the hereditary sovereign's power should be limited in favour of the people (i.e., the Council and the Estates). The political and legal agenda they proposed had its roots in the Middle Ages, and has been described as either constitutionalism, or "Council-constitutionalism" (*rådskonstitutionalism*). In the early 1570s, Hogenskild Bielke even seems to have been considering the overthrow of John III to replace him with a regent and rule via the Council as had been done in the fifteenth century. It seems Hogenskild Bielke and Erik Sparre were not engaging in these activities only to better their agency as councillors, but to represent the highest aristocracy as a group.[62]

Erik Sparre's pamphlet *Pro Lege, Rege et Grege* from the 1580s, was actually written with John III's consent and was directed against Duke Charles' aspirations for power. It marked a turning point in its legalistic anti-absolutist stance and with its references to Roman law. Indeed, it effectively challenged the assumptions on which the Vasa monarchy rested. According to Kerstin Strömberg-Back, Sparre's arguments were influenced by other councillors, especially his father-in-law, Secret Councillor Per Brahe. Brahe was also concerned about the nobility's lost privileges and shared Sparre and Bielke's sympathies towards Catholicism. Otherwise Brahe, already an older man, adopted a moderate position and avoided taking too overt a stance in the power struggle that ensued.[63]

Axel Stensson (Leijonhufvud) (1554–1619) was the only councillor who came to the Diet of Arboga in 1597, when Duke Charles virtually carried out a coup d'état and made himself the regent (*riksföreståndare*).[64] Axel Stensson's agency as a councillor stands out in opposition to the rest of the group concerning this. As a cousin to both John III and Duke Charles he had a renowned social status.[65] Explanations for the volatility of his agency can be found in his personality: he was a political opportunist and, according to contemporaries, was quick to lose his temper. Leijonhufvud started out as royalist but soon channelled his loyalty towards Duke Charles in spite of the opinions of the other councillors, and he eventually ended up as judge at their trial.[66]

The councillors now found themselves in a situation with "evil on all sides", as Gustav Banér wrote to Hogenskild Bielke. They did not want to surrender to Duke Charles, yet despite their efforts, they could not agree on a joint policy against him. Their ranks started to break, until by the spring of 1597 Erik Stenbock (1538–1602), Sten Banér, Göran Knutsson Posse (1556–1616) as well as Erik Sparre himself had left Sweden to seek help in Poland.[67]

In the civil war that followed, Charles cruelly crushed any dreams the aristocracy may have had of power. The former leading councillors were either sentenced to death or went into exile, and the Council as good as disappeared in these chaotic years. In Linköping, March 1600, Duke Charles (from 1605 officially King Charles IX) arranged a show trial with a tribunal of 155 judges, some of them councillors themselves. Seven councillors were accused and Ture Bielke, Erik Sparre, Gustaf Banér, and Sten Banér were executed.[68]

It is clear then that sixteenth-century councillors had quite limited political agency, and from the 1570s onwards most of this centred on efforts to get the king to delegate some of his power to them. This was therefore an era in which councillors attained a new political consciousness. The leading group adopted an approach novel to aristocrats: actively using their agency to gain a secure position in central administration. However, they were a small group without an independent feudal background or strong leader, and while opposed by the Vasa monarchs, they lacked the means to achieve their goals before the 1620s.

The fate of the elderly Hogenskild Bielke serves as a fitting epilogue to the councillors' limited agency in the sixteenth century. He was imprisoned in Linköping in 1600 and had the dubious honour of becoming the last councillor to be executed in the Swedish realm in 1605 because of his incautious letters regarding Charles IX.[69] This sudden end to the executions that had shadowed Swedish political life up to this point leads one to ask, what had changed between the Council aristocracy and the king so that such displays of power were no longer needed?

## *The Council of the Realm is restored and given greater agency*

In October 1601 the remaining last councillor, Nils Gyllenstierna (1526–1601), died and the Council of the Realm ceased to exist for all practical purposes; but only for a while, as it soon became clear that the kingdom could not be ruled without it. There were so many administrative tasks now, that the king and his secretaries could not manage everyday operations alone. And without councillors, other countries found it difficult to negotiate with Sweden, as they thought the country now lacked credible negotiators.[70]

The old institution was restored without major modifications at the Diet of 1602, with Duke Charles appointing 15 new counsellors.[71] He found it sufficient to state that, to avoid the earlier troubles, the Council was there only to give counsel, and not to rule (*råda, ej regera*);[72] yet he still had to trust the same noble families who had formerly been members of the Council. Of the 15 new councillors seven had fathers, one a father-in-law, and four had grandfathers (on their mothers' side) who had also been councillors. Only three had no relatives previously in the Council of the Realm.

The king had nonetheless made some quite important changes to the Council, as he still did not trust the higher nobility. Now there were only a few members representing them. These were led by the two Brahe brothers, ranked first among the handful of counts in Sweden. Jan Samuelson has studied the geographical composition of the Council and found that Charles IX favoured his former duchy with regard to the nominees for the new Council. All the provinces were represented, but there were now more councillors from Västergötland and Södermanland.[73] But Charles IX not only turned to those who had previously served as counsellors in his dukedom Ludbert Kauer (d. 1608), Johan Oxenstierna (1557–1607), Seved

Ribbing (1552–1613) and Jöran Stiernsköld (1552–1611)); he also wanted to reward those who had changed side during the crisis: Göran Boije (d. 1617), Mauritz Leijonhufvud (1559–1607), Erik Ribbing (1558–1612), and Arvid Horn (d. 1606/7).[74] This both legitimized their status and his as a ruler. Göran Boije had originally belonged to Sigismund's party and played a big role in defending the eastern border against the Russians. Boije had chosen Sigismund, because he saw cooperation between Poland and Sweden as essential to protect the realm against Russia. Nevertheless, because of his former allegiance, Charles IX stripped Boije of his position as a Chief Judge and Commander-in-Chief in Estonia, leaving him as simply the Commander of Tallinn Castle. Then, in 1602, Charles IX visited Tallinn and pardoned Boije, making him once again the Chief Judge in Estonia and appointing him to the Council of the Realm. After this, Göran Boije was given many confidential posts to do with defending the eastern border.[75] His military expertise and knowledge of the local area were essential to gaining this greater agency for himself as a councillor.

Arvid Horn had also been a supporter of Sigismund, but he managed to remove himself in time, and became one of the key figures who signed a new oath of allegiance to Charles IX. In return, Charles IX appointed him to the Council of the Realm, but did not give him any significant tasks.[76] Meanwhile, Mauritz Leijonhufvud earnt Duke Charles' trust by being the active spokesperson of the duke at the Diet of 1602.[77] Although Erik Ribbing had stayed with Sigismund in Poland, he returned to Sweden in 1595 and earnt Duke Charles' trust as a judge both in Linköping (1600) and Stockholm (1605). He was also the brother of Seved Ribbing (1552–1613), who was an acquaintance of Charles IX.[78] Due to the circumstances of their appointments, made on the slimmest benefit of the doubt, both Mauritz Leijonhufvud and Erik Ribbing were somewhat restrained in their roles as councillors. Their personal agency was only as great as the trust in which they were held, and at the start of the seventeenth century, this was not a great deal. In fact the Council of the Realm had little real power at this stage.

For example, the Chancellor of the Realm, Svante Bielke (1567–1609), did not receive any actual instructions and thus spent most of his time taking care of personal business on his estate. Meanwhile, the everyday tasks of the Royal Chancellery were taken care of by Royal Chancellor (*swe: hovkansler*) Nils Chesnecopherus (1574–1622) (also appointed in 1602). He had been educated in Marburg University and was not from the nobility. Svante Bielke had been one of the judges in Linköping in 1600, but he was afraid that he had fallen from Duke Charles' grace after the Linköping trials. His wife urged him to ask Duke Charles to reassure him of his trust, which he duly did, with the result that Bielke was appointed to the Council of the Realm.[79] From the personal agency point of view, this case is interesting because, although Duke Charles made Bielke Chancellor of the Realm, Chesnecopherus had more real power than him. This suggests that Duke Charles was afraid to give any real power to the nobility, which might have given them greater individual agency.[80]

Indeed, Charles IX had only a few trusted councillors. One of them, Axel Ryning (1552–1620), had been the negotiator between him and the

Council of the Realm after the death of John III. Axel had made a personal oath of allegiance with Charles IX and was given special tasks. He was in charge of several diplomatic negotiations, but also played an integral part in the duke's marriage negotiations. The trust of Charles IX was the fount of Axel's agency as councillor, and thanks to it he was able to work in many different sectors of the administration. He was even chosen to be admiral without any substantial experience of seafaring and later, under Gustavus Adolphus, he was made a Field Marshal (though without any administrative responsibilities).[81] The other councillor Duke Charles had used as a negotiator was Jöran Ulfsparre (1544–1612). His job had been to negotiate with Sigismund about Sweden's freedom of religion, which was one factor in the internal crisis of the 1590s.[82]

If Axel Ryning was an important and powerful member of the Council of the Realm, then Seved Ribbing, appointed as Lord High Treasurer in 1602, was even more so. One of his responsibilities as chief of Stockholm Castle was its fortification and arranging supplies for the troops, over which he had substantial personal agency.[83] One of Charles IX key strategies was to appoint very trusted men such as these in all the important castles of the realm to lead military operations (for example, Jöran Stiernsköld (1552–1611), Jöran Gyllenstierna 1575–1618), and Mats Kruus (d. 1606)).[84] In a world where controlling armed forces was crucial, it shows a huge amount of trust on both sides and strongly indicates these men had a greater degree of personal agency. This trust gave them more room to operate and plan individual actions. People earnt the ruler's trust in a variety of ways. In Charles' case, being a judge in critical situations where Sigismund's supporters could be punished seemed to work. Many of the new councillors had indeed proven themselves this way by condemning former fellow members of the nobility to death. Svante Bielke had been a judge in Linköping, as had Abraham (1569–1630) and Magnus Brahe (1564–1633); Erik Ribbing, Peder Ribbing (1544–1604), and Johan Oxenstierna had been judges in both Linköping and Stockholm; and Seved Ribbing and Jöran Ulfsparre had been judges in Jönköping and Linköping. Sometimes Charles IX demanded that families act against their best interests in order to gain his trust. Abraham and Magnus Brahe, for example, had to condemn their sister's husband to death, while Erik and Seved Ribbing had to condemn their wife's uncle to death.

Almost everybody from the 1602 Council of the Realm had relatives, usually a father or grandfather (on their mother's side), in the council before. The only odd man out was Ludbert Kauer who was hired as an administrator without the help of large aristocratic networks in Charles' dukedom, and then awarded a place in the Council of the Realm for, it seems, doing a good job.[85] Only two people in the Council were from a different social rank. Magnus[86] and Abraham[87] Brahe were counts (in fact, their father Per Brahe the elder was the first to have ever been awarded this title in Sweden),[88] and this gave them a certain agency. First of all, it gave them access to networks of power. Abraham Brahe escorted Duke Charles many times in his travels, and this not only gave him access to more information, but also the opportunity to provide the duke with advice and guidance.[89] The brothers also represented the government in official ceremonies such as weddings and funerals.

The Council of the Realm's collective agency was minimal in the early years of the seventeenth century; but being on the Council did make it easier for its individual members to influence things. Still these new councillors had to rely more on their personal agency than their peer group in later decades. By the reign of Charles IX, the lower nobility held most of the seats on the Council, but they were all from families who had previously provided councillors – usually their fathers or grandfathers (on the mother's side). The only real exception to this would seem to be the Banér family who were only able to return to the Council of the Realm after 1623. Even the Bielke family were not banished for so long, as by 1606 they had not one (the first came back in 1602), but two representatives on the Council.[90]

Charles IX did not really have the chance to develop his administration even if he had plans to do so. The priority in his reign became to secure the king's position by keeping the nobility under control and ensuring that they remained servants of the realm. But by the time he died in 1611, his son Gustavus Adolphus (1594–1632) could finally focus on restructuring the central government with the help of Axel Oxenstierna (1583–1654). Oxenstierna was a dynamic man who had gained diplomatic experience abroad, and with the threats of war that Sweden now faced, the time was ripe to create a more efficient chain of command at home so that not every decision would need to be directly made by the king.[91] The king would indeed spend most of his reign outside the country. This effectively meant that the Council of the Realm would have more responsibilities, as a caretaker government. But to ensure that there would be no danger of it usurping the king's authority, there needed to be clear instructions, which would set out the limits of the councillors' agency and their responsibilities to the king.

So it seems that the key to solving Sweden's domestic problems lay outside its borders. Gustavus Adolphus needed to rebuff claims to the Swedish Crown from Sigismund, who was now King of Poland. It took almost two decades to do this, but at the same time it catalysed the state-building process in Sweden. The first part of the administration to be reformed by Axel Oxenstierna was the Royal Chancellery, where tasks now became clearly delineated. Oxenstierna established office working hours and structured salaries for all workers (including councillors). In the process, the role of the Council of the Realm changed.[92] It became the top institution, whose task was to supervise the whole administration via separate Collegia (colleges), of which the head of each was naturally also a member of the Council; and its role grew even bigger during the extensive periods that the king spent abroad with his army.[93]

During the 1620s, the role of the Council became clearer as a result of specific instructions. Its prime function was to guarantee the administration ran smoothly in the absence of the king, but it had to keep a record of all of its actions, so the king could check the decisions made afterwards. From 1625 to 1630, there were new instructions every year. The first orders stipulated that it was mandatory for at least six councillors to always be present in Stockholm. In practice, this meant that they had to live in the capital at a time when most councillors had their own castles outside Stockholm. But the workload eventually proved to be so great that, in 1626, the stipulated minimum number of councillors required in the capital increased to ten.[94] From then on, the king was so often away that the number of council meetings grew enormously and the Council soon became the foremost institution for making domestic political decisions. Between 1625 and 1635, the number of council meetings grew from approximately 50 meetings a year to nigh on 200.[95] In practice this meant the councillors were no longer men who gave occasional counsel to the king; but had become fully professional administrative personnel who spent most of their time solving matters of national importance.

The nobility had gained new privileges from Gustavus Adolphus in 1617. They were now entitled to all high-ranking offices in the civil administration.[96] There was now a great need for nobles who were capable of doing the job required and it became a challenge for the noble Estate.[97] This need should have come as no surprise, as Per Brahe the elder had already stated in his guidebook for raising nobility in the 1570s, that part of their education should be in administrative skills.[98] In reality, however, many important figures in the administration had to be recruited from outside the nobility. This influx of commoners put some pressure on the higher nobility, but also had the effect of raising the status of the Council of the Realm.

By 1609, the Council had 20 members.[99] When the new rules for the Council came into force, this number jumped to 24, as stipulated by law. But the one striking feature was that all these new appointments came from the lower nobility. It was not until after Gustavus Adolphus' death during the interregnum, that members of the higher nobility were again appointed to the Council of the Realm. In fact, just a year after the king's death, the Council got six new members,[100] and during the 12 years of the interregnum, the higher nobility were able to return to power.[101]

As caretaker in the king's absence, the Council increased its workload, but the number of councillors stayed practically the same throughout the 1620s. In that time seven councillors passed away and eight new ones were appointed. Only two of them (Per Banér (1588–1644) and Claes Fleming (1592–1644)) were appointed for their administrative expertise; and both were appointed in 1625.[102]

Per Banér was perhaps King's most trusted officer, and when the new instructions for the Council came in 1625 and 1626, Banér was appointed head of the Royal Chancellery, making him ultimately responsible for the Council's decisions. Banér simultaneously held many offices and their combination meant he had significant personal agency. He was even able to act independently of Axel Oxenstierna and he used this rare freedom to plot his own agenda between different political camps. Per Banér was also a hard-working man who rarely missed a meeting, but by the end of 1632 he fell ill and never fully recovered. His work ethic became less important, he became indecisive, and he developed a negative approach to almost everything.[103]

Claes Fleming was appointed into the Council same year as Per Banér. He was also very active, but in many ways the total opposite of Banér. He was a firm supporter of Axel Oxenstierna and was in charge of the capital Stockholm (*överståthållare*). He worked hard to upgrade the look of the city by renewing the city planning, legislation and market regulations. But at the same time his primary responsibility was to develop the Swedish navy; and even though he was a busy man, or perhaps because of it, he had an eye for business. He secured himself the privilege of manufacturing the swords the army required, for example. To give himself more freedom and personal agency, he wisely decided to remain politically neutral within the Council of the Realm, and yet at the same time he was very actively present in the meetings. Fleming also belonged to Gustavus Adolphus' inner circle, and many times it was his duty to transport not only the king, but also the queen. This gave him almost constant access to the ruler, and royal proximity was a great source of agency in early modern society, of which Fleming was no doubt aware. One thing that describes Fleming's strong belief in his own personal agency is that he resigned by choice from the Council of the Realm, but he died only a few months later at sea, in the war against Denmark. The news of his death was hard for many residents of Stockholm, because he was very popular.[104]

The workload of councillors began to grow in the beginning of the 1620s and increased dramatically from 1626 onwards, when the Council started to meet almost on a daily basis. The whole culture of being a councillor changed. This transition was especially hard for those 14 councillors who had been appointed before the 1620s. Two of them, Bo Ribbing (1560-1640) and Erland Bååt (d. 1628), were already so old that they were no longer actively participating in meetings of the Council.[105] Three of them, Jacob De la Gardie (1583-1654), Carl Gyllenhielm (1574-1650) and Nils Stiernsköld (1583-1627), were also rarely present because they were away at war.[106] Meanwhile, Gustaf Stenbock (1575-1629) and Gabriel Bengtsson Oxenstierna (1586-1656) were absent from the council meetings because of foreign policy diplomatic assignments;[107] while Filip Scheiding (1578-1646) and Claes Horn (1583-1632) were only able to make the meetings from time to time as they were taking care of local assignments. This means that from the old guard, only four members (Abraham Brahe, Magnus Brahe, Gabriel Gustafsson Oxenstierna (1587-1640) and Johan Skytte (1577-1645)) were left as active members of the Council. All four were very highly educated and quite capable of taking care of official governmental business. Gabriel Gustafsson Oxenstierna was like a carbon copy of his brother Axel Oxenstierna in terms of his work ethic, and earlier he had played an important role in the diplomatic negotiations with Denmark.[108] Together with Per Banér and Claes Fleming, these six men formed the core of the domestic administration and because they were in places where they could really influence things, they had more room to act as they saw fit, which was a lot in the hierarchical system. In other words they had substantial personal agency. Perhaps the clearest point in common for these men was having a good connection to King Gustavus Adolphus.

Johan Skytte had been the king's teacher throughout Gustavus' adolescence, and that had created a strong emotional tie between the two. But because, relatively speaking, Skytte was an upstart, it also created rumours that he was the illegitimate son of Charles IX. Indeed, the connection to Charles and later to Gustavus was the source of Johan's agency, and because of his wide reading he became a very skilled office-holder. His area of responsibility became law and foreign diplomacy, which were both very important matters to the king. Even Charles IX trusted Johan; but it was his son Gustavus Adolphus who appointed him to the Council of the Realm in 1617 at his coronation ceremony. Johan Skytte had one skill in which he particularly excelled, social relations and rhetoric. Gustavus Adolphus had given Johan the task of taking care of the kingdom's treasury without any formal appointment and he did a good job, but this arrangement meant Johan was totally at the king's beck and call, so when Gustavus Adolphus died, Skytte lost the agency he had formerly enjoyed and gradually slipped into the margins of power.[109]

Gabriel Gustafsson Oxenstierna was Johan Skytte's opposite in many ways. Gabriel's agency came from family networks and like his brother Axel, he was a hard-working man at a time when this was much needed in an office-holder. Gabriel was the commander of the castles in both Stockholm and Uppsala, which were really important positions in the kingdom and gave him high prestige among the higher nobility. That position together the family background was the source of his agency and he liked the freedom of the job. But in 1624 came new instructions, and Gabriel no longer had the same degree of freedom in the job, so he decided to resign. Even his contemporaries said that Gabriel lacked social skills when he acted as mediator between the king and nobility. Like his brother, he believed that the kingdom came before the Estates and perhaps precisely because of this, he was used many times in diplomatic missions.[110]

By the time the interregnum was over and Christina (1626–1689) took charge of Sweden, the Council of the Realm had secured its position as a powerful part of the administration.[111] Before Christina councillors had always gone to the king to give counsel, but with Christina it was now the other way round. She was forced come to them for counsel, but this did not last for long. Christina played the high nobility at their own social network game rather than enter into open warfare with them. That is, she quickly created a large group of loyal supporters around her by ennobling lots of people and placing new people in the administration. She also started to make decisions outside the Council of the Realm with the help of her new secretaries. She also increased the number of councillors, to dilute the power of the original Council until by the end of her reign there were 48 councillors in Sweden. By the end of her ten year reign, she had appointed 45 new councillors.[112]

Christina's successor, Charles X Gustav (1622–1660), did not appoint so many councillors, but immediately after his death, the second interregnum started with nine new councillor appointments and a pattern similar to the first interregnum followed.[113] The last Swedish king that ruled together with the Council of the Realm was Charles XI (1655–1697), and he turned totally against it, finally replacing it in 1680 with the less powerful Royal Council.[114]

## From personal influence to collective practices

The seventeenth-century Swedish councillors testify to the birth of a profession,[115] even if this is in a premodern sense of the word. Their predecessors in the sixteenth century had been, in practice, provincial magnates uttering their advice on important matters only when asked by the king. After the 1620s however, they became a collective and permanent body of officials, running state affairs in a regulated and stable manner, living in Stockholm and working in their own official chamber in the Royal Castle.

However, as we have seen, the first shoots of change revealed themselves in the reigns of Eric XIV and John III. This began with the kings attempting to reorganize central government and then, from the 1570s onwards, the councillors too, trying to create more permanent and efficient institutions. These attempts often turned into a power struggle between the high aristocracy and the sovereign, as the king experienced the aristocracy's stronger role to be a direct threat to his own authority. The attempts of individuals alone were not enough to reform structures of the state; what was needed was a favourable context created by a variety of factors. This happened in the early seventeenth century, after some 50 years of trying.

Nevertheless, the change in attitude among the aristocracy in the 1570s is remarkable in itself. Up to this point, councillors had been reluctant to leave their landed properties and undertake burdensome work duties. Although Gustavus Vasa persuaded them to take up permanent service, it proved only temporary. Most of the aristocracy (and indeed the Council) clung to their traditional role as great men living in their countryside manors. They sought sources of influence that were separate from the king, each in their locality rather than in cooperation with the king at the centre of the state (where, in contrast, they had little agency).

The agency of councillors in the late sixteenth century took the form of giving collective advice to the king in a powerless manner, seeking and suggesting new forms of central government, mostly in vain, engaging in political writing, and finally, for some of them, taking part in plotting against the ruler, as other means proved insufficient. There were attempted or suspected coup d'etats in the reigns of Gustavus Vasa, Eric XIV, John III, Sigismund and Charles IX, and a few of them even proved successful. All of this testifies to the unstable nature of central politics in the realm.

A characteristic feature of the traditional, personal rule of the king and his advisors was a lack of clearly defined roles. There were no clear boundaries for personal agency spelled out within the system. The law and mandates did not give clear definitions regarding the tasks of the councillors, nor define limits for their agency; thus it was constantly being tested and redefined. It was shaped through personal interaction, on a case by case basis. Personal abilities thus played a key role here: the limits of agency expanded or decreased depending on the councillor's abilities, as well as his status, social network and relationship to the king. This bargaining on one's influence was part and parcel of the everyday working life of councillors.

As long as relations between king and Council were not clearly defined, there was a constant struggle to achieve the necessary power balance. At its worst, this resulted in the execution of councillors as the king would try to secure his position. Then, suddenly, the executions came to an end in 1605.

The question over who makes the decisions, the king alone or in consultation with the nobility, was gradually solved in the seventeenth century as a central administration was established. From the 1620s onwards, the Council of the Realm became the head of the administration. It became a truly administrative Council and a "corporation of civil servants". The king's position was established as a sovereign completely beyond the reach of the rest of the aristocracy. At the same time, Sweden was engaged in European wars, and it became the Council's task to run the kingdom's domestic issues while the ruler was fighting enemies abroad. With new administrative rules, the agency between king and councillors was now clearly defined in legal terms.

It seems obvious that death sentences were connected to disputes over the organisation of the central administration in the sixteenth century, and that they ended just as the administration was satisfactorily reorganized and the king's power secured at the beginning of the seventeenth century. The state-building process evidently required a shift in administrative practices from those defined by personal agency to those defined by an agency clearly framed in institutions and laws.

The big changes in Sweden's state formation happened in the early decades of the seventeenth century as the time was ripe for this change: the internal crisis had been mostly solved and the focus now shifted to foreign policy. The new king, Gustavus Adolphus, and his loyal chancellor of the realm, Axel Oxenstierna, shared the same vision about what had to be done. If Sweden, as a relatively small nation, wanted to be a strong player in European politics, the only way to build an outstanding army from minimal resources was to have a highly effective administrative machine to collect funds and men.

Piece by piece, Axel Oxenstierna and the king reformed the administration, especially at the central level. New collegia took care of the core areas and were led by members of the Council of the Realm. Together with the king, the councillors were monitoring the decision-making process within the new governmental institutions. For the first time, councillors had a clear mission instead of a vague role as the king's advisors. Instead of being a group of individuals who should give their personal view of matters, the Council became an institution: a permanent entity that was collectively consulted by the monarch as a matter of course.

By transforming themselves from a military asset into being also the sovereign's civil servants, the nobility created a situation where expertise became a necessary part of office-holding, and combined with an annual salary this also became an early form of profession. A clear sign of this transformation of the Council from being various powerful individuals to a collective group is the use of space: previously the Council of the Realm had physically gone to meet the sovereign, but when Christina of Sweden took charge of her realm, it was she who went to meet the Council in their official chamber and discussed matters with them as a collective.

In the first few decades of the seventeenth century, councillors who had previously been a constant threat to the monarch, now became loyal servants of the realm. Of course councillors still had their own agendas and used their position at the top of the society to increase their own power against the other Estates and within the nobility itself. But in the end, it was better to have a secure position within the central administration at the top of society than take a chance to reach ultimate power at a very high risk.

The research on which this publication is based was funded by the Academy of Finland (grant no. 137741).

## Notes

1. See for more, *Approaches and Perspectives* by Petri Karonen and Marko Hakanen.
2. Richard Bonney, *The European Dynastic States 1494–1660. The Short Oxford History of the Modern World* (Oxford University Press: Oxford, 1991), pp. 334–345.
3. See for more, *Approaches and Perspectives* by Petri Karonen and Marko Hakanen.
4. Jan Samuelson has listed councillors from the years 1523–1611 and analyzed their family relations and places of residence from this time. Kurt Ågren made an unpublished database about councillors' family relations from the years 1602–1647. Similar to Ågren, Björn Asker has examined seventeenth-century aristocracy, starting from the nomination policy and role of kin relationships in it from the years 1640–1680. Ulf Sjödell has also applied a database in his analyses that concentrate on the transformation of the Council of the Realm into the Royal Council. Ulf Sjödell, *Riksråd och kungliga råd. Rådskarriären 1602–1718*, (Gleerup: Västerås, 1975); Kurt Ågren, Rise and Decline of an Aristocracy. The Swedish Social and Political Elite in the 17th Century, *Scandinavian Journal of History*, vol. 1: 1–4, 1976, pp. 55–80; Björn Asker, "Aristocracy and Autocracy in Seventeenth-Century Sweden. The Decline of the Aristocracy within the Civil Administration Before 1680", *Scandinavian Journal of History*, vol. 15: 1–2, 1990, pp. 89–95; Jan Samuelson, *Aristokrat eller förädlad bonde? Det svenska frälsets ekonomi, politik och sociala förbindelser under tiden 1523–1611*. Bibliotheca Historica Lundensis 77. Lund: Lund Universitet, 1993).
5. Diana K. Jones, "Researching groups of lives: a collective biographical perspective on The Protestant ethic debate", *Qualitative Research* 1(3) (2001); Krista Cowman, "Collective Biography". In: Gunn, Simon, Faire, Lucy (ed.), *Research Methods for History* (Edinburgh: Edinburgh University Press, 2012).
6. Stone, "Prosopography"; Gunner Lind, "Prosopografi med relationelle databaser". In: Aronsson, Peter, Fagerlund, Solveig, Samuelsson, Jan (red.), *Nätverk i historisk forskning. Metafor, metod eller teori?* (Växjö: Växjö Universitet, 1999); Donald Broady, "French prosopography: definition and suggested readings", *Poetics* 30, 2002; Merja Uotila, *Käsityöläinen kyläyhteisönsä jäsenenä. Prosopografinen analyysi Hollolan käsityöläisistä 1810–1840*. Jyväskylä Studies in Humanities 237 (Jyväskylä: Jyväskylän yliopisto, 2014), pp. 32–33.
7. Marko Lamberg, "Prosopografian mahdollisuuksia". In: *Keskiajan avain*, (Helsinki: The Finnish Literature Society, 2008), pp. 230–232.
8. See for more, *Approaches and Perspectives* by Petri Karonen and Marko Hakanen. See for instance Erkki Lehtinen, *Hallituksen yhtenäistämispolitiikka Suomessa 1600-luvulla (1600-n. 1680)* (Helsinki: Finnish Historical Society, 1961); Marko Lamberg, *Dannemännen i stadens råd. Rådsmanskretsen i nordiska köpstäder under senmedeltiden*. Monografier utgivna av Stockholms stad 155 (Stockholm: Stockholmiaförlag, 2001).

9   Kristoffers landslag. Schlyters utgåva (SSGL 12), digital publication, Konungxbalker VIII [http://project2.sol.lu.se/fornsvenska/01_Bitar/B.L1.A-KrL.html], accessed March 27, 2015.
10  SAOB: Svenska Akademiens ordbok, "rättrådighet", accessed June 30, 2015. See also for one example, SRA AHTs1, Arvid Tawast to John III 29th of April, 1590, Kurjala: "will Jag ware Eders Kong. Mtt, rätrådi- och trogen".
11  Olli Matikainen, *Verenperijät. Väkivalta ja yhteisön murros itäisessä Suomessa 1500–1600-luvulla*. Bibliotheca historica 78 (Helsinki: The Finnish Literature Society, 2002), p. 65.
12  Lars Hermanson, *Släkt, vänner och makt: en studie av elitens politiska kultur i 1100-talets Danmark* (Göteborg: Göteborgs universitet, 2000), p. 197; Lars Hermanson, Vänskap som politisk ideologi i Saxo Grammaticus Gesta Danorum, *Historisk Tidskrift 123 (4) 2003*, pp. 533–534; Lars Hermanson, *Bärande band. Vänskap, kärlek och brödraskap i det medeltida Nordeuropa, ca 1000–1200* (Lund: Nordic Academic Press, 2009), p. 101.
13  Hans Gillingstam, "Rigsråd (Sverige)". In: *Kulturhistoriskt lexikon för nordisk medeltid från vikingatid till reformationstid, band XIV* (Helsingfors, 1969), pp. 230–233; Herman Schück, "Riksdagens framväxt: tiden intill 1611". In: Stjernquist, Nils (red.), *Riksdagen genom tiderna* (Stockholm: Sveriges riksdag & Riksbankens Jubileumsfond, 1985), pp. 7–19; Herman Schück, *Rikets råd och män. Herredag och råd i Sverige 1280–1480* (Stockholm: Kungl. Vitterhets Historie och Antikvitets Akademien, 2005), pp. 123–125; Björn Asker, *Hur riket styrdes. Förvaltning, politik och arkiv 1520–1920* (Stockholm: Riksarkivet, 2007), p. 53.
14  Gillingstam, "Rigsråd (Sverige)", pp. 230–233; cf. Schück, "Riksdagens framväxt", p. 15.
15  Torbjörn Eng, *Det svenska väldet: ett konglomerat av uttrycksformer och begrepp från Vasa till Bernadotte* (Uppsala: Uppsala universitet, 2001), pp. 75–76; Lars-Olof Larsson, *Arvet efter Gustav Vasa. En berättelse om fyra kungar och ett rike* (Stockholm: Prisma, 2005), p. 53; Harald Gustafsson, "A State that Failed? On the Union of Kalmar, Especially its Dissolution", *Scandinavian Journal of History 31 (3/4) 2006*, p. 209; Dick Harrison, Bo Eriksson, *Norstedts Sveriges historia 1350–1600* (Stockholm: Norstedts, 2010), p. 109.
16  Kristoffers landslag, Konungxbalker VIII: "Först sculu the swæria a gudh oc helgadoma som the ahalda, ath the scula konunge raada thet som the wita for gudhi honom oc lande hans nyttogt oc gagnligth wara, thet ey lata fore wild sculd, frendsæmio, maaghsæmio eller wenscap. Annat ath the scula han styrkia til rikesens ræth meth alle thera magt, ath han moghe alla the edha, som han hauer rikeno sworith oc almogen honom, wæl ath halda; och thet sama sculu the sielffua sik jætta ath halda. Tridia ær ath the scula alt thet lönlikit halda som konunger wil lönlikit haua, oc huargen vppenbara ther honom eller hans rike maa skadi aff koma." [http://project2.sol.lu.se/fornsvenska/01_Bitar/B.L1.A-KrL.html], accessed March 27, 2015.
17  Emil Hildebrand, *Svenska statsförfattningens historiska utveckling från äldsta tid till våra dagar* (Stockholm: P. A. Norstedt & söner, 1896), pp. 262, 266; Nils Herlitz, *Grunddragen av det svenska statsskickets historia* (Stockholm: P. A. Norstedt & Söners Förlag, 1928), p. 77.
18  Kristoffers landslag, Konungxbalker IV: "han scal meth sins raadz radhe j swerige rike sino swerike styra oc raada". [http://project2.sol.lu.se/fornsvenska/01_Bitar/B.L1.A-KrL.html], accessed March 27, 2015; Pentti Renvall, John E. Roos, "Keskitetyn hallintolaitoksen kehitys". In: Suolahti, Gunnar et al. (toim.), *Suomen Kulttuurihistoria II* (Jyväskylä: Gummerus, 1934), pp. 139–140.
19  Lauritz Weibull, *Stockholms blodbad och andra kritiska undersökningar* (Stockholm: Natur och Kultur, 1965), pp. 120–183; Poul Enemark, *Kalmarin unionista Tukholman verilöylyyn. Pohjoismainen unioniaika 1397–1521* (Helsinki:

Finnish Historical Society, The Finnish Literature Society, 1986), pp. 197–211; Gustafsson, "A State that Failed?", pp. 210–212; Bo Eriksson, *Svenska adelns historia* (Stockholm: Norstedts, 2011), pp. 163–164.

20   Christian Naumann, *Svenska statsförfattningens historiska utveckling* (Stockholm: P. A. Norstedt, 1866 & 1875), pp. 106–117; Emil Hildebrand, Oscar Alin, "Företal", *Svenska Riksdagsakter jämte andra handlingar som höra till statsförfattningens historia. Första serien: tidevarvet 1521-1718, avd. I: 1521-1544* (Stockholm: Svenska Riksarkivet, 1887), p. x; Eino Jutikkala, *Suomen talonpojan historia. Toinen, uudistettu ja lisätty laitos* (Helsinki: The Finnish Literature Society, 1958), pp. 97–99; Schück, *Rikets råd och män*, pp. 17–18, 123–129. For their mutual development, see Nils Ahnlund, "Ståndsriksdagens utdaning 1592–1672", *Sveriges Riksdag I: 3*. Red. Nils Edén (Stockholm: Sveriges Riksdag, 1933); Tor Berg, "Riksdagens utveckling under den äldre Vasatiden 1521–1592". In: Edén, Nils (red.), *Sveriges Riksdag I: 2*. (Stockholm: Sveriges Riksdag, 1935); Schück, "Riksdagens framväxt"; Schück, *Rikets råd och män*.

21   Herlitz, *Grunddragen av det svenska statsskickets historia*, p. 73; Renvall – Roos, "Keskitetyn hallintolaitoksen kehitys", pp. 140–141; Michael Roberts, *The Early Vasas. A History of Sweden, 1523-1611* (Cambridge: Cambridge University Press, 1968), pp. 187–194; Petri Karonen, *Pohjoinen suurvalta. Ruotsi ja Suomi 1521-1809* (Helsinki: The Finnish Literature Society, 2014), pp. 79–83.

22   An exception to this are the protocols of the so called *regementsråd* that was an administrative experiment in the late 1530s and early 1540s. Hildebrand – Alin, "Företal", viii–ix; Severin Bergh, *Rådsprotokoll och därmed jämförliga i riksarkivet förvarade protokoll* (Stockholm: P. A. Norstedt & söner, 1912), pp. 279–280.

23   Hildebrand, *Svenska statsförfattningens historiska utveckling*, p. 263; Nils Edén, *Om centralregeringens organisation under den äldre Vasatiden (1523-1594)* (Uppsala: Almqvist & Wikdells Boktryckeri, 1899), pp. 41–54; Herlitz, *Grunddragen av det svenska statsskickets historia*, pp. 74, 76; Renvall – Roos, "Keskitetyn hallintolaitoksen kehitys", p. 139; Schück, "Riksdagens framväxt", p. 40.

24   Naumann, *Svenska statsförfattningens historiska utveckling*, p. 100; Hildebrand, *Svenska statsförfattningens historiska utveckling*, pp. 265–266; Edén, *Om centralregeringens organisation*, p. 7; Lars-Olof Larsson, Eva Österberg, "Vasatiden och stormaktstiden". In: Behre, Göran, Larsson, Lars-Olof, Österberg, Eva, *Sveriges historia 1521-1809: stormaktsdröm och småstatsrealiteter* (Stockholm: Esselte Studium AB, 1985), pp. 46–47; Asker, *Hur riket styrdes*, p. 53.

25   Hildebrand, *Svenska statsförfattningens historiska utveckling*, pp. 262, 266–267; Edén, *Om centralregeringens organisation*, p. 7; Herlitz, *Grunddragen av det svenska statsskickets historia*, p. 77; Franklin D. Scott, *Sweden. The Nation's History* (Minneapolis: University of Minnesota Press, 1977), p. 147; Larsson, *Arvet efter Gustav Vasa*, p. 53.

26   Hildebrand, *Svenska statsförfattningens historiska utveckling*, p. 265; Gillingstam, "Rigsråd (Sverige)", p. 232.

27   Gillingstam, "Rigsråd (Sverige)", p. 232.

28   Bonney, *The European Dynastic States 1494-1660*, p. 335.

29   Hildebrand, *Svenska statsförfattningens historiska utveckling*, pp. 262–263: "den finaste eller mest lysande blomman af adeln"; Ulf Sjödell, *Infödda svenska män av ridderskapet och adeln: Kring ett tema i Sveriges historia under 1500- och 1600-talen* (Lund: Gleerup, 1976), pp. 12–13; Database of Councillors of the Swedish Realm, 1523–1680 [http://urn.fi/URN:NBN:fi:jyu-201710043922]. Eds Marko Hakanen & Ulla Koskinen.

30   [http://urn.fi/URN:NBN:fi:jyu-201710043922].

31   Hildebrand, *Svenska statsförfattningens historiska utveckling*, p. 264, footnote 3; Edén, *Om centralregeringens organisation*, p. 17.

32   Samuelson, *Aristokrat eller förädlad bonde?*, p. 121, tabell 19; [http://urn.fi/URN:NBN:fi:jyu-201710043922].

33 Hildebrand, *Svenska statsförfattningens historiska utveckling*, p. 266; Herlitz, *Grunddragen av det svenska statsskickets historia*, p. 77; Wilhelm Tham, *Den svenska utrikespolitikens historia I: 2. 1560–1648* (Stockholm: P. A. Norstedt, 1960), pp. 9–11.

34 Hildebrand, *Svenska statsförfattningens historiska utveckling*, pp. 263–264; Edén, *Om centralregeringens organisation*, p. 134.

35 Bonney, *The European Dynastic States 1494–1660*, pp. 334–340; Jan Glete, *War and the State in Early Modern Europe: Spain, the Dutch Republic and Sweden as fiscal-military states, 1500–1650* (London: Routledge, 2002), pp. 10–16, 181, 196.

36 Pentti Renvall, *Klaus Fleming und der Finnische Adel in den Anfangsphasen der Krise der neunziger Jahre der 16. Jahrhunderts* (Turku: Turun Yliopisto, 1939), p. 6; Scott, *Sweden*, p. 146; Jan Lindegren, "The Swedish "Military State", 1560–1720", *Scandinavian Journal of History* 10, 1985, p. 309; Larsson - Österberg, "Vasatiden och stormaktstiden", pp. 45–46; Larsson, *Arvet efter Gustav Vasa*, p. 53.

37 *Svenskt biografiskt lexikon*, A–Stålhammar (SBL) (Stockholm: Riksarkivet, 1917–2013) (Ivan Svalenius), Sten Eriksson (Leijonhufvud) [http://sok.riksarkivet.se/sbl/artikel/11175], accessed May 26, 2015; SBL (Georg Landberg): Per Brahe [http://sok.riksarkivet.se/sbl/artikel/18053], accessed March 10, 2015; Bo Eriksson, *I skuggan av tronen. En biografi över Per Brahe d.ä* (Stockholm: Prisma, 2009), pp. 133–258.

38 After issuing them with death sentences in an improvised court session, Eric XIV personally killed Councillor Svante Sture in Uppsala castle on 24th of May, 1567, and ordered the deaths of his two sons, two other noblemen and finally his own tutor, the Frenchman Councillor Dionysius Beurraeus, who was also Master of the Bursary (*räntemestare*). SBL (Jan Samuelson): Svante Sture [http://sok.riksarkivet.se/sbl/artikel/34643], accessed March 13, 2015; SBL (Georg Landberg): Dionysius Beurræus [http://sok.riksarkivet.se/sbl/artikel/18140], accessed May 21, 2015; Lars O. Lagerqvist, *Svensk historia* (Stockholm: Svenska institutet, 2001), pp. 48–49; Larsson, *Arvet efter Gustav Vasa*, p. 52; Harrison - Eriksson, *Norstedts Sveriges historia 1350–1600*, p. 544; Eriksson, *Svenska adelns historia*, pp. 164–165.

39 Hildebrand, *Svenska statsförfattningens historiska utveckling*, pp. 263–264; Edén, *Om centralregeringens organisation*, p. 134.

40 SBL (Ivan Svalenius): Sten Eriksson (Leijonhufvud) [http://sok.riksarkivet.se/sbl/artikel/11175], accessed March 10, 2015; SBL (Georg Landberg): Per Brahe, [http://sok.riksarkivet.se/sbl/artikel/18053], accessed March 10, 2015; Edén, *Om centralregeringens organisation*, pp. 149–151; Scott, *Sweden*, p. 147; Eriksson, *I skuggan av tronen*, pp. 310–311.

41 SBL (Ivan Svalenius): Sten Eriksson (Leijonhufvud), [http://sok.riksarkivet.se/sbl/artikel/11175], accessed March 10, 2015.

42 SBL (Lars-Olof Larsson): Gustaf Olsson (Stenbock), [http://sok.riksarkivet.se/sbl/artikel/20067], accessed March 10, 2015.

43 Hildebrand, *Svenska statsförfattningens historiska utveckling*, p. 267; Edén, *Om centralregeringens organisation*, pp. 161–170; Herlitz, *Grunddragen av det svenska statsskickets historia*, p. 77; Sjödell, *Infödda svenska män av ridderskapet och adeln*, pp. 15–18; Larsson, *Arvet efter Gustav Vasa*, pp. 53, 272–276; Lars Ericson Wolke, *Johan III. En biografi* (Lund: Historiska Media, 2006), pp. 120–122.

44 In 1590, virtually all John III's councillors were part of a mutual family network. Samuelson, *Aristokrat eller förädlad bonde?*, pp. 130–132, figure 4; Larsson, *Arvet efter Gustav Vasa*, p. 273.

45 Sten Lindroth, *Svensk lärdomshistoria. Medeltiden, reformationstiden* (Stockholm: P. A. Norstedt & Söners Förlag, 1975), pp. 310–316; Scott, *Sweden*, pp. 147–148; Glete, *War and the State in Early Modern Europe*, p. 196.

46 Edén, *Om centralregeringens organisation*, p. 161; Roberts, *The Early Vasas*, pp. 300–308.

47   Bonney, *The European Dynastic States 1494–1660*, p. 334.
48   Sven A. Nilsson, *Kampen om de adliga privilegierna 1526–1594* (Lund: Gleerup, 1952); see also Samuelson, *Aristokrat eller förädlad bonde?*, pp. 35–36 and Larsson, *Arvet efter Gustav Vasa*, pp. 274–275.
49   Ericson Wolke, *Johan III*, p. 120.
50   Renvall & Roos, "Keskitetyn hallintolaitoksen kehitys", p. 141.
51   Sven A. Nilsson, *Krona och frälse i Sverige 1523–1594. Rusttjänst, länsväsende, godspolitik* (Lund: Gleerup, 1947), pp. 122–130, 142–166.
52   Glete, *War and the State in Early Modern Europe*, pp. 196–197.
53   Renvall, *Klaus Fleming und der Finnische Adel*, p. 7; Pentti Renvall, "Baltian kysymyksen kriisi". In: Korhonen, Arvi (toim.), *Suomen historian käsikirja I* (Helsinki: WSOY, 1949), p. 338.
54   SBL (Bengt Hildebrand): Pontus De la Gardie [http://sok.riksarkivet.se/sbl/artikel/17387], accessed May 22, 2015; *Kansallisbiografia-verkkojulkaisu* (KB) (Suomalaisen Kirjallisuuden Seura, Helsinki, 1997–) (Veli-Matti Syrjö 1998), De la Gardie, Pontus (noin 1520–1585) [http://www.kansallisbiografia.fi/kb/artikkeli/529/], accessed May 22, 2015; Renvall, *Klaus Fleming und der Finnische Adel*, pp. 8–10; Scott, *Sweden*, p. 147; Samuelson, *Aristokrat eller förädlad bonde?*, p. 131; Eriksson, *Svenska adelns historia*, pp. 160–161.
55   Hildebrand, *Svenska statsförfattningens historiska utveckling*, pp. 267–268; Edén, *Om centralregeringens organisation*, pp. 180–181; Eric Anthoni, *Till avvecklingen av konflikten mellan hertig Carl och Finland I: konfliktens uppkomst och hertigens seger* (Helsingfors: Mercators tryckeri, 1935), pp. 5–7; Renvall, *Klaus Fleming und der Finnische Adel*, pp. 24–25; Roberts, *The Early Vasas*, pp. 318–319.
56   Edén, *Om centralregeringens organisation*, pp. 179–181; Hugo Sommarström, *Finland under striderna mellan Sigismund och hertig Karl. I: Klas Flemings tid* (Stockholm: Björck och Börjessons bokförlag, 1935), pp. 22–24; Renvall, *Klaus Fleming und der Finnische Adel*, pp. 20–26; Renvall, "Baltian kysymyksen kriisi", pp. 339–341; Schück, *Riksdagens framväxt*, p. 49; Larsson, *Arvet efter Gustav Vasa*, pp. 277–279, 287–293; Stefan Östergren, *Sigismund. En biografi över den svensk-polske monarken* (Stockholm: Katolsk Historisk förening, 2005), pp. 53–59.
57   SBL (Ingvar Andersson): Nils Gyllenstierna [http://sok.riksarkivet.se/sbl/artikel/13414], accessed May 22, 2015.
58   KB (Ari-Pekka Palola 2001): Tott, Klaus Åkenpoika (noin 1530–1590) [http://www.kansallisbiografia.fi/kb/artikkeli/3808/], accessed May 26, 2015; [http://urn.fi/URN:NBN:fi:jyu-201710043922].
59   KB (Kari Tarkiainen 2001): Fleming, Klaus (noin 1535–1597) [http://www.kansallisbiografia.fi/kb/artikkeli/526/], accessed May 22, 2015; SBL (Berndt Federley): Klas Fleming [http://sok.riksarkivet.se/sbl/artikel/14215], accessed May 22, 2015; Larsson, *Arvet efter Gustav Vasa*, pp. 342, 355.
60   Anthoni, *Till avvecklingen av konflikten*, pp. 14–16; Sommarström, *Finland under striderna*, pp. 20–21; Renvall, *Klaus Fleming und der Finnische Adel*, pp. 16–19; Rainer Fagerlund, *Finlands historia 2*. Huvudredaktör Märtha Norrback (Esbo: Schildt, 1996), p. 75; Larsson, *Arvet efter Gustav Vasa*, pp. 352–356; Östergren, *Sigismund*, pp. 56, 105–106.
61   Edén, *Om centralregeringens organisation*, pp. 184–190; Herlitz, *Grunddragen av det svenska statsskickets historia*, pp. 75–76; Renvall & Roos, "Keskitetyn hallintolaitoksen kehitys", p. 142; Glete, *War and the State in Early Modern Europe*, p. 196.
62   SBL (Tor Berg): Hogenskild Bielke [http://sok.riksarkivet.se/sbl/artikel/18165] and SBL (Bo Eriksson Janbrink): Erik Sparre [http://sok.riksarkivet.se/sbl/artikel/6186], accessed March 13, 2015; Ahnlund, "Ståndsriksdagens utdaning 1592–1672", pp. 15–19; Nilsson, *Kampen om de adliga privilegierna*, pp. 100–131; Kerstin Strömberg-Back, *Lagen rätten läran. Politisk och kyrklig idédebatt i Sverige under Johan III:s tid* (Lund: Lunds universitet, 1963), pp. 17–20; Lindroth, *Svensk lärdomshistoria*, pp. 315–316; Larsson, Österberg, "Vasatiden och stormaktstiden",

p. 56; Lindegren, "The Swedish 'Military State'", p. 308; Schück, "Riksdagens framväxt", pp. 45–50; Samuelson, *Aristokrat eller förädlad bonde?*, pp. 35–36; Larsson, *Arvet efter Gustav Vasa*, pp. 273–277, 347; Harald Gustafsson, *Nordens historia. En europeisk region under 1200 år* (Stockholm: Studentlitteratur, 2007), p. 103.

63   SBL (Georg Landberg): Per Brahe, [http://sok.riksarkivet.se/sbl/artikel/18053], accessed March 10, 2015; Nilsson, *Kampen om de adliga privilegierna*, pp. 39–40; Strömberg-Back, *Lagen rätten läran*, pp. 102–104; Roberts, *The Early Vasas*, pp. 304–305; Lindroth, *Svensk lärdomshistoria*, p. 316; Scott, *Sweden*, p. 148; Schück, "Riksdagens framväxt", pp. 47–48; Samuelson, *Aristokrat eller förädlad bonde?*, p. 36; Larsson, *Arvet efter Gustav Vasa*, pp. 276–277; Ericson Wolke, *Johan III*, pp. 122–123; Eriksson, *I skuggan av tronen*, pp. 331–340; Eriksson, *Svenska adelns historia*, pp. 161–162.

64   Ahnlund, "Ståndsriksdagens utdaning 1592–1672", pp. 51–57; Roberts, *The Early Vasas*, pp. 367–368; Fagerlund, *Finlands historia 2*, p. 77; Karonen, *Pohjoinen suurvalta*, pp. 105–106, 113.

65   His father Sten was brother to Margareta Eriksdotter Leijonhufvud, Gustav Vasa's second wife and mother to John and Charles. [http://urn.fi/URN:NBN:fi:jyu-201710043922].

66   SBL (Birgitta Lager-Kromnow): Axel Stensson (Leijonhufvud), [http://sok.riksarkivet.se/sbl/artikel/11161], accessed March 18, 2015; KB (Petri Karonen 2001): Leijonhufvud, Axel (1554–1619) [http://www.kansallisbiografia.fi/kb/artikkeli/3234/], accessed May 22, 2015; Larsson, *Arvet efter Gustav Vasa*, pp. 292–293, 358.

67   Roberts, *The Early Vasas*, pp. 369–371.

68   Roberts, *The Early Vasas*, p. 388; Mirkka Lappalainen, *Susimessu. 1590-luvun sisällissota Ruotsissa ja Suomessa* (Helsinki: Siltala, 2009), pp. 259–261.

69   SBL (Tor Berg): Hogenskild Bielke [http://sok.riksarkivet.se/sbl/artikel/18165], accessed March 13, 2015.

70   Hildebrand, *Svenska statsförfattningens historiska*, p. 268; Roberts, *The Early Vasas*, pp. 428–431.

71   Charles IX had also planned to appoint six members from the Estonian nobility, but had to give up because of strong resistance from the Estates. Roberts, *The Early Vasas*, p. 429; Michael Roberts, *The Swedish Imperial Experience 1560–1718* (Cambridge: Cambridge University Press, 1979), p. 93. In 1609, the Swedish higher nobility stipulated that every councillor had to be native Swedish and a knight. Severin Bergh, *Karl IX och den svenska adeln 1607–1609* (Uppsala: Akademiska boktryckeriet, 1882) p. 106. The first foreign-born councillors were appointed by Queen Christina, but overall the number of foreign-born councillors remained very low. There were only six in the seventeenth century. Sjödell, *Riksråd och kungliga råd*, p. 25.

72   Naumann, *Svenska statsförfattningens historiska utveckling*, p. 101; Hildebrand, *Svenska statsförfattningens historiska utveckling*, p. 262, 268; Nils Edén, *Den svenska centralregeringens utveckling till kollegial organisation i början af sjuttonde århundradet (1602–1634)* (Uppsala: Almqvist & Wiksells, 1902) p. 5; Herlitz, *Grunddragen av det svenska statsskickets historia*, p. 77; Roberts, *The Early Vasas*, p. 429.

73   Samuelson, *Aristokrat eller förädlad bonde?* p. 122.

74   [http://urn.fi/URN:NBN:fi:jyu-201710043922].

75   SBL (B. Boëthius): Göran Boije, [http://sok.riksarkivet.se/SBL/Presentation.aspx?id=17885], accessed February 17, 2015; KB (Veli-Matti Syrjö) Göran Boije, [http://www.kansallisbiografia.fi/kb/artikkeli/522/], accessed February 17, 2015; Mirkka Lappalainen, *Suku, valta, suurvalta. Creutzit 1600-luvun Ruotsissa ja Suomessa* (Helsinki: WSOY, 2005), p. 100.

76  SBL: Horn, släkt, [http://sok.riksarkivet.se/SBL/Presentation.aspx?id=13802#Forfattare], accessed February 17, 2015.
77  SBL (Birgitta Lager-Kromnow): Moritz Stensson (Leijonhufvud), [http://sok.riksarkivet.se/SBL/Presentation.aspx?id=11171#Forfattare], accessed February 17, 2015.
78  SBL (HG-m): Ribbing, släkt, [http://sok.riksarkivet.se/SBL/Presentation.aspx?id=6656], accessed February 17, 2015.
79  SBL (Tor Berg): Svante Bielke, [http://sok.riksarkivet.se/SBL/Presentation.aspx?id=18182], accessed February 17, 2015.
80  Charles IX was also suspicious towards family networks and tried to limit family connections in the Council of the Realm. Bergh, *Karl IX och den svenska*, p. 106.
81  SBL (Hans Gillingstam): Ryning (Rönning), släkt, [http://sok.riksarkivet.se/SBL/Presentation.aspx?id=6436], accessed February 17, 2015.
82  Gustaf Elgenstierna, *Den introducerade svenska adelns ättartavlor* (Elektronisk resurs, version 3.0. Riddarhusdirektionen, Stockholm, 2002), Ulfsparre af Broxvik, nr. 9.
83  SBL (Stefan Östergren): Seved Ribbing, [http://sok.riksarkivet.se/SBL/Presentation.aspx?id=6705], accessed February 18, 2015.
84  SBL: Gyllenstierna, släkt, [http://sok.riksarkivet.se/SBL/Presentation.aspx?id=13393], accessed February 18, 2015; NFB (Uggleupplagan. 26. Slöke - Stockholm, 1351-1352): Jöran Stiernsköld [http://runeberg.org/nfcf/0720.html], accessed 2015 February 18; KB (Veli-Matti Syrjö) Mats Kruus, [http://www.kansallisbiografia.fi/kb/artikkeli/538/], accessed February 18, 2015; SBL: Kruus, släkt, [http://sok.riksarkivet.se/SBL/Presentation.aspx?id=11829], accessed 2015 February 18, 2015.
85  [http://urn.fi/URN:NBN:fi:jyu-201710043922], NFB (Uggleupplagan. 13. Johan - Kikare, 1313-1314): Ludbert Kauer [http://runeberg.org/nfbm/0689.html], accessed February 18, 2015; SHM 1836, 113.
86  SBL (B. Broëthius): Magnus Brahe, [http://sok.riksarkivet.se/SBL/Presentation.aspx?id=18045#Forfattare], accessed February 19, 2015.
87  SBL (B. Broëthius): Abraham Brahe, [http://sok.riksarkivet.se/SBL/Presentation.aspx?id=18038], accessed February 19, 2015.
88  Gustaf Forsgrén, *Bidrag till Svenska gref- och friherreskapens historia 1561-1655 I, Erik XIV's och Johan III's tid* (Stockholm: Ivar Hæggströms boktryckeri, 1885), p. 12; Eriksson, *I skuggan av tronen*, pp. 262-263.
89  Abraham Brahe, *Abraham Brahes tidebok* (Stockholm: P. A. Norstedt & söners förlag, 1920), pp. 1-84.
90  [http://urn.fi/URN:NBN:fi:jyu-201710043922].
91  SBL (Sven A. Nilsson): Axel Oxenstierna, [http://sok.riksarkivet.se/SBL/Presentation.aspx?id=7882#Forfattare], accessed February 19, 2015; KB (Petri Karonen) Axel Oxenstierna, [http://www.kansallisbiografia.fi/kb/artikkeli/3236/], accessed February 19, 2015. See also Nils Ahnlund, *Axel Oxenstierna intill Gustav Adolfs död* (P. A. Norstedt & söner, Stockholm, 1940); Sven A. Nilsson, Gustav II Adolf och Axel Oxenstierna: en studie i maktdelning och dess alternativ *(Scandia 62,* 1996), pp. 169-194; Gunnar Wetterberg, *Kanslern Axel Oxenstierna i sin tid*, del 1 (Atlantis, Stockholm, 2002).
92  Nils Forssell, "Kansliet från Gustav II Adolf till år 1660". In: Wieselgren, Oscar, Forssell, Nils, Munthe, Arne, Forssell, Arne, Liljedahl, Ragnar (red.), *Kungl. Maj:ts kanslis historia del I: kansliets uppkomst, organisation och utveckling intill 1840* (Uppsala: Almqvist & Wiksells boktryckeri, 1935), pp. 23-54.
93  Edén, *Den svenska centralregeringens utveckling*, pp. 47-56; A. B. Carlsson, *Den svenska centralförvaltningen 1521-1809. En historisk översikt* (Stockholm: Beckmans, 1913), pp. 17-18; Herlitz, *Grunddragen av det svenska statsskickets historia*, pp. 101-103; Asker, *Hur riket styrdes*, pp. 54, 80-82; Marko Hakanen, *Vallan verkostoissa. Per Brahe ja hänen klienttinsä 1600-luvun Ruotsin valtakunnassa.*

Jyväskylä Studies in Humanities 157 (Jyväskylä: Jyväskylän yliopisto, 2011), pp. 51–54.
94 ICF 1856, pp. 295–305; Bergh, *Rådsprotokoll*, pp. 279–289.
95 [http://urn.fi/URN:NBN:fi:jyu-201710043922].
96 Naumann, *Svenska statsförfattningens historiska utveckling*, pp. 167–173; Jan von Konow, *Sveriges adels historia* (Karlskrona: Axel Abrahamsons Förlag, 2005), pp. 96–98.
97 Hakanen, *Vallan verkostoissa*, pp. 55–56.
98 Per Brahe, *Oeconomia eller Hushållsbok för ungt adelsfolk*. Utgiven med inledning, kommentar och ordförklaringar av John Granlund och Gösta Holm. Nordiska museets Handlingar 78 (Lund: Berlinska boktryckeriet, (1971)), pp. 13–25. Education was demanded even more on lower level of administration. Svante Norrhem, *Uppkomlingarna. Kanslitjänstemännen i 1600-talets Sverige och Europa* (Stockholm: Almqvist & Wiksell International, 1993), pp. 39–41.
99 [http://urn.fi/URN:NBN:fi:jyu-201710043922].
100 [http://urn.fi/URN:NBN:fi:jyu-201710043922].
101 Hakanen, *Vallan verkostoissa*, pp. 164–169.
102 Svante Banér and Gustaf Horn were professional soldiers who participated in council meetings rarely. Three new councillors, Carl Oxenstierna, Mattias Soop and Johan Sparre, did not hold any important offices and they sat rarely in council meetings and were selected mainly to give extra support to Oxenstierna's views. Meanwhile, Lindorm Ribbings' appointment was a reward for life-long loyalty to the king. He was only able to enjoy his position for three years before passing away. CSRDB; SBL (Hans Gillingstam): Oxenstierna, släkt, [http://sok.riksarkivet.se/SBL/Presentation.aspx?id=7880], accessed February 20, 2015; SBL (Hans Gillingstam): Soop, släkt, [http://sok.riksarkivet.se/SBL/Presentation.aspx?id=6141#Forfattare], accessed February 20, 2015; SBL (Hans Gillingstam): Sparre, släkt, [http://sok.riksarkivet.se/SBL/Presentation.aspx?id=6160#Forfattare], accessed February 20, 2015; SBL (HG-m): Ribbing, släkt, [http://sok.riksarkivet.se/SBL/Presentation.aspx?id=6656#Forfattare], accessed February 20, 2015.
103 SBL (B. Boëthius): Per Banér, [http://sok.riksarkivet.se/SBL/Presentation.aspx?id=19048], accessed February 19, 2015.
104 SBL (Bengt Hildebrand): Klas Fleming, [http://sok.riksarkivet.se/SBL/Presentation.aspx?id=14217#Forfattare], accessed 2015 February 19, 2015; KB (Aimo Halila and Anneli Mäkelä-Alitalo): Klaus Fleming, [http://www.kansallisbiografia.fi/kb/artikkeli/2311/], accessed February 19, 2015; Piia Einonen, *Poliittiset areenat ja toimintatavat. Tukholman porvaristo vallan käyttäjänä ja vallankäytön kohteena n. 1592–1644*. Bibliotheca Historica 94. (Helsinki: The Finnish Literature Society, 2005), pp. 55–57.
105 [http://urn.fi/URN:NBN:fi:jyu-201710043922]; SBL (HG-m): Ribbing, släkt, [http://sok.riksarkivet.se/SBL/Presentation.aspx?id=6656#Forfattare], accessed February 20, 2015; SBL (G. Carlsson): Bååt, släkt, [http://sok.riksarkivet.se/SBL/Presentation.aspx?id=16242], accessed February 20, 2015.
106 [http://urn.fi/URN:NBN:fi:jyu-201710043922]; Grill 1949, 76–90; SBL (B. Boëthius): Jakob P. De la Gardie, [http://sok.riksarkivet.se/SBL/Presentation.aspx?id=17379#Forfattare], accessed February 23, 2015; KB (Veli-Matti Syrjö): Jacob De la Gardie, [http://www.kansallisbiografia.fi/kb/artikkeli/527/], accessed February 23, 2015; SBL (Erik Granstedt): Karl Karlsson Gyllenhielm, [http://sok.riksarkivet.se/SBL/Presentation.aspx?id=13376#Forfattare], accessed February 23, 2015; NFB (Uggleupplagan. 26. Slöke – Stockholm, 1351–1352): Nils Stiernsköld [http://runeberg.org/nfcf/0720.html], accessed February 23, 2015.
107 SBL (Hans Gillingstam): Stenbock, släkt, [http://sok.riksarkivet.se/SBL/Presentation.aspx?id=20066#Forfattare], accessed February 23, 2015; SBL (HG-m): Oxenstierna, släkt, [http://sok.riksarkivet.se/SBL/Presentation.aspx?id=

7880], accessed February 23, 2015; KB (Petri Karonen): Gabriel Bengtinpoika Oxenstierna, [http://www.kansallisbiografia.fi/kb/artikkeli/3239/], accessed February 23, 2015.

108 [http://urn.fi/URN:NBN:fi:jyu-201710043922]; NFB (Uggleupplagan. 24. Ryssläder – Sekretär, 999–1000): Filip Scheiding [http://runeberg.org/nfcd/0526.html], accessed 2015 February 23; Elgenstierna 2002, Horn af Kanckas, nr. 12, TAB 8; NFB (Uggleupplagan. 11. Harrisburg – Hypereides, 1113–1115): Klas H. [http://runeberg.org/nfbk/0586.html], accessed 2015 February 23; SBL: Horn, släkt, [http://sok.riksarkivet.se/SBL/Presentation.aspx?id=13802#Forfattare], accessed February 23, 2015. Both SBL and NFB mistakenly records Claes' patronym as Henriksson. His father was Carl Henriksson Horn; SBL (B. Broëthius): Magnus Brahe, [http://sok.riksarkivet.se/SBL/Presentation.aspx?id=18045#Forfattare], accessed February 23, 2015; SBL (B. Broëthius): Abraham Brahe, [http://sok.riksarkivet.se/SBL/Presentation.aspx?id=18038], accessed February 23, 2015.

109 SBL (Erland Sellberg): Johan Skytte, [http://sok.riksarkivet.se/SBL/Presentation.aspx?id=6037#Forfattare], accessed February 24, 2015.

110 SBL (Robert Sandberg): Gabriel Gustafsson Oxenstierna, [http://sok.riksarkivet.se/SBL/Presentation.aspx?id=7932#Forfattare], accessed February 23, 2015.

111 Charles IX had agreed with nobility that the Council of the Realm would include the eight highest officeholders of the Realm and 12 other councillors who should be knights and born in Sweden. Finally in the 1634 Instrument of Government the top five offices became the central power group of the administration, even above the Council of the Realm. Bergh, *Karl IX och den svenska adeln*, p. 106; Naumann, *Svenska statsförfattningens historiska utveckling*, p. 151; Sven Nilsson, "1634 års regeringsform", *Scandia 10, 1937*, pp. 36–37; Sven A. Nilsson, "1634 års regeringsform i det svenska statssystemet", Statsvetenskaplig tidskrift, Årgång 87, 1984, p. 303; Asker, *Hur riket styrdes*, p. 54.

112 [http://urn.fi/URN:NBN:fi:jyu-201710043922]; Sven Stolpe, *Drottning Kristina* (Helsingfors: WSOY, 1988), pp. 109–111; Peter Englund, *Kuningatar Kristiina Elämäkerta*. Suom. Rauno Ekholm (Helsinki: WSOY, 2007), pp. 64–68; Hakanen, *Vallan verkostoissa*, pp. 58–59.

113 [http://urn.fi/URN:NBN:fi:jyu-201710043922].

114 Hildebrand, *Svenska statsförfattningens historiska utveckling*, pp. 408–410; Ulf Sjödell, *Kungamakt och högaristokrati. En studie i Sveriges inre historia under Karl XI* (Lund: Gleerups, 1966), pp. 355–362; Dahlgren, Stellan, "Estates and Classes". In: Roberts, Michael (ed.), *Sweden's Age of Greatness 1632–1718* (London and Basingstoke: Macmillan, 1973), pp. 119–120.

115 See for more, *Approaches and Perspectives* by Petri Karonen and Marko Hakanen.

# Sources

## Archival sources

Svenska Riksarkivet (SRA), Stockholm (Swedish National Archives)
Arvid Henriksson Tavasts samling, vol. 1.

## Electronic sources

Swedish Councillors of the Realm, 1523–1680 (SCR) JYX: [http://urn.fi/URN:NBN:fi:jyu-201710043922]
Assembled by Marko Hakanen & Ulla Koskinen.

## Information collected from:

Elgenstierna, Gustaf 2002(ES): *Den introducerade svenska adelns ättartavlor*. Elektronisk resurs, version 3.0. Stockholm: Riddarhusdirektionen.
*Kansallisbiografia* (KB). Helsinki: The Finnish Literature Society 1997–. http://www.kansallisbiografia.fi/]
*Kristoffers landslag*. Schlyters utgåva (SSGL 12), digital publication [http://project2.sol.lu.se/fornsvenska/01_Bitar/B.L1.A–KrL.html].
Nordisk familjebok (NFB): *Nordisk familjebok* 1876–1899: Konversationslexikon och realencyklopedi. Första utgåvan. Stockholm: Expeditionen af Nordisk familjebok.
*Nordisk familjebok* 1904–1926: Konversationslexikon och realencyklopedi (huvudred. Bernhard Meijer). Stockholm: Nordisk familjeboks förlags aktiebolag, Stockholm. [http://runeberg.org/nf/]
Samuelson, Jan 1993 (JS): *Aristokrat eller förädlad bonde? Det svenska frälsets ekonomi, politik och sociala förbindelser under tiden 1523–1611*. Bibliotheca Historica Lundensis 77. Lund: Lund University Press (bilaga 8).
SAOB: *Svenska Akademiens ordbok* [http://g3.spraakdata.gu.se/saob/].
Schlegel & Klingspor (SK): Schlegel, Bernhard, Klingspor, Carl Arvid 1875: *Den med sköldebref förlänade men ej å riddarhuset introducerade svenska adelns ättar-taflor*. Stockholm 1875.
Stiernman, Anders Ant. von 1835, 1836 (SHM): *Swea och Götha Höfdinga-Minne*, I–II delen.
Svenska riksrådets protokoll (SRP): *Svenska riksrådets protokoll* 1878–1959: Handlingar rörande Sveriges Historia, Tredje serien. Stockholm: Kungl. boktryckeriet P. A. Norstedt & söner.
*Svenskt biografiskt lexikon* 1917–2013 (SBL): A–Stålhammar. Stockholm: Riksarkivet. [http://sok.riksarkivet.se/SBL/Start.aspx]
Äldre svenska frälsesläkter (ÄSF): *Äldre svenska frälsesläkter*: Ättartavlor utgivna av riddarhusdirektionen I:1 (red. Folke Wernstedt). Stockholm: Riddarhusdirektion 1957.
*Äldre svenska frälsesläkter*: Ättartavlor utgivna av Riddarhusdirektionen I:2 (red. Folke Wernstedt). Stockholm: Riddarhusdirektion 1965.
*Äldre svenska frälsesläkter*: Ättartavlor utgivna av Riddarhusdirektionen I:3 (red. Folke Wernstedt, Hans Gillingstam, Pontus Möller)). Stockholm: Riddarhusdirektion 1989.

## Printed sources

Brahe, Abraham 1920: *Abraham Brahes tidebok*. Stockholm: P. A. Norstedt & söners förlag.
Brahe, Per (1971): *Oeconomia eller Hushållsbok för ungt adelsfolk*. Utgiven med inledning, kommentar och ordförklaringar av John Granlund och Gösta Holm. Nordiska museets Handlingar 78. Lund: Berlinska boktryckeriet.
*Samling av instructioner rörande den civila förvaltning i Sverige och Finland 1856*. Red. C.G. Styffe. Stockholm: Hörbergska boktryckeriet (ICF).

## Literature

Ahnlund, Nils 1933: "Ståndsriksdagens utdaning 1592–1672", *Sveriges Riksdag I: 3.* Red. Nils Edén. Stockholm: Sveriges Riksdag.

Ahnlund, Nils 1940: *Axel Oxenstierna intill Gustav Adolfs död.* Stockholm: P. A. Norstedt & söner.

Anthoni, Eric 1935: *Till avvecklingen av konflikten mellan hertig Carl och Finland I: konfliktens uppkomst och hertigens seger.* Helsingfors: Mercators tryckeri.

Asker, Björn 1990: "Aristocracy and Autocracy in Seventeenth-Century Sweden. The Decline of the Aristocracy within the Civil Administration before 1680", *Scandinavian Journal of History 15 (1–2).*

Asker, Björn 2007: *Hur riket styrdes. Förvaltning, politik och arkiv 1520–1920.* Stockholm: Riksarkivet.

Berg, Tor 1935: "Riksdagens utveckling under den äldre Vasatiden 1521–1592". In: Edén, Nils (red.), *Sveriges Riksdag I: 2.* Stockholm: Sveriges Riksdag.

Bergh, Severin 1882: *Karl IX och den svenska adeln 1607–1609.* Uppsala: Akademiska boktryckeriet.

Bergh, Severin 1912: *Rådsprotokoll och därmed jämförliga i riksarkivet förvarade protokoll.* Stockholm: P. A. Norstedt & söner.

Bonney, Richard 1991: *The European Dynastic States 1494–1660. The Short Oxford History of the Modern World.* Oxford: Oxford University Press.

Broady, Donald 2002: "French prosopography: definition and suggested readings", *Poetics 30 (5–6).*

Carlsson, A. B. 1913: *Den svenska centralförvaltningen 1521–1809. En historisk översikt.* Stockholm: Beckmans.

Cowman, Krista 2012: "Collective Biography". In: Gunn, Simon, Faire, Lucy (ed.), *Research Methods for History.* Edinburgh: Edinburgh University Press.

Dahlgren, Stellan 1973: "Estates and Classes". In: Roberts, Michael (ed.), *Sweden's Age of Greatness 1632–1718.* London: Macmillan.

Edén, Nils 1899: *Om centralregeringens organisation under den äldre Vasatiden (1523–1594).* Uppsala: Almqvist & Wiksells Boktryckeri.

Edén, Nils 1902: *Den svenska centralregeringens utveckling till kollegial organisation i början af sjuttonde århundradet (1602–1634).* Uppsala: Almqvist & Wiksells Boktryckeri.

Enemark, Poul 1986: *Kalmarin unionista Tukholman verilöylyyn. Pohjoismainen unioniaika 1397–1521.* Helsinki: Finnish Historical Society & The Finnish Literature Society.

Eng, Torbjörn 2001: *Det svenska väldet: ett konglomerat av uttrycksformer och begrepp från Vasa till Bernadotte.* Acta Universitatis Upsaliensis 201. Uppsala: Uppsala universitet.

Englund, Peter 2007: *Kuningatar Kristiina. Elämäkerta* (suom. Rauno Ekholm). Helsinki: WSOY.

Ericson Wolke, Lars 2006: *Johan III. En biografi.* Lund: Historiska Media.

Eriksson, Bo 2009: *I skuggan av tronen. En biografi över Per Brahe d.ä.* Stockholm: Prisma.

Eriksson, Bo 2011: *Svenska adelns historia.* Stockholm: Norstedts.

Fagerlund, Rainer 1996: *Finlands historia 2.* Huvudredaktör Märtha Norrback. Esbo: Schildt.

Forssell, Nils 1935: "Kansliet från Gustav II Adolf till år 1660". In: Wieselgren, Oscar, Forssell, Nils, Munthe, Arne, Forssell, Arne, Liljedahl, Ragnar (red.), *Kungl. Maj:ts kanslis historia del I: kansliets uppkomst, organisation och utveckling intill 1840.* Uppsala: Almqvist & Wiksells boktryckeri.

Forsgrén, Gustaf 1885: *Bidrag till Svenska gref- och friherreskapens historia 1561–1655. I, Erik XIV's och Johan III's tid*. Stockholm: Ivar Hæggströms boktryckeri.

Gillingstam, Hans 1969: "Rigsråd (Sverige)", *Kulturhistoriskt lexikon för nordisk medeltid från vikingatid till reformationstid, band XIV*. Helsingfors: Akademiska bokhandeln.

Glete, Jan 2002: *War and the State in Early Modern Europe: Spain, the Dutch Republic and Sweden as fiscal-military states, 1500–1650*. London: Routledge.

Grill, Erik 1949: *Jacob De la Gardie. Affärsmannen och politikern 1608–1636*. Göteborg: Wettergren & Kerbergs förlag.

Gustafsson, Harald 2006: "A State that Failed? On the Union of Kalmar, Especially its Dissolution", *Scandinavian Journal of History 31 (3/4)*.

Gustafsson, Harald 2007: *Nordens historia. En europeisk region under 1200 år*. Stockholm: Studentlitteratur.

Hakanen, Marko 2011: *Vallan verkostoissa. Per Brahe ja hänen klienttinsä 1600-luvun Ruotsin valtakunnassa*. Jyväskylä Studies in Humanities 157. Jyväskylä: Jyväskylän yliopisto.

Harrison, Dick, Eriksson, Bo 2010: *Norstedts Sveriges historia 1350–1600*. Stockholm: Norstedts.

Herlitz, Nils 1928: *Grunddragen av det svenska statsskickets historia*. Stockholm: P. A. Norstedt & Söners Förlag.

Hermanson, Lars 2000: *Släkt, vänner och makt: en studie av elitens politiska kultur i 1100-talets Danmark*. Avhandlingar från Historiska institutionen, Göteborgs universitet, 24. Göteborg: Göteborgs universitet.

Hermanson, Lars 2003: "Vänskap som politisk ideologi i Saxo Grammaticus Gesta Danorum", *Historisk Tidskrift 123 (4)*.

Hermanson, Lars 2009: *Bärande band. Vänskap, kärlek och brödraskap i det medeltida Nordeuropa, ca 1000–1200*. Lund: Nordic Academic Press.

Hildebrand, Emil 1896: *Svenska statsförfattningens historiska utveckling från äldsta tid till våra dagar*. Stockholm: P. A. Norstedt & söner.

Hildebrand, Emil, Alin, Oscar 1887: *Företal. Svenska Riksdagsakter jämte andra handlingar som höra till statsförfattningens historia*. Första serien: tidevarvet 1521–1718, avd. I: 1521–1544. Stockholm: Svenska Riksarkivet.

Jones, Diana K. 2001: "Researching groups of lives: a collective biographical perspective on the Protestant ethic debate", *Qualitative Research 1 (3)*.

Jutikkala, Eino 1958: *Suomen talonpojan historia*. Toinen, uudistettu ja lisätty laitos. Helsinki: The Finnish Literature Society (first published 1942).

Karonen, Petri 2014: *Pohjoinen suurvalta. Ruotsi ja Suomi 1521–1809*. Helsinki: The Finnish Literature Society.

Konow, Jan von 2005: *Sveriges adels historia*. Karlskrona: Axel Abrahamsons Förlag.

Lagerqvist, Lars O. 2001: *Svensk historia*. Stockholm: Svenska institutet.

Lamberg, Marko 2001: *Dannemännen i stadens råd. Rådmanskretsen i nordiska köpstäder under senmedeltiden*. Monografier utgivna av Stockholms stad 155. Stockholm: Stockholmiaförlag.

Lamberg, Marko 2008: "Prosopografian mahdollisuuksia", *Keskiajan avain*. Helsinki: The Finnish Literature Society.

Lappalainen, Mirkka 2005: *Suku, valta, suurvalta. Creutzit 1600-luvun Ruotsissa ja Suomessa*. Helsinki: WSOY.

Lappalainen, Mirkka 2009: *Susimessu. 1590-luvun sisällissota Ruotsissa ja Suomessa*. Helsinki: Siltala.

Larsson, Lars-Olof 2005: *Arvet efter Gustav Vasa. En berättelse om fyra kungar och ett rike*. Stockholm: Prisma.

Larsson, Lars-Olof, Österberg, Eva 1985: Vasatiden och stormaktstiden. In: Behre, Göran, Larsson, Lars-Olof, Österberg, Eva, *Sveriges historia 1521–1809: stormaktsdröm och småstatsrealiteter*. Stockholm: Esselte Studium AB.

Lind, Gunner 1999: "Prosopografi med relationelle databaser". In: Aronsson, Peter, Fagerlund, Solveig, Samuelsson, Jan (red.), *Nätverk i historisk forskning. Metafor, metod eller teori?* Växjö: Växjö Universitet.

Lehtinen, Erkki 1961: *Hallituksen yhtenäistämispolitiikka Suomessa 1600-luvulla (1600-n. 1680).* Historiallisia Tutkimuksia 60. Helsinki: Finnish Historical Society.

Lindegren, Jan 1985: "The Swedish "Military State", 1560–1720", *Scandinavian Journal of history* 10.

Lindroth, Sten 1975: *Svensk lärdomshistoria. Medeltiden, reformationstiden.* Stockholm: P. A. Norstedt & Söners Förlag.

Matikainen, Olli 2002: *Verenperijät. Väkivalta ja yhteisön murros itäisessä Suomessa 1500–1600-luvulla.* Bibliotheca historica 78. Helsinki: The Finnish Literature Society.

Naumann, Christian 1866–1875: *Svenska statsförfattningens historiska utveckling.* Stockholm: P. A. Norstedt.

Nilsson, Sven A. 1937: "1634 års regeringsform", *Scandia* 10.

Nilsson, Sven A. 1947: *Krona och frälse i Sverige 1523–1594. Rusttjänst, länsväsende, godspolitik.* Lund: Gleerupska univ. bokhandeln.

Nilsson, Sven A. 1952, *Kampen om de adliga privilegierna 1526–1594.* Skrifter utgivna av vetenskaps-societeten i Lund 41. Lund: C. W. K. Gleerup.

Nilsson, Sven A. 1984: "1634 års regeringsform i det svenska statssystemet", *Statsvetenskaplig tidskrift* 87.

Nilsson, Sven A. 1996: "Gustav II Adolf och Axel Oxenstierna: en studie i maktdelning och dess alternativ", *Scandia* 62.

Norrhem, Svante 1993: *Uppkomlingarna. Kanslitjänstemännen i 1600-talets Sverige och Europa.* Stockholm: Almqvist & Wiksell International.

Renvall, Pentti, Roos, John E. 1934: "Keskitetyn hallintolaitoksen kehitys". In: Suolahti, Gunnar et al. (toim.), *Suomen Kulttuurihistoria II.* Helsinki: Gummerus.

Renvall, Pentti 1939: *Klaus Fleming und der Finnische Adel in den Anfangsphasen der Krise der neunziger Jahre der 16. Jahrhunderts.* Turun Yliopiston Julkaisuja B: 24. Turku: Turun yliopisto.

Renvall, Pentti 1949: "Baltian kysymyksen kriisi". In: Korhonen, Arvi (toim.), *Suomen historian käsikirja I.* Helsinki: WSOY.

Roberts, Michael 1968: *The Early Vasas. A History of Sweden, 1523–1611.* Cambridge: Cambridge University Press.

Roberts, Michael 1979: *The Swedish Imperial Experience 1560–1718.* Cambridge: Cambridge University Press.

Samuelson, Jan 1993: *Aristokrat eller förädlad bonde? Det svenska frälsets ekonomi, politik och sociala förbindelser under tiden 1523–1611.* Bibliotheca Historica Lundensis 77. Lund: Lund University Press.

Schück, Herman 1985: "Riksdagens framväxt: tiden intill 1611". In: Stjernquist, Nils (red.), *Riksdagen genom tiderna.* Stockholm: Sveriges riksdag & Riksbankens Jubileumsfond.

Schück, Herman 2005: *Rikets råd och män. Herredag och råd i Sverige 1280–1480.* Stockholm: Kungl. Vitterhets Historie och Antikvitets Akademien.

Scott, Franklin D. 1977: *Sweden. The Nation's History.* Minneapolis: University of Minnesota Press.

Sjödell, Ulf 1966: *Kungamakt och högaristokrati. En studie i Sveriges inre historia under Karl XI.* Bibliotheca Historica Lundensis XVII. Lund: Lunds universitet.

Sjödell, Ulf 1975: *Riksråd och kungliga råd. Rådskarriären 1602–1718.* Bibliotheca Historica Lundensis XXXVIII. Lund: Lunds universitet.

Sjödell, Ulf 1976: *Infödda svenska män av ridderskapet och adeln: Kring ett tema i Sveriges historia under 1500- och 1600-talen.* Skrifter utgivna an Vetenskapssocieteten i Lund 72. Lund: Gleerup.

Sommarström, Hugo 1935: *Finland under striderna mellan Sigismund och hertig Karl. I: Klas Flemings tid*. Stockholm: Björck och Börjessons bokförlag.
Stolpe, Sven 1988: *Drottning Kristina*. Helsinki: WSOY.
Stone, Lawrence 1971: "Prosopography", *Daedalus 100*.
Strömberg-Back, Kerstin 1963: *Lagen rätten läran. Politisk och kyrklig idédebatt i Sverige under Johan III:s tid*. Bibliotheca Historica Lundensis XI. Lund: Lunds universitet.
Tham, Wilhelm 1960: *Den svenska utrikespolitikens historia I: 2. 1560–1648*. Stockholm: P. A. Norstedt.
Uotila, Merja 2014: *Käsityöläinen kyläyhteisönsä jäsenenä. Prosopografinen analyysi Hollolan käsityöläisistä 1810–1840*. Jyväskylä Studies in Humanities 237. Jyväskylä: Jyväskylän yliopisto.
Weibull, Lauritz 1965: *Stockholms blodbad och andra kritiska undersökningar*. Stockholm: Natur och Kultur.
Wetterberg, Gunnar 2002: *Kanslern Axel Oxenstierna i sin tid, del 1*. Stockholm: Atlantis.
Ågren, Kurt 1976: "Rise and Decline of an Aristocracy. The Swedish social and political elite in the 17th century", *Scandinavian Journal of History 1 (1–4)*.
Östergren, Stefan 2005: *Sigismund. En biografi över den svensk-polske monarken*. Stockholm: Katolsk Historisk förening.

# Royal Secretaries III

Marko Hakanen
http://orcid.org/0000-0002-4214-960X

Ulla Koskinen
http://orcid.org/0000-0002-3430-9810

# Secretaries as Agents in the Middle of Power Structures (1560–1680)

Access of information, possession of information, and distribution channels of information have always been key elements in efficient power networks. Often the information needs to be kept secret, but how good are secretaries at keeping secrets, and how is their trustworthiness measured anyway? Because of the nature of government, it needs structure, and so it creates loci of power; places where different streams of information merge to be used as an integral part in the decision-making process and so sent off elsewhere. The problem is, of course, that people in power cannot be present at every important locus at one and the same time, yet they still need the information. So they naturally turn to the people who happen to stand in the middle of that information traffic, but who cannot use it directly for their own benefit because they lack the formal position of power. The world knows these people as secretaries.

Secretaries wielded formal power that was invested in their formal post and duties, as well as informal power which derived from practical factors: their position at the core of the central power, their proximity to the king, social relations, and access to knowledge. Positioned at the nexus of power networks, secretaries gained information from various sources and persons and could perform as mediators between the ruler and his or her subjects. In this way, they gained influence over decision making, even though it was not part of their official duties. This situation was promoted by the Vasa kings, who treated secretaries as their allies in trying to keep the aristocracy in check.

In this chapter we look at the Royal Chancery secretaries[1] (*sekreterare*) in sixteenth and seventeeth century Sweden. It is a period when the administrative structures of Sweden went through remarkable changes in a relatively short period of time.[2] The expanding administration and bureaucracy created a new operational environment for secretaries which simultaneously increased their informal power to influence matters, because they had greater access to the flow of information and the inner circle of people who made the decisions. This personal contact made it much easier to influence decisions.

In the sixteenth century, the administrative structures in Sweden were so basic that the king was personally running the whole administration, or at least supervising it. The latter part of the century is known for being the time when there was a power struggle between the monarch and nobility, and it was also around this time that secretaries began to have more influence over decisions, even making some independently for themselves. In fact, it was during this period of transition that they perhaps had the most power, or at least certainly more than in later centuries, when the bureaucracy caught up with them. By the seventeenth century the formerly powerful position of secretaries was just a distant memory, but that did not mean that secretaries had become completely powerless. They just adapted, and dived into the world of social networks in the knowledge that control of information is also power.

Even though secretaries played a significant role in the early modern administrative system, they have still been mostly seen as office workers, and have therefore been given surprisingly short shrift in historical studies. In this chapter we aim to lift them from this obscurity into the limelight. Firstly, we will study the official instructions that were given to secretaries, to better understand the structural context in which they worked, as this clearly determined much of their agency. In these normative operational environments like the Royal Chancellery, Council of the Realm, and collegia, secretaries had to work under certain rules, but in the long run, the norm was actually constant change, so it meant that the secretaries had to be ready to adapt their agency around these changes. By studying secretaries over a relatively long time period (sixteenth and seventeeth centuries) we can track the formal changes, and see how they affected secretaries' agency in real terms.

In previous research, it has usually been thought that the power of secretaries ended in Sweden by the end of the sixteenth century.[3] In some sense this is correct, but in another it is not that simple. It is true that in the sixteenth century, monarchs ruled Sweden largely with the help of secretaries, whereas by the next century they were helped by the Council of the Realm and its accompanying administrative bureaucracy. But this does not mean that secretaries lost their power all together; it just took on a more informal shape. For the years it covers, Ivan Svalenius' seminal work on the history and composition of the chancellery, *Rikskansliet i Sverige 1560–1592*, provides a solid context for analyzing this informal power, as it presents the socio-economic background of its secretaries, their careers, networks, and detailed biographies.[4] Meanwhile, Svante Norrhem has studied the officials of the Royal Chancellery in the seventeenth century and compared them with those of Spain, France, and England. He shows that a very important part of agency for secretaries relied on the patronage networks they belonged to.[5]

Secretaries have often been neglected by historical studies or, at best, are mentioned randomly. So to be able to create a more solid database, we have used collective biography as a quantitative method together with more traditional qualitative source materials like official instructions, minutes, royal letters, and personal correspondence. Using prosopographical methods to collect information like this from several different biographical collections (including official rolls) allows us, not only to analyze the role of secretaries in their operational environment, but also to generalize more reliably about them. For instance, we have a better idea of the usual length of their careers, their age when appointed, the kind of tasks they handled, and how often they changed office. Our hypothesis is that the longer a secretary's career was, the more information and skills he would have. Secretaries were able to create a personal network where their role was to act like a nexus that connected members from different social networks, especially with regard to patronage. By connecting biographical and private sources with normative material, we hope to thereby shed more light on the actions of the secretaries and interpret their agency more effectively.

## The Royal Chancellery as a nexus for power

In his well-known treatise *Del Secretario* (1564), the Italian scholar Francesco Sansovino popularised a theological metaphor describing secretaries as being as close to their prince as angels are to God.[6] Although the administrative context of Sansovino's secretaries was quite different, the same could be said of the royal secretaries of sixteenth and seventeenth century Sweden. All over Europe, in fact, the significance of secretaries grew during this period, and as modern states developed, they became important wielders of power, assisting their sovereigns in foreign politics and domestic administration. As the demands placed upon the secretaries increased, there was a need for education, training, expertise, and even specialisation. These were the first steps in the professionalization of secretaries into skillful state officials who commanded respect.[7]

Secretaries grew more prominent within the Swedish government during the 1530s and '40s, when the Royal Chancellery was established and set up according to German imperial principles. The innovator behind this and other reorganizations of the central administration was Conrad von Pyhy (d. 1553), a well-educated jurist who had served the German Holy Roman Emperors before he came to Sweden in 1538. The Royal Chancellery henceforth became a central administrative body consisting of Swedish and German (and Latin) departments, run by a chancellor and under the close surveillance of Gustavus Vasa.[8]

Some highly trusted secretaries acquired a lot of influence from their kings in this way. For example, there was Jöran Persson (c. 1530–1568) (Eric XIV), Johan Henriksson (d. 1592) (John III) as well as Nils Chesnocopherus (1574–1622), Erik Jöransson (Tegel) (1563–1636) and Johan Bengtsson Skytte/Schroderus (1577–1645) (Charles IX).[9] Their position was in practice that of a minister, and it resonates well with Spain, England and France, where one of the most powerful offices of state, by the mid-sixteenth century, became the Secretary of State – held by some prominent individuals, such as Thomas Cromwell.[10]

However, in Sweden the royal secretaries' position remained informal and very much dependent on their personal relationship to the king. Apart from his favourites, even the ordinary royal secretaries working in the chancellery had practical power because of their proximity to the king and the fact that they were the ones who presented governmental matters to him. Their influence in fact grew so strong in the 1530s and 1540s, that the period became referred to as the "rule of the secretaries" (*sekreterareregementet*).[11] The aristocracy and councillors of the realm frowned on this for decades, until in the 1620s a restructuring of the administrative system took effect. The end result was a collegiate system where secretaries' apparent positions of power turned into more discreet forms of influence.

In the power struggle of the 1590s, most secretaries remained on the lawful king's side, even if he did not have the full support of the ruling elite. From an administrative point of view, secretaries were the king's personal servants and so when King Sigismund did eventually lose his battle against Duke Charles, they all lost their jobs; and none were appointed to the new chancellery that was set up in 1602. Charles, who became King Charles IX, understandably wanted to start with a clean slate, knowing full well what an important position they had in an administration. Using the experiences he had gained previously in his dukedom, he pushed for further centralization of the administration,[12] but with the same number of secretaries. Many see this as the point when the power of secretaries began to wane, and the process was completed under the next king, Gustavus Adolphus, when he eventually put the high aristocracy in control of all the major organs of the central administration.[13]

In 1611, the new king appointed Axel Oxenstierna (1583–1654) as Lord High Chancellor[14] and under this man's guidance, a new collegial form of government took shape. The Royal Chancellery was now led by Oxenstierna with help of two councillors of the realm and the royal chancellor (*hovkansler*). In effect, it meant that all the important decisions were made by members of the higher nobility now, instead of secretaries as it had been in the previous century. The other change was that, from 1618 onwards, their work was now clearly regulated by a specific job description and instructions concerning it. These reforms did not happen overnight though; in fact, it was not until 1626 that these chancellery instructions finally included such important details as their working hours. During the week they were expected to work from 6 to 10 am and from 2 to 5 pm, except on Wednesdays and Fridays when work started later at 8 am. On Saturdays, they only worked in the mornings from 6 till 10. The work done everyday was also controlled, as every secretary had to keep a record of what they had done so they could be checked by the Lord High Chancellor.[15]

However, these reforms to the administration[16] increased the overall amount of bureaucracy that was needed in government, and this in turn increased the need for further secretaries. In the sixteenth century, however, secretaries were resented by the nobility to such an extent that they pushed through new privileges which guaranteed that all high offices in the administration were only open to the noble estate. The problem was, however, that there were not enough skilful people among the nobility capable of doing the required jobs. This potentially difficult situation actually benefited the high nobility though, who through patronage of their own ennobled secretaries could now control various parts of the administration. It was a win-win situation for both the secretaries, ensured of a job; and the high nobility, ensured of a large number of gratefully loyal servants. The result was a new estate of noble civil servants in Sweden.

By the end of the seventeenth century, 258 civil servants had been ennobled, and 46 of these were actually secretaries. Appointment as a secretary did not instantly guarantee a noble title though; sometimes they had to wait years, and it also depended on the post's location. If it was in the central administration, the average waiting time was five years, while in local government it was 8½. The best option, career-wise, seems to have been to serve either in the Chancellery Collegium or Crown Repossessions Collegium, where the average age for an officeholder to become noble was 38. In other collegia, it was over 40, with the worst option being the Admiralty, where it was 46.

Gustavus Adolphus and Oxenstierna's first orders for the Royal Chancellery were that the Lord High Chancellor was now in charge of it.[17] The first clear structural reform happened in 1618, when it was ruled that only one person was now responsible for forming an official archive in the chancellery, so that all important documents could be found quickly. The number of actual 'secretaries' may not have grown, nevertheless three skilful clerks were ordered to serve the secretary in charge of the archive – normally secretaries only got two.[18] The workload nevertheless kept increasing, so that only 18 months later the number of secretaries hired by the chancellery had risen to nine. At the same time, a second clerk joined the Archive and some secretaries now had three clerks helping them, so overall the number of personnel had grown.[19]

By the end of the 1620s, the reforms to the Royal Chancellery had stabilized and Gustavus Adolphus paid more attention to the Council of the Realm's role in supervising the administration. The Council not only got a clear description of its precise role, but it also had to draw up minutes for every meeting, so that king could check on what had been decided later.[20] Henceforth reforms to the high administration continued steadily, as from 1625 to 1630 the Council of the Realm got new instructions annually.[21] Its most important task was to ensure the safe running of the administration when the monarch was abroad leading the army. The instructions stated that six councillors of the realm needed to stay permanently in Stockholm and attend the council meetings, so there would be no interruptions in the day-to-day running of the administration.[22] The number of councillors required to stay in the capital city soon became ten, however,[23] and because the workload of the higher administration was now clearly greater (with the number of council meetings increasing), so was there a need for more secretaries.[24]

As the tasks of the Royal Chancellery steadily increased, so did the accompanying bureaucracy, and the diversity of staff it employed.[25] In 1639, there were amanuenses, introducers, clerks, copyists, caretakers, hired men, and carriers working alongside secretaries at the chancellery.[26] By 1661 the reforms at the Royal Chancellery were pretty much complete and after that it operated without any major changes for another 140 years. As the number of secretaries grew, it became evident that some kind of ranking would be necessary. For instance, 'Royal Chancellor' (*hovkansler*) became the title of the secretary in charge of all others, and 'Secretary of State' was another honorary title received by some.[27]

## The rule of secretaries (1560–1600)

In the late sixteenth century, the Swedish realm was administered by the king and whoever he graced as a close trustee at the time. Increasingly those most favoured were found to be among his non-noble secretaries, much to the resentment of the nobility.[28]

Though most of his German-inspired reforms to the central administration were too specialized and eventually had to be abandoned, Gustavus Vasa's simple idea behind organizing the chancellery proved to be permanent. The 'Swedish department' took care of domestic correspondence, presented matters to the king, and copied and archived documents. Other ways to distribute the workload within the apartment were attempted, but most stayed on paper. However, practical specialization within the home office did take place, as some secretaries specialised in correspondence with bailiffs, others in appeals from the king's subjects, and others in 'important letters'.[29]

Meanwhile, foreign policy was mostly the responsibility of the 'German department' of the chancellery, which maintained contacts with foreign princes as well as organized delegations and envoys.[30] The leading secretaries were even present in face-to-face negotiations with foreign powers, as diplomatic delegations usually consisted of two to three councillors of the realm and a secretary.[31] Some of these experts in the chancellery, like Erik Matsson (1520s–1593) and Hans Eriksson Kranck (before 1571–after 1626), gained a status that was effectively comparable to noble office holders.

After Gustavus Vasa's "German period" the number of secretaries in the Swedish department went up as more Swedish-born men from the bourgeoisie and clergy acquired a higher education. Many of them were educated in jurisprudence, and this also made them an asset in other matters of the realm.[32] Six secretaries worked permanently in the chancellery during the reigns of Eric XIV and (apparently) John III. Each was responsible for a particular policy area and assisted by scribes and copyists. In addition, there were usually seven other secretaries or "more qualified people" with varying temporary commissions.[33] Eric XIV, John III and Charles IX all nominated an aristocratic Chancellor of the Realm to lead the chancellery, but this was largely a symbolic and titular post.[34]

When John III seized power in 1569, the chancellery underwent some serious changes. In order to make some concessions to the aristocracy as well as distinguish his rule from the previous administration, John III renamed some secretaries of the former administration mere "chancellery staff". Four one-time supporters of Eric XIV were condemned to death or replaced, and several others died of natural causes around the same time.[35] In the last years of John III's reign, the number and political influence of office staff in central government increased once again. This clearly coincided with the king's growing alienation from the aristocracy. Indeed, during the internal crisis that followed his death in 1592, the staff numbers went down again to ten people.[36]

The length of secretaries' careers varied widely. They were most volatile in the German department where careers lasted typically 1–5 years, whereas they were notably longer and more established in the Swedish department.

A third of the secretaries there (14 to be precise) worked in the chancellery for 20 years or more, another third for 10–19 years, and only five for less than eight years. The most senior was a Finn called Erik Matsson, who was first employed by Gustavus Vasa and remained in service until 1593 – a total of almost 50 years. He began his career in the Chamber and was made Chamberlain (*kammarråd*) by Eric XIV. Even though he had been one of the dethroned monarch's closest servants he managed to maintain his influential position even after Erik's deposition. According to Bengt Hildebrand, this continuity testifies either to his meagre political influence, or to his personal flexibility and indispensable value in the chancellery.[37]

Clemet Hansson Oliveblad, the son of a burgher, had almost as long a career (45 years), and so did the genealogist, Rasmus Ludvigsson (d. 1594) (41 years). Both were born in Stockholm. Oliveblad's work in the chancellery was continued by his son Ivar Clemetsson. Ludvigsson, whose nickname among colleagues was "Sapientia" or "Sapientia in confusione" had studied in Rostock in his youth. There were also some that had a career of almost 30 years even in the German department, namely Ambrosius Palmbaum, Herman Bruser (d. 1588) and Mattias Schubert (d. 1611).[38]

The influential position of royal secretaries was a novelty in Sweden's sixteenth century administration that became most prominent under the reign of Eric XIV and had a resurgence again in John III's time. It was an important factor that rocked the delicate balance of power between the king and aristocrats in the Council of the Realm. Because of their low birth, secretaries were outside the traditional aristocratic power networks at the core of the realm. At a time when the significance of written documents rose hand in hand with the bureaucratization of state structures, all documents concerning the king went through the hands of these low-born secretaries. They composed the official documents and letters, and presented or read documents that arrived to the ruler, as well as reported on statements received from foreign envoys.[39]

To the aristocracy's horror, their influence grew beyond this too. In principle, the chancellery was just an executive body, but it seems clear that secretaries had influence over more than just the form of the documents they composed. A massive amount of minor documents were actually left to the secretaries to compose, and some royal letters were not even signed by the king. Occasionally the secretary even made a note that the king approved the document without reading the whole text. In the reign of Eric XIV, common civil servants thus achieved previously unheard of political importance and some even had the possibility to exert real political power. According to Michael Roberts, in this way they became instruments in fostering the king's anti-aristocratic policy.[40]

This was sure to provoke resentment among the aristocracy, who were used to having this kind of influence for themselves. Secretaries presented a threat simply by being physically close to the sovereign. They were constantly in a position to exert influence over his decisions, whereas the Council of the Realm gathered only occasionally with the councillors staying mostly away from the centre of power on their estates in the country.[41]

According to many researchers, power fell into the secretaries' hands because of the political situation in Sweden, as the sons of Gustavus Vasa were trying not to delegate their power to the aristocracy. Both Eric XIV and John III were almost paranoid about the high nobility's lust for power, so it was natural that they relied on lower estate secretaries who owed their new status personally to the king. Through them, the rulers could be sure that they had reliable control over the central administration and archived state documents.[42]

The royal secretaries thus became known for being an institution of commoners. There were virtually no sons of noblemen as secretaries in the sixteenth century, and the secretaries were usually not ennobled during their career. Most of them came from a bourgeois background in Stockholm. Leading secretaries had the chance to become wealthy and many of them were rewarded with fiefs and ended up owning stone houses in the capital. Some of them even lent great sums of money to the Crown. In line with Michael Roberts, Ivan Svalenius sees favouring the secretaries as the sovereigns' attempt to create a functional bureaucracy by engaging the bourgeoisie in central administration to capitalize on their royalist tendencies. This connects Sweden to the overall pattern of state-building that was going on across Europe too. As the expansion of princely power was achieved at the expense of the Church and aristocracy, royalty across the continent sought political support from the burghers and merchant estates. In Sweden, they were relatively few in number and low in influence, but apparently eager to fill the political power vacuum left by the clergy after the Reformation.[43]

Another fact worth noting is how the overall political importance of the eastern part of the realm grew. By the time John III died, 11 of the 15 secretaries were either born in Finland or connected to that part of the realm through marriage.[44] This was an effect of the war against Russia that dominated John's foreign policy, diplomacy, and inner administration. A better known result of the war was the special position and privileges that the Finnish nobility gained for being mainly in charge of the Swedish war efforts. During the next century, there were always people in the chancellery that took care of Finnish matters and understood the Finnish language.[45]

There were continuous demands in the constitutional negotiations between king and aristocracy during John III's reign that the nobility be more actively involved in the chancellery; and this increased in the ensuing inner power struggle following his death. In 1585 and 1593, the Council of the Realm even had plans to recruit and train sons of the aristocracy for the king's service, but they never came to fruition. Ivan Svalenius has pointed out that, despite these plans, in practice the aristocracy were not so eager to train their sons up for royal service as secretaries. His interpretation is that they instead wished to transform the whole system by making the humble secretaries previously dependent on the king into prestigious aristocratic state officials working in the chancellery. In the following century, this finally happened and once again king and aristocracy were allied; but in comparison with the rest of Scandinavia it took a long time. In Denmark, for instance, this kind of aristocratic-royal alliance had occurred already in the early sixteenth century.[46]

However, the "rule of secretaries" need not to have been a poor choice per se. Its bad reputation stemmed from aristocracy's fierce political denigration. It was mainly the Swedish councillors and other high aristocracy who gave secretaries as a whole a bad reputation, thus demonising the whole administrational practice and making the most prominent secretaries infamous as individuals. The aristocracy had over the centuries developed a discursive practice of nominating Swedish-born noblemen as the primary group whenever there was talk about granting privileges or appointing powerful positions. For a time, however, they were satisfied with the prominent position they gained when John III dethroned his brother in 1568.[47]

After 1575, however, the king started relying on his secretaries in dealing with controversial ecclesiastical matters and economic negotiations vis-à-vis the nobility. The frustrated aristocracy targeted their consequent resentment against the secretaries. Hogenskild Bielke (1538–1605) called them "a loose party" that cannot be relied on.[48] This contemporary formulation is worth noting: since the bourgeois secretaries were outsiders to the reciprocal aristocratic networks of trust and solidarity, there were no pre-existing bonds of loyalty to guide mutual interaction. The essential elements of social relations – predictability, loyalty and trust – were missing, thus making the secretaries dubious 'others' in the eyes of the aristocracy.

How the secretaries actually viewed this has received far less publicity in the literature however. After all, in the history of winners, there is no space for an alternative view of the "rule of the secretaries". Most of the secretaries were educated and had gained years of expertise in administration, unlike the high-born aristocrats, who only realized the importance of education from the secretaries' example. As Ulf Sjödell has pointed out, members of the nobility did not traditionally even meet the qualifications for working in the chancellery, such as linguistic skills, university education and experience abroad. On the other hand, the other central body that took care of finances, the Chamber was traditionally led by an aristocratic Chamberlain (Sw. *kammarråd*).[49]

As B. Boëthius has pointed out, the agency of secretaries was personal and informal in nature and therefore has generally left no historical traces. The echoes preserved of the secretaries' own voices stress their competence, even in contrast to the aristocrats. In fact, one gets the impression that it was the secretary who took care of the actual matters in diplomatic missions, while the aristocratic members were there to give a good impression of the realm.[50] There are only some hints as to what their actual agency consisted of. One outstanding case concerns Johan Berndes (d. 1602), who allied with his colleagues and successfully elaborated for the sovereign the necessity of a milder policy, when John III had ordered the confiscation of noble properties in the newly conquered Estonian area.[51]

One reason behind much of the aristocracy's bitterness towards the secretaries was that Eric XIV created a system in which they were used to keep a check on the aristocracy; as the king suspected them of trying to gain more power. At the master controls of this machinery was procurator Jöran Persson. Eric XIV created this post for him as head of the chancellery, but in practice it meant that Persson was in control of the judicial system. Jöran Persson has become a historically well-known figure as a personification of the many grievances associated with Erik's rule. Because Persson's story has been told by his opponents, he has become a scapegoat; research has in fact shown that he may have striven to balance the whims of an unstable king. He was succeeded in his role as "minister of control" by the active Catholic and Jesuit supporter, Johan Henriksson, who became as hated as his predecessor. Henriksson had the added honour of being suspected of poisoning Eric XIV after he had been deposed and imprisoned, and was tried in court for another murder as well.[52]

Another influential secretary was Sven Elofsson (b. 1533), son of a pastor, who was hired to the chancellery when in his 20s by Gustavus Vasa. His job as a royal trustee involved participating in several foreign missions and he gained considerable wealth. Sven Elofsson stands out for his Self-confidence, as he resigned from service under John III for religious reasons. Instead he entered Charles IX's service and remained there for the rest of his working life. In his retirement, he wrote his memoirs on recent Swedish history (1556–79) called 'Paralipomena'. This is extraordinary in the Swedish context for this time period and reflects a certain trust in his own worth and capabilities. A later publisher added a note to say, "The very well-known secretary of King Gustav and his sons". The memoirs mark the beginning of a lasting tradition that would portray Gustavus Vasa as a heroic state-builder – a measure against whom all his successors were judged, and often found to be lacking. Elofsson even went so far as to note that "together with King Gustav, the realm's vigour and well-being have been laid in tomb and are gone".[53]

*Powerful secretaries and the nobility – forming networks of agency*

In 1589, the councillors of the realm openly confronted John III, and forced him to abandon his plan to bring his son, King Sigismund of Poland, back to Sweden. The humiliated king was furious, calling some of the councillors traitors, and threatening to suspend them, among other things. However, the councillors' reaction gives an idea of where lay the real power to influence decision making. They chose to send a letter to secretary Olof Sverkersson (d. after 1609) asking him to placate the enraged king, even though Sverkersson was the person who had delivered the king's infuriated answer to the aristocrats in the first place. The secretary was not on good terms with the lords; in Sweden, he was called "Vändekåpa" (coat turner) and in Finland, "Perkelsson" (devil's son). The plea was unsuccessful, but it reveals that even the aristocrats felt obliged to rely upon the disrespected secretary's help as their best option to influence the king.[54]

This was by no means a unique example of noblemen collectively appealing to royal secretaries. The following year the commanders of Narva castle wrote a letter addressed to the "secretaries and staff of the chancellery", plainly asking them to use their "good advice and influence" on the king, so that the starved mercenaries in Narva would get provisions. At the same time the noblemen asked the secretaries to further their own cause, so that they might have their estates returned after having them confiscated the year before.[55] Even the reviled procurator, Jöran Persson, received petitions from the highest aristocracy in the 1560s.[56] It was thus necessary and practical to recognise the power of the secretaries.

An earlier, as illustrious example of relying onto secretaries' help is Mikael Agricola (c. 1510–1557), the famous Finnish reformator and later bishop, who was in 1548 replaced as rector in Turku. Via a middleman, Agricola had a plea written to the royal secretary Olof Larsson to maintain his position. The try was, however, unsuccesful.[57]

To illustrate how the secretaries mediated on behalf of the nobility's power networks, and integrated themselves into them, it is worth looking at some more concrete examples. Here again, the secretaries' own voice is seldomly preserved; their agency has to be reconstructed from other sources. Especially people living in the peripheries of the realm had very limited possibilities to access the king in person. A much-used strategy was to contact a secretary first and try to enlist his help in the matter at hand. This worked best for people in a considerably good social position who could rely on a strategy of reciprocal exchange, being themselves in a position to offer some valued counter services.

One such person was nobleman Arvid Henriksson Tawast (c. 1540–1599), who served throughout the 1580s as commander of Swedish infantry. He was born into Finnish nobility but made a successful career in the military and civil administration, was ennobled and became one of the leading figures in the eastern part of the realm. His mansions were located inland in the province of Tavastia.[58]

In fact, Tawast's letter collection is one of the rare ones from the Finnish part of the realm that has been even partly preserved in the archives from that era. His letters address other noblemen with the polite title "brother", creating a symbolic brotherhood between peers. The word had a strong reference to equality and solidarity. The noble "brothers" formed a steadfast network of friends always ready to help one another. But there was one who received the honour of being called "brother" without being a noble – Secretary Hans Eriksson Kranck. This is remarkable in itself, but Tawast went even further, in 1583, when he wrote to Kranck with the plea, "I trust you, dear brother of my heart, that you are helpful […]".[59] The term "heart" is usually reserved for correspondence with family only, and outside his family, Tawast uses it only when talking to a couple of noblemen who seem to be his closest friends.[60]

Why does this secretary occupy such a special position in Tawast's social network? Hans Eriksson Kranck was born in Turku, the son of an office-holder in the local administration. He started working as a scribe in the chancellery from 1571, and was promoted to secretary between 1578 and 1581. Over the years he had become a specialist on politics in the Eastern Baltic, which perhaps explains why the commander of infantry was so eager for his attention. Kranck's Finnish origins and his large family networks there made it easier for the nobility in Finland to connect with him. His importance to foreign policy was substantial. Kranck was also in with the pro-Catholic circles, becoming Sigismund's secretary in Sweden after John III's death. This means that during the civil conflict that followed, he was an extremely important supporting connection for the royalists in Finland.[61]

Arvid Henriksson Tawast asked for Kranck's help on two major occasions in his career. The first was when he was trying to rid himself of an assignment to build a fortress in Ingria in 1583; and the second when he tried to secure himself position as a district judge in 1590. In both cases, Tawast also wrote to the king, but he clearly made sure that he was in the secretary's good books first. Because Kranck's responses have not survived, we only have Tawast's letters to base an evaluation of their relationship on. It is clear that Tawast considered their relationship important, and it seems it was also confidential. Kranck seemed to benefit from his good relations with the nobility in the form of gifts. This reciprocal exchange is hard to distinguish from a kind of bribery or corruption. For instance, Tawast sent Kranck's wife a roll of cloth as a gift to accompany his pledge concerning his request to not have to build the fortress in Ingria. Tawast also assured his readiness in the future, promising to compensate Kranck's "benevolent brotherly goodwill with all that is good".[62]

Another royal secretary with whom Arvid Henriksson Tawast networked was Erik Eriksson Bris (1550s–after 1623) (scribe 1587, secretary 1591–98). It is also worth noting that he was born on the Finnish side of the realm (in Helsinki).[63] Tawast wrote a letter to clear himself regarding severe complaints made about his actions before Duke Charles and the Council. Tawast began his undated, extensive letter by asking that the secretary "do the best for me as my good friend and be benevolent and helpful to me in this matter, as much as the law and justice permit". This shows the grey zone between help and corruption that secretaries had to navigate in their everyday agency between the king and his subjects.[64]

Tawast had probably chosen Erik Eriksson to write to because of his close relations to Duke Charles. It is also interesting that later, Eriksson switched sides and became a royalist, in the end fleeing the country with his colleague Olof Sverkersson, converting to catholicism and entering Sigismund's service in Poland and Livonia.[65] The crisis in the 1590s put the royal secretaries that had cooperated with Duke Charles into an ambiguous position and forced them to take a stance. Tawast as a known royalist maybe had knowledge of Erik's inclinations already at the time of writing.

Another powerful secretary was Michel Olofsson (1550s–1615), who served Duke Charles in 1591 and was one of his most trusted men. He received pleas from a number of high-ranking royalists, and one of them was Arvid Tawast, who asked him to act as his "patron" (*fordrare*) in helping him to obtain a repayment from the Duke, to whom Tawast had loaned 1000 daler.[66] Again, Tawast promised future services in return for the secretary's good will.[67]

The deviant use of rhetorics places secretaries completely apart other non-noble office holders with whom Tawast was in correspondence. Being in a high position himself, Tawast rarely uses the word *fordrare* at all; it only occurs when addressing Marshal Claes Fleming (1535–1597), the highest-ranking person in Finland.[68] One can only assume that the practical power that royal secretaries wielded was more than a match for the foremost members of the aristocracy; and this was exactly what they constantly complained about to John III.

It is remarkable that informal influence worked the other way round too. John III also used his secretaries as brokers in his attempts to influence noblemen. If there was a fine line between noble networks and corruption, there was an even finer line between royal persuasion and blackmail. For instance, in 1576 Henrik Claesson Horn (1512–1595) had (face to face) refused the king's request to accept an assignment to negotiate with the nobility in Finland. He left the royal premises, reached his ship, and was just setting sail for Finland, when Hans Kranck arrived to remind him of what the king had asked, so Horn felt obliged to accept the assignment against his will.[69] It is hardly coincidental that John III used his most influential Finnish secretary to persuade a Finnish nobleman; on the contrary, it shows that he was aware of their mutual networks and chose the secretary he deemed would have the most clout.

## Secretaries as brokers and their patronage networks

Meritocracy was an unknown concept in the Swedish administration of the seventeenth century.[70] A more important factor in deciding recruitment and careers was social connections.[71] In seventeenth century Sweden, patronage was an open and morally accepted part of personal agency. In practice, this meant finding a good patron to support one's job search within the royal administration.[72] Secretaries were no exception, in fact they were almost the opposite. Their job was so sought after by non-nobles, that by the 1650s the competition was already very stiff. Nevertheless, some skills were still of course needed.

One of the key skills secretaries have always needed is the ability to protect information. And the secrets they were charged to keep were often more intangible and troublesome than what the royal guards were protecting. In 1592, Duke Charles (later to become King Charles IX) gave orders as to how his chancellery should be organised. The first regulation dealt with the secrecy of files, and orders were given as to which secretaries should keep the key for the files.[73] But before a secretary could be given such key, the king had to know if he could trust that person. Trust has always played a big part in human relations and always been greatly valued.

By the start of the seventeenth century, the "reign of the secretaries" was but a distant memory for most of the high nobility. They certainly did not want those days back, and the best way to keep the secretaries under their thumb was through patronage. By using patronage networks both parties got what they wanted, but it required reciprocal trust with both sides expected to abide by existing social and moral codes. In patronage relationships, trust was built by repeated actions without self-interest.[74] Edvard Ehrensteen

(1620–1686) was born in a lower order clerical family, but with his social skills he managed to get connected to the high nobility and eventually with loyal service he was able to gain the trust of the King Charles X Gustav. He became a royal secretary and the king's trusted man who advised him on almost every matter and prepared all the important documents. He was described as a trustworthy, quick-witted, experienced servant, but his best feature was the ability to create social and unofficial (intelligence) networks to access information.[75] A similar kind of description was given to the other secretary from the king's chancery, Johan Fagraeus (Strömfelt) (1587–1644), whose qualities were alertness, practicality, and trustworthiness.[76] Access to secrets and keeping a secret was part of the operational environment especially for those secretaries whose responsibilities were to record important meetings. For example, all the Council of the Realm meetings needed to be transcripted, exactly as matters were discussed in the meeting (with no editing) and more often than not, members did not agree on things. Because of the nature of these minutes, secretaries were not allowed to discuss them with anyone either, without clear instruction.[77]

In the seventeenth century, the pen became as important a tool as the sword; and gaining skills in writing and organizing documents meant good career opportunities. The whole government was run via written documents (such as letters of order, instructions, donations, and letters of attorney), and letter writing had become a fixed part of everyday life. It helped maintain or create social relationships.[78] Because letters were such an important channel for passing information, secretaries were vital in high-level administrative work. In practice this meant that secretaries had to read all incoming letters, if they were not indicated as private, and then present them to the office-holder. All outgoing letters were written by secretaries too, if the matter was not really private.[79] This practical aspect of secretarial work placed them at the nexus of flows of information crucial for the exercise of power. They were also in a place where they could show their trustworthiness or exploit it for their own good. Being a secretary was thus a source of individual personal agency, and there was the chance that the job could further their own personal goals in life.

The vast expansion of Sweden's administration at the beginning of the seventeenth century created a good market for the secretaries, as the administration was always short of quality secretaries. When Gustavus Adolphus stepped outside Sweden to lead his army in 1621, he ordered nine Councillors of the Realm to stay in Stockholm and rule the country through the Council.[80] In a few years the meetings of the Council of the Realm went from only a few meetings per month to over 20.[81] The workload of secretaries was growing and the demand for new recruits was constantly there in the 1630s and 1640s. This growing need was already being seen in the growing salaries that the Royal Chancellery had to find for the secretaries that it did already have.[82]

In the seventeenth century, the privileges of the nobility guaranteed them all the high administrative offices in the government. But it was also now accepted that secretaries had a fair share of official power in their hands and their job was well respected, to such an extent that it was now considered a position worthy of a noble. But the situation in the sixteenth and at the turn of the seventeenth century was that none of the secretaries were nobility. This situation did not sit well among the mindset of the nobility, but the problem was they could not offer good secretaries from among themselves, as their education and goals were still centred around the military. The solution was thus to ennoble the best secretaries, or at least those who had the best connections – with the idea that 'making them one of us' would be the best way for the nobility to regain some influence.[83] Transforming the environment in this way created totally new ways to advance or fail the careers of secretaries. Patronage became the key element in starting and advancing secretaries' careers, and both sides benefited from the arrangement. The commoners who once clamoured for a secretarial position now got social status too, while nobles got loyal clients. The everyday agency of secretaries thus became less formally defined as it became subject to the more informal networks of patronage, and the patron-client relationship.

The number of ennobled civil officials rose steeply after the 1620s. In fact, almost half of all ennoblements in the seventeenth century were of civil servants and 26% of that half were of those in the central administration. Working in government administration generally meant a good chance of getting ennobled, because 66% of those who were not ennobled for being in the military came from the administration or judiciary. If we include the diplomats in this figure – they usually worked as secretaries before – the number goes up to 71%.[84] In France there was a similar practice. The distinguished position of a *secrétaire du roi*, writer of the royal documents, was seen to be so prestigious, that whoever bought this venal office, got nobility for their whole family. Thus it was a highly valued and understandably expensive post to buy. We can see this, from the Swedish perspective, as another example of a practice which, as Collins has mooted,[85] further enhanced the monopoly of noble power rather than undermining it – as others have sometimes suggested.

Almost everybody then who worked as a secretary in the Royal Chancellery from the 1620s onwards was ennobled.[86] The most secure way to receive a noble title was to work as personal secretary to the Lord High Chancellor of the Realm – Axel Oxenstierna. Anyone who held this position went on to be ennobled.[87] The expansion of the Royal Chancellery and its responsibilities happened almost in tandem with the rise in noble civil servants, albeit with a delay of about two years to allow for the ennoblement. Nils Tungel (1592–1665), who had been trained at Uppsala university and abroad, followed his older brother Lars Tungel (1582–1633) into the Royal Chancellery. Lars had been appointed as a secretary in 1621 and had a solid position in the chancellery.[88] In 1625, Nils was appointed as a clerk and almost immediately he was relocated to work for Axel Oxenstierna.[89] In addition to his work as a clerk he also had to do some work as an official representative, but throughout all this time the cooperation between Tungel and Oxenstierna stayed very cold.[90]

But Nils Tungel's luck turned quickly, because in 1626 Axel Oxenstierna had to travel abroad to take care of governmental business, and the Royal Chancellery had two nobles put in charge of it at the same time. The first,

Carl Eriksson Oxenstierna died early in 1629, and Per Gustafsson Banér (1588–1644), the second noble, singlehandedly took over responsibilities of the Royal Chancellery as Vice-Chancellor of the Realm. In this time, Per Banér had became Tungel's patron and in October 1629, Tungel was appointed as his secretary and worked as Banér's close subordinate and client.[91]

But Per Banér and Nils Tungel's patron-client relationship took a dramatic turn in the summer of 1644. During a meeting of the Council of the Realm, Banér got seriously ill. He bravely participated in meetings for the next two days, but after three weeks he died at the age of 56. With the loss of Per Banér, Nils Tungel lost his patron, which not only affected his present job but also his career and life in general.[92] He had to make quick decisions and act accordingly, so by letter he informed the Lord High Chancellor, Per Brahe the younger (1602–1680), that Per Banér had passed away.[93] This information did not come as a surprise for Brahe, because he had been present at those meetings when Banér got sick. The real reason to approach Brahe was, of course, to let him know that he was ready and willing to serve him and was asking him to be his patron.[94]

This illustrates how social networks had become essential for secretaries to operate. Nils Tungel had to rebuild his own because without a high profile patron he could not carry out his job, let alone advance his career. This urgency made him approach Per Brahe again just few days later, even though he did not have anything new to report, perhaps just to show his willingness to serve the Count. In his previous letter to him he had simply addressed him by his title, but in this one he was already describing Brahe as a "magnificent patron".[95] Nils Tungel survived a predicament which could have cost him his career and cut off his agency;[96] so to prove his worth to Brahe he began to report on what was going on in the Royal Chancellery and Stockholm in general.[97] This relationship benefited both parties: Brahe's patronage network gave Tungel a social security, while Brahe was able to keep tabs on the flow of information in the capital, now that he had Tungel listening in. Perhaps most important for Brahe though, was that through Tungel he was able to influence the king's decisions, as he was physically present when matters were decided and could relay this unofficial information back.[98] This extra dimension to the work of a secretary was a key element and created a major part of their agency. In fact, this kind of influence was so valuable that sometimes secretaries were able to profit from it further.[99]

Secretaries usually acted as a broker, because their instructions usually came from their patrons. Sometimes these instructions were vague: for example, Tungel reported to Brahe that he would do as much he could to get Brahe's bailiff (*hopman*) ennobled;[100] other times, when it was a matter of appointments, the instructions were more specific. In 1658, Per Brahe, as Chancellor of the Royal Academy of Turku, informed the king that there would be an opening for a history and politics professor at the Academy, and that the Academy had elected two candidates for the position. One of the nominees was Brahe's client and the other belonged to a rival's network. Brahe naturally sang the praises of his own client and merely mentioned the other by name, so that there would be no misunderstanding as to who the king should appoint for this 'open' job.¹⁰¹ Just to make doubly sure though, Brahe contacted the king's secretary and let him know too, at the same time instructing him to persuade the king (as if it were his own opinion) who the best man for the job was.¹⁰² For secretaries acting as a broker in this way, it was a chance to grow their agency by gaining both the king's and the patron's trust, but there was always a risk that they might misjudge the political situation and end up limiting their agency in the future. In this respect, their power was largely based on their social skills and sensitivity to situations in which decisions were made and where they were often personally present.¹⁰³

Per Brahe had a great need for information, because of his position as second in rank to the king. To be able to act intelligently in his many different offices he needed a constant flow of information about what was going on. It was particularly important that he had access to the information nexus of the Royal Chancellery. All the correspondence concerning the kingdom's affairs went through it, via the secretaries there. Brahe was not able to personally tap into this information flow all the time, however, because of the other social commitments to attend to. Every year around November time, for example, he travelled with his family from the capital down to his fiefdom in Visingsborg,¹⁰⁴ so he had to rely on his client Nils Tungel to report on all the important happenings in Stockholm.

Tungel was very happy to be able to serve Brahe in this way, it seems judging from the kinds of rhetorical expressions he uses in his letters to his patron.¹⁰⁵ They not only reveal that this was one source of his agency (giving him strong status among other secretaries and inside the administrative hierarchy), but also what kind of social codes Tungel had to use to fulfil his role as Brahe's client. Tungel's reports included information on the movements of the Swedish navy among other war efforts. For instance, he vividly described Admiral Claes Fleming's unfortunate sea battle in which he was fatally wounded, his struggle for life lasting no more than two hours before he finally died at 6 am on 27 July 1644. In the same letter he also included an extensive description of the political situation in Central Europe.¹⁰⁶

From the kingdom's point of view, the war news was important, but Per Brahe was also very keen to hear about the movements of important people. Tungel had to report when foreign ambassadors arrived or left Stockholm and where they were being accommodated. Sometimes Tungel also even reported on what kind of catering was being arranged.¹⁰⁷ But most important of all was to report on the movements of the ruler, because the power was very much tied to the physical presence of the monarch; although Tungel only reports on the movements of foreign leaders once, when he informs Brahe of the death of Czar Michael I of Russia and the succession of his son.¹⁰⁸

Per Brahe also wanted to monitor the core of administrative power, so Tungel's job was to inform him of all the movements of the councillors of the realm, of who was dying, and of any new appointments made.¹⁰⁹ All this affected everybody's personal agency, because the core of the high power network was so small. Any shift in personal relations or positions there could have an effect on the larger operational environment. Tungel's personal reports also usually included copies of the most important documents that had arrived in the Royal Chancellery. He did not feel that his task of fulfilling Brahe's wishes had been an onerous one, as only once he writes that he is in a rush because of a heavy workload.[110]

With the right social connections, Nils Tungel was able to advance his career even though he had lots of troubles in his personal life. Thanks to Per Brahe he was able to push his personal agency further than many of his other colleagues, but even his agency had limits. He could not help but get himself mixed up in one too many misdemeanours from which his mighty patron could not save him anymore. The cost of crossing the limits of his personal agency were huge. Nils Tungel lost his job and reputation and lived the rest of his life in obscurity. Rather than being remembered as a great royal secretary and court chancellor, people remember him more for his failings.[111]

## From formal power to informal power

In major European countries, the sixteenth century was the era of powerful secretaries, working in close contact with the monarchs.[112] In this chapter, we have examined how this changed in Sweden in the long run, especially after the governmental reformation in the 1620s. It has been assumed that the power of secretaries diminished as administrational structures expanded. On closer examination, the actual differences appear to lie in the change of the operational surroundings which expanded remarkably, thus making the secretaries less visible within the government.

The specific situation in Sweden was due to the aristocracy's concern in the late sixteenth century with the "rule of the secretaries". In the eyes of the aristocracy, the practical but informal power wielded by these commoners that remained outside the aristocratic networks of trust and loyalty was a central administrational problem. As they saw it, secretaries were a hindrance to aristocratic endeavours at creating a governmental structure that would secure for the aristocracy a formal, recognised position and actual influence in central government and the decision-making processes.

For kings, secretaries were seen as trustworthy because they were personally dependent on the king for their social status, whereas for the nobility, they represented a threat. The solution was to try to find a way to somehow assimilate the secretaries into aristocratic networks. In the sixteenth century, the nobility's strategy of calling them "brothers" or "patrons" and establishing reciprocal exchange relations with them were attempts in this direction. During the following century, this took the form of a system of patronage.

This resulted in the administrative reforms of the 1620s made between the king and aristocracy. The power exercised by the royal secretaries was now shrouded, but it did not necessarily disappear at all. Their agency simply became more informal, to suit the new administrative structure. The question remains as to whether the "reign of the secretaries" really had been a problem, or whether it was just a convenient target for the aristocracy who felt marginalized from the real sources of power. As far as the secretaries themselves were concerned, they saw themselves as educated, experienced, and seasoned practitioners, who were true servants of the king and the backbone of Sweden's administration.

The 1620s in Sweden marked the beginning of a new era as some members of the nobility decided to serve the king as civil servants rather than militarily in the king's army. At the same time, the noble estate was infused with new blood with the many civil servants that were ennobled as the state's governing apparatus grew. This change had a huge effect on the agency of secretaries. Even though they may have lost their direct power, they gained social recognition for the time period when it really mattered; and they became part of a large social group in the vastly growing administrative machinery where influence was real power. In some senses, secretaries' operational environment actually grew larger, so their potential for agency was increased, but operating inside it became more complicated when they had to navigate so carefully the private and public spheres of patronage networks – personal connections were valuable and social skills vital.

The research on which this publication is based was funded by the Academy of Finland (grant no. 137741).

## Notes

1. Persons employed in the Royal Chancellery to carry out correspondence and administrative tasks.
2. See Figure 1. The administration and legislature of Sweden 1560–1720 in *Personal Agency and State Building in Sweden, c. 1560–1720: Approaches and Perspectives* by Petri Karonen and Marko Hakanen, p. 26.
3. Richard Bonney, *The European Dynastic States 1494–1660* (Oxford: Oxford University Press, 1991), p. 334; Svante Norrhem, *Uppkomlingarna. Kanslitjänstemännen i 1600-talets Sverige och Europa* (Stockholm: Almqvist & Wiksell international, 1993), pp. 29–31; Michael Roberts, *The Early Vasas. A History of Sweden, 1523–1611* (Cambridge: Cambridge University Press, 1968), pp. 436–437.
4. Ivan Svalenius, *Rikskansliet i Sverige 1560–1592* (Stockholm: Riksarkivet, 1991).
5. Norrhem, *Uppkomlingarna*, p. 165.
6. Francesco Sansovino, *Del Secretario, o vero formulario de lettere missive e responsive* (unknown publisher, 1569; first edition by Francesco Rampazzetto, Venetia, 1564), p. 1.
7. Richard Bonney, *The European Dynastic States*, pp. 331–334; Christopher Black, *Early Modern Italy: A Social History* (London: Routledge, 2002), p. 96; Nancy Kollmann, *Crime and Punishment in Early Modern Russia* (Cambridge: Cambridge University Press, 2012), p. 50.
8. Björn Asker, *Hur riket styrdes. Förvaltning, politik och arkiv 1520–1920* (Stockholm: Riksarkivet, 2007), p. 80; Petri Karonen, *Pohjoinen suurvalta. Ruotsi ja Suomi 1521–1809* (Helsinki: The Finnish Literature Society, 2014), p. 83; Dick Harrison, Bo Eriksson, *Norstedts Sveriges historia 1350–1600* (Stockholm: Norstedts, 2010), p. 450.
9. Harrison - Eriksson, *Norstedts Sveriges historia*, pp. 454–455; Roberts, *The Early Vasas*, p. 436.

10 Nils Herlitz, *Grunddragen av det svenska statsskickets historia* (Stockholm: P. A. Norstedt & Söners Förlag, 1928), p. 75; Bonney, *The European Dynastic States*, pp. 331-334; Lars-Olof Larsson, *Arvet efter Gustav Vasa. En berättelse om fyra kungar och ett rike* (Stockholm: Prisma, 2005).

11 Roberts, *The Early Vasas*, p. 42; Ulf Sjödell, *Infödda svenska män av ridderskapet och adeln: kring ett tema i Sveriges inre historia under 1500- och 1600-talen* (Lund: Gleerup, 1976), p. 13.

12 Mats Hallenberg, Johan Holm, Dan Johansson, "Organization, Legitimation, Participation. State formation as a dynamic process – the Swedish example, c. 1523–1680", *Scandinavian Journal of History* 33, 2008, pp. 255–256.

13 Svalenius, *Rikskansliet i Sverige*, pp. 58–59.

14 The office had been empty after Svante Bielke died in 1609.

15 Nils Forssell, "Kansliet från Gustav II Adolf till år 1660". In: Wieselgren, Oscar, Forssell, Nils, Munthe, Arne, Forssell, Oscar, Liljedahl, Ragnar (eds), *Kungl. Maj:ts kanslis historia del I: kansliets uppkomst, organisation och utveckling intill 1840* (Uppsala: Almqvist & Wiksells boktryckeri, 1935), p. 25.

16 See figure 1, *Approaches and Perspectives* by Petri Karonen and Marko Hakanen, p. 26.

17 *Samling av instructioner rörande den civila förvaltning i Sverige och Finnland* (ICF) (Stockholm: Hörbergska boktryckeriet, 1856), pp. 295–297. A few years later the job descriptions and arrangements were reorganized by order of the king, because the number of secretaries was expanding. ICF, pp. 298–299.

18 ICF, pp. 300–302.

19 ICF, pp. 302–305.

20 N. A. Kullberg, "Förord". In: Bergh, Severin (red.), Svenska riksrådets protokoll i 1620–1629 (Stockholm: Kungl. boktryckeriet P. A. Norstedt & söner, 1878), pp. 7–10.

21 *Svenska riksrådets protokoll* 1878–1959 (Stockholm: Kungl. boktryckeriet P. A. Norstedt & söner, 1878–1959), I, pp. I–XLVI.

22 *Svenska riksrådets protokoll*, I, pp. IX–X.

23 *Svenska riksrådets protokoll*, I, p. XIII.

24 In 1622 and 1624 one secretary would introduce matters on the agenda, but after that the number starts to increase steadily. By 1626, three secretaries were doing this, in 1627 the number was six, in 1628 eight, and in 1629 there were nine secretaries doing the job. *Svenska riksrådets protokoll*, I.

25 The growing diversity of jobs is reflected in the wages: Lord High Chancellor of the Realm 4000–6000 silver daler, Councillor of the Realm 1000–1500, Chancellor 1200–1800, Secretary of State 1000–1500, secretary 800–1200, presenting official 400–750, clerk of Lord High Chancellor 300–450, actuary 450, registrar 400, office clerk 250–375, copyist 150–225, hired man 100–150, and courier 52–78. Forssell, *Kungl. Maj:ts kanslis historia*, p. 41.

26 Administrative personnel rapidly expanded from 1620s onwards. Ingvar Elmroth, *För kung och fosterland: studier i den svenska adelns demografi och offentliga funktioner 1600–1900* (Lund: Gleerup, 1981), pp. 207–209.

27 Forssell, *Kungl. Maj:ts kanslis historia*, pp. 35–36, 47–48; James Cavallie, Jan Lindroth (eds), *Riksarkivets beståndsöversikt, Del 1: Medeltiden, Kungl. Maj:ts kansli, Utrikesförvaltningen. Band 2*. Skrifter utgivna av Svenska Riksarkivet 8 (Stockholm: Riksarkivet, 1996b), p. 582; James Cavallie, Jan Lindroth (eds), *Riksarkivets beståndsöversikt, Del 1: Medeltiden, Kungl. Maj:ts kansli, Utrikesförvaltningen. Band 1*. Skrifter utgivna av Svenska Riksarkivet 8 (Stockholm: Riksarkivet, 1996a), p. 62.

28 Nils Edén, *Om centralregeringens organisation under den äldre Vasatiden (1523–1594)* (Uppsala: Almqvist & Wiksells Boktryckeri, 1899), p. 209; Herlitz,

Grunddragen, p. 75; Jerker Rosén, Svensk historia I: tiden före 1718 (Stockholm: Svenska Bokförlaget, 1962), p. 445.

29 Edén, Om centralregeringens organisation, pp. 54–57, 98–107, 210–214; Pentti Renvall, John E. Roos, "Keskitetyn hallintolaitoksen kehitys". In: Suolahti, Gunnar et al. (eds), Suomen Kulttuurihistoria II (Jyväskylä: Gummerus, 1934), pp. 139–140; Svalenius, Rikskansliet i Sverige, pp. 28–29, 37–44; Karonen, Pohjoinen suurvalta, p. 83.

30 Svalenius, Rikskansliet i Sverige, p. 29; Harrison – Eriksson, Norstedts Sveriges historia, p. 450.

31 Wilhelm Tham, Den svenska utrikespolitikens historia I: 2. 1560–1648 (Stockholm: P. A. Norstedt, 1960), pp. 9–10.

32 Edén, Om centralregeringens organisation, pp. 103–105; Sjödell, Infödda svenska män, p. 13.

33 Edén, Om centralregeringens organisation, pp. 203–209; Svalenius, Rikskansliet i Sverige, pp. 15, 27–37. The number of secretaries seems to drop in John III's early reign, but according to Svalenius, this is likely to be an illusion due to different principles in naming the people in salary registers.

34 Asker, Hur riket styrdes, p. 80. Councillor Nils Gyllenstierna was appointed Chancellor of the Realm (Sw. rikskansler) by Eric XIV and remained in the post for 30 years (1560–90). Councillor Erik Sparre was the next to receive the title in 1593 from Sigismund and to keep it during the inner crisis until his execution in 1600. Edén, Om centralregeringens organisation, pp. 195–201.

35 Svalenius, Rikskansliet i Sverige, p. 15; Larsson, Arvet efter Gustav Vasa.

36 Roberts, The Early Vasas, p. 307; Svalenius, Rikskansliet i Sverige, pp. 34–35.

37 Svenskt biografiskt lexikon (SBL), A–Stålhammar (Riksarkivet, Stockholm, 1917–2013) (Bengt Hildebrand), Erik Matsson, [http://sok.riksarkivet.se/sbl/artikel/15404], accessed November 24, 2015; Svalenius, Rikskansliet i Sverige, pp. 29–30.

38 SBL (Hans Gillingstam), Rasmus Ludvigsson, [http://sok.riksarkivet.se/sbl/artikel/7561], accessed November 24, 2015; Svalenius, Rikskansliet i Sverige, pp. 26, 105, 107, 162, 168–170, 173–174.

39 Edén, Om centralregeringens organisation, pp. 218–219; Herlitz, Grunddragen, pp. 74–75; Svalenius, Rikskansliet i Sverige, p. 32.

40 Edén, Om centralregeringens organisation, pp. 219–222; Herlitz, Grunddragen, pp. 74–75; Roberts, The Early Vasas, pp. 224–225; Svalenius, Rikskansliet i Sverige, pp. 32–33.

41 Rosén, Svensk historia, p. 445; Roberts, The Early Vasas, p. 307; Svalenius, Rikskansliet i Sverige, p. 51; Larsson, Arvet efter Gustav Vasa.

42 Edén, Om centralregeringens organisation, pp. 154–155, 209–210; Herlitz, Grunddragen, p. 74–75; Sjödell, Infödda svenska män, pp. 13–14; Svalenius, Rikskansliet i Sverige, p. 51; Lars Ericson Wolke, Johan III. En biografi (Lund: Historiska Media, 2006), p. 132.

43 Sjödell, Infödda svenska män, pp. 14–15; Svalenius, Rikskansliet i Sverige, pp. 25, 52.

44 Svalenius, Rikskansliet i Sverige, p. 57.

45 Kari Tarkiainen, Finnarnas historia i Sverige 1: Inflyttarna från Finland under det gemensamma rikets tid (Helsingfors: Finnish Historical Society, 1990), pp. 109–110.

46 Edén, Om centralregeringens organisation, pp. 209–210; Roberts, The Early Vasas, p. 307; Sjödell, Infödda svenska män, pp. 16–20; Svalenius, Rikskansliet i Sverige, pp. 52–53, 56.

47 Sjödell, Infödda svenska män, pp. 11–21; Svalenius, Rikskansliet i Sverige, pp. 16–17, 52.

48 Svalenius, Rikskansliet i Sverige, p. 6: "lösa parti som man litet på byggja kan", p. 52; Roberts, The Early Vasas, p. 307.

49 Sjödell, *Infödda svenska män*, pp. 14–15; Svalenius, *Rikskansliet i Sverige*, pp. 6–7.
50 Svalenius, *Rikskansliet i Sverige*, pp. 51–52 presents some examples of the secretaries' own points of view.
51 SBL (B. Boëthius), Johan Berndes, [http://sok.riksarkivet.se/sbl/artikel/18094], accessed November 24, 2015.
52 SBL (Jerker Rosén), Jöran Persson [http://sok.riksarkivet.se/sbl/artikel/12296], accessed November 9, 2015; Svalenius, *Rikskansliet i Sverige*: 27–28, 56–57; SBL (Ivan Svalenius), Johan Henriksson [http://sok.riksarkivet.se/sbl/artikel/12104], accessed November 5, 2015; Edén, *Om centralregeringens organisation*, pp. 201–203; Larsson, *Arvet efter Gustav Vasa*.
53 Sven Elofsson, "Paralipomena". In: *Handlingar rörande Skandinaviens historia XII* (Stockholm: Elméns och Granbergs Tryckeri, 1825; original 1599), p. 122: "samt med honom i grafven är ock Riksens karskhet och välmåga nederlagd och försvunnen"; Larsson, *Arvet efter Gustav Vasa*.
54 SBL (Ivan Svalenius), Olof Sverkersson Elfkarl (Potomander) [http://sok.riksarkivet.se/sbl/artikel/7750], accessed November 9, 2015; Pentti Renvall, *Klaus Fleming und der Finnische Adel in den Anfangsphasen der Krise der neunziger Jahre der 16. Jahrhunderts* (Turku: Turun Yliopisto, 1939), p. 56; Larsson, *Arvet efter Gustav Vasa*.
55 SRA, Kanslitjänstemäns koncept och mottagna skrivelser, vol. 9, Arvid Tawast, Henrik Abel (von Minden) and Erik Johansson to the secretaries and staff of the chancellery, November 8, 1590, Narva: "secreterare och Cantzelij förwantter", "der god rådh och tilskyndhen".
56 SBL (Jerker Rosén), Jöran Persson [http://sok.riksarkivet.se/sbl/artikel/12296], accessed November 9, 2015.
57 Viljo Tarkiainen, Kari Tarkiainen, *Mikael Agricola, Suomen uskonpuhdistaja* (Helsinki, Otava, 1985), pp. 86–87, 315–316; Anu Lahtinen, "Mikael Agricola aatelisvallan verkostoissa". In: Häkkinen, Kaisa, Vaittinen, Tanja (toim.), *Agricolan aika* (Helsinki, BTJ Kustannus, 2007), pp. 31–32.
58 Ulla Koskinen, *Hyvien miesten valtakunta. Arvid Henrikinpoika Tawast ja aatelin toimintakulttuuri 1500-luvun lopun Suomessa*. Bibliotheca Historica 132 (Helsinki: The Finnish Literature Society, 2011).
59 SRA Arvid Henriksson Tawasts samling (AHTs), vol. 1, Arvid Tawast to Hans Kranck, 2nd of June, 1583: "Jag förseer mig och till tig min h[järtats] käre broor attu är behielplig".
60 Koskinen, *Hyvien miesten valtakunta*, pp. 137–142.
61 Svalenius, *Rikskansliet i Sverige*, pp. 100–101.
62 SRA AHTs1, Arvid Tawast to Hans Kranck, 2nd of June, 1583: "din welwillig brod:ligit benegenhett mz alt gott förskylle och förtiene"; Koskinen, *Hyvien miesten valtakunta*, pp. 381–382.
63 SBL (Erik Anthoni), Erik Eriksson Bris [http://sok.riksarkivet.se/sbl/artikel/15398], accessed November 9, 2015; Svalenius, *Rikskansliet i Sverige*, pp. 59, 72, 97–98, 100–101.
64 SRA AHTs1, Arvid Tawast to Erik Eriksson, undated: "i wille göre wäll sosom mijn godhe wän och ware migh i saachen Befordelig och hielplig så mykit lagh och rätt kan medgifue".
65 SBL (Erik Anthoni), Erik Eriksson Bris [http://sok.riksarkivet.se/sbl/artikel/15398], accessed November 9, 2015.
66 SBL (Lars-Olof Skoglund), Mickel Olofsson [http://sok.riksarkivet.se/sbl/artikel/9344], accessed November 9, 2015.
67 SRA AHTs1, Arvid Tawast to Michel Olofsson, undated.
68 Koskinen, *Hyvien miesten valtakunta*, pp. 123–124.
69 SRA AHTs1, Henrik Claesson (Horn) to Arvid Tawast, 3rd of February, 1576, Haapaniemi.

70 See more about professionalism, *Approaches and Perspectives* by Petri Karonen and Marko Hakanen, p. 26.
71 For example Professor Michael Gyldenstolpe (1608/9–1670) urged his son Nils to advance his father's matters by asking help from the secretaries Johan Schäder (who was working as a personal secretary of Per Brahe) and Henrik Tawast (who was working in the Royal Chancellary). A. A. A. Laitinen, *Michael Wexionius* (Helsinki, K. F. Puromiehen kirjapaino, 1912) pp. 137–138; Marko Hakanen, "Career Opportunities. Patron-Client Relations Used in Advancing Academic Careers". In Karonen, Petri (ed.), *Hopes and Fears fort he Future in Early Modern Sweden, 1500–1800* (Helsinki, The Finnish Literature Society, 2009), pp. 112–114.
72 S. N. Eisenstadt, Louis Roniger, *Patrons, Clients and Friends. Interpersonal Relations and the Structure of Trust in Society* (Cambridge: Cambridge University Press, 1984), p. 205; Norrhem, *Uppkomlingarna*, p. 165; Marko Hakanen, Ulla Koskinen, "From 'friends' to 'patrons': Transformations in the social power structure as reflected in the rhetoric of personal letters in sixteenth- and seventeenth- century Sweden", *Journal of Historical Pragmatics, 2009, pp. 15–17;* Hakanen, "Career Opportunities", pp. 100–101.
73 ICF, pp. 294–295.
74 Bernard Barber, *The Logic and Limits of Trust* (New Brunswick & New Jersey: Rutgers University Press, 1983), pp. 9, 16–21; Norrhem, *Uppkomlingarna*, p. 52; Piotr Sztompka, *Trust: A Sociological Theory* (Cambridge: Cambridge University Press, 1999), pp. 99–101.
75 SBL (S. U. Palme): Edvard Philipsson Ehrensteen [https://sok.riksarkivet.se/SBL/Presentation.aspx?id=16711], accessed October 27, 2015.
76 SBL (Roger Axelsson): Strömfelt, släkt [https://sok.riksarkivet.se/SBL/Presentation.aspx?id=34602], accessed October 27, 2015.
77 Severin Bergh, *Rådsprotokoll och därmed jämförliga i Riksarkivet förvarade protokoll.* Meddelanden från Svenska riksarkivet (Stockholm: Riksarkivet, 1912), p. 293.
78 Lars-Arne Norborg, *Källor till Sveriges historia* (Lund: Gleerups, 1968), pp. 217–218; Toivo J. Paloposki, *Suomen historian lähteet* (Helsinki: Gaudeamus, 1972), pp. 161–167; Stina Hansson, *Svensk brevskrivning: teori och tillämpning* (Göteborg: Göteborgs universitet, 1988), pp. 39–41; Anu Lahtinen, *Sopeutuvat, neuvottelevat, kapinalliset: naiset toimijoina Flemingin sukupiirissä 1470–1620.* Bibliotheca historica 108 (Helsinki: The Finnish Literature Society, 2007), pp. 30–31; Janne Haikari, *Isännän, Jumalan ja rehellisten miesten edessä. Vallankäyttö ja virkamiesten toimintaympäristöt satakuntalaisessa maaseutuyhteisössä 1600-luvun jälkipuoliskolla.* Bibliotheca Historica 121 (Helsinki: The Finnish Literature Society, 2009), p. 28. Apart from communication letters functioned also as an official document of donations or appointment to the office etc. Seija Tiisala, "Power and Politeness: Languages and Salutation Formulas in Correspondence Between Sweden and the German Hanse", *Journal of Historical Pragmatics*, 5:2, 193–206, p. 194.
79 Minna Nevala, "Accessing Politeness Axes: Forms of Address and Terms of Reference in Early English Correspondence", *Journal of Pragmatics* 36, p. 2127; Terttu Nevalainen, "Letter Writing: Introduction", *Journal of Historical Pragmatics*, 5:2, p. 187.
80 Bergh, *Rådsprotokoll*, pp. 279–280. The Council minutes can be partly compared to records of received and sent letter records in the sixteenth century, because the Council of the Realm's duty was to issue administrative instructions. Meetings usually began by secretaries reading out loud received letters.
81 Bergh, *Rådsprotokoll*, p. 287.
82 Forssell, *Kungl. Maj:ts kanslis historia*, pp. 73–76.
83 Norrhem, *Uppkomlingarna*, p. 36, see also p. 183; Ingvar Elmroth, *Från överklass till medelklass: studier i den sociala dynamiken inom Sveriges adel 1600–1900*, (Lund: Nordic Academic Press, 2001), pp. 142–144.

84 For more on the professions of ennobled civil servants, see Elmroth, *Från överklass till medelklass*, p. 145.
85 James B. Collins, *The State in Early Modern France* (Cambridge: Cambridge University Press, 1995), p. xxxii.
86 Bergh, *Rådsprotokoll*, pp. 283–284.
87 Forssell, *Kungl. Maj:ts kanslis historia*, p. 44. Before the 1620s, only six civil servants were ennobled, two from the Royal Court, two from local administration, and two from the judiciary. Fahlbeck 1898, pp. 184–185.
88 Forssell, *Kungl. Maj:ts kanslis historia*, p 29; Gustaf Elgenstierna, *Riddarhusets stamtavlor* (Elektronisk resurs, version 3.0. Riddarhusdirektionen, Stockholm, 2002), Tungel, Table 2 and 3.
89 Forssell, *Kungl. Maj:ts kanslis historia*, p. 30.
90 Anders Fryxell, *Berättelser ur swenska historien* (Stockholm: Åttonde delen. L. J. Hierta, 1838), p. 178; Forssell, *Kungl. Maj:ts kanslis historia*, p. 43.
91 Forssell, *Kungl. Maj:ts kanslis historia*, pp. 29–30.
92 SBL, Band 2, p. 665; NFL II 1904, p. 834; *Svenska riksrådets protokoll*, X pp. 551–553.
93 Nils Tungel wrote that Banér died on 12$^{th}$ of July, a day later than other biographical sources maintain.
94 Nils Tungel to Per Brahe 16$^{th}$ of July, 1644, SRA, SS II, E8150.
95 Nils Tungel to Per Brahe 24$^{th}$ of July, 1644, SRA, SS II, E8150.
96 Patron-client-relationship might broke, if the other party could not fulfil the expectations of the role. Look for example the case of Israel Schultz. Fabian Persson, "Att leva på hoppet: om misslyckade klienten", *Historisk tidskrift*, 112, pp. 316–329.
97 Nils Tungel to Per Brahe 8$^{th}$ of August, 1644, SRA, SS II, E8150.
98 Per Brahe to royal secretary 21$^{st}$ of February, 1658 PBB I 1932, 50. Cf. Ulla Koskinen, "Friends and Brothers: Rhetoric of Friendship as a Medium of Power in Late 16th-Century Sweden and Finland", *Scandinavian Journal of History*, 30, 2005, p. 245.
99 Royal secretaries were well aware of their possibilities to influence and use their informal personal power. Usually people who were about to get their ennoblement documents from the Royal Chancellery had to pay for the secretaries. Nils Tungel was no exception in this matter. Forssell, *Kungl. Maj:ts kanslis historia*, pp. 78–80.
100 Nils Tungel to Per Brahe 10$^{th}$ of December, 1648 SRA, SS II, E8150.
101 Per Brahe to King Charles X Gustav 19$^{th}$ of February, 1658 PBB I 1922, p. 49.
102 Per Brahe to the royal secretary 21$^{st}$ of February, 1658 PBB I 1922, p. 50.
103 Nils Runeby, *Monarchia mixta: maktfördelningsdebatt i Sverige under den tidigare stormaktstiden*. Studia Historica Upsaliensia VI (Uppsala: Uppsala universitet, 1962), pp. 392–404. For more on the importance of secretaries, see also Koskinen, "Friends and Brothers", p. 245.
104 Brahe 1806, pp. 48, 51–52, 54, 70, 78, 81–82. The letters Tungel sent to Brahe were usually dated between December and February. SRA, SS II, E8150.
105 Nils Tungel to Per Brahe 10$^{th}$ of December, 1645, SRA, SS II, E8150.
106 Nils Tungel to Per Brahe 8$^{th}$ of August, 1644, SRA, SS II, E8150.
107 Nils Tungel to Per Brahe 24$^{th}$ of July, 1644, 10$^{th}$ of January, 1646, SRA, SS II, E8150.
108 Nils Tungel to Per Brahe 10$^{th}$ of December, 1645, SRA, SS II, E8150.
109 Nils Tungel to Per Brahe 16$^{th}$ of July, 1644, 10$^{th}$ of December, 1645, 13$^{th}$ of December, 1645, 10$^{th}$ of December, 1648 and in January 1656, SRA, SS II, E8150.
110 Nils Tungel to Per Brahe 7$^{th}$ of February, 1646, SRA, SS II, E8150.
111 Svenskt biografiskt handlexikon: [http://runeberg.org/sbh/b0644.html]; Nordisk familjebok: [http://runeberg.org/nfcj/0185.html]
112 Norrhem, *Uppkomlingarna*, p. 163.

# Sources

## Archival sources

Svenska Riksarkivet (SRA), Stockholm (Swedish National Archives)
Arvid Henriksson Tavasts samling, vol. 1.
Kanslitjänstemäns koncept och mottagna skrivelser, vol. 9.
Skokloster samlingen II, E8150.

## Printed sources

Brahe, Per (d.y.) 1806: *Svea rikes drotset Grefve Per Brahes tänkebok.* Utgifven af D. Krutmejer. Carl Delén: Stockholm.
Elofsson, Sven 1599 (1825): "Paralipomena". In: *Handlingar rörande Skandinaviens historia XII.* Stockholm: Elméns och Granbergs Tryckeri (printed 1825, original 1599).
*Samling av instructioner rörande den civila förvaltningen i Sverige och Finland 1856* (ICF): Red. C.G. Styffe. Stockholm: Hörbergska boktryckeriet.
Svenska riksrådets protokoll 1878–1959. *Handlingar rörande Sveriges historia*, Tredje serien. Stockholm: Kungl. boktryckeriet P. A. Norstedt & söner.

## Electronic sources

Elgenstierna, Gustaf 2002 (ES): *Den introducerade svenska adelns ättartavlor.* Elektronisk resurs, version 3.0. Stockholm: Riddarhusdirektionen.
*Kansallisbiografia* (KB). Helsinki: The Finnish Literature Society 1997–. [http://www.kansallisbiografia.fi/]
*Svenskt biografiskt lexikon* 1917–2013 (SBL): A–Stålhammar. Stockholm: Riksarkivet. [http://sok.riksarkivet.se/SBL/Start.aspx]

## Literature

Asker, Björn 2007: *Hur riket styrdes. Förvaltning, politik och arkiv 1520–1920.* Stockholm: Riksarkivet.
Barber, Bernard 1983: *The Logic and Limits of Trust.* New Brunswick & New Jersey: Rutgers University Press.
Bergh, Severin 1912: *Rådsprotokoll och därmed jämförliga i Riksarkivet förvarade protokoll.* Meddelanden från Svenska riksarkivet. Stockholm: Riksarkivet.
Black, Christopher 2002: *Early Modern Italy: A Social History.* London: Routledge.
Bonney, Richard 1991: *The European Dynastic States 1494–1660. The Short Oxford History of the Modern World.* Oxford: Oxford University Press.
Cavallie, James, Lindroth, Jan (red.) 1996a: *Riksarkivets beståndsöversikt, Del 1: Medeltiden, Kungl. Maj:ts kansli, Utrikesförvaltningen. Band 1.* Red. James Cavallie och Jan Lindroth. Skrifter utgivna av Svenska Riksarkivet 8. Stockholm: Riksarkivet.
Cavallie, James, Lindroth, Jan (red.) 1996b: *Riksarkivets beståndsöversikt, Del 1: Medeltiden, Kungl. Maj:ts kansli, Utrikesförvaltningen. Band 2.* Red. James Cavallie och Jan Lindroth. Skrifter utgivna av Svenska Riksarkivet 8. Stockholm: Riksarkivet.
Collins, James B. 1995: *The State in Early Modern France.* Cambridge: Cambridge University Press.

Edén, Nils 1899: *Om centralregeringens organisation under den äldre Vasatiden (1523–1594)*. Uppsala: Almqvist & Wiksells Boktryckeri.

Einonen, Piia 2005: *Poliittiset areenat ja toimintatavat. Tukholman porvaristo vallan käyttäjänä ja vallankäytön kohteena n. 1592–1644*. Bibliotheca Historica 94. Helsinki: The Finnish Literature Society.

Eisenstadt, S. N., Roniger, Louis 1984: *Patrons, Clients and Friends. Interpersonal Relations and the Structure of Trust in Society*. Cambridge: Cambridge University Press.

Elmroth, Ingvar 1981: *För kung och fosterland. Studier i den svenska adelns demografi och offentliga funktioner 1600–1900*. Bibliotheca Historica Lundensis L. Lund: Lunds universitet.

Elmroth, Ingvar 2001: *Från överklass till medelklass. Studier i den sociala dynamiken inom Sveriges adel 1600–1900*. Lund: Nordic Academic Press.

Ericson Wolke, Lars 2006: *Johan III. En biografi*. Lund: Historiska Media.

Forssell, Nils 1935: "Kansliet från Gustav II Adolf till år 1660". In: Wieselgren, Oscar, Forssell, Nils, Munthe, Arne, Forssell, Oscar, Liljedahl, Ragnar (red.), *Kungl. Maj:ts kanslis historia del I: kansliets uppkomst, organisation och utveckling intill 1840*. Uppsala: Almqvist & Wiksells.

Fryxell, Anders 1838: *Berättelser ur swenska historien*. Åttonde delen. Stockholm: L. J. Hierta.

Haikari, Janne 2009: *Isännän, Jumalan ja rehellisten miesten edessä: vallankäyttö ja virkamiesten toimintaympäristöt satakuntalaisessa maaseutuyhteisössä 1600-luvun jälkipuoliskolla*. Bibliotheca Historica 121. Helsinki: The Finnish Literature Society.

Hakanen, Marko 2009: "Career Opportunities. Patron-Client Relations Used in Advancing Academic Careers". In: Karonen, Petri (ed.), *Hopes and Fears for the Future in Early Modern Sweden, 1500–1800*. Studia Historica 79. Helsinki: The Finnish Literature Society.

Hakanen, Marko, Koskinen, Ulla 2009: "From 'friends' to 'patrons': Transformations in the social power structure as reflected in the rhetoric of personal letters in sixteenth- and seventeenth-century Sweden", *Journal of Historical Pragmatics* 10.

Hallenberg, Mats, Holm, Johan, Johansson, Dan 2008: "Organization, Legitimation, Participation. State formation as a dynamic process – the Swedish example, c. 1523–1680", *Scandinavian Journal of History* 33.

Hansson, Stina 1988: *Svensk brevskrivning: teori och tillämpning*. Göteborg: Göteborgs universitet.

Harrison, Dick, Eriksson, Bo 2010: *Norstedts Sveriges historia 1350–1600*. Stockholm: Norstedts.

Herlitz, Nils 1928: *Grunddragen av det svenska statsskickets historia*. Stockholm: P. A. Norstedt & Söners Förlag.

Karonen, Petri 2014: *Pohjoinen suurvalta. Ruotsi ja Suomi 1521–1809*. Helsinki: The Finnish Literature Society.

Kollmann, Nancy 2012: *Crime and Punishment in Early Modern Russia*. Cambridge: Cambridge University Press.

Koskinen, Ulla 2005: "Friends and Brothers: Rhetoric of Friendship as a Medium of Power in Late 16th-Century Sweden and Finland", *Scandinavian Journal of History* 30.

Koskinen, Ulla 2011: *Hyvien miesten valtakunta. Arvid Henrikinpoika Tawast ja aatelin toimintakulttuuri 1500-luvun lopun Suomessa*. Bibliotheca Historica 132. Helsinki: The Finnish Literature Society.

Kullberg, N. A. 1878: "Förord". In: Bergh, Severin (red.), *Svenska riksrådets protokoll. I. 1620–1629*. Handlingar rörande Sveriges Historia, Tredje serien. Stockholm: Kungl. boktryckeriet P. A. Norstedt & söner.

Lahtinen, Anu 2007: "Mikael Agricola aatelisvallan verkostoissa". In: Häkkinen, Kaisa, Vaittinen, Tanja (toim.), *Agricolan aika*. Helsinki: BTJ Kustannus.

Lahtinen, Anu 2007: *Sopeutuvat, neuvottelevat, kapinalliset: naiset toimijoina Flemingin sukupiirissä 1470–1620*. Bibliotheca Historica 108. Helsinki: The Finnish Literature Society.

Laitinen, A. A. A. 1912, *Michael Wexionius*. Helsinki: K. F. Puromiehen kirjapaino.

Larsson, Lars-Olof 2005: *Arvet efter Gustav Vasa. En berättelse om fyra kungar och ett rike*. Stockholm: Prisma.

Ljung, Sven 1939: *Erik Jöransson Tegel. En biografisk-historiografisk studie*. Lund.

Nevala, Minna 2004: "Accessing Politeness Axes: Forms of Address and Terms of Reference in Early English Correspondence", *Journal of Pragmatics* 36.

Nevalainen, Terttu 2004: "Letter Writing: Introduction", *Journal of Historical Pragmatics*, 5:2.

Norborg, Lars-Arne 1968: *Källor till Sveriges historia*. Lund: Gleerups.

Norrhem, Svante 1993: *Uppkomlingarna. Kanslitjänstemännen i 1600-talets Sverige och Europa*. Stockholm: Almqvist & Wiksell International.

Paloposki, Toivo J. 1972: *Suomen historian lähteet*. Helsinki: Gaudeamus.

Persson, Fabian 1992: "Att leva på hoppet: om misslyckade klienten", *Historisk tidskrift* 112.

Renvall, Pentti, Roos, John E. 1934: "Keskitetyn hallintolaitoksen kehitys". In: Suolahti, Gunnar et al. (toim.), *Suomen Kulttuurihistoria II*. Helsinki: Gummerus.

Renvall, Pentti 1939: *Klaus Fleming und der Finnische Adel in den Anfangsphasen der Krise der neunziger Jahre der 16. Jahrhunderts*. Turun Yliopiston Julkaisuja B: 24. Turku: Turun yliopisto.

Roberts, Michael 1968: *The Early Vasas. A History of Sweden, 1523–1611*. Cambridge: Cambridge University Press.

Rosén, Jerker 1962: *Svensk historia I: tiden före 1718*. Stockholm: Svenska Bokförlaget.

Runeby, Nils 1962: *Monarchia mixta: maktfördelningsdebatt i Sverige under den tidigare stormaktstiden*. Studia Historica Upsaliensia VI. Uppsala: Uppsala universitet.

Sansovino, Francesco 1569: *Del Secretario, o vero formulario de lettere missive e responsive*. Publisher unknown (first edition Francesco Rampazzetto, Venetia 1564).

Sjödell, Ulf 1976: *Infödda svenska män av ridderskapet och adeln: kring ett tema i Sveriges inre historia under 1500- och 1600-talen*. Lund: Gleerup.

Svalenius, Ivan 1991: *Rikskansliet i Sverige 1560–1592*. Skrifter utgivna av Svenska Riksarkivet 7. Stockholm: Riksarkivet.

Sztompka, Piotr 1999: *Trust: A Sociological Theory*. Cambridge: Cambridge University Press.

Tarkiainen, Kari 1990: *Finnarnas historia i Sverige 1: Inflyttarna från Finland under det gemensamma rikets tid*. Helsinki: Finnish Historical Society.

Tarkiainen, Viljo, Tarkiainen, Kari 1985: *Mikael Agricola, Suomen uskonpuhdistaja*. Helsinki: Otava.

Tiisala, Seija 2004: "Power and Politeness: Languages and Salutation Formulas in Correspondence between Sweden and the German Hanse", *Journal of Historical Pragmatics*, 5:2.

Tham, Wilhelm 1960: *Den svenska utrikespolitikens historia I: 2. 1560–1648*. Stockholm: P. A. Norstedt.

# Governors IV

MIRKKA LAPPALAINEN
http://orcid.org/0000-0002-5674-3597

# Loyal Servants of the King and the Crown (1620–1680): Stewards and Governors in Sweden before the Age of Absolutism

A well-functiNoning local administration is perhaps the most important prerequisite of state-building. A centralized state cannot exist without loyal officers, whose role is to watch over its authority at the local level. In Europe, local magnates maintained a contradictory relationship with central power: at the same time as the king and his administration were dependent on these noblemen, their strong local networks formed a constant obstacle for centralization and control.

In the Realm of Sweden the situation was somewhat different than in Central Europe. In Sweden there were no powerful medieval centres of power and no local noblemen, whose ancient status could be compared to those of, for example, France. In Sweden, the greatest challenges to state-building were the realities dictated by geography and climate. Because of distances, snow, sleet, ice and darkness it was a realm most difficult to rule.[1]

The purpose of this chapter is to study how, in seventeenth century Sweden, the system of stewards (*ståthållare*) and governors (*landshövding*) was created. These offices formed the backbone of local administration and played a pivotal role in centralizing power in seventeenth century Sweden. Stewards were the civil servants that replaced governors in 1630s, to oversee that the centralized system was uniformly implemented. But what, for example, were the precise roles and duties of stewards and governors? How did they carry them out? What were their boundaries of personal agency; and what form did this agency take? The chapter concentrates on the period before the 1680s, as in that decade absolutism was established and it naturally changed the relationship between the administration, officials and ruler.

With regard to the state-building process, stewards and governors had a dual role. At the same time as being active subjects, who built up the centralized system and wielding state power over others, they were themselves objects of centralization, and their subordination was inevitable. This chapter shows how the position of steward was based on personal loyalty to the king and served various military purposes.

How did the stewards and governors perform as agents of the king and the state? The growth of centralized state power is directly reflected in the increasingly detailed orders given out to define the duties of stewards and governors. From the 1630s onwards, the governors were expected to carry out their duty within an extremely structured framework, which left little opportunity to adapt one's actions to local circumstances.

This study is based on three kinds of sources: (i) instructions and mandates issued by the Crown to new stewards and governors at the beginning of their term in office; (ii) general statutes concerning local administration; and (iii) the accounts of their terms in office that governors were required to keep from 1662 onwards. These instructions, statutes and accounts have been published in printed form, mostly in *Samling af Instructioner för högre och lägre tjänstemän vid landt-regeringen i Sverige och Finland* (1852), *Handlingar rörande Skandinaviens historia* (vol. 31, 1851), *Rikskansleren Axel Oxenstiernas skrifter och brevväxling*, and Waaranen's series *Samling af urkunder*. Also Karl Tigersted's collections *Handlingar rörande Finlands historia kring medlet af 17t:de århundradet* (1849/1850) and *Bref från Generalguvernörer och Landshövdingar i Finland* (1869) have been used.

One should bear in mind that the sources used in this chapter reflect the formal relationship between central government and its stewards and governors. Especially when it comes to their personal agency, it is important to understand what function these orders and accounts served. The accounts were clearly not "realistic" reports of the comings and goings within a certain province. Rather, they were almost certainly created to prove that the governor complied with the stipulations.

Some remarks must be made about the terminology. The term *ståthållare* essentially derives from the German word *statthalter*. In the early seventeenth century, even the form *Stadtholder*[2] was used. It has usually been translated as *governor*, since this is a general enough term to describe the leader of an area of local administration. Meanwhile, the term *landshövding* is always translated as *governor*. However, considering that the point of this chapter is to examine how the steward system developed into the governor system, it is hardly sensible to translate both offices as "governor". Furthermore, the word "governor" does not adequately convey the archaic nature of the *ståthållare*. Therefore, the term *ståthållare* has been translated as *steward* and *landshövding* as *governor*.[3]

In general, there is plenty of research on stewards, governors and their position. However, the focus of most of this historical research has not been on the stewards and governors themselves, but rather the administrative structures surrounding them (*länsförvaltningen*). Stewards and governors do, however, feature heavily in the research simply because it is virtually impossible to write about early modern Swedish history without doing so. Stewards and governors were important actors, who were involved in everything that was going on in the realm. Biographical studies, such as the *Svenskt biografiskt lexikon* and Finnish *Suomen kansallisbiografia*, naturally include articles about people who, at some point in their career, functioned as governors; but only the most successful individuals have been included in these works. Their work as a governor has seldom been the focus of these studies, since most often it is not the most interesting part of some high-powered nobleman's career path.[4]

The position of stewards has, for the most part, been analyzed in the context of the Swedish civil war of the 1590s in both biographical studies and local histories. The stewards played a crucial role in the political disturbances of the late sixteenth century, and there is plenty of research on them and on the civil war in general. The important office of *överståthållare* in Stockholm has particularly commanded much attention. However, the stewards system in general is still somewhat poorly understood, mainly because of the variety of roles this office afforded. Perhaps the most comprehensive study on the stewards is in Olof Sörndal's research concerning the development of provincial administration in Sweden (*Den svenska länsstyrelsen*, 1937). Also Pentti Renvall's studies on Finnish administration in the sixteenth century (1939, 1949) and Folke Lindberg's article on the stewards in Östergötland (1939) are important pieces of work.

Historical research covering the governors is much more abundant. Björn Asker complements Olof Sörndal's work with a detailed picture of the administrative system in *I konungens stad och ställe. Länstyrelser in arbete 1635–1734* (2004). In addition, the governors not only crop up in many extensive studies of administrative and judicial processes, but also in the local history of different provinces. However, in such historical research the governors are seldom given the leading role.

The most comprehensive study of governors is almost certainly Alexander Jonsson's *De norrländska landshövdingarna och statsbildningen 1634–1769* (2005). Jonsson emphasizes the importance of governors in the process of state-building. Meanwhile, Piia Einonen has researched the spatial aspects of the office in her article – *A travelling governor* (2011), while I myself have written about the role of governor in one noble family's rise to wealth and power in *Suku, valta, suurvalta. Creutzit 1600-luvun Ruotsissa ja Suomessa* (2005).[5]

## The Steward system – Representatives of the King

The first steward in the Realm of Sweden was Gustaf Olsson Stenbock (1502–1571), who was given the title of steward (*stadthollere*) of Västmanlad in 1540, during the reign of Gustavus Vasa (1521/23–1560). Gustavus Vasa reorganized and built the administration largely on the German model. In the Habsburg Empire, a *statthalter* had represented the ruler in various parts of the realm since the Middle Ages. The use of the title was, however, indefinite, as holders of larger fiefs could also be called stewards. However, Stenbock's office included distinctly administrative and judicial duties in Västmanland overall.[6] In the late sixteenth century, several stewards were appointed, and from 1560 onwards the term *ståthållareskapet* came to signify an administrative area and was no longer connected to the fiefs of the steward in question.[7]

The steward system was not actually a system as such, for the role and duties of a steward varied greatly.[8] A steward was a representative of the king and used his authority, but this authority was not bound into solid administrative structures or orders. The amount of power given to a steward was dependent on the monarch whose servant he was. Axel Leijonhufvud (1554–1619), for instance, who was steward of the whole of Finland (1587–1592), administrated a huge area and exercised a new, larger authority over the taxation system. Petri Karonen points out that his role is comparable to that of the governor-generals of Finland in the seventeenth century.[9] Leijonhufvud was a purposeful man, but complained that the bailiffs (*fogde*) were not especially keen to follow his orders. According to Pentti Renvall, this was due to the unclear role of the stewards and the arbitrariness of the whole administrative system. Folke Lindberg points out that the situation was similar in Östergötland too, where the steward institution had not yet gained the degree of stability that was perhaps needed for the stewards to be seen as obligatory links between the local bailiffs and central administration.[10]

However, this instability allowed for a certain flexibility, characteristic of late sixteenth century political culture, which proved expedient in the changing role and authority of the stewards. For example, in the political disturbances of the 1590s, the stewards played an important military role. When Sigismund, became King of Sweden and Poland in 1593, he was deeply suspicious of the intentions of his uncle, Duke Charles. So to protect his interests in the North, Sigismund appointed loyal stewards in all the important castles of the realm.[11] Meanwhile, Finland was in the hands of Claes Fleming (c.1535–1597), King Sigismund's most important supporter in the 1590s. Fleming, who exercised total control over Finland, was both Supreme Commander of the Army and stewards of Finland and Estonia, while his follower, Arvid Stålarm (1549–1620), was also called steward of Finland. Both Fleming and Stålarm proved important figures in the Swedish civil war, being first and foremost the soldiers and military leaders who wielded Sigismund's royal authority in the North. During times of political turbulence, they were literally *statthalter*s of the absent king, and therefore they were given an exceptionally large military and civil authority; and the as yet unformalized nature of the steward office and title certainly enabled this.[12] To usurp the throne, which he eventually did, Duke Charles had to effectively overthrow the stewards of Sigismund and conquer the castles. The civil war thus clearly indicates that the role of a steward in late sixteenth, early seventeenth century Sweden was to protect the king's authority by using military power. However, during the following decades this was all about to change.

Once Duke Charles was Crowned King Charles IX (1604–1611), his aim was to get the taxation system under control and to ensure the political loyalty of officials to make it more effective overall. This work was continued and completed by his son Gustavus Adolphus (1611–1632). Nevertheless, before the 1620s, the system was still archaic and the duties of the steward varied greatly according to the area or castle the steward was responsible for. Indeed, their letters of appointment make a point of clearly specifying the particular castle and surrounding area that each steward was responsible for.[13] Herman Wrangel (1584/87–1643), who was appointed in 1616 to the militarily important Kalmar fortress, was even called *ståthållare och Öffwerste på Calmar och dess län* (Steward and Colonel of Kalmar and its

Province).¹⁴ In September 1611, Charles IX appointed Johan de la Gardie as the Steward of Turku Castle. His letter of commission begins with the stipulation that the Turku fortress be taken care of, renovated, and defended; and goes on to clarify that the steward promises to keep the *fortress* loyal to "us, our heirs" and "no other".¹⁵

During the first decades of the seventeenth century, Swedish rulers were afraid that Sigismund might plan to return to Sweden. An invasion was expected, and both Charles IX and Gustavus Adolphus feared that supporters of Sigismund were infiltrating both Sweden and Finland, and lying in wait for their master to arrive. Stewards thus had an important political role to ensure that no spies got into the realm and to confiscate any suspicious letters.¹⁶ It was also extremely important that the stewards were politically loyal, like Johan de la Gardie (1582–1640), who belonged to the powerful network of family and friends that centred around chancellor Axel Oxenstierna (1583–1654). Nevertheless, two years after his appointment, Johan de la Gardie got into trouble for not noticing one of Sigismund's supporters, who had come to Turku and stayed in a well-known mansion in the area under his jurisdiction.¹⁷

When Herman Wrangel was appointed as Steward of Kalmar in 1616, his letter of instruction stated firstly that he should make sure the "King of Poland" and his supporters did not get into the castle. Evidently the Crown was still afraid that Sigismund's supporters would once more try to take hold of important castles. In the second paragraph, he was told to secure the loyalty of the people and make sure that nobody was circulating letters from the King of Poland or the Swedes who had escaped to Poland.¹⁸ It is remarkable that there was no mention of any threat from the Danes, in spite of the fact that there had been a war between Denmark and Sweden. We can presume that the Danes therefore did not pose a threat to the position of the Swedish king.

Warfare, in general, was a natural part of life for a steward. Few noblemen had obtained a formal education, but they were trained in warfare. Arvid Tönneson Wildeman (c.1570–1617), who was steward of Vyborg (Viborg) from 1603 up to his death in 1617, is a good example of an early seventeenth century stewards. Not only did he take care of everyday local administration, but he played a significant role in bolstering the reign of the young Gustavus Adolphus (1611–1632) in Finland, carrying out diplomatic duties on behalf of the kingdom vis-à-vis the Russians and ambassadors of other countries. In addition, he negotiated the surrender of Käkisalmi (Priozersk) after the siege of 1611 and, before his death, attended the peace negotiations which culminated in the Treaty of Stolbovo. Arvid Tönneson had a military background, like most of his fellow peers and family members – in fact he had even been an admiral in Sigismund's Finnish fleet. This background might explain why on his tombstone, he is depicted in armour.¹⁹

Arvid Tönneson's career path was evidently not an easy one. Firstly, he had to bury his ambiguous past as an admiral of Sigismund, and to do this he had to prove his loyalty to the new king. This may have been made even more difficult by the fact that Charles IX had slaughtered members of his own kin. But there is no doubt that he was a keen supporter of Charles' son,

Gustavus Adolphus. When the new king rose to power, Arvid Tönneson was quick to swear allegiance long before he was ordered to do so. He was a loyal servant who escorted his king throughout Finland and entertained the regent in his mansion there. The crucial difference between Arvid Tönneson and his successors was that Tönneson and his fellow stewards' role was a great deal more flexible. There were still no generally formalized instructions that clearly defined the duties and responsibilities of a steward. His most important qualification was his eagerness to be politically loyal during times of war and fear.[20]

According to Alexander Jonsson, the office of steward was established to exert greater control over the bailiffs. The means offered to the stewards for doing so were nevertheless inadequate.[21] Yet the history of the stevard system should not be observed solely within the context of taxation. Stewards were not just predecessors of governors, but also belonged to an earlier kind of power structure. The broad and flexible authority of a steward was once well-suited for its purpose. He used considerable power in a world where structures of administration were as yet primitive and so the position of his master, the ruler, was continuously under threat. His main duty was thus not simply to control minor local officials, but also to be the guardian of his master's mandate.

## Overhaul of the system

During the reign of Gustavus Adolphus there was a general overhaul of the whole state, particularly with regard to the judicial and administrative system. In fact, it is often claimed that Gustavus Adolphus, and his chancellor Axel Oxenstierna, created the foundations of the effective early modern Swedish centralized state, and in this process, stewards understandably played an important role.

In May 1616, Gustavus Adolphus sent a letter of instruction to Johan de la Gardie, Steward of Turku. This letter shows how the amount of detailed instructions being issued was increasing. Again, the steward's duty to prevent hostile people from entering the country was mentioned in the opening paragraphs, but the long letter went on to stipulate how judicial matters and various orders of the Crown should be implemented. For instance, it was made clear that the steward should see to it that regulations concerning trade and the municipalities within his jurisdiction be observed (Gustavus Adolphus wanted the country's economy to run according to strict mercantile principles).[22] This was a foretaste of what was to come. A steward could no longer be a medieval-style knight whose main duty was to protect a military fortress. In a peaceful, but in many ways more complex society, this kind of figure was fast becoming obsolete. Instead, the Crown now needed men who could effectively implement and monitor the increasing number of rules that the new administrative system required.

In April 1620, the king gave new orders about how the taxes in the realm should be collected. Taxation was, of course, vital for the existence of the realm, and consistent problems in collecting taxes and other revenues had been a major obstruction in Sweden's path to becoming a great power. Because the land was relatively poor and sparsely populated, collecting taxes was a major undertaking, and in the early seventeenth century financial administration was primitive, which made taxation hard to enforce. Not only was it hard for the Crown to control the flow of tax revenues, but also to know how they had been used, or whether they had been embezzled or not. Bailiffs were thus constantly under suspicion and often threatened with inspections.[23] But this was in many ways counter-productive as it was essential to build a system where control did not simply come from Stockholm but was instead clearly embedded in the structure of the administration. It was not until May 1620 that it was clearly stipulated that the bailiffs were subordinates of the stewards. The instructions also prescribed how a steward should compile cameral records of his province – on the 15$^{th}$ and 30$^{th}$ day of every month, the bailiffs were obliged to write to the steward and report on various different cameral aspects of their area. The instructions reflect the Crown's belief that constant monitoring of the bailiffs was necessary to prevent misdeeds.[24]

In July 1624, new orders were sent out with 25 paragraphs that laid out the role of a steward in far greater detail. The reforms to the steward system were part and parcel of those made to the central administration – in particular the Treasury, the Chancery and the taxation system as a whole. The appointment of Nils Bielke (1569–1639), in 1623, as the first Governor-General of Finland was an important step in the state-building process. Bielke was a tireless supporter of centralization and though the relationship between the stewards and governor-general was not specifically defined in the order of 1624, Bielke's own letter of appointment declared that the stewards and bailiffs must obey him. What this actually meant in practice, however, was not defined.[25]

It was now decreed that each steward was responsible for local governmental and juridical matters such as monitoring the Crown's revenues and interests, i.e., collecting taxes from "bailiffs, customs collectors, clerks, leaseholders, sheriffs and whatever they are called." The instructions of 1624 also specified the different structures for taxation and cameral administration. One consequence of this was that the duties of stewards were defined in greater detail. Bailiffs were ordered to give regular accounts of the finances in their area, and cameral records had to be compiled carefully and receipts preserved. The obligation to supervise the bailiffs was of a concrete nature. If a bailiff was caught stealing from tax revenues, the stewards were ordered to report it, and if misappropriation could be proved, the culprit was sentenced to death.[26]

Given the actual state of the administration system in the early 1620s, the contents of the orders of 1620 and 1624 may understandably seem strikingly unrealistic. Simply giving more detailed orders is clearly not enough to change an administrative culture in the course of a few years. One of the greatest obstacles in developing an effective administrative culture was the lack of readily available professionals. During his time in Turku (1611–1626), Johan de la Gardie often complained of a lack of educated staff and the overwhelming problem of disobedient bailiffs, clergymen and judges.[27]

The new system presented great challenges for officials and their education. The world in which warfare and practical skills linked to this had defined the whole existence of noblemen had ceased to exist.[28]

Previously, the duties of stewards had been vaguely defined and their jurisdiction had been in many ways unlimited. They had been loyal guardians of their master's interests, both in economic and military terms. But with the development of a centralized state, it was not enough that simply the relationship between stewards and his subordinates be more clearly defined; the jurisdiction a steward itself needed clarification, so that he would be powerful as part of the system but not too powerful as to pose a threat to it. The Crown must be the sole source of royal authority. In this repect, rather than carry out reforms within the framework of the old steward system, a whole new structure with new titles was created.

## Governor, *servant of a centralized state*

In 1634, two years after death of Gustavus Adolphus, Sweden's first constitution was enacted. The Instrument for Government (*regeringsform*) was thus one of the great milestones in the history of Sweden and Finland. It established a new structure of administration on both central and local levels. The main idea behind the Instrument was a centralized administration consisting of *collegia* for every branch of government. This system was tailored to meet the demands of a realm which now had the status of a great power in the Baltic Area. After Gustavus Adolphus, the realm was governed by an aristocratic regency. In effect, chancellor Axel Oxenstierna was the driving force behind the Instrument for Government, and the new system was essentially based on his ideas.[29]

In his proposition for the *regeringsform* of 1634, Oxenstierna showed considerable interest in the role of governors. They should not only work for centralization, he believed, but also be subjected to controls. The traditional independence of the steward was thus henceforth to be demolished. Oxenstierna made several suggestions to ensure that the governors were agents of the Crown, rather than independent local magnates. Governors should be changed every three years, and after a governor had left his province he was expected to travel to Stockholm to give a detailed report of his administration to "convince the King of his loyal service". If someone had made complaints about his administration, he should answer for them in court. Although one of the most important tasks of the governor was to monitor law and justice within his area, he was not allowed to work as a judge (*lagman*), nor had he any right to intervene in military affairs and the command of fortresses. Thus Oxenstierna clearly intended to consign the old military and legal powers of the stewards to history. Instead, the new governors were supposed to be high-profile civil servants who derived all their power from Stockholm. Oxenstierna even suggested that every governor should own a house in Stockholm, and after leaving his office an ex-governor should indeed move to Stockholm.[30] The actual Instrument for Government followed Oxenstierna's suggestions for the most part, although it was slightly less detailed and so, for example, the claim that governors had to reside in Stockholm was abandoned.

All mediaeval-style administrative structures were now dismantled. The new basic unit for local administration was the province (*län*), and the old title of steward was discarded. The provinces were governed by men who carried the title of governor. This title has already been used before, although sporadically. Indeed, in the late sixteenth century, the aristocracy had suggested establishing seven large, permanent provinces, each with a governor at its head. But the purpose of this had been to enhance the power of the aristocracy.[31] Now, however, governor had became instrumental in ensuring the power of the Crown within Sweden as a great power. According to the Instrument of Government there would now be 23 governors in the whole of Sweden, Finland and other occupied areas.

Under this constitution, the governor now had to supervise all jurisprudence and make sure that no serious crimes were concealed or hushed up; that sentences were properly executed; that soldiers were recruited properly, that they were kept in the service of the Crown; and that there were no malpractices going on in their province. The main duty of a governor was to guard the Crown's possessions and to ensure the proper collection of taxes. He not only ensured that towns and roads were kept in proper condition, but that peaceful conditions prevailed and that uprisings, disagreements and other disturbances did not occur. This duty extended also to the clergy, but otherwise the governors were forbidden to interfere in affairs of the Church.[32]

The following year there were even more detailed instructions for the governors. There were now 45 paragraphs covering practically all activities in the everyday life of a province, including subjects such as religious matters, hospitals, roads, towns, financial administration, orphanages, and beggars. Whereas the stewards instructions of the 1620s had emphasized the stewards' role in supervising bailiffs, the role of the governors was more general and wide-ranging. As representative of the Crown, it was now his duty to systematically watch over everything that was going on in his province. His responsibilities were divided into six categories: affairs of the church, justice, army, navy, administration, and finance. This division was connected to the structure of the central administration.[33] It was a huge leap from the previous nebulous definitions towards a more modern administration, where every branch of administration clearly had its own responsibilities.

The instructions still mentioned the "King of Poland" and staying on guard for any possible suspicious deeds, such as spies or letters he might send in his efforts to "open the door" to the realm. The regency also seemed a little uncertain of its own position, because §3 stipulated that a governor must make it clear to the public that the regency was working tirelessly, "and by doing so plant in their hearts a good will" towards the regency.[34] Like the stewards, the governors were presumed to ensure the loyalty of the subjects. This paragraph was, at the time, perhaps the most important part of the order, but it soon lost its relevance. The threat of Poland had become a thing of the past (King Sigismund had died, and his sons had little interest in Sweden) and no one seriously questioned the legitimacy of the regency or the monarchs that followed.

The change of a governor's role in military and judicial administration was particularly emphasized. Paragraph 12 noted that governors were now forbidden, under pain of penalty, to interfere in any military affairs, such as armaments, military exercises and defence. In practice however, military experience was still required – especially during times of war and in the border areas. For instance Johan Graan (c. 1610–1679), Governor of Norrland and Lapland, was responsible for arranging the defences of his province during the war with Russia in the 1650s.[35] As for the judicial side of things, a governor was now no longer allowed to be a judge, although it had "been common up to this day". He was still, however, responsible for the overall functioning of the judicial system and was to make sure that court records were entered correctly, serious crimes resolved, and sentences carried out, so that "the land would not be contaminated by grave blood-debts".[36] In this respect, governors were watching over the morals and right behaviour of the people.

The order of 1635 described in great detail how the the governor's office (*landskansli*) should be organized, how all the papers should filed, how many archival cabinets there should be, and how such things as *diarium* and *registratur* should be compiled. Orders were also given with regard to timetables and the number of rooms allowed in the governor's house of residence, and there would be a governor's clerk, who would follow his every move.[37] This "micro-management" may seem rather odd, but in the historical context it seems perfectly reasonable in fact. The goal of these instructions were to ensure uniformity and repeatable, reliable administrative practices that would facilitate the flow of information between the centre and peripheries. In a centralized state, local administration could not be allowed to arrange its routines freely. Flimsy ever-changing practices and a lack of information were considered the major obstacles to ensuring an efficient administration, so documents were valuable and the development of archival practices became an integral part of state-building. In this respect, governors and their officials were important actors.

The orders of 1635 were so comprehensive that they remained in force for over 50 years, in spite of the rapidly changing face of Swedish society. New orders were eventually issued in 1687, however, with the establishment of absolutism in Sweden, and therefore the order needed revising. Everything aimed at uniformity and harmony in seventeenth century Sweden. The new administration was supposed to function smoothly, without any local hiccups. Everyone, in fact, had his or her place and its corresponding duties determined by almighty God. The way estates were run, and the way mercantile economic policy worked, were manifestations of the same idea. Administration and economic life were thus overflowing with regulations, orders and privileges. A particularly striking feature of the governors' orders were that they were supposed to cover and assess all aspects of life in the provinces. As in economic life, there was a huge gap between the practicalities of executing the orders and instructions, and what was theoretically reflected in them. Theoretically, the governors were not supposed to have any agency above and beyond their orders. The ability of a governor was thus determined by his ability to juggle the complex and mundane demands of actually governing his province with the formal and usually more idealistic demands from above.

The belief that uniform regulation would nevertheless create harmony was deep-rooted in seventeenth century Sweden. But in reality, things were much more complex and even chaotic. Enormous distances, the small number of officers (all with a large workload), and a lack of reliable information were common problems.

## *Appointment and duties*

Previously, the steward had been given varying and often cursory letters of appointment. With the establishment of the new system this totally changed. The general instructions of 1635 were copied and sent out to every new governor; with only the caption at the beginning changed according to the posting. Any demands there might have been for the instructions to be modified according to local circumstances were soon forgotten. The instructions clearly reflect the government's wish for centralization, uniformity, and smoothly functioning administrative practices.[38]

Beforehand, the steward had enjoyed more or less direct contact with his master – he was literally, after all, a servant of the ruler. In this respect, the steward system had been essentially medieval in character. It was based on personal loyalty and the obligations that came with the relationship between a lord and his servant.[39] The governor, in turn, was loyal to the Crown and the system he was part of, but the connection between a governor and his ruler was bureaucratized and most often indirect – blocked by the *collegia* of central government.

The situation changed somewhat in 1687 however, when governors became subject to the direct powers of an absolute monarch.[40] Historians are relatively unanimous in their opinion that the control of governors became more acute during absolutism.[41] However, this is not to say that the relationship between absolute monarch and governor returned to the way it had been between king and steward. By the late seventeenth century, Sweden had become a thoroughly bureaucratized state, where, in practice, both the absolutist monarch and governors were still very much tied to the administrative system.

Recruitment of seventeenth century governors turned into something of a contest, embedded in important patron-client relationships. The increasing number of noblemen with a formal higher education, combined with the shortage of personnel soon transformed itself into a struggle for good positions. Patrons and recommendations became very important when an aspiring nobleman wanted to make his way up the ladder of the administration system.[42]

There was no such thing as a typical seventeenth century governor, and being a governor was not a career in itself. The position played a different role in career paths, depending on the status and aspirations of the office-holder in question. For those who aimed high and who were already well-connected (i.e., someone born to a high-ranking noble family), being a governor – even in central Sweden – was just a part of their career path. These people were often appointed as governors at a relatively young age. Lars Fleming (1621–1699), for instance, was appointed Governor of Uppland at the age of 31, later becoming President of the Dorpat Court of Appeal and a Member of the Council of the Realm. Meanwhile, Knut Kurck (1622–1690) was 29 when he became Governor of Västmanland, before being a Member of the Council of the Realm and President of the Svea Court of Appeal. Gustav Soop (1624–1679) and Krister Bonde (1621–1659) were others who had similar career paths. For those who were not so well-connected however, the position of governor was the culmination of a career. According to the SBL, the late seventeenth century saw several ennobled or foreign men who ended their civil career as governors.[43]

There were once again differences in the nature of various governor postings. In the now firmly established centralized state, all aspiring noblemen wanted to work in and around Stockholm, close to the ruler and court, whereas somewhere like Finland was considered to be on the periphery and a less influential position to be governor in the seventeenth century. Within Finland itself, the same logic applied, as the most southwestern province (i.e., closest to Sweden) was seen to be the most influential. So Governor of Turku was a position that was generally more sought after than Governor of Vyborg (Viborg) on the Russian border. However, these offices could have different meanings for different people. For instance, in his letter to his patron Magnus Gabriel de la Gardie, Lorentz Creutz strongly recommended his currently unemployed brother-in-law, Jacob Duwall (1625–1684), as Governor of Vyborg by virtue of the fact that he knew Finnish, which was necessary in the region. It probably seemed a reasonably well-founded request, as in the previous decade two noblemen had consecutively refused their appointment to Vyborg. Duwall did not get the job however, and the man who was eventually appointed – Swedish diplomat, Gustaf Lilliecrona (1623–1683) – never even went to Vyborg. Lilliecrona instead bided his time, as he was later appointed first Governor of Kronoberg and then of Uppsala Län in Central Sweden.[44]

The Crown tried to efface the differences between provinces, but in practice these differences were huge and local circumstances also dictated who could be appointed to a certain office. Although the governors were forbidden to interfere in military affairs, men with military background were often appointed as governors of border areas. Likewise, some understanding of the Finnish language was necessary for a governor in the Finnish provinces.[45] Uniformity remained the ideal, but it was not possible to build a uniform centralized state without taking local circumstances into account.

In December 1637, the Government wrote to Per Brahe (1602–1680), the Governor-General of Finland about the Governor of Hämeenlinna (Tavastehus). The governor, Arvid Horn (1590–1653) had been in office for six months, and now Stockholm wanted to know if he was "sufficient and capable" enough to be fully appointed. If Brahe thought he was not suitable, then he was asked to propose another in his place, with the aim being to find *någon dugelig man* (some skilful man) for the position.⁴⁶ Times had changed, as in the 1620s political loyalty still played a leading role in appointments for important offices. Gustavus Adolphus had not appointed Finns to Finnish Castles, for example, as he thought they might yet turn to Sigismund.⁴⁷

At first, no governor was to work in the same province for more than three years. This was rarely carried out however, as it often proved impractical and unnecessary. In 1660 this was therefore changed: if a governor did his work well, he was not to be replaced without good reason.⁴⁸ This is an interesting development, directly connected to state-building. Before, rulers had been chronically suspicious of their government officials. Bailiffs were constantly changed,⁴⁹ and it was feared that if the same was not done with local officials, then they would gain too much power and become local magnates. The three-year term of office was a relic from this old attitude. However, with an increasingly complex society and centralized state, competence became more and more important. It was not practical to change governors all the time, when there were more effective ways to control their actions.

In the orders of 1635, it was made clear to governors that they were representing their king (*att han står där i Konungens stadh och ställe*); and as they were taking care of matters in his absence they were still, in effect, called the king's steward.⁵⁰ It is interesting that it still had to be emphasized that a governor was representing the absent king. The historical roots of this idea are much older than the position of steward, however. In medieval Sweden, the king was always on the go, as he had to regularly tour the country with his convoy. Gustavus Adolphus was even forced to do this during the early years of his regency. One important initiative for constructing the new administrative and legal system was thus to free the king from this frustrating task.⁵¹

Constructing a system that was relatively independent from the ruler himself meant a huge leap from a medieval-style government to modern bureaucracy. The most acute problem was actually the stubbornness of the king's subjects. Peasants and townspeople trusted the king but were suspicious of aristocracy and the nobility. The main problem was therefore that the king's representatives were noblemen. The peasants and the bourgeoisie had to be reassured that a governor was not simply there to safeguard the interests of his own noble family. The instructions of 1635 thus stated clearly that "[b]ecause he is the head or chief of the province (*Landzens huffwud eller Höffdingh*), his main priority is to do what is best for the king, the Crown, the province as well as the people".⁵² These instructions compared the duties of a governor to those of the king: he ruled both earthly (through five collegia) and church affairs of the state. Likewise, the governor, "as the king's *vicarius* and executor of the five *collegia*", was resposible for surveying affairs of the church, and the five earthly categories of justice, army, navy, administration (*landzregeringen*), and finance.⁵³ This analogy between the role of the king and the role of the governor is of great importance. The governor was not only acting vicariously on behalf of the king, but his province was seen to be like the realm in miniature.

## Control and obedience

The governors were themselves subject to controls and inspection, although this was not systematically applied. The orders of 1635 stated that they were to travel to Stockholm once a year to give a report, just as the bailiffs' had previously been duty bound to travel to Stockholm. But eventually, in 1662 it was officially enacted that governors were obliged to compose a written report every year.[54] At first, this new principle was taken seriously, although the Governor of Kronoborg underlined that he had already been to Stockholm and given a verbal report.[55] But then the demand for written accounts was gradually abandoned to the point where it was not mentioned in the orders of 1687.[56]

In practice, probably the most important means of control was the constant exchange of letters between the governor and his superiors. The *collegia* of central administration supervised that the governors executed whatever was on their agenda. In Finland, the establishment of the governor system was supported by the governor-general, Per Brahe, whose duty it was to organize the new provinces and their administration within Finland, and who also showed interest in keeping an eye on the governors. In 1648 and 1650, he thus enacted two complementary orders for governors in Finland.[57]

The main challenge facing any controlling of the system, was discovering the reasons for the problems with tax collection. In the face of what was sometimes unnecessarily heavy taxation, it was often difficult for a governor to meet the demands of central government due to poverty, harvest failure and soldier recruitments, and the Crown was generally reluctant to acknowledge these problems. Instead, the Crown usually foisted blame onto the officials.

The Governor of Turku, Bror Andersson Rålamb (1568–1647), for example, was deeply offended by the letter he had received from the *kammarkollegium* in 1635. The college had urged him to send some "means" to Stockholm and, according to the governor, had threatened him. He wrote back that he had always done his best in his difficult (*beswärlige*) office, but it was not in his power to take any more taxes from "this great desolate land". Those, who were with him at the office every day, as well as many others, could bear witness as to how diligently he worked and pursued the interests of the Crown. In his letter, Rålamb was adopting a martyr-like attitude that was typical of his contemporaries. He wrote that he would rather see that someone else be appointed to his office, than to incur the disfavour of the regency.[58]

The accounts of the governors (*Landshövdingarnas berättelser*) from the 1660s are quite uniform in character, regardless of the fact that the governors had no specific instructions as to how to write them.[59] In their accounts, the governors highlighted their loyalty and willingness to work hard, as well as their successes in carrying out instructions and orders in their provinces. The Governor of Stora Kopparberget, Jacob Duwall, even wrote that he used his instructions as a guideline for writing his account. In this way he could clarify how he had "adapted his performances" as laid out in the orders and in accordance with the king's will.[60]

It is clear that in these documents the governors did not generally dwell so much on the difficulties they faced, and yet there is some variety in the accounts. For instance, the Governor of Uppland painted a surprisingly gloomy picture of his province, even though it was the most central in Sweden and hardly the most difficult to administrate. He even complains how the bad weather and darkness caused problems in arranging court sessions.[61] Many governors wrote about local difficulties, such as poverty, long distances and damage caused by war. Sometimes seemingly minor issues were obstacles to uniformity. The Governor of Öster- and Västerbotten, which were sparsely populated areas, explained that he could not follow the archive practices required of him, because one of his residences had only a small cupboard for storage.[62]

The governors' accounts were not so much reports about the situation in the provinces. Their sole purpose was to present how a governor had managed to follow his orders. The king's letter stated clearly, that the governors should clarify how they had "followed, paid attention to and fulfilled" their orders.[63] Of course, it was impossible to monitor just how truthful these accounts actually were, and their role as an effective means of control was thus dubious. However, by at least confirming their willingness to obey every detail of their instructions, the governors were contributing to the hierarchical political reality of the Swedish centralized state. These rhetorical assurances of loyal service were an integral part of the centralized system. Things may have been more complicated in reality, but at least everyone knew how they *should* function and they shared the same idea of order and harmony.

Governor Carl Sparre (1627–1702), who had served three years as Governor of Gestrikland, Helsingland, Medelpad, Jämtland, Härjedalen and Ångermanland, wrote in his account, that according to his call and duty he was a good, loyal and upright servant of the Swedish Crown. He did his best to contribute to its best interests and well-being. His duty was to keep an eye out for anything that may hinder this, keep subjects obedient, and ward off any disagreements that may have caused "much disorder and have dangerous *Consequentier*".[64]

Likewise, Jakob Törnsköld (1625–1674) Governor of Vyborg (Viborg) and Savonlinna (Nyslott), wanted first to insist on his humble duty and loyalty to the King and Crown of Sweden. He stressed that his deeds should bear witness as to how hard he had been working to fulfill his obligations as a "faithful, honest, obedient and humble servant and subject". He was doing his best to keep the common people devoted to the Crown and to ensure that there were no revolts and disturbances.[65]

Besides simply carrying them out, the governors were also obliged to make the endless number of mandates and orders given by the central government public. And judging from the *berättelser*, the governors were quite aware of just how important this task was to a central government that held regulations so dear. For instance, Gustav Duwall, Governor of Stora Kopparberget, listed all the orders he had made public as well as a detailed description of how certain mandates had been carried out. This latter task was, in reality, anything but straightforward, due to a lack of resources and the Crown's unwillingness to acknowledge the local realities in provinces. For instance, the Governor of Öster- och Västerbotten, Johan Graan, explained that he tried to carry out the king's order regarding "old monuments and *antiqviteter*", but no one knew of any such things in his province. Duwall, on the other hand, had found several who did.[66]

## Between the centre and periphery

The governors derived their authority directly from the Crown. From the perspective of centralization, it was clearly essential that governors were not tempted to merge with local society and its interests. They had to be above them. This was done by ensuring that the status of the governor was higher than members of the local elite, and that the Crown was the most important source of wealth and power.

This development is linked to three major changes that occurred in early seventeenth century Swedish society: the rise in power of the nobility, fundamental changes in the role of the nobility, and the demolition of local networks of power. The nobility now turned their attention to Stockholm and its surroundings. It became less important to wield power locally and getting involved in local intrigues which might diminish the power of the Crown was generally frowned upon.[67]

The position of a governor was not an easy one. His workload was enormous. According to the Instrument for Government, a governor was to be assisted by a "good clerk", a bookkeeper, a *landsprofoss*, an *underprofoss*, and a servant. In the context of Swedish history, a *profoss* was usually employed in the army and his duty was to execute sentences;[68] but according to the Instrument for Government, the governor's *profoss* sometimes had to follow the governor, but also patrol the main roads, guard the peace, and carry out orders.[69] Considering the huge distances and sheer amount of duties involved, the number of administrative staff was very modest indeed. The governors were supposed to watch over the interests of the Crown while simultaneously guarding and looking after the residents in their jurisdiction. According to Björn Asker, it was clearly stated that a governor was to represent the Crown in the local community, not the other way round. However, in practice, governors understandably represented their own province and promoted their own affairs in the administration system.[70] Alexander Jonsson points out too that, even in the instructions, a governor was described as the head of the province and must take into account the interests of its people. These somewhat contradictory claims could cause problems.[71]

A governor had to balance his responsibilities towards the Crown with the demands of infuriating people in his province. Sometimes the tasks given to the governor were harsh – like ordering the governor of Värmland and Dalarna to catch the so-called "forest Finns" and send them to the Swedish colonies in North America (or work as forced labour for the Crown).[72] In this respect a governor's challenges were not so different from a bailiff's, as Janne Haikari has pointed out.[73]

In practice, the authority of a governor was challenged all the time, and the lack of staff only exacerbated the problem. In the seventeenth century world, it was simply quite easy to be disobedient. In 1638, Melchior von Falkenberg (1597–1651) complained to Governor-General Brahe about Finnish officials: "God knows how it is possible to get these thick-witted people to obey; they do not care about threats or imprisonment".[74] A couple of weeks later, he wrote to add that he might have to punish certain bailiffs "by gauntlet", or in some other humiliating manner, so they would not so easily forget their disobedience.[75] Not surprisingly, Falkenberg was at odds with a number of people – his "old enemies", a *profoss*, and some of his former colleagues – who had all mocked him in public at some point. Falkenberg suspected that no honest man in his right mind would want to be a governor in Finland, if he had to endure such mistreatment. Falkenberg's difficulties were not lessened by the fact that he was born in Livonia and spent his earlier years abroad; therefore he could not speak Finnish adequately and was generally unfamiliar with the local circumstances. He was often arguing with his staff and his subordinates, and was even questioned by the Council of the Realm about some confusion over collecting taxes. So it is of some interest to note that the central government did not sack him – on the contrary, Falkenberg asked several times if he could be "released" from his office, but his request was repeatedly ignored.[76] At that point in time, the administration system was new and the demand for educated noblemen was high. Falkenberg was clearly good enough; and fighting with local people was not considered a serious offence. A governor's role was to place Stockholm's authority in the provinces, regardless of the "thick-wittedness" of people.

Claes Rålamb, Governor of Uppland, wrote in his account that certain people "object to sentences being carried out, scorn arrest, and do not obey orders".[77] Governors also complained of the reluctance of judges to bring copies of their court records to the governor's office. Sometimes there were even more severe problems within the community. Jacob Duwall once wrote that the peasants of Mora hated all things military and made it customary to mistreat governors.[78] Meanwhile, the Governor of Inkerinmaa and Käkisalmi was forced to take in members of the town of Narva's law court and protect them from the violence of the bourgeoisie.[79]

The story of Ernst Johan Creutz (1619–1684), Governor of Helsinki and Uusimaa (1652–1666), and of Västmanland (1666) provides a great example of the kind of difficulties a governor could encounter. He was a member of an old Finnish noble family with excellent connections to the aristocracy and especially the powerful de la Gardie family, with whom his family had a patron-client relationship.[80] He was also supported by his successful brother, Lorentz. Ernst Johan studied abroad and began his career in the Svea Court of Appeal. However, his violent temper caused problems, and a young boy was killed in unclear circumstances in his house. In the early 1650s he was sent away from Stockholm to work as a governor in Helsinki. Some years after his appointment he had an embarrassing drunken outburst in Stockholm Castle. The Chancellor must have wondered what Creutz would do as governor of the province that had been entrusted to him.[81]

Creutz was born in nearby Pernaja, where his family had its manors and fiefs and exercised considerable local power. Therefore he was familiar with local circumstances and possibly knew some Finnish. Despite this, he encountered problems that were surprisingly similar to Falkenberg's. He built a huge and magnificent residence in Helsinki, a kind of monument to the governor's power over the townspeople. As governor, he did not tolerate any objections, and when someone in his province questioned his authority, his response was often violent. One of his biggest enemies was the mayor of Helsinki, and after one particularly drunken party he even ordered his servants to fire cannons at the mayor's house. On another occasion, during a seemingly minor argument with some sailors, Creutz flew into a rage, struck out at them with his cane and shouted "haven't you heard of Creutz?"[82] In his account for the years 1652–1666, Creutz was surprisingly open about his various conflicts with officers and noblemen, like the judge who purposefully arranged his court sessions so that the governor was not able to be present. The reasons he included these details was perhaps because he thought insolence towards him was disobedience towards the Crown. He even uses the expression *Embetets Respect*.[83]

In 1666, Ernst Johan Creutz was finally awarded with a better position and became the Governor of Västmanland which was more central. In Västmanland he was again subjected to insubordination, when a secretary got cross with him and left for two weeks taking the key to the office with him.[84] Despite his violent rages, Ernst Johan Creutz was not an unsuccessful governor. Maybe his administrative methods were harsh, but from Stockholm's point of view, the fact that he identified himself with the power of the Crown was a good thing. One should not disobey the governor, who represented the Crown.

The role of a governor was thus a difficult one, taking into account both the Crown and the local community – trying to a balanced harmony in a society that was filled with intrigues and problems. Nevertheless, the Crown was successful in binding governors to the system. The letters and accounts reveal that the governors were constantly afraid of their position; afraid of accusations and bad rumours and worried that their actions would cause anger in Stockholm[85]. This may have furthered unification and control, but it is questionable whether it actually made for a more efficient administration.

## Conclusion

The transition from steward to governor system is an important development in Swedish state-building in the seventeenth century. A well-functioning, uniform local administration was a precondition for the birth of a centralized state. Provinces had to be tightly connected to Stockholm, and the official who was in charge had to be a loyal servant of the system itself. His personal agency was intrinsically linked to pursuing the interests of central government. It was a system that was made to benefit both the Crown and the governors themselves.

Although the first stewards were nominated by Gustavus Vasa, the office had many medieval characteristics. Even in the early seventeenth century the stewards were representatives of the ruler himself and their authority was broad and vaguely defined. They resided in robust castles and fortresses, and had civil, military and judicial tasks. Their most important duty was to protect the power of their master, by arms if necessary.

The broad and flexible authority of the steward served its purpose in the early stages of state-building in Sweden, when governmental institutions were still relatively primitive and the central administration was plagued by a lack of information and educated staff. And this particular brand of political loyalty among stewards was also crucially useful during the civil war and the two decades that followed. But as the reign of Gustavus Adolphus progressed, this began to change. As the principal elements of a highly centralized state system became established, the stewards became important cornerstones in the overall process of state-building. The most valuable qualification of a steward was no longer his political loyalty but his eagerness to work as a part of the system. Loyalty towards a certain regent, in person, was thus gradually changed into loyalty towards the Crown and state.

In the 1620s it was decided that bailiffs and other civil officers should be made subjects of the stewards, which meant a clarification of hierarchical chains of command and responsibility. The duties of stewards were now defined much more clearly and they were no longer allowed to act as judges. In other words, the stewards had become overall supervisors of perhaps the most important feature of a centralized state – collecting taxes. At the same time, more specific orders from the king prevented them from garnering too much local power and possibly posing a threat to the Crown.

In 1634, the whole administration system was overhauled. The newly created central administration was now backed up by a more rigorous local administration in each of the provinces, where a governor was now in charge. A governor was a high-profile civil officer and more of a governor than a steward now. His duties and tasks were defined in greater detail in the general order of 1635. He was no longer allowed to interfere in military or judicial affairs. His role was now one of supervisor for his particular province in the realm. It was the governor's duty to ensure that all orders that came from Stockholm were executed, and sentences carried out. Repeatable administrative practices were important, as well as systematic archiving of the documents so that it was easier to compare like with like and make assessments. Every governor, regardless of the local circumstances in his province, was thus given similar instructions.

Governors were now essential actors in the centralized state; and the system would quickly have been untenable without their devotion to their occupation and the Crown. Moreover, the governors were not expected to just guard simply the interests of the Crown in their provinces, but also to govern according to the principles detailed in the order of 1635. The shift from the more improvised administration of the early seventeenth century to the carefully orchestrated system built from the 1630s onwards was extremely rapid, and this also explain why orders were taken so seriously.

The seventeenth century Swedish state system was built on the principles of hierarchy and order. Likewise, economic life was fettered under strict mercantile principles. The governors became guardians of this system on the local level. Their duty was not only to ensure that these and other orders were put into effect, but also to execute and realize this ideology in their own actions and governance. Therefore, the accounts that the governors wrote to Stockholm were formal, and their most important feature was to make assurances that the governor was a loyal part of the system and he was governing as instructed. Formally, a governor was not supposed to have any personal agency outside the order, but in practice it was essential, as there was a sharp contradiction between political and administrative ideology and the mundane reality.

The circumstances in different provinces varied, and very often there was a lack of information and dire poverty. The governors' duty was to represent the interests of central power on the local level, but in practice he often needed to become a spokesman for his province. The interests of Stockholm and the interests of local peasants and merchants were often contradictory, and the Crown's unwillingness to take into account local circumstances was striking. Another problem was that the governors' authority was constantly challenged by other officials and the bourgeoisie.

A successful governor was one who could govern in spite of these contradictory interests, and could strike a balance between orders from the Crown and provincial reality. From Stockholm's point of view, a governor's most important qualification was his eagerness to pursue the Crown's interests. Therefore, even Ernst Johan Creutz and his otherwise terrible outbursts were tolerated.

One should not be misled by the whining tone in many of the governors' letters and accounts. Self-pity and dramatic expressions were typical of seventeenth century rhetorical culture. The position of a governor was certainly challenging however, as he had to prove his authority, implement orders and balance several different interests at once. It was thus relentlessly hard work and presumed a certain degree of toughness.

In general, the governors were eager to prove their abilities and were committed to their work. It was simply in their interest to serve the Crown as well as possible. In seventeenth century Sweden, the nobility was, in this way tightly bound to the state system. Success owed itself to the state and a career in either the administration or the army. There simply was no other source of wealth and power, and therefore it was in the best interest of governors to pursue the Crown's interests. Competition for a place in the sun was harsh and, of course, one's success was not dependent on just ability. Family and patron-client relationships also seemed to play a great role, as we see in the case of Ernst Johan Creutz, whose career was bolstered by the aristocratic de la Gardie family.

The stewards were servants of a king or duke, and guardians of his interests in a world where robust castles were centres of (often violent) political life. The governor, however, was a civil officer, guardian of the newly established and carefully organized system and the ideas behind it. When the governors were told how to organize the papers in their archival cabinets, it was not only a question of finding these papers again. The cabinets reflected how society was, it was hoped, controlled with orders, privileges and hierarchy.

In reality, the administrative system did not function as harmoniously as originally intended though. In practice, many of the detailed orders and *placates* were impossible to put into effect, and a governor could not supervise if the rules were followed. The realm suffered from poverty and a lack of information. The number of officials was small, and, despite the detailed regulations, there was no modern administrative infrastructure. Nevertheless, the Swedish system was effective in its own time and the principles of an effective administration proved to be much more durable than Sweden's status as a great power.

## NOTES

1 See for instance Mirkka Lappalainen, *Jumalan vihan ruoska. Suuri nälänhätä Suomessa 1695–1697* (Helsinki: Siltala, 2012) pp. 39–40, 80–82, 131–137; Kimmo Katajala, "Maps, Borders and State-building". In: Lamberg, Marko, Hakanen, Marko, Haikari, Janne (ed.), *Physical and Cultural Space in Pre-Industrial Europe. Methodological Approaches to Spatiality* (Lund: Nordic Academic Press, 2011), pp. 58–59, 81–85, Ulla Koskinen, "Distance as an Argument". In: Lamberg, Hakanen, Haikari (ed.), *Physical and Cultural Space*, pp. 158, 166–168; Matts Hallenberg, *Statsmakt till salu. Arrendesystemet och privatiseringen av skatteuppbörden i det svenska riket 1618–1635* (Lund: Nordic Academic Press 2008).

2 *Fulmacht för Johan de la Gardie*, 15th of September, 1611. Johan E. Waaranen, Handlingar upplysande Finlands historia under Karl IX:s tid utgifna af Dr Johan E. Waaranen. III. 1609–1611. Samling af urkunder rörande Finlands historia III (Helsingfors, 1866), p. 160.

3 Today, *ståthållare* is the head of "Ståthållareämbetet" who guards and takes care of the Royal Swedish castles. Nationalencyklopedin [www.ne.se], "Ståthållare" and "Ståthållareämbetet", accesed February 10, 2015.

4 *Svenskt biografiskt lexikon*, [www.sbl.se], "utökad sökning", landshövding 1634–1680, Kansallisbiografia (the Finnish National Biography), "maaherra" 1600–1700.

5 The book has been published also in Swedish (*Släkten, makten, staten*, 2007).

6 SBL (Lars-Olof Larsson), "Gustaf Olsson (Stenbock)", [https://sok.riksarkivet.se/sbl/Presentation.aspx?id=20067], pp. 266–267; Alexander Jonsson, *De norrländska landshövdingarna och statsbildningen 1634–1769*. Skrifter från institutionen för historiska studier 10 (Umeå: Umeå universitet, 2005), pp. 47–49; Olof Sörndal, *Den svenska länsstyrelsen. Uppkomst, organisation och allmänna maktställning* (Lund: Sundqvist & Emond, 1937), pp. 9–12; Nils Herlitz, *Grunddragen av det svenska statsskickets historia* (Stockholm: Svenska bokförlaget, Norsteds, 1927), pp. 72–73; J. A. Almquist, *Den civila lokalförvaltningen i Sverige 1523–1630. Med särskild hänsyn till den kamerala indelningen*, I. Meddelanden från Svenska riksarkivet: ser. 2, 6 (Stockholm, 1917), pp. 47–57; *Nordisk familjebok* 1904–1926, pp. 568–569; Emil Hildebrand, *Svenska statsförfattningens historiska utveckling från äldsta tid till våra dagar* (Stockholm: P. A. Norstedt & Söners Förlag, 1896), p. 282.

7 Jonsson, *De norrländska landshövdingarna*, pp. 49–50; Folke Lindberg, "Till frågan om landshövdingeämbetets äldsta historia. Östergötlands län före 1635", *Historisk Tidskrift* 1939, pp. 138–139; Sörndal, *Den svenska länsstyrelsen*, pp. 13–14.

8 The position of a steward (*ståthållare*) should not be mixed up with *riksföreståndare*, who represented the absent monarch as a regent.

9  KB (Petri Karonen), Leijonhufvud, Axel, [http://www.kansallisbiografia.fi/kb/artikkeli/3234/], accessed November 24, 2015.
10 Pentti Renvall, *Kuninkaanmiehiä ja kapinoitsijoita Vaasa-kauden Suomessa* (Helsinki: Tammi, 1949), pp. 115–138; Pentti Renvall, "Suomen tilintarkastuksen organisointi 1500-luvulla", *Historiallinen Aikakauskirja* (1/1939), p. 29; Lindberg, "Till frågan om landshövdingeämbetets äldsta historia", pp. 141–146.
11 Mirkka Lappalainen, *Susimessu. 1590-luvun sisällissota Suomessa ja Ruotsissa* (Helsinki, Siltala, 2009), pp. 132–133, 204–205; Michael Roberts, *The Early Vasas. A History of Sweden, 1523–1611* (Cambridge: Cambridge University Press, 1968), pp. 338–384; Sörndal, *Den svenska länsstyrelsen*, p. 15.
12 SBL (Lars Ericson Wolke), "Arvid Eriksson Stålarm" [https://sok.riksarkivet.se/sbl/Presentation.aspx?id=34659], accessed November 25, 2015; Lappalainen, *Susimessu*, pp. 69–88, 145–158, 185–195, 213–215, 264–266; KB (Veli-Matti Syrjö), "Stålarm, Arvid" [http://www.kansallisbiografia.fi/kb/artikkeli/257/]; KB (Kari Tarkiainen), "Fleming, Klaus",[http://www.kansallisbiografia.fi/kb/artikkeli/526/]; SBL (Berndt Federley), "Klas Fleming" [https://sok.riksarkivet.se/sbl/Presentation.aspx?id=14215]; Renvall, *Kuninkaanmiehiä ja kapinoitsijoita*, pp. 239–258.
13 *Fulmacht för Johan de la Gardie* 15th of September, 1611, Waaranen, Samling af urkunder rörande Finlands historia III, pp. 160; *Fulmacht för Erich Hare* 31st of March, 1612, 26th of December, 1612, Waaranen, *Samling af urkunder rörande Finlands historia* IV, p. 37, 105; *K. Instruction för Herman Wrangel*, November 28th 1616, C. G. Styffe, Samling af instructioner för högre och lägre tjenstemän vid landt-regeringen i Sverige och Finnland (Stockholm, 1852) s. 103; *K. Instruction för Peder Göransson*, 22nd of March, 1616, Styffe, *Samling af instructioner*, p. 127.
14 Riksarkivet (SRA) (Swedish National Archive, Stockholm), Riksregistratur (RR) (Swedish National Records) 29th of November, 1616, p. 550.
15 SRA RR 15th of September, 1611, Waaranen, Samling af urkunder rörande Finlands historia III, pp. 160–161.
16 Mirkka Lappalainen, *Pohjolan leijona. Kustaa II Aadolf ja Suomi 1611–1632* (Helsinki: Siltala, 2014); pp. 155–159; Erkki Lehtinen, *Hallituksen yhtenäistämispolitiikka Suomessa 1600-luvulla (1600–n. 1680)*, Historiallisia Tutkimuksia 60 (Helsinki: Finnish Historical Society, 1961), pp. 59–61.
17 Lappalainen, *Pohjolan leijona*, p. 156; Lehtinen, *Hallituksen yhtenäistämispolitiikka*, p. 53.
18 *K. Instruction för Herman Wrangel*, 28th of November, 1616, Styffe, *Samling af instructioner*, p. 103.
19 Lappalainen, *Pohjolan leijona*, pp. 118–133.
20 Lappalainen, *Pohjolan leijona*, pp. 122–133.
21 Jonsson, *De norrländska landshövdingarna*, p. 270.
22 *K. Instruction för Frih. Johan de la Gardie* (...), 15th of May, 1616. Styffe, *Samling af instructioner* pp. 99–103.
23 Lappalainen, *Pohjolan leijona*, pp. 51–53; Mirkka Lappalainen, "Den lokala eliten och uppkomsten av maktstaten. Egenmäktiga ämbetsmän och svag kunglig överhöghet i det tidiga 1600-talets Finland", *Historisk Tidskrift för Finland 85*, 2000, pp.11–14, see also Erkki Lehtinen, "Suomen kameraalinen keskushallinto 1600-luvun alkupuolella", *Historiallinen Arkisto 57* (Helsinki: Finnish Historical Society, 1961).
24 *Kongl. Maj:ts Memorial för Ståthållarne om uppbördsverket*, April 6th 1620, Styffe, *Samling af instructioner*, pp. 142–149; Sörndal, *Den svenska länsstyrelsen*, pp. 24–25.
25 Lappalainen, *Pohjolan leijona*, 2014 s. 147–149, 199–208; Michael Roberts, "Gustavus Adolphus and the Rise of Sweden" (London: The English Universities Press Ltd, 1973), pp. 86–88; Sörndal, *Den svenska länsstyrelsen*, 1937 p. 24.
26 *K. Gustaf II Adolfs "Ordning hwar effter Chronones Ränthor* (...)", 27th of July, 1624,

Styffe, *Samling af instructioner*, pp. 169-184; Sörndal, *Den svenska länsstyrelsen*, pp. 25-28; K. R. Melander, *Kuvaus Suomen oloista vuosina 1617-1634* (Helsinki, 1887), pp. 35-45.

27 SBL (Bertil Boëthius), Johan Pontusson De la Gardie [https://sok.riksarkivet.se/sbl/Presentation.aspx?id=173789], accessed November 25, 2015.

28 Lappalainen, *Pohjolan leijona*, pp. 79-81, 142-146.

29 About the Instrument for government, see for instance Björn Asker, *I Konungens stad och ställe. Länstyrelser i arbete 1635-1734* (Uppsala: Stiftelsen för utgivande av Arkivvetenskapliga studier, 2004) pp. 120-125; Petri Karonen, *Pohjoinen suurvalta. Ruotsi ja Suomi 1521-1809* (Helsinki: The Finnish Literature Society 2014), pp. 185-197; Nils Runeby, *Monarchia mixta. Maktfördelningsdebatt i Sverige under den tidigare stormakstiden*, Studia Historica Upsaliensia VI (Uppsala: Uppsala universitet, 1962); pp. 211-236; Sven A. Nilsson, "1634 års regeringsform i det svenska statssystemet", *Scandia* 10, 1937.

30 *Förslag till Regeringsform (...)* 29th of July, 1634. Rikskansleren Axel Oxenstiernas skrifter och brefvexling. Utgifna af kong. vitterhets-historie- och antiqvitetsakademien. I:1, Historiska och politiska skrifter (Stockholm: P. A. Norstedt & Söners förlag,1888) pp. 266-270; Lehtinen, *Hallituksen yhtenäistämispolitiikka*, p. 253; see also Alexander Jonsson, "'Försumblige i deras kall och ämbete...' 1600-talets debatt om den nya regionalförvaltningen". In: Harnesk, Börje (red.), *Maktens skiftande skepnader. Studier i makt, legitimitet och inflytande i det tidigmoderna Sverige*, Historiska Perspektiv (Umeå: Umeå Universitet, 2003), pp. 122-126.

31 Lindberg, *Till frågan om landshövdingeämbetets äldsta historia*, pp. 151-153.

32 *Regeringsform* 1634, Hildebrand, Emil, Sveriges regeringsformer 1634-1809 samt konungaförsäkringar 1611-1800. ed. Emil Hildebrand (Stockholm: P. A. Norstedt & Söner, 1891), pp. 1-41; Sörndal, *Den svenska länsstyrelsen*, pp. 39.

33 Jonsson, *De norrländska landshövdingarna* pp. 55-56.

34 *Instruction och...1635*. § 3-4, Styffe, *Samling af instructioner*, pp. 191-192.

35 Lehtinen, *Hallituksen yhtenäistämispolitiikka*, pp. 250-261; KB (Pentti Virrankoski), Graan, Johan [http://www.kansallisbiografia.fi/kb/artikkeli/2321/] accessed November 24, 2015.

36 *Instruction och...1635*. §9, § 12, Styffe, *Samling af instructioner*, pp. 195, 197-198.

37 *Instruction* of 1635 §27-42, Styffe, *Samling af instructioner*, pp. 207-261; Jonsson, *De norrländska landshövdingarna*, p. 55, 58-60.

38 Sörndal, *Den svenska länsstyrelsen*, pp. 43-44; Lehtinen, *Hallituksen yhtenäistämispolitiikka*, p. 120.

39 About the mediaeval idea of service, see Peter Reinholdsson, *Uppror eller resningar. Samhällsorganisation och konflikt i senmedeltidens Sverige*, Studia Historica Upsaliensia 186 (Uppsala: Uppsala universitet, 1998), pp. 150-180.

40 Jonsson, *De norrländska landshövdingarna*, pp. 60-61.

41 Asker, *I Konungens stad och ställe*, p. 234.

42 Marko Hakanen, *Vallan verkostoissa. Per Brahe ja hänen klienttinsä 1600-luvun Ruotsin valtakunnassa*. Jyväskylä Studies in Humanities 157 (Jyväskylä: Jyväskylän yliopisto, 2011), pp. 46-59, 124-136; Lappalainen, *Suku, valta, suurvalta*, pp. 53-55, 156-157, 343-354; Lehtinen, *Hallituksen yhtenäistämispolitiikka*, pp. 257-259.

43 See "Lars Fleming", "Knut Kurck", "Gustav Soop", "Krister Bonde", "Polycarpus Cronhielm", "Abraham Cronhjort", "Clas Dankwardt-Lillieström", "Hans von Dellingshausen", "Lars Larsson Eldstierna", "Anders Grelsson Lindehielm". In: Svenskt biografiskt lexikon, www.sbl.se.

44 SRA, De la Gardieska samlingen, E 1375, Lorentz Creutz to Magnus Gabriel de la Gardie, Vyborg 10th of April, 1674; Antti Kujala, *Viipurin Karjala, Käkisalmen lääni ja Inkerinmaa Ruotsin suurvaltakaudella 1617-1710*. In: Kaukiainen, Yrjö, Marjomaa, Risto, Nurmiainen, Jouko (toim.), *Suomenlahdelta Laatokalle. Viipurin läänin historia III* (Lappeenranta: Karjalan kirjapaino, 2010), pp. 374-375, 395;

Lappalainen, *Suku, valta, suurvalta,* p. 287; SBL (Lars-Olof Skoglund), Gustaf Lilliecrona, [https://sok.riksarkivet.se/sbl/Presentation.aspx?id=10320], accessed December 10, 2015.
45 Lehtinen, *Hallituksen yhtenäistämispolitiikka,* pp. 245–263.
46 SRA RR 22nd of December, 1637, Karl Tigerstedt, *Handlingar rörande Finlands historia kring medlet af 17:de århundradet, i akademiska disputationer utgifne af Karl Tigerstedt* (Helsingfors, 1849, 1850), pp. 87–88.
47 Lehtinen, *Hallituksen yhtenäistämispolitiikka,* pp. 60–61, 250–251.
48 Sörndal, *Den svenska länsstyrelsen,* pp. 53–54.
49 Lappalainen, "Den lokala eliten", p. 13.
50 *Instruction* of 1635 §6, Styffe 1852 p. 193; Instruction for Melchior von Falkenberg §5, Karl Tigerstedt, *Handlingar rörande Finlands historia,* p. 5.
51 Lappalainen, *Pohjolan leijona,* 295.
52 *Instruction* of 1635 §6, Styffe, *Samling af instructioner,* p. 193.
53 *Instruction* of 1635 §7, Styffe, *Samling af instructioner,* pp. 193–194.
54 SRA RR 2nd of May, 1662, ff. 474–474v; Sörndal, *Den svenska länsstyrelsen,* pp. 54–55.
55 The account of Georg Gyllenstierna, 1662, *Handlingar rörande Skandinaviens historia* 31, p. 166.
56 *Handlingar rörande Skandinaviens historia* 31, pp. 1–2 (Introduction).
57 *General Gouverneuren Grefve Per Brahes "Instruction och påminnelse för Landzhöfdingarna här i Stoorfurstendömet Finland (...)",* 13th of September, 1648, Styffe 1852 pp. 240–249; *General Gouverneuren Grefve Per Brahes "Bij Instruction för Landzhöfdingerne (...),* 29th of April, 1650, Styffe, *Samling af instructioner* pp. 249–253; See even Per Brahe's letters to governeurs in Karl Tigerstedt, *Handlingar rörande Finlands historia* and *Bref från Generalguvernörer och Landshöfdingar i Finland, förnämligast under Drottning Kristinas tid. Utgifne af Karl K. Tigerstedt* (Åbo 1869); Lehtinen, *Hallituksen yhtenäistämispolitiikka,* pp. 120–121.
58 Bror Andersson Rålamb to *Kammarkollegium,* Turku castle, 20th of June, 1635. Tigerstedt, *Bref från Generalguvernörer och Landshöfdingar i Finland,* p. 183; Bror Andersson Rålamb to *Kammarkollegium,* Turku, September 1635, Tigerstedt, *Bref från Generalguvernörer och Landshöfdingar i Finland,* p. 187.
59 The account of Erik Sparre, 1661–1662, *Handlingar rörande Skandinaviens historia* 31, p. 148.
60 The account of Gustav Duwall, 1666, *Handlingar rörande Skandinaviens historia* 31 (1850), p. 206.
61 The account of Claes Rålamb, 1661, *Handlingar rörande Skandinaviens historia* 31 (1850), pp. 91–98; see also Jonsson, *De norrländska landshövdingarna,* p. 106.
62 The account of Johan Graan, probably 1668, *Handlingar rörande Skandinaviens historia* 31, pp. s. 306–307; about distances, Piia Einonen, "A travelling governor". In: Lamberg, Marko, Hakanen, Marko, Haikari, Janne (eds), *Physical and Cultural Space in Pre-Industrial Europe. Methodological Approaches to Spatiality* (Lund: Nordic Academic Press, 2011).
63 SRA RR 2nd of May, 1662 f. 474v.
64 The account of Carl Sparre, 1664–1666, *Handlingar rörande Skandinaviens historia* 31 (1850), pp. 255–256.
65 The account of Jacob Törneskiöd, 1662, *Handlingar rörande Skandinaviens historia* 31 (1850), p. 480.
66 The account of Johan Graan, 1668, *Handlingar rörande Skandinaviens historia* 31 (1850), p. 299–300; The account of Jacob Duwall, 1666, Handlingar rörande Skandinaviens historia 31 (1850), p. 234–235; about Graan and his career: Jonsson, *De norrländska landshövdingarna;* KB (Pentti Virrankoski), Falkenberg, Melchior von [http://www.kansallisbiografia.fi/kb/artikkeli/2349/], accessed November 24, 2015.

67 About this development see for instance Lappalainen, *Suku, valta, suurvalta;* Fredric Bedoire, *Guldålder. Slott och politik i 1600-talets Sverige* (Stockholm: Albert Bonniers förlag, 2001); Mirkka Lappalainen, "Regional Elite Group and the Problem of Territorial Integration. The Finnish Nobility and the Formation of the Swedish 'Power State', c. 1570–1620", *Scandinavian Journal of History* 26, 2001; Reinhard Bendix, *Kings or People. Power and the Mandate to Rule* (Berkeley and Los Angeles: University of California Press, 1980), p. 220; Lehtinen, *Hallituksen yhtenäistämispolitiikka.*

68 *Svenska Akademins ordbok*, www.saob.se, "profoss", *Nationalencyklopedin*, www.ne.se, "profoss". Accessed November 24, 2015.

69 *Regeringsform 1634*, Hildebrand, Sveriges regeringsformer, pp. 1–41; Jonsson, *Försumblige i deras kall och ämbete*, p. 122.

70 Asker, *I Konungens stad och ställe*, p. 239.

71 Jonsson, *De norrländska landshövdingarna*, p. 147; Jonsson, *Försumblige i deras kall och ämbete*, pp. 131–133.

72 *Kongl. Regerings Bref till Landshöfdingen öfwer Wermland och Dal Olof Stake*, 16th of April, 1641, Handlingar rörande Skandinaviens historia XXIX (1848), pp. 218–219.

73 Janne Haikari, *Isännän, Jumalan ja rehellisten miesten edessä. Vallankäyttö ja virkamiesten toimintaympäristöt satakuntalaisessa maaseutuyhteisössä 1600-luvun jälkipuolella*. Bibliotheca Historica 121 (Helsinki: The Finnish Literature Society, 2009), pp. 121–122, 152–166, 224–235.

74 Melchior von Falkenberg to Per Brahe, Turku, 3rd of March, 1638, Tigerstedt, *Bref från Generalguvernörer och Landshöfdingar i Finland*, p. 209.

75 Melchior von Falkenberg to Per Brahe, Turku, 19th of March, 1638, Tigerstedt, *Bref från Generalguvernörer och Landshöfdingar i Finland*, p.212; Jonsson, *De norrländska landshövdingarna*, pp. 132–134.

76 Melchior von Falkenberg to Per Brahe, Kokemäki vicarage, 5th of June, 1641, Tigerstedt, *Bref från Generalguvernörer och Landshöfdingar i Finland*, p. 235; SBL (Emil Hildebrand), Falkenberg, Melchior [https://sok.riksarkivet.se/SBL/Presentation.aspx?id=15077], accessed December 10, 2015; KB (Pentti Virrankoski), Falkenberg, Melchior von [http://www.kansallisbiografia.fi/kb/artikkeli/2349/], accessed November 24, 2015.

77 The account of Claes Rålamb, 1661, *Handlingar rörande Skandinaviens historia* 31 (1850), p. 89.

78 The account of Gustaf Duwall, 1666, *Handlingar rörande Skandinaviens historia* 31 (1850), p.215.

79 The account of Simon Grundel Helmfelt, 1662, *Handlingar rörande Skandinaviens historia* 31 (1850), p. 502.

80 Lappalainen, *Suku, valta, suurvalta*, pp. 145–207, 343–344.

81 Lappalainen, *Suku, valta, suurvalta*, pp. 162–172, 184–191.

82 Lappalainen, *Suku, valta, suurvalta*, pp. 191–206.

83 The account of Ernst Johan Creutz, 1652–1666, *Handlingar rörande Skandinaviens historia* 31, pp. 465–478. The problems Ernst Johan Creutz encountered in Helsinki can be compared with governor Johan Graan's disputes with the mayor of Oulu. Jonsson, *De norrländska landshövdingarna*, pp. 140–142.

84 Lappalainen, *Suku, valta, suurvalta*, pp. 206–211.

85 See also Jonsson, *De norrländska landshövdingarna*, pp. 144–145.

# Sources

## Archival sources

Svenska Riksarkivet (SRA), Stockholm (Swedish National Archives)
Riksregistratur (Swedish National Records) (SVAR-database)

## Printed sources

Handlingar rörande Skandinaviens historia, vol. 29. Stockholm 1848.
Handlingar rörande Skandinaviens historia, vol. 31. *Landshöfdinge-berättelser från sjuttonde åhrhundradet.* Stockholm 1850.
Hildebrand Emil (utg.) 1891. *Sveriges regeringsformer 1634–1809 samt konungaförsäkringar 1611–1800.* Utg. af. Emil Hildebrand. Stockholm: P. A. Norstedt & Söner.
*Rikskansleren Axel Oxenstiernas skrifter och brefvexling.* Utgifna af kong. vitterhets-historie- och antiqvitets-akademien. I:1, Historiska och politiska skrifter. Stockholm: P. A. Norstedt & Söners förlag 1888.
Styffe, C. G. 1852: *Samling af instructioner för högre och lägre tjenstemän vid landtregeringen i Sverige och Finnland.* Stockholm: Hörbergska boktryckeriet.
Tigerstedt Karl K. 1869: *Bref från Generalguvernörer och Landshöfdingar i Finland, förnämligast under Drottning Kristinas tid.* Utgifne af Karl K. Tigerstedt. Åbo.
Tigerstedt Karl 1849, 1850: *Handlingar rörande Finlands historia kring medlet af 17:de århundradet,* i akademiska disputationer utgifne af Karl Tigerstedt. Helsingfors.
Waaranen Johan E. 1866: *Handlingar upplysande Finlands historia under Karl IX:s tid utgifna* af Dr Johan E. Waaranen. III. 1609–1611. Samling af urkunder rörande Finlands historia III. Helsingfors.
Waaranen Johan E. 1874: *Handlingar upplysande Finlands historia under Gustaf II Adolfs tid* samlade af dr Johan E. Waaranen. I. 1611–1614. Samling af urkunder rörande Finlands historia IV. Helsingfors.

## Electronic sources

Nationalencyklopedin, http://www.ne.se
*Nordisk familjebok,* http://runeberg.org/nf/

## Literature

Almquist, J.A. 1917: *Den civila lokalförvaltningen i Sverige 1523–1630. Med särskild hänsyn till den kamerala indelningen.* I. Meddelanden från Svenska riksarkivet 2, 6. Stockholm: Riksarkivet.
Asker, Björn 2004: *Konungens stad och ställe. Länstyreselser i arbete 1635–1734.* Uppsala: Stiftelsen för utgivande av Arkivvetenskapliga studier.
Federley, Berndt 1964–1966: "Klas Fleming", *Svenskt biografiskt lexikon.* Stockholm: Svenskt biografiskt lexikon.
Bedoire, Fredric 2001. *Guldålder. Slott och politik i 1600-talets Sverige.* Stockholm: Albert Bonniers förlag.
Bendix, Reinhard 1980: *Kings or People. Power and the Mandate to Rule.* Berkeley and Los Angeles: University of California Press.

Boëthius, Bertil 1931: "Johan Pontusson De la Gardie", *Svenskt biografiskt lexikon*. Stockholm: Svenskt biografiskt lexikon.

Einonen, Piia 2011: "A travelling governor". In: Lamberg, Marko, Hakanen, Marko, Haikari, Janne (eds), *Physical and Cultural Space in Pre-Industrial Europe. Methodological Approaches to Spatiality*. Lund: Nordic Academic Press.

Haikari, Janne 2009: *Isännän, Jumalan ja rehellisten miesten edessä. Vallankäyttö ja virkamiesten toimintaympäristöt satakuntalaisessa maaseutuyhteisössä 1600-luvun jälkipuolella*. Bibliotheca Historica 121. Helsinki: The Finnish Literature Society.

Hakanen, Marko 2011: *Vallan verkostoissa. Per Brahe ja hänen klienttinsä 1600-luvun Ruotsin valtakunnassa*. Jyväskylä Studies in Humanities 157. Jyväskylä: Jyväskylän yliopisto.

Hallenberg, Matts 2008: *Statsmakt till salu. Arrendesystemet och privatiseringen av skatteuppbörden i det svenska riket 1618–1635*. Lund: Nordic Academic Press.

Herlitz, Nils 1927: *Grunddragen av det svenska statsskickets historia*. Stockholm: Svenska bokförlaget/Norsteds.

Hildebrand, Emil 1956: "Melchior Falkenberg", *Svenskt biografiskt lexikon* 15. Stockholm: Svenskt biografiskt lexikon.

Jonsson, Alexander 2003: "Försumblige i deras kall och ämbete..." 1600-talets debatt om den nya regionalförvaltningen". In: Harnesk, Börje (red.), *Maktens skiftande skepnader. Studier i makt, legitimitet och inflytande i det tidigmoderna Sverige*. Umeå: Umeå Universitet.

Jonsson, Alexander 2005: *De norrländska landshövdingarna och statsbildningen 1634–1769*. Skrifter från institutionen för historiska studier 10. Umeå: Umeå universitet.

Karonen, Petri 2005: "Leijonhufvud, Axel", *Suomen kansallisbiografia*. Helsinki: The Finnish Literature Society.

Katajala, Kimmo 2011: "Maps, Borders and State-building". In: Lamberg, Marko, Hakanen, Marko, Haikari, Janne (eds), *Physical and Cultural Space in Pre-Industrial Europe. Methodological Approaches to Spatiality*. Lund: Nordic Academic Press.

Koskinen, Ulla 2011: "Distance as an Argument". In: Lamberg, Marko, Hakanen, Marko, Haikari, Janne (eds), *Physical and Cultural Space in Pre-Industrial Europe. Methodological Approaches to Spatiality*. Lund: Nordic Academic Press.

Kujala, Antti 2010: "Viipurin Karjala, Käkisalmen lääni ja Inkerinmaa Ruotsin suurvaltakaudella 1617–1710". In: Kaukiainen, Yrjö, Marjomaa, Risto, Nurmiainen, Jouko (toim.), *Suomenlahdelta Laatokalle. Viipurin läänin historia III*. Lappeenranta: Karjalan kirjapaino.

Lappalainen, Mirkka 2000: "Den lokala eliten och uppkomsten av maktstaten. Egenmäktiga ämbetsmän och svag kunglig överhöghet i det tidiga 1600-talets Finland", *Historisk Tidskrift för Finland* 85.

Lappalainen, Mirkka 2001: "Regional Elite Group and the Problem of Territorial Integration. The Finnish Nobility and the Formation of the Swedish "Power State", c. 1570–1620", *Scandinavian Journal of History 26*.

Lappalainen, Mirkka 2005: *Suku, valta, suurvalta. Creutzit 1600-luvun Ruotsissa ja Suomessa*. Helsinki: WSOY (Swedish translation: *Släkten, makten, staten. Familjen Creutz i 1600-talets Sverige och Finland*. Stockholm: Norstedts 2007).

Lappalainen, Mirkka 2009: *Susimessu. 1590-luvun sisällissota Suomessa ja Ruotsissa*. Helsinki: Siltala.

Lappalainen, Mirkka 2012: *Jumalan vihan ruoska. Suuri nälänhätä Suomessa 1695–1697*. Helsinki: Siltala.

Lappalainen, Mirkka 2014: *Pohjolan leijona. Kustaa II Aadolf ja Suomi 1611–1632*. Helsinki: Siltala.

Larsson, Lars-Olof 2007–2011: "Gustaf Olsson (Stenbock)", *Svenskt Biografiskt Lexikon*. Stockholm: Svenskt biografiskt lexikon.

Lehtinen, Erkki 1961: *Hallituksen yhtenäistämispolitiikka Suomessa 1600-luvulla (1600–n. 1680)*. Historiallisia Tutkimuksia 60. Helsinki: Finnish Historical Society.

Lehtinen, Erkki 1961a: "Suomen kameraalinen keskushallinto 1600-luvun alkupuolella", *Historiallinen Arkisto 57*. Helsinki: Finnish Historical Society.

Lindberg, Folke 1939: "Till frågan om landshövdingeämbetets äldsta historia. Östergötlands län före 1635", *Historisk Tidskrift*.

Melander, K.R. 1887: *Kuvaus Suomen oloista vuosina 1617–1634*. Akatemiallinen väitöskirja. Helsinki.

Nilsson, Sven A. 1937: "1634 års regeringsform i det svenska statssystemet", *Scandia* 10.

Reinholdsson, Peter 1998: *Uppror eller resningar. Samhällsorganisation och konflikt i senmedeltidens Sverige*. Studia Historica Upsaliensia 186. Uppsala: Uppsala universitet.

Renvall, Pentti 1939: "Suomen tilintarkastuksen organisointi 1500-luvulla", *Historiallinen Aikakauskirja*.

Renvall, Pentti 1949: *Kuninkaanmiehiä ja kapinoitsijoita Vaasa-kauden Suomessa*. Helsinki: Tammi.

Roberts, Michael 1968: *The Early Vasas. A History of Sweden, 1523–1611*. Cambridge: Cambridge University Press.

Roberts, Michael 1973: *Gustavus Adolphus and the Rise of Sweden*. London: The English Universities Press Ltd.

Runeby, Nils 1962: *Monarchia mixta. Maktfördelningsdebatt i Sverige under den tidigare stormakstiden*. Studia Historica Upsaliensia VI. Uppsala: Uppsala universitet.

Skoglund, Lars-Olof 1980–1981: "Gustaf Lilliecrona", *Svenskt biografiskt lexikon 23*. Stockholm: Svenskt biografiskt lexikon.

Syrjö, Veli-Matti 2007: "Arvid Stålarm", *Suomen kansallisbiografia*. Helsinki: The Finnish Literature Society.

Sörndal, Olof 1937: *Den svenska länsstyrelsen. Uppkomst, organisation och allmänna maktställning*. Lund: Sundqvist & Emond.

Tarkiainen, Kari 2003: "Fleming, Klaus", *Suomen kansallisbiografia*. Helsinki: The Finnish Literature Society.

Virrankoski, Pentti 1998: "Graan, Johan", *Suomen kansallisbiografia*. Helsinki: The Finnish Literature Society.

Virrankoski, Pentti 2001: "Falkenberg, Melchior von", *Suomen kansallisbiografia*. Helsinki: The Finnish Literature Society.

Wolke, Lars Ericson 2013: "Stålarm, Arvid Eriksson", *Svenskt biografiskt lexikon*. Stockholm: Svenskt biografiskt lexikon.

# Judges V

Olli Matikainen

# Judges, Law-readers and Malpractice (1560–1680)

In May 1639, a group of local judges were invited to Stockholm to meet with the Council of the Realm. Chancellor Axel Oxenstierna (1583–1654) began their meeting by reflecting on the true calling of a judge, and what such an office entailed.[1]

> The government understands very well what a difficult office [law-readers] hold, since they must not let their own emotions interfere with how justice is dispensed. There are, however, some who exceed their authority and are not true to their vocation and office.

The meeting with the Council had been called to ease internal unrest in a country that was embroiled in a difficult phase of war abroad in Germany. The chancellor felt irritated that local conflicts were not being resolved effectively enough by the judges. Not only did this abet social unrest, in his opinion, but it added a further burden to the higher levels of administration that already had enough on their hands with the war. According to Oxenstierna, the judges were too ready to 'press their seal' on letters to the central government containing "inappropriate claims" by common people. Judges should instead investigate these cases more carefully and hear all the parties equally. As Oxenstierna had hoped for, the appearance of judges with local judicial problems at the level of the Council was rare, and Oxenstierna's critical comments hardly testify, as such, to any widespread crisis of the Swedish legal system.[2] This collective reprimand before the Council of the Realm did, however, show the importance of the office of judge. After all, the "welfare of the fatherland depended on their vocation".

The aim of this chapter is to analyze how the role and status of judges developed in Sweden before the important reforms of 1680, which granted them a life-time tenure. The general concept of 'judge' (*domare*) refers here to a person that 'in practice' exercises judicial power and judges people according to law and custom in local courts (*ting*) with the help of a local jury (*nämnd*). In Sweden, regional judges were known as *häradshöfding*; and the office is mentioned for the first time by the middle of the 14th century, which is a few years before the first law code was compiled for the Swedish realm (1350). By the sixteenth and seventeeth centuries *häradshöfding* had become an office that could be made part of a 'donation'. In practice this meant that an aristocratic office-holder was in charge of the revenues and hired a substitute to take charge of some or all of the court sessions. These substitutes were called law-readers.[3]

Oxenstierna stressed in his speech the important social role of judges and their constructive agency; and yet this subject has raised surprisingly little interest in historical studies. Nevertheless, Max Weber has written in *Economy and Society* about law being a "craft", and in which he examined legal *honoratiores* – a group of prestigious people that played a central role in building the legal structures of society;[4] while Harvard legal scientist, John P. Dawson, published *The Oracles of the Law* in 1968 – a modern classic of legal history in which he compares the position of judges in different legal cultures. Meanwhile more recent research has stepped out of the court rooms and analyzed the agency of judges in the wider context of society, like John McLaren's study of 19th century British colonial judges.[5]

The personal agency of judges has gone largely unnoticed perhaps because the profession of judge was traditionally perceived as a calling, or vocation, to act impartially as an oracle of sacred truth. The Reformation in the sixteenth century strengthened the idea that God sees everything and punishes all crimes that are hidden, and so judges were part of this process of uncovering the truth. Severe crimes like homicide needed to be strictly investigated and punished accordingly. Customary compensation, which was negotiated between the parties, was typical both to accusatory medieval legal culture and reciprocal relationships between kin-groups. During the course of the sixteenth and seventeenth centuries, however, the increasing centralization of the state meant that these customary communal practices became gradually more limited.[6] It is clear that, if the judge performed his task properly, his agency would also usually remain invisible for later researchers. Olaus Petri's (1493–1552) famous sixteenth century formulation of these principles in "Instructions for Judges" was that the judge "should always have God in his mind".[7] The Law Commission of 1643, which began to prepare reforms to the medieval code of law, stressed similar ideals; the "judge should have a growing moral reputation".[8] Mats Pålsson worked for decades as a law-reader in Ostrobothnia without any great conflict, and at his funeral in 1685, his obituary suggests the importance of moral conduct above all else.[9]

> He took good care of his office,
> As many can amply prove;
> He lived profoundly engaged with the world,
> And did not ask for glory.

Earlier studies on judges from the early modern period have mainly focused on their career, social background, and education. In the 1950s, for instance, Yrjö Blomstedt studied the social background and careers of sixteenth and seventeenth century judges extensively in the Finnish part of the realm. Law-readers were recruited from among bailiffs, scribes, burghers, and even clergymen. Blomstedt showed that the custom of finding law-readers from among socially lower stratum did not lead to a decline in judicial security as some contemporaries seemed to think.[10] In 1598 Duke Charles (1550–1611) thought that many law-readers were "not even capable of reading or writing".[11] On the contrary, Blomstedt argues that being a law-reader prepared the ground for them then developing into a more professional group of judiciary.[12] This profession began to take shape quickly after the establishment of the Court of Appeal (Svea 1614, Turku 1623), which encouraged the professional education of law-readers. David Gaunt has followed the careers of the seventeenth century judges recruited and trained by the Court of Appeal and describes the professionalization of judges as a successful incorporation strategy by the Crown. Abolishing the law-reader system in the reforms of 1680 was thus made technically easier, since many law-readers could now simply become permanent judges with tenure.[13]

Legal history has touched on the problem of judges' agency mostly in the interaction between judge and jury in reaching verdicts. Besides handling criminal and civil cases, local courts throughout the Realm of Sweden provided a public forum for the Crown to meet people. Indeed, a typical feature of the legal culture in Nordic countries has been that it strongly involves the common people.[14] It is thus surprising that not so much attention has been paid to how the administration and local community interacted; in other words, how the status and role of the judge was defined in practice. To properly evaluate this, other sources need to be considered than the usual political debates or normative sources of justice.[15]

Another factor contributing to the invisibility of judges in the seventeenth century – especially in Finland – is because the minutes for the Turku Court of Appeal dating from that period have been almost completely destroyed.[16] Although records of the local court sessions from then exist, and are well preserved, judges rarely feature in them as actors. This is probably because, if the agency of judges was noticed at all, it was usually when there were accusations of malpractice, and in that case there would have then been an appeal and it would have passed to the higher court. Indeed, Blomstedt describes several cases where the judges were tried for such reasons in the sixteenth and seventeenth centuries, but as a classical historian wanting to build an objective picture of the past, he stresses that the value of these individual cases should not be extended to generalizations about the overall state of judicial ethics or security of the profession. In Blomstedt's opinion, such accusations and defamations against judges were often caused by personal bitterness.[17] There is, however, some room for rethinking and rereading these cases. As will be shown below, a closer study of these conflicts, even when they proved to be false accusations, can often prove rewarding and reveal something of the usual state of affairs which other studies may often have ignored.

## Historical sources of judicial power

There is already substantial literature on how the role of judge developed historically in connection with the shifting balance of political power.

According to the medieval codes of the realm (1350, 1442), regional judges (*häradshöfding*) were elected by the local community in a meeting that was led by the "lawspeaker" (*lagman*) – a position appointed by the king.[18] Some information on the process of electing judges is provided in two letters concerning election of regional judges in the Piikkiö district of Southwestern Finland in 1468.[19] In one letter (from June 1469 and addressed to his "beloved common people"), the king confirms that "you have legally elected Sten Henriksson to be your *häradshöfding*". However, as the *lagman* and others informed him, Sten Henriksson had not even been nominated as a candidate. A meeting led by local sheriffs (*länsman*) and six peasants from every parish in the district had, nevertheless, pushed for Sten Henriksson to be appointed.

If we were to generalize about the process of electing regional judges in late medieval Finland from this evidence, we might suppose that the letter of the law was followed, and the community played the principal role in electing the judge. Sten Henriksson also seems to have had the typical background for the makings of a regional judge, as he was a member of the local well-respected and wealthy elite.[20] Meanwhile in the province of Eastern Savo there was no aristocracy. One 'judge' (*domare*) of obviously peasant origins, Pekka Utriainen, is mentioned in a document from Eastern Finland describing the establishment of the parish of Juva in 1442. His appointment as judge has puzzled historians, but perhaps the most probable explanation is again the medieval law code. Utriainen had the status of *häradsdomare*, which meant that, according to the law, he would be nominated by the jury to act as judge if a *häradshöfding* was not available for some reason. Indeed, rather than being the vestiges of an old form of Finnish folk justice, Utriainen's case seems to illustrate more the way in which the Swedish legal system was consolidating itself, even in remote areas of Finland.[21]

However, during the early sixteenth century, the disintegration of the Union of Calmar and the accompanying political turmoil led to rulers often nominating judges without election or hearing the opinion of local communities.[22] The founding father of the modern Swedish state, King Gustavus Vasa (1496–1560), was already maintaining in the 1540s that the right of the ruler to personally nominate judges had "always" been a legitimate practice. The king thought the idea of the local community taking part in electing their own judges was "insane" (*vansinnigt*), although he did graciously promise to consider candidates that might "please" the local peasants too.[23] But this was a hollow promise considering what happened in the 1550s when the locals of Lappee in Eastern Finland tried to remove their unpleasant judge by complaining to the king. Not only did he ignore their request, but when eventually a riot broke out, he ordered two of the peasant leaders to be executed as rebels.[24]

Throughout the sixteenth century, the Vasa kings offered many posts for the aristocracy within the realm's military and administration. In fact, one way to reward faithful service to the king was to 'donate' offices such as *häradshöfding* to nobles, and this profitable reward soon became eagerly sought after by them.[25] A noble awarded such an office was a regional judge only nominally though. In practice, he was simply expected to collect the revenues and be in charge of an annual judicial session, while all the other tasks were delegated to the law-readers hired for the task. The prospect of attending provincial local courts sometimes two or three times a year in remote areas of the Finnish countryside, and often in difficult conditions, was obviously not attractive to many of the nobility; and yet many sixteenth century *häradshöfding* office-holders sat in on a good number of the sessions personally. The office of Savo regional judge was donated to leading Finnish aristocrat Arvid Eriksson Stålarm (1549–1620), who held the post from 1583 to 1599. Stålarm was highly respected among his peers and very busy with many military and administrative tasks, yet he understood that showing up in person at least once every couple of years was vital for building authority among tax-paying peasants and the local community.[26]

Executive and judicial power often overlapped in Sweden's sixteenth century administration; and it was not really until the new constitution of 1634 that, holding the posts of governor and judge at the same time, for instance, was officially ruled out. Gustav Fincke (d. 1566) was one of King Gustavus Vasa's trusted men, as he was personally indebted to the king for intervening on his behalf in the 1530s, when Fincke had committed a homicide in Denmark. He was thus a military commander, the Crown's bailiff, and the regional judge of Savo province all at the same time from the 1540s to the early 1560s. In 1556, the king's secretary received various complaints about Fincke's conduct, and it looked fairly evident that Fincke had been using his position as a judge, more or less within the law, to amass quite a fortune;[27] and there are a number of descriptions of how he 'did business' in the literature.

> When Gustav Fincke attends to the court, no peasant is able to complain to him without first visiting his chamber and bringing him presents. It often happens that these presents amount to a greater value than what His Majesty collects for a fine.[28]

As is often the case, the accusations against Fincke that he was taking bribes appeared too difficult to verify. His son Gödik (d. 1617) succeeded him in the same post as Crown's bailiff 1582. Gödik Fincke's letters are interesting in that they show how private and public interests were often mixed in sixteenth century administration. Fincke's fellow aristocrat, Arvid Stålarm, handed part of his personal *häradshöfding* revenues to Fincke as a sign of goodwill, to help with the maintenance of the Crown's central castle.[29]

In the course of the seventeenth century it became customary that only a few of the regional judges from the upper aristocracy visited their judicial districts at all. According to Blomstedt, between 1625 and 1653, none actually appeared in the court room personally in Finland. The system was criticized for being prone to incompetence and malpractice particularly because the law-readers were so dependent on the absent office-holder.[30] The relationship between law-readers and their regional judge is interesting, but there seems to be limited evidence available. For instance, the law-reader Herman Böcke's letter of 1639 to his *häradshöfding* Matthias Soop (1585–1653) shows, how the latter was mostly interested in collecting revenues.

Böcke was facing problems with peasants that had fled to Russia, and so the law-reader was left with incomplete tax rolls and gaps in tax incomes. Böcke hoped that he would not see this as a case of him "fiddling taxes", and that "God may help him in his calling as an honest man".[31]

Björn Asker has analyzed in detail, how the office of regional judge became an important part of a long political struggle, where the upper aristocracy holding donations stood against the king and lower estates. The king wanted to cancel the *häradshöfding* office as a donation and create in its place a system of permanent and professional Crown judges with tenure. One particular conflict in the early 1640s illustrates this tension. The Council of the Realm and *häradshöfding* Matthias Soop sent a new law-reader to his judicial district in the province of Kexholm without consulting the Turku Court of Appeal. Unaware of Soop's actions, the Court of Appeal ordered its own judge to sit for the local court sessions in the province, but when he got there Soop's judge was already in session and prevented the Turku judge from entering. Eventually the Courts of Appeals managed to undermine the right of office-holders to choose their law-readers; and then the law-reader system was abandoned altogether as part of the Great Reduction reforms in 1680 that simultaneously got rid of the donations.[32]

One leading seventeenth century ideologue to take part in this debate, from the Swedish high aristocracy, was Count Per Brahe (1602–1680). As a holder of large donations in Finland, he knew the problems of jurisdiction personally. Brahe considered the office of *häradshöfding* to lawfully belong to the aristocracy, but he also maintained that the judge should at least be resident in his judicial district and he should not employ law-readers, if possible. Brahe's views reflected his semi-feudal ideology, i.e., peasants and common people should not be considered as direct subjects of the Crown, but only indirectly so via patronage of the aristocracy.[33] In other words, Brahe's patriarchal model would have meant a return to medieval practice, where the local elite took charge of jurisdiction.

Brahe made these views clear to the Turku Court of Appeal in the early 1660s, when the jurisdiction of his large donation in Northern Finland (*Cajaneborg*) was called into question. After the war against Russia in the 1650s, justice in Brahe's donation left much to be desired. The Turku Court of Appeal received various complaints about dubious verdicts and illegal imprisonments. Accusations were directed against Brahe's judges, Johan Curnovius and Zacharias Palmbaum.[34] One problem seemed to be that the personal relationship between the two judges was rather tense.[35] Brahe was the most powerful man in Sweden after the king, but the Court of Appeal took the accusations seriously and was not shy in reminding him that neglecting such complaints could easily escalate into serious unrest. It was therefore decided that a special commission should be sent up north to investigate the accusations.

In his response, Brahe made it pretty clear that there was really no need, as this was very much in his jurisdiction (*min jurisdiction*); and that it was his duty to investigate and punish judges, if he was to find that any malpractice had taken place. Indeed, Brahe had already asked his judges to clarify the matter, underlining that he held the power of lawspeaker (*lagman*) in his donation. Nevertheless, since he could not sit in the sessions in person, he appointed a substitute *underlagman* to act on his behalf. Besides attending to judicial matters, this *underlagman* was also chief supervisor of social and economic affairs in the area.[36] Brahe dared not openly oppose the Crown by preventing the planned commission from entering his donation, but he made it clear to them that it was "usual" for the quarrelling peasants to exaggerate their problems.

The Court of Appeal noticed the hint of irritation in the letter, and replied that perhaps no special commission would be needed if things could be sorted out otherwise. The Court of Appeal continued, however, to show its superiority in legal matters by criticizing Brahe for failing to deliver court records from his donation to the Court of Appeal. The style of the letter was openly ironic, since as he had been appointed the Lord High Chancellor (*drots*), he "should not be ignorant" of the right (*riktig*) practices. It went on to suggest that actually sending the records had perhaps "slipped his mind".[37] In the 1670s, Brahe did criticize his judge Nikolaus Petrellius for neglecting his duties; and he clarified the new constellation of power by adding that "politeness" required all matters of justice be first reported to him, even if *ultimate legal power* lay in the hands of the Royal Court of Appeal.[38]

## *The limits of agency: the role of judge redefined*

In their struggle over judicial power, both the Crown and high aristocracy comfortably forgot the medieval law code, which nevertheless remained in force up to 1734. Early legal scientists could not simply close their eyes to the fact that the right of the community to take part in the election of judges was firmly within the law. In the 1660s, the issue was discussed by the Svea Court of Appeal, and the possible role of the local community was seriously taken into consideration. After some deliberation, the judiciary reached the conclusion that the right of the community to take part in the election had, in practice (*in utendo*), been abolished.[39] But the memory of the common people was much longer. Legal historian Pia Letto-Vanamo has studied the judicial process of sixteenth century local courts and shown that the local community and jury certainly played a central role in reaching verdicts,[40] and this went on into the following century. This hypothesis could perhaps be supported by some of the scandals caused by Governor Herman Fleming (1579–1652) during local court sessions in Savo province during 1644. At the same time, it also illustrates the changing role of judges once the Court of Appeal had been established.

Law-reader Knut Bock reported how his local court session was suddenly interrupted, when Bailiff Ture Persson physically attacked one member of the jury and tried to drag him out of the court room. The bailiff accused the commoner of neglecting his duty to deliver fish to the governor. The jury member replied, "let go of me, I have court people (*käräjäkansa*) here". Indeed, the common people present clearly reacted against the bailiff's aggression and shouted him down "with one mouth". The law-reader was forced to stand up and call for order, while Governor Fleming himself said neither "good or bad" of the matter, watching passively from the side. Later Fleming did, however, criticize the bailiff with some harsh words, but Bock found it strange that Fleming was not chastising the bailiff for violating court proceedings so much, as for letting the law-reader give him orders. Irritated by this criticism, Bock announced that he would send a report to the Court of Appeal complaining of the governor's "lack of action".[41]

On another occasion though, Herman Fleming perhaps took too much action when he personally dragged out another bailiff, Johan Falk, in the middle of a court session. Bock described this as "illegal and against all Christian behaviour". When he decided to interrupt the session, he was again met by a stormy reaction from the common people. The conclusion by the people was that "the rabble (*metelikansa*) had taken over". Law and order needed to be maintained so that the session could continue, otherwise "they [the aristocrats] would act with impunity, as it was before, when law and order were not respected".[42] The years of the late sixteenth century peasant uprising were still fresh in the collective memory, and so the real motives of the aristocracy were held in some doubt.

Herman Fleming was son of Claes Hermansson Fleming (d. 1616), who was remembered by the oldest people in Savo as a military leader and member of the 1595 border commission that conducted the peace negotiations with Russia. The Fleming family belonged to the upper strata of the nobility in Finland.[43] Herman Fleming had made his career in the Turku Court of Appeal; which in many ways made his behaviour all the more difficult to fathom. Law-reader Bock's complaints eventually reached the highest level, and the king promised that he would settle the conflict "impartially" – Fleming was nonetheless removed from his post. As a last resort, Herman Fleming tried to appeal to Count Per Brahe since he was "an old man and had already served our late King (Gustavus Adolphus, 1594–1632)". A new man had, however, already been assigned to his post and Fleming's petition, signed with shaky handwriting, did nothing to further his cause.[44] Indeed, Herman Fleming's unusual aggression may even have had something to do with ageing. Aggressive outbursts by disappointed and bitter parties in court sessions were not exceptional, but in this case questioning the fundamental legitimacy of the judge's authority was considered a step too far.

In the conflict between Bock and Fleming, the main point was in principle the same as in the tensions of colonial justice that have been studied by McLaren. The issue was whether the "executive [in this case Fleming] in exercising the royal prerogative was seen by the judiciary [in this case Bock] as trenching upon its powers in the administration of justice and rule of law sensibilities".[45] Meanwhile, in Sääksmäki the roles were reversed in the 1650s when ageing judge Krister Nilsson Rosencrantz caused serious problems for Governor Ernst Johann Creutz (1619–1684). The governor complained that he was unable to arrange his duties (*publica negotia*) since Rosencrantz did not announce the schedule of his court sessions in enough time. The latter's excuse that it was due to the poor postal service was not acceptable it seems, especially as the Turku Court of Appeal had also received a mass of complaints from people of both high and low status on his dubious and random verdicts. Lady Margareta Boije was furious, for instance, that Rosencrantz had judged against her tenant Jaakko Ruuskanen in Rautalampi without her knowledge. It resulted in her losing half of one island, although she had a document proving that the land had been in her family's possession for over 60 years.[46]

According to the Turku Court of Appeal's investigation, the faults found in the judge's court records (*feel och exorbitantier*) were "more numerous than one might think". The letter of the law was often not cited in an appropriate way, and the judge seemed to have given verdicts too "freely" (*pro libitu*). The Court of Appeal concluded that Rosencrantz "should have known" his vocation and office better, as a man of his experience. The final straw for Rosencrantz was to be accused of bribery and fraud. In many cases he had judged that routine fines should be paid, but they were not all found accounted for in the fine rolls for the Crown. In one case of adultery the judge had made a deal with the wife that her unfaithful husband could return back without further sanctions, in return for some pieces of cloth.

The religious element was a strong factor in building the legitimacy of justice, and the Vicar of Jämsä complained that he had difficulty getting cases of adultery handled by Rosencrantz in the local court – which did not help his case. In fact, having court sessions and church services on the same day remained a regular practice in the countryside for centuries.[47] One must also remember that clergymen could still act as substitute judges (i.e., law-readers) in the sixteenth century – the latest date known by Blomstedt for Finland is actually 1591.[48] But by the seventeenth century the idea of a 'clergyman judge' with "one foot in the court room and the other in the pulpit" was deemed unacceptable, even if the clergy often helped out the judges in many less formal ways. After all, many earthly crimes did often involve what the Church would consider 'sin', and this collaboration actually grew during the latter part of seventeenth century when the campaign against adultery intensified.[49]

Governor Johan Rosenhane's (1611–1661) diary from the 1650s shows, how the roles were not always clearly defined and conflicts emerged. At Puumala in 1653, for instance, the vicar called the law-reader a "liar" and "forger".[50] Rosenhane also describes how the Bishop of Vyborg (Viborg) almost ended up in a fist fight with the representatives of the Turku Court of Appeal when he asked to check the court records, and was met with the response that such "earthly matters" did not concern the bishop at all.[51] In fact, Rosenhane wrote many examples in his diary of the uneasy waltz between the actors within the administration. At Pellosniemi in 1653, for instance, both the law-reader and bailiff emerged before the court hopelessly drunk (*öffwerst fulla och druckna*). On top of this, the governor did not uncritically subscribe to the views presented by local officials – the bailiff had, for example, shown his bias to defend the interests of the donation-holder in a conflict over statute labour. Governor Rosenhane commented: "today the king, tomorrow dead".[52]

The governor, law-reader and bailiff thus formed the holy trinity of seventeenth century local administration; and in Kexholm, in the 1640s, it was widely suspected that they actually clubbed together to ensure the highest revenues and actually added to the burden on the common people.

Like Gustav Fincke a century earlier, law-reader Anders Lytthraeus was accused of transforming court sessions into a market place open to the highest bidder.[53] Kexholm was an exceptional province, since Sweden had won it from Russia in 1617 and so administration in the area was still suffering from irregularities as resettlement was still ongoing.[54] This fact is reflected in the minutes of Karelia's Lagman's Court between 1635 and 1645. The Lagman's Court was mentioned in medieval law code as an institution for mediating between local courts and the king. The institution has received little attention in the seventeenth century context, since the Court of Appeal has usually been considered the central institution for justice in this period.[55] However, the Lagman's Court usually handled litigation cases, such as land disputes which had not been successfully resolved by the local courts, yet considered to be of too little significance to burden the Court of Appeal with in Turku. The Lagman's Court could handle cases, for example, where the local judge was personally implicated, or legally disqualified (*interessert*).[56]

Lagman Anders Swart in Savo asked Governor Reinhold Metstake, Bailiff Henrik Piper and Law-reader Herman Böcke in neighbouring Kexholm province whether any sessions of the Lagman's Court were needed in Kexholm 1639. Swart received the answer that they were not, though later it became evident that the revenues for having court sessions were collected (even though the Lagman's Court never actually sat).[57] This was understandably causing growing unrest among common people and the Crown was forced to step in. Eventually, in 1642 it was declared at every court session that "Her Majesty will do everything" to restore law and order in the province.[58] Nevertheless, the first round of local court sessions in 1642 had failed because Law-reader Peder Nilsson Raam could not speak or understand Finnish, let alone any of the local customs. Swart therefore overruled as *lagman* a sentence given by Raam in the case of an assault where a man was almost lethally hit with a stone. The offender was asked to pay a substantial compensation to go free. This verdict was thus obviously quite against the letter of the law and passed instead according to local customs only.[59]

Law-reader Raam's shortcomings are perhaps quite simply explained by his outsider status in the community, but the question of a judge's integration into the local community was a double-edged issue. Local knowledge was considered important for the judge, but an involvement in community affairs that went too deep could also jeopardize his judicial independence. This problem became topical during the transition period that followed the establishment of the Court of Appeal in the 1620s. Many Finnish law-readers had a local community background as bailiffs, and this group especially was often criticized by the Court of Appeal for judging against the letter of the law – even for serious crimes like manslaughter. Many law-readers were still following old customary practices, which would usually include negotiating various forms of informal compensation between the families involved.[60] Ostrobothnian law-reader, Gabriel Påhlsson, was removed for these reasons, even though he wrote a long explanatory letter to the Court of Appeal. The law-reader described himself as an "uncomprehending, sick old man", who was powerless against other actors of administration and members of local jury.[61]

The improved education of law-readers after the establishment of the Court of Appeal led to more self-assertive behaviour among the judiciary. This becomes evident when one compares the law-readers of the 1620s to some of their better trained colleagues two decades later. As shown above, for example, the law-reader of Savo – Knut Bock – was not afraid of the governor when defending the autonomy of the judiciary. But Bock also found himself on the other side of the court table too, when the burghers of Lappeenranta accused him of disturbing the peace in 1645, when he landed a boat at their market place purportedly full of tar (this was his business), that inspectors considered suspicious as they were too light. When they smashed some of the barrels to pieces, a furious Bock and those he had come with in the boat attacked them with oars and stakes. The local burghers found the situation threatening and rebellious and charged him. Nevertheless, in the local court session Bock emerged as self-confident and even gave a lecture at the beginning on how court sessions should be correctly summoned.[62]

Meanwhile, at the Lagman's Court in Vyborg (Viborg), October 1642, Law-reader Erik Hansson complained that his "vocation and office" (*kall och ämbete*) had been wrongly called into question by a Krister Simonsson. The latter had been involved in a land dispute with the commoner Antti Salakka, and when they met in a village alley had once threatened each other with weapons – Simonsson with a sword and Salakka with an axe. According to Simonsson, who introduced himself as an "old servant of the Crown" it was only Salakka who was guilty of disturbing the peace. Erik Hansson, however, did not subscribe Simonsson's interpretation – perhaps because he seemed to be hinting that he was somehow more 'above the law' than the peasant. Instead he began literally to "read the law" to a nervous Simonsson, who then reacted by accusing the law-reader of "forging the law" and taking bribes from Salakka. He quickly realized, however, the seriousness of his accusations and took his words back, explaining the behaviour in the court as being due to drunkenness. The law-reader then made a bit of a show about the power of his leniency, and mercifully announced that he was not willing to cause Simonsson "any further harm" – with the result that he was only charged a minor fine for the slander.[63]

Two years later the same local judge got in another clash. This time it was with Lt. Col. Berndt Taube who complained that Hansson had been in his judicial district with some "loose characters" (*löösgäster*), demanding food, drinks and other benefits on the basis of his status alone. Especially irritating for the officer, was that Erik Hansson had declared that as a law-reader, he was actually their superior when they were not on a battlefield. Not only was Hansson appearing to undermine the officer's authority, but he was even trying to physically chastise Taube's men. So Taube insisted that the Lagman's Court put the law-reader back in his place, since military issues (*krigz staten*) were none of his business.

> Just as soldiers have their court martials, the king's chamber is set up to supervise that law-readers do not spend the Crown's wages on loose characters.

As usual, Erik Hansson replied to this by reading aloud the law code to argue for his rights. He also represented himself as a defender of peasant's rights against violations committed by the military. But then the conflict took on an even stranger turn, when Taube began to insinuate that Erik Hansson was guilty of causing one particular peasant's death. Taube dared not officially present such a serious accusation, however, and so he "left the court room silently" with the insinuation hanging. Erik Hansson went on to admit that he had once hit a peasant with a stick, and this person had died later, but it had been from natural causes. The injuries of the peasant had already been checked by Governor Erik Gyllenstierna (1602–1657), and they were considered too minor to have caused death.[64]

Common people also knew their rights and were quick to react to any signs of malpractice by judges, either in the court room or outside. One such commoner was a "poor soldier's wife" – Riitta Matintytär of Halikko – who complained to the Court of Appeal that the local judge, Arvid Matsson, had mistreated her. According to Riitta, the drunken judge had rushed in to her cottage in the middle of the night and accused her of being a child murderer, even though Riitta could show that she had recently given birth to a child that was still very much alive. Despite this, Matsson had called her an "obvious whore" and ordered one member of the jury to "milk" her, and proceeded to grab one of her breasts himself. Nevertheless, the judge saw himself simply as a loyal servant of the Crown – controlling the behaviour of loose characters.[65] Arvid Matsson continued to get involved in other conflicts in his local community, but these were all directly handled at the level of the local court by his regional superior – Magnus Rålambsstierna (1606–1666). The judge (*häradshöfding*) thus personally sat on these local court sessions. Mattson won the cases against the peasants, who ended up resorting to calling him a "false judge" and the "Crown's thief."[66]

## Conclusion

Studying the agency of judges in an early modern Finnish context is challenging, not only because of the destroyed archives in Turku. The vocation and office of a judge was associated with the idea that they performed their task best when their agency went undetected. The conflicts and accusations of malpractice against the judges described above should therefore not be generalized from too liberally; although in practice the role and status of judges was defined in interaction with other men of the administration (governors, bailiffs, clergy, military) and the local community. The real state of affairs is thus not discovered by only studying normative sources.

There was often more at stake in the conflicts between actors than just the personal qualities of an individual judge or the rightness of his actions. In the course of the early modern "judicial revolution" the role of judges and the limits of their agency were renegotiated. A fundamental question is how judicial and executive powers began to separate in practice at the grass-roots level. Judges in the sixteenth century could have both considerable executive and judicial powers. With the professionalization of a judge's calling and office came a testing of the limits of a judge's agency. Thus we have cases such as those of Knut Bock, Erik Hansson, Anders Lytthraeus and Arvid Matsson in the 1640s and 1650s which show to what extremes this could be pushed. It was surely no coincidence that all of these were judges of the same generation trained by the Turku Court of Appeal. The new power of the judiciary was also noted by Count Per Brahe, when the Court of Appeal was not shy in criticizing the state of legal security in his donations.

Although, in general, the status of judges improved with professionalization and their new-found assertiveness, the limits of their agency got at the same time narrower and more exactly defined, as the bureaucratic state with its various division of roles developed. Like a number of other actors in the administration, the judges were controlled by the local community. In the seventeenth century, the essential source of legitimacy for justice was still therefore very much rooted in the "people", and at the local level.

The research on which this publication is based was funded by the Academy of Finland (grant no. 137741).

NOTES

1 Severin Bergh (ed.), *Svenska riksrådets protokoll: 7* (Stockholm 1892), p. 520.
2 Björn Asker, Striden om häradshövdingeämbetena under 1600-talet", *Historiskt Tidskrift för Finland* 72, 1987, p. 232.
3 Yrjö Blomstedt, *Laamannin- ja kihlakunnantuomarinvirkojen läänittäminen ja hoito Suomessa 1500- ja 1600-luvuilla (1523-1680). Oikeushistoriallinen tutkimus.* Historiallisia Tutkimuksia 51 (Helsinki: Finnish Historical Society, 1958), pp. 21-29; Asker, "Striden om häradshövdingeämbetena", pp. 224-225; Sten Claeson, *Häradshövdingeämbetet i senmedeltidens och Gustav Vasas Sverige.* Skrifter utgivna av Institutet för rättshistorisk forskning. Serien 1, Rättshistoriskt bibliotek 39 (Stockholm: Institutet för rättshistorisk forskning, 1987), pp. 197-198. The judicial administration of towns is not discussed in this chapter. For more on this, see Petri Karonen, "*Raastuvassa tavataan*". *Suomen kaupunkien hallinto- ja oikeuslaitoksen toimintaa ja virkamiehiä suurvalta-aikana* (Jyväskylä: Jyväskylän yliopisto, 1995).
4 Max Weber, *Economy and Society. An Outline of Interpretive Sociology* (University of California Press, 1978), pp. 784-802.
5 John McLaren, *Bewigged, Bothered and Bewildered: British Colonial Judges on Trial 1800-1900* (Toronto [Ont.]: University of Toronto Press, 2011).
6 On Early Modern "Judicial Revolution" and violence, see Bruce Lenman, Geoffrey Parker, "The State, the Community and Criminal Law in Early Modern Europe". In: Gatrell, V. A. C., Lenman, Bruce, Parker, Geoffrey (eds), *Crime and the Law: the social history of Crime in Western Europe since 1500* (London 1980), pp. 11-48; Österberg, Eva, Sogner, Sølvi (eds), *People meet the law: control and conflict-handling in the courts. The Nordic countries in the post-Reformation and pre-industrial period* (Oslo: Universitetsforlaget, 2000); Heikki Ylikangas, "What happened to violence? An analysis of the development of violence from mediaeval times to the early modern era based on Finnish source material". In: Lappalainen, Mirkka (ed.), *Five centuries of violence in Finland and the Baltic* (Helsinki: Suomen Akatemia, 1998), pp. 7-128; Olli Matikainen, *Verenperijät. Väkivalta ja yhteisön murros itäisessä Suomessa 1500-1600-luvulla.* Bibliotheca Historica 78 (Helsinki: The Finnish Literature Society, 2002).

7  Jan Eric Almquist, *Domarregler från den yngre landslagens tid* (Uppsala 1951).
8  C. J. Wahlberg, *Åtgärder för lagförbättring 1633–1665* (Upsala, 1878), pp. 89–92.
9  Armas Luukko, *Etelä-Pohjanmaan historia. 3, Nuijasodasta Isoonvihaan* (Seinäjoki: Etelä-Pohjanmaan maakuntaliitto, 1987), p. 344.
10  Blomstedt, *Laamannin- ja kihlakunnantuomarinvirkojen läänittäminen*, pp. 150–151, 203–204, 264, 327–335; On judges and law-readers in Sweden, compare also Jan Eric Almquist, *Lagsagor och domsagor i Sverige med särskild hänsyn till den judiciella indelningen* (Stockholm: Norstedt, 1954).
11  Johan Schmedemann, *Kongl. stadgar, förordningar, bref och resolutioner: ifrån åhr 1528, in til 1701, angående justitiæ och executions-ährender...* (Stockholm 1706), p. 113.
12  Blomstedt, *Laamannin- ja kihlakunnantuomarinvirkojen läänittäminen*, p. 353.
13  David Gaunt, *Utbildning till statens tjänst. En kollektivbiografi av stormaktstidens hovrättsauskultanter* (Uppsala: Uppsala universitet, 1975), pp. 177–180; Asker, "Striden om Häradshövdingeämbetena", pp. 246–251; see also Marianne Vasara-Aaltonen, "From well-travelled "Jacks of all-trades" to Domestic Lawyers: the educational and career backgrounds of Svea Court of Appeals Judges 1614–1809". In: Korpiola, Mia (ed.), *The Svea Court of Appeal in the Early Modern Period: Historical Reinterpretations and New Perspectives*. Rättshistoriska studier 26 (Stockholm: Institutet för rättshistorisk forskning, 2014), pp. 301–354.
14  For an overview of the Nordic development, see Österberg, Sogner (ed.), *People meet the Law*.
15  On interaction between judges and local community in seventeenth century criminal investigation, see Kustaa Vilkuna, *Neljä ruumista* (Helsinki: Teos, 2009); Riikka Miettinen, *Suicide in Seventeenth-Century Sweden: The Crime and Legal Praxis in the Lower Courts* (Tampere, 2015), pp. 164–191. On power relations of Finnish seventeenth century local rural communities, see Janne Haikari, *Isännän, Jumalan ja rehellisten miesten edessä. Vallankäyttö ja virkamiesten toimintaympäristöt satakuntalaisissa maaseutuyhteisöissä 1600-luvun jälkipuoliskolla* (Helsinki: The Finnish Literature Society, 2009).
16  Aulis Oja, "Turun hovioikeuden 1827 vanhempi arkisto". In: Blomstedt, Yrjö (toim.), *Turun hovioikeus 1623–1973* (Helsinki 1973).
17  Blomstedt, *Laamannin- ja kihlakunnantuomarinvirkojen läänittäminen*, p. 2.
18  Blomstedt, *Laamannin- ja kihlakunnantuomarinvirkojen läänittäminen*, pp. 21–29.
19  Erik Anthoni, "Sten Henrikssons häradshövdingebrev för Pikis härad", *Historist tidskrift för Finland* 34, 1950, p. 129.
20  On the role of the community, see Mia Korpiola, "Not without the Consent and Goodwill of the Common people: The community as a legal authority in Medieaval Sweden", *The Journal of Legal History* vol 35: 2 (2014), pp. 95–119.
21  Henrik Munktell, "Häradsrätt och häradsnämnd. En rättshistorisk översikt". In: *Domsagorna i Sverige* (Uppsala: Almqvist & Wiksell, 1944), p. 15; Jukka Korpela, *Viipurin läänin historia. 2, Viipurin linnaläänin synty* (Lappeenranta: Karjalan kirjapaino, 2004), p. 206.
22  Blomstedt, *Laamannin- ja kihlakunnantuomarinvirkojen läänittäminen*, pp. 31–34; Claeson, *Häradshövdingeämbetet*, p. 234.
23  Blomstedt, *Laamannin- ja kihlakunnantuomarinvirkojen läänittäminen*, p. 35.
24  Kimmo Katajala, *Suomalainen kapina. Talonpoikaislevottomuudet ja poliittisen kulttuurin muutos Ruotsin ajalla (n. 1150–1800)* (Helsinki: The Finnish Literature Society, 2002), pp. 168–179.
25  Ulla Koskinen, *Hyvien miesten valtakunta: Arvid Henrikinpoika Tawast ja aatelin toimintakulttuuri 1500-luvun lopun Suomessa* (Helsinki: The Finnish Literature Society, 2011), p. 245.
26  Blomstedt, *Laamannin- ja kihlakunnantuomarinvirkojen läänittäminen*, p. 143–145; Kauko Pirinen, *Savon historia. 2:1, Rajamaakunta asutusliikkeen aikakautena*

1534–1617 (Kuopio: Kustannuskiila, 1982), p. 483. On importance of authority and personal presence, See Dag Retsö, "Med hand och mun, med bud och brev. Närvaro och auktoritet i Sverige 1300–1560". In: Hallenberg, Mats, Linnarsson, Magnus (ed.), *Politiska rum* (Lund: Nordic Academic Press, 2014), pp. 101–117.

27  Helge Pohjolan-Pirhonen, *Olavinlinnan historialliset vaiheet* (Savonlinna: Pyhän Olavin kilta, 1973), pp. 204–205.

28  Kansallisarkisto (KA), Helsinki (Finnish National Archives). Voudintilit: Yleisiä asiakirjoja (Accounts of the Bailiffs: General dokuments) KA 215j: 23–30; Blomstedt, *Laamannin- ja kihlakunnantuomarinvirkojen läänittäminen*, p. 103.

29  Olli Matikainen, "Gödik Fincke ja aatelin ryhmäidentiteetin kriisi 1500-luvulla". In: Katajala-Peltomaa, Sari, Niemi, Marjaana, Sulkunen, Irma (toim.), *Usko, tiede ja historiankirjoitus. Suomalaisia maailmankuvia keskiajalta 1900-luvulle*. Historiallisia Tutkimuksia 271 (Helsinki: The Finnish Literature Society, 2016).

30  Wahlberg, *Åtgärder för lagförbättring*, pp. 16–17, 19–20; Blomstedt, *Laamannin- ja kihlakunnantuomarinvirkojen läänittäminen*, pp. 267–272, 345; Asker, "Striden om häradshövdingeämbetena", pp. 230–233;

31  Riksarkivet (SRA), Stockholm (Swedish National Archives). Skolosterssamlingen II. Herman Böcke to Matthias Soop 15th of May, 1639; Herman Böcke to Matthias Soop 8th of March, 1640.

32  Yrjö Blomstedt (toim.), *Turun hovioikeus 1623–1973* (Helsinki 1973), p. 153.

33  Asker, "Striden om häradshövdingeämbetena", p. 233. On Brahe and his influence, see Erik Pettersson, *Vicekungen. En biografi över Per Brahe den yngre* (Stockholm: Natur och Kultur, 2009); Marko Hakanen, *Vallan verkostoissa. Per Brahe ja hänen klienttinsä 1600-luvun Ruotsin valtakunnassa*. Jyväskylä Studies in Humanities 157 (Jyväskylä: Jyväskylän yliopisto, 2011).

34  SRA Skoklostersamlingen II vol.11: Turku Court of Appeal to Per Brahe 23rd of February, 1660; Per Brahe to Turku Court of Appeal 14th of March, 1660; Turku Court of Appeal to Per Brahe 5th of April, 1661.

35  SRA Rydboholmssamlingen vol 13: Zacharias Palmbaum to Per Brahe 15th of February, 1659.

36  SRA Rydboholmssamlingen vol 13: Johan Wassenius to Per Brahe 11th of February, 1661.

37  SRA Skoklostersamlingen II vol 11: Turku Court of Appeal to Per Brahe 30th of May, 1661.

38  Mauno Jokipii, *Suomen kreivi- ja vapaaherrakunnat II*. Historiallisia Tutkimuksia 58: 2 (Helsinki: Finnish Historical Society,1960), pp. 32–33.

39  Blomstedt, *Laamannin- ja kihlakunnantuomarinvirkojen läänittäminen*, p. 314.

40  Pia Letto-Vanamo, *Käräjäyhteisön oikeus. Oikeudenkäyttö Ruotsi-Suomessa ennen valtiollisen riidanratkaisun vakiintumista* (Helsinki 1995).

41  KA, Laamanninoikeuksien renovoidut tuomiokirjat, Karjala 1635–1645 (Judgment books of the Lagman's Court), KA ä 1, 335, 396.

42  Matikainen, *Verenperijät*, p. 83.

43  On Fleming family, see Anu Lahtinen, *Sopeutuvat, neuvottelevat, kapinalliset: Naiset toimijoina Flemingin sukupiirissä 1470–1620* (Helsinki: The Finnish Literature Society, 2007).

44  SRA Skoklostersamlingen II. Herman Fleming to Per Brahe 19th of March, 1646; Erkki Lehtinen, *Hallituksen yhtenäistämispolitiikka Suomessa 1600-luvulla* (Helsinki: Finnish Historical Society, 1961), p. 257.

45  McLaren, *Dewigged, Bothered, and Bewildered*, p. 283.

46  The sources for Rosenkrantz case: SRA Hovrätternas skrivelser till K.M. Åbo Hovrätt vol 3a. Turku Court of Appeal to Royal Majesty 16th of March, 1661, 10th of April, 1662; SRA Skoklostersamlingen II: Turku Court of Appeal to Per Brahe 12th of February, 1664; Krister Rosencrantz to Per Brahe 29th of April, 1664 ; Blomstedt, *Laamannin- ja kihlakunnantuomarinvirkojen läänittäminen*, p. 305.

47 Pentti Lempiäinen, *Oikeusjumalanpalvelus ja oikeussaarna* (Helsinki: Suomalainen teologinen kirjallisuusseura, 1981).
48 Blomstedt, *Laamannin- ja kihlakunnantuomarinvirkojen läänittäminen*, p. 151.
49 Seppo Aalto, *Kirkko ja kruunu siveellisyyden vartijoina. Seksuaalirikollisuus, esivalta ja yhteisö Porvoon kihlakunnassa 1621–1700* (Helsinki: Finnish Historical Society, 1996), pp. 156–160.
50 *Johan Rosenhanes dagbok 1652–1661*. Utgiven genom Arne Jansson (Stockholm: Samfundet för utgivande av handskrifter rörande Skandinaviens historia 1995), p. 60; On Rosenhane, see Piia Einonen, "Travelling Governor". In: Lamberg, Marko, Hakanen, Marko, Haikari, Janne (eds), *Physical and Cultural Space in Pre-industrial Europe. Methodological Approaches to Spatiality* (Lund: Nordic Academic Press, 2011), pp. 124–151.
51 *Johan Rosenhanes dagbok 1652–1661*, p. 17.
52 *Johan Rosenhanes dagbok 1652–1661*, p. 62.
53 Blomstedt, *Laamannin- ja kihlakunnantuomarinvirkojen läänittäminen*, p. 22; Olli Matikainen, *Iskuin ja lyönnein. Väkivalta ja käräjät Käkisalmen läänissä 1618–1651* (Jyväskylä: Jyväskylän yliopisto, 1995), p. 25.
54 See Antti Kujala, "Det svenska riket och dess undersåtar i Ingermanland och i Kexholms län på 1600-talet (1617–1658): kronans dialog med den lokala adeln och de ortodoxa bönderna och köpmännen", *Historisk tidskrift för Finland* 2011, pp. 131–161.
55 See Rudolf Thunander, *Hovrätt i Funktion. Göta hovrätt och brottmålen 1635–1699*. Skrifter utgivna av institutet för rättshistorisk forskning 49 (Stockholm: Institutet för rättshistorisk forskning, 1993); Korpiola (ed.), *The Svea Court of Appeal*.
56 *Johan Rosenhanes dagbok 1652–1661*, p. 61.
57 KA, Laamannioikeuksien renovoidut pöytäkirjat (Judgment books of the Lagman's Court), KA ä 1, 102.
58 KA, Laamannioikeuksien renovoidut pöytäkirjat (Judgment books of the Lagman's Court), KA ä 1, 209.
59 KA, Laamannioikeuksien renovoidut pöytäkirjat (Judgment books of the Lagman's Court), KA ä 1, 216–217v.
60 Blomstedt, *Kihlakunnan- ja laamanninvirkojen läänittäminen*, pp. 215–217; Aalto, *Kirkko ja kruunu siveellisyyden vartijoina*, pp. 131–133; Mirkka Lappalainen, *Pohjolan leijona. Kustaa II Adolf ja Suomi 1611–1632* (Helsinki: Siltala, 2014), pp. 230–233.
61 K.R. Melander, *Drag ur Åbo hovrätts äldre historia och ur rättsliv i Finland under förra hälften av 1600-talet* (Helsingfors: Juridiska föreningens i Finland, 1936), pp. 153–163.
62 KA, Kihlakunnanoikeuksien renovoidut pöytäkirjat ((Judgment books of the Judicial Districts), KA jj 6: 73.
63 KA, Laamannioikeuksien renovoidut pöytäkirjat (Judgment books of the Lagman's Court), KA ä 1, 230–231v.
64 KA, Laamannioikeuksien renovoidut pöytäkirjat (Judgment books of the Lagman's Court), KA ä 1, 343–343v.
65 KA, Kihlakunnanoikeuksien renovoidut pöytäkirjat ((Judgment books of the Judicial Districts), KA cc7: 325–326; *Blomstedt, kihlakunnan- ja laamanninvirkojen läänittäminen*, p. 306.
66 KA, Kihlakunnanoikeuksien renovoidut pöytäkirjat ((Judgment books of the Judicial Districts), KA cc7: 177v; 184v, 208, 305.

# Sources

## Archival sources

Kansallisarkisto (KA), Helsinki, (Finnish National Archives), Finland
    Kihlakunnanoikeuksien renovoidut tuomiokirjat (Judgment books of the Judicial Districts) (KA cc; jj)
        Laamannioikeuksien renovoidut tuomiokirjat (Judgment books of the Lagman's Court) (KA ä)
        Voudintilit: Yleisiä asiakirjoja (Accounts of the Bailiffs: General dokuments) (KA 215)
Riksarkivet (SRA), Stockholm, (Swedish National Archives), Sweden
    Hovrätternas skrivelser till K.M: Åbo Hovrätt
    Rydboholmssamlingen
    Skoklostersamlingen II.

## Printed sources

Almquist, Jan Eric 1951: *Domarregler från den tyngre landslagens tid*. Uppsala.
Bergh, Severin (red.) 1892. *Svenska riksrådets protokoll: 7*. Stockholm: Kungl. boktryckeriet P. A. Norstedt & söner.
Rosenhane, Johan (1995): *Johan Rosenhanes dagbok 1652–1661*. Utgiven genom Arne Jansson. Stockholm: Samfundet för utgivande av handskrifter rörande Skandinaviens historia.
Schmedemann, Johan 1706: *Kongl. stadgar, förordningar, bref och resolutioner: ifrån åhr 1528,in til 1701, angående justitiæ och executions-ährender...* Sålunda med flijt samlade och genom trycket i dagsliuset befordrade Joh. Schmedeman. Stockholm.
Wahlberg, C. J. 1878: *Åtgärder för lagförbättring 1633–1665*. Uppsala.

## Literature

Aalto, Seppo 1996: *Kirkko ja kruunu siveellisyyden vartijoina. Seksuaalirikollisuus, esivalta ja yhteisö Porvoon kihlakunnassa 1621–1700*. Bibliotheca Historica 12. Helsinki: Finnish Historical Society.
Almquist, Jan Eric 1954: *Lagsagor och domsagor i Sverige med särskild hänsyn till den judiciella indelningen*. Stockholm: Norstedt.
Anthoni, Erik 1950: "Sten Henrikssons häradshövdingebrev för Pikis härad", *Historiskt tidskrift för Finland 34*.
Asker, Björn 1987: "Striden om häradshövdingeämbetena under 1600-talet", *Historiskt Tidsrift för Finland 72*.
Blomstedt, Yrjö 1958: *Laamannin- ja kihlakunnantuomarinvirkojen läänittäminen ja hoito Suomessa 1500- ja 1600-luvuilla (1523–1680). Oikeushistoriallinen tutkimus.* Historiallisia Tutkimuksia 51. Helsinki: Finnish Historical Society.
Blomstedt, Yrjö (toim.) 1973: *Turun hovioikeus 1623–1973*. Helsinki.
Claeson, Sten 1987: *Häradshövdingeämbetet i senmedeltidens och Gustav Vasas Sverige*. Skrifter utgivna av Institutet för rättshistorisk forskning. Serien 1, Rättshistoriskt bibliotek 39. Stockholm: Institutet för rättshistorisk forskning.
Dawson, John P. 1968: *The Oracles of The Law*. Ann Arbor: The University of Michigan School of Law.

Einonen, Piia 2011: "Travelling Governour". In: Lamberg, Marko, Hakanen, Marko, Haikari, Janne (ed.), *Physical and Cultural Space in Pre-industrial Europe. Methodological Approaches to Spatiality.* Lund: Nordic Academic Press.

Gaunt, David 1975: *Utbildning till statens tjänst. En kollektivbiografi av stormaktstidens hovrättsauskultanter.* Studia Historica Upsaliensia 63. Uppsala: Uppsala universitet.

Haikari, Janne 2009: *Isännän, Jumalan ja rehellisten miesten edessä. Vallankäyttö ja virkamiesten toimintaympäristöt satakuntalaisissa maaseutuyhteisöissä 1600-luvun jälkipuoliskolla.* Bibliotheca Historica 121. Helsinki: The Finnish Literature Society.

Hakanen, Marko 2011: *Vallan verkostoissa. Per Brahe ja hänen klienttinsä 1600-luvun Ruotsin valtakunnassa.* Jyväskylä Studies in Humanities 157. Jyväskylä: Jyväskylän yliopisto.

Jokipii, Mauno 1960: *Suomen kreivi- ja vapaaherrakunnat I.* Historiallisia Tutkimuksia 58: 2. Helsinki: Finnish Historical Society.

Karonen, Petri 1995: *"Raastuvassa tavataan". Suomen kaupunkien hallinto- ja oikeuslaitoksen toimintaa ja virkamiehiä suurvalta-aikana.* Studia Historica Jyväskyläensia 51. Jyväskylä: Jyväskylän yliopisto. also [https://jyx.jyu.fi/dspace/handle/123456789/19532]

Katajala, Kimmo 2002: *Suomalainen kapina. Talonpoikaislevottomuudet ja poliittisen kulttuurin muutos Ruotsin ajalla (n. 1150–1800).* Historiallisia Tutkimuksia 212. Helsinki: The Finnish Literature Society.

Korpela, Jukka 2004: *Viipurin läänin historia. 2, Viipurin linnaläänin synty.* Lappeenranta: Karjalan kirjapaino.

Korpiola, Mia 2014: "Not without the Consent and Goodwill of the Common people: The community as a legal authority in Medieaval Sweden", *The Journal of Legal History vol 35: 2.*

Korpiola, Mia (ed.) 2014: *The Svea Court of Appeal in the Early Modern Period: Historical Reinterpretations and New Perspectives.* Rättshistoriska studier 26. Stockholm: Institutet för rättshistorisk forskning.

Koskinen, Ulla 2011: *Hyvien miesten valtakunta. Arvid Henrikinpoika Tawast ja aatelin toimintakulttuuri 1500-luvun lopun Suomessa.* Bibliotheca Historica 132. Helsinki: The Finnish Literature Society.

Kujala, Antti 2011: "Det svenska riket och dess undersåtar i Ingermanland och i Kexholms län på 1600-talet (1617–1658): kronans dialog med den lokala adeln och de ortodoxa bönderna och köpmännen", *Historisk tidskrift för Finland.*

Lahtinen, Anu 2007: *Sopeutuvat, neuvottelevat, kapinalliset: Naiset toimijoina Flemingin sukupiirissä 1470–1620.* Bibliotheca Historica 108. Helsinki: The Finnish Literature Society.

Lappalainen, Mirkka 2014: *Pohjolan leijona. Kustaa II Adolf ja Suomi 1611–1632.* Helsinki: Siltala.

Lehtinen, Erkki 1961: *Hallituksen yhtenäistämispolitiikka Suomessa 1600-luvulla (1600–n. 1680).* Historiallisia Tutkimuksia 60. Helsinki: Finnish Historical Society.

Lempiäinen, Pentti 1981: *Oikeusjumalanpalvelus ja oikeussaarna.* Helsinki: Suomalainen teologinen kirjallisuusseura.

Lenman, Bruce, Parker, Geoffrey 1980: "The State, the community and criminal law in Early Modern Europe". In: Gatrell, V.A.C., Lenman, Bruce, Parker, Geoffrey (eds), *Crime and the Law: the social history of Crime in Western Europe since 1500.* London: Salem House Academic Division.

Letto-Vanamo, Pia 1995: *Käräjäyhteisön oikeus. Oikeudenkäyttö Ruotsi-Suomessa ennen valtiollisen riidanratkaisun vakiintumista.* Oikeushistorian julkaisuja 2. Helsingin yliopisto. Rikos- ja prosessioikeuden sekä oikeuden yleistieteiden laitos. Helsinki: Helsingin yliopisto.

Luukko, Armas 1987: *Etelä-Pohjanmaan historia. 3, Nuijasodasta Isoonvihaan.* Seinäjoki: Etelä-Pohjanmaan maakuntaliitto.

Matikainen, Olli 1995: *Iskuin ja lyönnein. Väkivalta ja käräjät Käkisalmen läänissä 1618–1651.* Suomen historian julkaisuja 22. Jyväskylä: Jyväskylän yliopisto.

Matikainen, Olli 2002: *Verenperijät. Väkivalta ja yhteisön murros itäisessä Suomessa 1500–1600-luvulla.* Bibliotheca Historica 78. Helsinki: The Finnish Literature Society.

Matikainen, Olli 2016: "Gödik Fincke ja aatelin ryhmäidentiteetin kriisi 1500-luvulla". In: Katajala-Peltomaa, Sari, Niemi, Marjaana, Sulkunen, Irma (toim.), *Usko, tiede ja historiankirjoitus. Suomalaisia maailmankuvia keskiajalta 1900-luvulle.* Historiallisia Tutkimuksia 271. Helsinki: The Finnish Literature Society.

McLaren, John 2011: *Dewigged, Bothered, and Bewildered. British Colonial Judges on Trial,* 1800–1900. Toronto [Ont.]: University of Toronto Press.

Melander, K.R. 1936: *Drag ur Åbo hovrätts äldre historia och ur rättsliv i Finland under förra hälften av 1600-talet.* Helsingfors: Juridiska föreningens i Finland.

Miettinen, Riikka 2015: *Suicide in Seventeenth-Century Sweden: The Crime and Legal Praxis in the Lower Courts.* Tampere.

Munktell, Henrik 1944: "Häradsrätt och häradsnämnd. En rättshistorisk översikt". In: *Domsagorna i Sverige,* Uppsala: Almqvist & Wiksell.

Oja, Aulis 1973: "Turun hovioikeuden 1827 vanhempi arkisto". In: Blomstedt, Yrjö (toim.), *Turun hovioikeus 1623–1973.* Helsinki.

Pettersson, Erik 2009: *Vicekungen. En biografi över Per Brahe den yngre.* Stockholm: Natur och Kultur.

Pirinen, Kauko 1982: *Savon historia. 2:1, Rajamaakunta asutusliikkeen aikakautena 1534–1617.* Kuopio: Kustannuskiila.

Pohjolan-Pirhonen, Helge 1973: *Olavinlinnan historialliset vaiheet.* Savonlinna: Pyhän Olavin kilta.

Retsö, Dag 2014: "Med hand och mun, med bud och brev. Närvaro och auktoritet i Sverige 1300–1560". In: Hallenberg, Mats, Linnarsson, Magnus (red.), *Politiska rum.* Lund: Nordic Academic Press.

Thunander, Rudolf 1993: *Hovrätt i funktion. Göta hovrätt och brottmålen 1635–1699.* Rättshistoriskt bibliotek. Skrifter utgivna av institutet för rättshistorisk forskning 49. Stockholm: Institutet för rättshistorisk forskning.

Vasara-Aaltonen, Marianne 2014: "From well-travelled "Jacks of all-trades" to Domestic Lawyers: the educational and career backgrounds of Svea Court of Appeals Judges 1614–1809". In: Korpiola, Mia (ed.), *The Svea Court of Appeal in the Early Modern Period: Historical Reinterpretations and New Perspectives.* Rättshistoriska studier 26. Stockholm: Institutet för rättshistorisk forskning.

Weber, Max 1978: *Economy and Society. Economy and society. An outline of interpretive sociology.* Vol. 2. Berkeley: University of California Press.

Vilkuna, Kustaa 2009: *Neljä ruumista.* Helsinki: Teos.

Ylikangas, Heikki 1998: "What happened to violence? An analysis of the development of violence from mediaeval times to the early modern era based on Finnish source material". In: Lappalainen, Mirkka (ed.), *Five centuries of violence in Finland and the Baltic.* Helsinki: Suomen Akatemia.

Österberg, Eva, Sogner, Sølvi (eds) 2000: *People meet the law: Control and conflicthandling in the courts. The Nordic countries in the post-Reformation and pre-industrial period.* Oslo: Universitetsforlaget.

# VI Bailiffs

Janne Haikari

# The Bailiff: Between a Rock and a Hard Place (1600–1690)?

Bailiffs were one of the key groups to contribute in the formation process of the Swedish state in the early modern period. Gustavus Vasa (1496–1560) needed them to provide the Crown with access to local resources: taxes and military recruitment. Consequently crown bailiffs (*befalningsman, crono fougde*) became the lowest rung on the ladder of the emerging administrative organisation. A bailiff could be defined as the single most prominent person within early modern Swedish local communities in embodying the Crown and its bureaucracy, given that tax collection is considered one of the key symbols of legitimacy in society.[1]

The main task of crown bailiffs was still basically quite simple in the seventeenth century. They were supposed to take care of the practical logistics of tax collection. It was their duty to raise the money or other payments due to the Crown. Their bailiwick, which was often referred to as a 'hundred' (*härad*), could sometimes cover more than one parish and have been comprised of several hundred farms. Overall, the finances of the Crown were heavily dependent on the performance of the bailiffs, as it was down to their ability to accumulate the Crown's assets each year. This meant they were under constant pressure from above, and yet remain sensitive to the problems of those being taxed, who often wanted concessions for a variety of reasons.[2]

Such an environment raises interesting questions about personal agency. What were the ideal personal characteristics required for a bailiff to fulfil these often conflicting demands? What factors limited his activities? What was it like to be in a community that was accustomed to constant interaction with the authorities? How did the community generally view the actions of the bailiff?

In this chapter, the personal agency of bailiffs will be outlined from the various perspectives of different sources. In the first case, the perspective is from that of administrative officials who worked in the County of Pori,[3] and this will provide the starting point for a general model of agency. In the second, Finnish local history studies and biographical studies and records[4] will provide more detailed information about the personal agency of bailiffs in terms of their day-to-day local work, and the careers of those in the office. The third perspective will be in terms of the official instructions bailiffs received from the Crown. This will be analysed whilst also bearing in mind other laws and codes that defined the agency of those in office. As we shall see, the agency under discussion is actually not just the agency of crown bailiffs but also of those officials who carried out similar duties even if they had a different title.

The difficult position of bailiffs stuck between the Crown and the common people has certainly been recognised, but only a few researchers have focused on the realities of their work in detail. Mats Hallenberg has approached the case of sixteenth century bailiffs of the Swedish Realm from the perspective of organisational theories, especially New Institutional Economics theory (NIE). In his extensive study, Hallenberg argues that during the sixteenth and early seventeenth centuries, bailiffs essentially became brokers in facilitating the exploitation of resources for the Crown through their personal abilities and various ties to the community, which were of course backed up by royal authority. Since people paid their dues not only in money, but also in kind (with the various products they produced), the bailiff had to be able to give these goods a value, and if necessary, to negotiate an adequate amount of them and in a form the Crown could use. The transportation, storage and sale of these goods also demanded logistical skills from the bailiff. If there had been a crop failure or any other disaster, the bailiff had to also take these into account. At times something had to be given in exchange, for example, postponements of payment and certain tax allowances. Consequently the relationship between the bailiffs and the people being taxed became mutual and confidential.[5]

This brokerage seems to play a familiar role throughout European early modern societies, and Hallenberg shows that it is a useful concept in Swedish history too. However, his perspective comes more from the official hierarchy above bailiffs, rather than from the bailiffs themselves. Indeed, the theories behind Hallenberg's compelling overview seem to emphasise that the chief motive behind bailiffs' exploitation of resources was the state formation process; and while he does not totally neglect the individual nature of each bailiff's agency, he is clearly focusing more on organisational logic rather than on the personal sphere of the individual. Hallenberg thus pays less attention to the actual interaction involved in this brokerage, not to mention the dynamics of each local community that the bailiff was responsible for. Another point to bear in mind is that Hallenberg's study discusses primarily the sixteenth century. Equally, many other previous studies on bailiffs have also approached the subject from the view of central administration and in terms of the long-term historical development of the modern state.[6]

This chapter focuses solely on the seventeenth century bailiffs, because during the sixteenth century the agency of bailiffs was still in the making. Their position was not cemented in the Crown's organisation despite their obvious contribution to effectiveness of taxation system. It was only in the next century when the office of bailiff became an established part of administrative organization, although the position and duties of crown bailiffs evolved even then. Overall, the history of crown bailiffs in the seventeenth century is a twofold story of development and division. The profession was consolidated through the same major reforms that restructured the administration as a whole, not least by the reconstruction of provincial administration in 1635. The position of bailiffs became more established and distinct, as general administrative norms became more precise. At the same time, however, their sphere of operations became subject to constant experiments and changes.[7]

In the 1620s and 1630s, the Crown leased out taxation rights to private tax collectors (*arrendators*), and although this system was abandoned, in 1640s and 1650s the Crown granted increasing numbers of landed properties to the nobility. These 'donations' included taxation rights. Consequently, the crown bailiffs had often had to hand over some of their duties to colleagues, who worked for those of the nobility who had been given the right to levy taxes. These factors fragmented the work of bailiffs but also expanded the profession. Despite the increasing number of donations made, the Crown did not cut down its own administration completely, because the Crown did still have some claims in the donated areas. Consequently, there could be two bailiffs working in the same area in many parts of the country from the 1650s to 1680s, whose tasks were similar. Once these were pruned back in the "Great Reduction" in the 1680s, the taxation rights were once more sold off again to private tax collectors.[8]

In the 1650s there were 20 counties (*grevskap*) and 34 baronies (*friherrskap*) in Sweden. They were the most extensive form of donations measured in both numbers of farms and transferred power, as the noble holders of the counties and baronies received various administrative rights in addition to the rights to collect taxes. Therefore they usually set up their own administration that took care of tax collection. However, they were still obliged to follow the same patterns of governance as the Crown's administration, and in many cases the key figure in the new county or barony administration was also called 'bailiff' whose job description was similar to the crown bailiff's. In some donations, the bailiff acted alone, while in others he had a superior who was expected to coordinate the management of the donated area while the bailiff concentrated on tax collection. Another bailiff category consisted of those servants who were hired to take care of the mansions or the smaller donations under the nobility's jurisdiction. They were often called bailiffs too, and although their sphere of administration was considerably smaller than that of the colleagues in larger units, they were principally in a similar position to them.[9]

In the case of Björneborg County (Pori), two officials were hired at the beginning of 1651. Påwal Callia (d. 1692) was installed as a bailiff and Hans Hansson Gode (c. 1620–1685), became his 'inspector' (*inspektor*). Callia took care of the practical tasks, including tax collection, while Gode was primarily responsible for coordination and the transportation of goods from Finland to Stockholm. Both Callia and Gode were expected to correspond with Count Gustaf Horn (the noble who had received the donation, 1592–1657), and then Countess Sigrid Bielke (1620–1679) after his death in 1657. This changed, however, in 1671 when Bielke suspended Gode for alleged malpractices and ordered Callia to take over all administrative tasks in the county. Pori County had crown bailiffs operating alongside county officials in the same parishes too, because some of the taxes were still due to the Crown despite the donation; while sometimes in other counties and baronies, both Crown and county might even be served by the same official.[10]

Another change that occurred during the seventeenth century was that crown bailiffs, although officially on the lowest rung of the administrative ladder, began to delegate the practicalities of tax collection to lower administrative officials, such as the rural police chief (*länsman*).[11] Indeed, studies of Finnish local history show that, at the start of the seventeenth century, the rural police chief was the person most involved with tax collection in those parishes that were not already part of counties or baronies. As his superior, the crown bailiff mainly monitored this collection process and only intervened if there was some issue that needed to be resolved.[12]

There have been previous studies on Swedish local communities, which have been described as either 'political' or 'interactional', because there were official and legitimate channels for common people to have an influence on matters such as taxation or military recruitment. But in most cases the main focus of these studies has been on the institutions and structures themselves, rather than the bailiffs.[13] Generally speaking, the only time the role of bailiffs has come to the fore is when there were reports of conflict within local communities. In such conflicts over taxation or military recruitment, the bailiff would be the one to bear the brunt of opposition, as those being taxed often suspected the officials nearest them as being the ones responsible for any perceived injustices, leaving them exposed to accusations and suspicions.[14] Such findings are significant, but because they only crop up in times of crisis, so they perhaps do not adequately portray the normal state of affairs.

The notion of bailiffs being stuck between a rock and a hard place in this manner, is not exactly new, as the wording of the 1688 instructions for crown bailiffs reveal. The formula for the oath of office required the bailiff to pledge himself accountable for all his duties "in front of God, his Royal Majesty, his Chamber Collegium, and every honest man".[15] This same statement describes the starting point of agency for bailiffs, which is examined in this chapter too. Demands were posed on bailiffs from a number of different directions, some of which related to his practical tasks while others urged him to consider his actions in moral or cultural terms.

## *Defining agency – the regulations and norms that applied to bailiffs*

In the seventeenth century, crown bailiffs were obliged to follow written instructions. They were usually drafted individually, but they all followed roughly the same pattern. Duke Charles (1550–1611) had published common instructions for all bailiffs in Finland back in 1602, but it was not until 1688 that the first general directive for crown bailiffs across the whole country was published. Other bailiffs serving donation-holders usually received similar written instructions from their respective masters, but these obviously varied a lot.[16]

The crown bailiff instructions of 1688 contain a lengthy list of tasks divided into 25 chapters. The main role of the bailiff remained the same, even though political power became more centralized in the 1670s and 1680s with the accession Charles XI (1655–1697) to the Swedish throne. The overall priority was still to collect all the various taxes and to deliver them to the Crown's depots on time. The instructions provided step-by-step guidelines on the best way to carry this out. They specified the documents required for the different phases of tax collection; the correct procedures for securing the legitimacy of all activities; the decrees and royal orders that had to be taken into account in the process; and how the bailiff was supposed to cooperate with other crown officials.[17] Most importantly of all, the crown bailiffs had to take an oath to carry out their duties in front of the local court, which made people aware of both the bailiff's authority and his obligations. As they heard him take his oath, the common people were both symbolically and literally granted the position of supervising the actions of the bailiff.[18]

The instructions of 1688 are significantly longer than, for example, the instructions of Duke Charles from 1602, and they show a shift towards systematizing the bureaucracy. Yet they are far from comprehensive, and remain rather abstract. Instead of detailing the work more thoroughly, the 1688 instructions nebulously demand that the bailiff should personally acquire the knowledge of how to take care of the task. One stipulated requirement, for example, is simply to have a "penetrating insight" into administrative matters; another is to keep a "watchful eye" over them; and another is to "be informed" of crucial "factors" whatever they might be. In this respect, the instructions place expectations more on the personality of the bailiff rather than on the precise nature of the tasks themselves. In most cases this meant for the bailiff was expected to act "diligently" or "with all his might" to fulfil his duties (in other words, to be loyal).[19]

These generalised guidelines suggest that, in practice, bailiffs often had to take the initiative and be personally responsible for their actions, as it seemed clear for most of the time that the bailiff would face unforeseen circumstances. Thus the exact details of each bailiff's agency were defined more by his individual skills, and the demands specific to his surroundings, than the guidelines. What the oath of office from 1688 did, was put into words the already commonly accepted belief that bailiffs should have a strong moral conscience and commitment, not only to the Crown, but also to God.

This wording was evidently familiar to the officials of Pori County, for example when, in 1672, both Påwal Callia and Hans Hansson Gode defended their actions in correspondence by insisting that their conscience was pure and that, if necessary, they would be willing to stand in front of God to answer any accusations. This is also apparent in Countess Bielke asking them if there was anything "on their conscience". Paradoxically, the fundamental law which presupposed any member of society taking an oath in public, was that he was clearing his name of any suspicious criminal activity. Another factor to bear in mind, was that Lutheranism was at the heart of state-building in seventeenth century Sweden. Not only did its teachings serve the interests of the Crown in terms of how resources were exploited, but pastors could also urge their congregation to also keep an eye on whether there were any corrupt officials (as well as pay their taxes on time). The role of pastors in local community is discussed in another chapter of this book.[20]

Administrative work's moral core reflected the commonly accepted notion that God was arbitrating over what was good and bad; and this naturally increased the pressure of work on bailiffs and other state officials. People were always accountable to God in the end. In fact, this idea that "you only reap what you sow" was referred to on several different occasions by people in Pori County. For example, Sigrid Bielke referred to it when she fired Gode in 1672. Perhaps these kinds of statements were simply rhetorical formulas repeated as a matter of routine, and it is indeed difficult to know just how religious these people were being, seeing as none of them contemplates this in detail; but neglecting these statements altogether would be equally wrong, as they at least represented the ideals of good governance. Church and God was therefore disciplining not just the common people, but the administration too.[21]

In Pori County, officials willingly defended and explained their actions using biblical arguments. For example, Påwal Callia was a bailiff who fought with his brother Henrich Callia (d. 1675) for decades. During this time and to complicate matters, Henrich himself had two crown bailiff appointments, so the family feud soon turned into a larger administrative issue at times (rising to a head in the 1670s). Both brothers tried to harm each other's reputation by accusing the other of all kinds of misconduct, and then when suddenly Henrich Callia died from a disease in the spring of 1675, his brother felt it was the ultimate sign of God's blessing. Påwal Callia had previously asked God mete out "the punishment and shame" he felt that his brother deserved. "Please God, don't let him go unpunished," he had urged, and when his brother died, he explained in a letter that God "in his amazing wisdom, has punished my brother's house with a black cross". Before his death, Henrich Callia had foreseen similar fate to his brother. Henrich had pledged his innocence to his superior governor (*landshövding*) Harald Oxe (1628–1689) and sworn that he was ready to stand in front of God with a clear conscience, reassuring his superior that it was Påwal Callia who was destined to the ultimate penalty of death. Henrich predicted that "[t]he head of the instigator will fall".

There was always a moral dimension to the bailiff's agency, with the question looming over him of whether his conduct was just in the eyes both of the Crown and the people he collected taxes from. Another 'unwritten' code (at least for the most part), was related to domestic household conventions of the time. Being in front of the king, or nobility responsible for taxation in an area, was in many ways the same as a servant presenting himself before his master, and it meant following the rules of patriarchal hierarchy. Tax administration therefore followed the principles that determined nearly all other social interaction, i.e., the rules of a domestic household, where family was the most important ideal. Accordingly, this relationship was not based on a salary, but more like a familial connection where the bailiff had the 'junior' role.[22]

Loyalty and devotion were expected from juniors in a society where the norms of patriarchal family life were familiar to everyone. Indeed, the rules for behaviour inside a family were not just biblically defined, but also found in the so-called 'oeconomic' literature. These books aimed at educating nobility in becoming good masters and managers of property. Essentially, the main message was that there were no shortcuts for achieving this. The nobility had to devote themselves to agriculture and in so doing, would contribute to the fundamental reorganisation of society along the lines of a smooth-running household. Oeconomics championed the noble household (or estate doctrine), rather than that of the Crown or lower estates, to such a point that the agency of its officials were virtually synonymous with the ideals and virtues of a good nobleman. This personal devotion was enough to endorse the office-holder.[23]

Oeconomic literature also contained information on how to manage the landed properties, thus providing guidelines for officials who managed the donations, even though they were not usually of noble origin. Bailiffs were expected to dedicate themselves intensively to all the details of management. The ideals were presented in the context of a single manor economy, but again they were expandable to larger settings. Concrete examples of good conduct could be applied to any scale of management. The guides instructed how the bailiff should behave in everyday life. For example, it was recommended that the bailiff enjoy his meals among the servants so that there would be no reason for them to believe that the bailiff was having the best pieces of meat. Transparency was needed, because the bailiff had to be morally superior to the servants below him, and honourable conduct would help him gain respect and loyalty from his subordinates.[24]

Eventually oeconomic thought promoted the idea that bailiffs should be like fathers of a family, who should treat their 'estate' in the same way as they would raise their own children. The bailiff's agency was therefore not simply focused on the practicalities of securing the best possible revenue. Ultimately, they also had to be sensitive to promoting the right mentality and morality among the people they worked with. Bailiffs thus not only had to show obedience, but also to breed it in those around them.

## *The process of collecting taxes*

The Swedish taxation system in the seventeenth century consisted of a number of taxes that all were related to the capacity of each farm. The size and quality of landed properties defined the tax rates; and the manpower in each farm also counted to a certain degree. The tax rates were recorded in the Crown's account books, and although tax collectors at the local level regularly assessed the conditions in which their taxpayers lived, the key figures marked in the Land Charge Register (*jordebok*) were rarely changed during the seventeenth century; and this provided a solid foundation for taxation. And yet, although the basics of the system did not change radically, there were several new taxes that were introduced in the first decades of the seventeenth century. As a whole, the taxation system was now therefore a complex set of different contributions, which were deliverable to a number of parties: the Crown, the nobility, local trustees and the Church.

The taxes were collected according to an established schedule. In most regions they were traditionally paid on certain days, which were usually in the autumn after the crop had been harvested. Once collected, the taxes were thoroughly verified on their way to the Crown's warehouses to make sure they got there. The crown bailiffs kept accounts of all the tax revenue collected, and if it had not been paid in full, they had to provide a verifiable explanation for the amount missing. Without an acceptable excuse they were considered personally responsible for the loss, and it shows just how much pressure they were under from the hierarchical crown administration. A confirmation for the reasons as to why an amount was missing would have to be obtained from the local court, and the bailiffs working for the nobility usually followed a similar procedure too, if they had an amount missing from their coffers and needed to account for it.[25]

In normal local circumstances, the established system left little room for negotiation between the tax collector and taxed. However, it was fairly common for these circumstances to not be normal. In fact, the climate in Sweden became colder in the seventeenth century and crop failures often hampered agriculture throughout the century, culminating in a great famine in the 1690s. In Finland alone, the population decreased by 30%, with more than 100,000 people dying through famine and disease.[26]

It was not unusual that the bailiffs failed to secure the tax reliefs from the authorities that they had promised the poverty-stricken farmer. In these cases the crown bailiff was usually suspended from his position and had to pay the missing amount from his own pocket. The alternative was for the bailiff to try and get the money from the farmer after all. If he was a wealthy man, he could survive his dismissal from office but it could also mean a loss of stable income. Grels Eskilsson worked as the crown bailiff for the area of Ylä-Satakunta (1639–1640) and accumulated a debt of 800 *riksdaler* for uncollected taxes. Eventually, the Crown decided to confiscate all his landed properties – at least two farms – to recover the debt. Grels Eskilsson did not deny the debt as such, but he felt injustice at the confiscation process and eventually burned his farms out of anger and desperation.[27]

Even in the midst of a famine it could be difficult for bailiffs to convince those higher in the administration that it would be difficult to collect taxes in full. Perhaps one of the most extreme examples of this, is the case of Jacob Saringius (d. 1714). He worked as a manor bailiff in the 1690s under Count Axel Julius De la Gardie (1637–1710) and baroness Sofia Juliana Forbus (1649–1701), nobility who had lost much of their tax income in the Great Reduction. They were reluctant to accept any tax reliefs the bailiff was suggesting despite the great famine of 1696–1697 that had stricken their manors and those working in them. The bailiff hoped that the nobility in charge might instead send grain to ease the plight of the people, as one could expect honourable master to do, but the countess mostly neglected his reports and instead blamed Saringius for writing too rarely.[28]

It was common that nobility who lived far from their possessions were suspicious of their servants. Countess Sigrid Bielke, for instance, had misgivings about the honesty of Hans Gode (the inspector of Pori County) for years, but she dismissed him only after she had arrived personally from Stockholm to Pori to supervise the management of the county. It was in fact the only time the countess had deigned to visit, and even though it was difficult to find clear-cut evidence for corruption, she dismissed Gode, not only blaming him for the low tax income, but also for infrequent communication. As such, the suspicions were not unusual, but considering the amount of agency bailiffs usually had, these doubts were worst when a bailiff could not be supervised face-to-face.

Up to a certain point, bailiffs were free agents, in spite of the pressures on them from various directions. For sure they had to correspond with their superiors by letter and send them records of everything, but for day-to-day activities they were left to be the unsupervised leader of a group. This was very much the case for bailiffs operating on behalf of donation-holders, who were often several hundred kilometers away in Stockholm or elsewhere. The setting gave them space, but at the same time it was the ultimate source for distrust, and one of the main reasons for demanding accurate records and regular correspondence. Securing the confidence of the higher authorities was thus one of the key requirements for bailiffs who wished to maintain their agency, whether serving the Crown or nobility. One of the best ways to maintain this confidence was to actively investigate situations where the official rates of tax could not be met, and documenting the reasons for the deficit.

The tax collector had to find valid reasons to explain why sometimes the correct amount of tax could not be paid, and after assessing the level of poverty, it was necessary to define a reasonable level of tax that could be met. This process presupposed localised knowledge of the parish. Had there been climate factors contributing to the crop failure? Were specific fields more prone to frost or flooding? The tax collectors had to have precise information on each farm in their tax area, and whatever they settled on as the level of required taxes they had to be able to justify firmly but sensitively. In Pori County, the bailiff Påwal Callia spared no efforts in trying to gather such relevant information from every corner of the county, but there was no way he could cover hundreds of farmsteads by himself, so he hired assistants to help him in the task; and it eventually became common practice that various officials and servants of authority in the local area would assess the ability to pay tax as a group.[29]

The same pattern was followed elsewhere too, so that the bailiffs (working for both the Crown and donation-holders) could get a better overview of the local conditions. Of all the people in the seventeenth century who became roped into this task, the local court and its jurors became perhaps the most important organ for assessing the degree of hardship that taxpayers were suffering. Bailiffs became officially obliged to seek confirmation on key information for tax collection from the court. The jurors were supposed to confirm the list of unpaid taxes that had been a result of negotiations between the various taxpayers and the official responsible for collecting their tax. The local community itself selected the jurors to their position and, by being the ones to give them the authority to assess hardship, added an element of negotiation into the process.[30]

It is also worth noting that, in the seventeenth century, although bailiffs were supposed to be in the front line of negotiations about the level of tax between the common people and the higher authorities, the process was starting to be less in their hands. Instead, they were the ones who coordinated and supervised tax collection (and any tax relief decisions) while the actual fieldwork was assigned to servants and trustees in the local community. The rural police chief, jurors, and other local officials were often the people who actually faced the common people in many districts; and local historical studies unequivocally suggest that rural police chief became the main executive for tax collection at the local level during the seventeenth century.

But arrangements varied for those collecting on behalf of the nobility with taxation rights. In Pori County, the rural police chief remained a peripheral administration figure. Inspector Hans Hansson Gode was responsible for coordinating taxation, while Påwal Callia (the bailiff) was regularly in contact with the people, keeping an eye on the harvest in all districts of the county. He had assistants helping him gather information, but he was the one who seems to have been at the 'chalkface' between the administration and common people. He knew what the nobility in charge expected, and he knew what folk were able to actual deliver. In the Barony of Kimito, the key figure in sole charge for the whole process of collecting taxes, keeping records (and transporting the taxes collected) was known as the *amtman*. He had assistants, but he was the one who went face-to-face with the common people in the barony, or at least he was expected to do so. When, after a poor tax income, Count Axel Oxenstierna (1583–1654) would give the go-ahead for a tax investigation and collection to be made, the amtman was urged to be personally involved in the process.[31]

Although there was local expertise among tax collectors, there was of course always the potential for conflict. There would be disagreements over just how serious the damages were that made it difficult to pay taxes, even after the case had been addressed in the court. This was the moment when the agency of the bailiffs and their team was truly tested. After the jurors had confirmed the fact that there were taxes left unpaid, the tax collector could try to repossess the debt against the will of tax debtors, and the seizure of goods could turn into a heated conflict involving physical force.

Several local historical studies report that it often occurred that punches were thrown and insults exchanged when tax was being collected. For example in the parish of Raisio, the crown bailiff, Henrik Isaksson, and his servants went to the farm of Jöran Thomasson to repossess unpaid taxes in 1625. The farmer first tried to resist by grabbing the bailiff by the throat, but the bailiff was stronger and pushed him away, so then he tried to prevent the bailiff's servants from taking away his oxen; but in the end they managed to take it anyway. Meanwhile, in Kalajoki, the wife of the farmer Matti Leppänen confronted the rural police chief's servant who had come in 1639 for the same reason with a punch in the face. Also in Kalajoki, Sipi Tulppo tried to strike a juror and bailiff's servant with an axe in 1695.[32] So it seems clear that the bailiff or any official about to seize goods for taxes unpaid had to be prepared for the possibility of a violent reaction. At the very least, the tax collector had to be able to defend himself, but it was better if the aggressive behaviour could also be restrained (and physically if necessary).

The agency of a tax collector could thus require a certain physical character, but the tensions did not always end in a brawl – insults were sometimes enough. In Ulvila, Anders Pedersson and his family greeted the crown bailiff's tax collectors with foul language in 1639, and refused to open their granary or to assist the bailiff in any way; so the bailiff was apparently forced to break down the door of the granary and measure out the right amount of grain that would equal the tax owed. He then ordered Pedersson to carry the grain sacks down to the river bank, but he refused again to cooperate, and the two men started pushing each other. It did not escalate into a full-scale fight, but the end result was that the bailiff could not take the sacks with him.[33] In such cases, forced confiscation was thus not an option, and instead the bailiff would try and calm things down, in the hope that compliance would be achieved this way instead. Eloquence was one example of the kind of interactional skill that would certainly help the tax collector in this respect; and the ability to handle insults with apt remarks about common human decency could prove very helpful to a bailiff.

During the course of his whole career as a bailiff, it seems Påwal Callia only had a couple of really major conflicts over tax collection. For example, he fought with Markus Matsson Kouvo over a period of several years in the 1650s, as he was unwilling to pay taxes according to the official rates. Eventually Callia went to his farm with his servants and repossessed a set of goods against Kouvo's will. Among other things, they took 14 barrels of grain, five cows, one ox and confiscated the key to his granary. Kouvo appealed to Count Gustaf Horn and Countess Sigrid Bielke, who returned the case to the local court. In addition to complaining about the repossessed items, Kouvo blamed the bailiff for cheating and abusing his power. He said that the bailiff had been using false meters on the tax parcels he had already sent and that he had therefore not properly recorded the amount of tax paid. At this point, Kouvo's complaints were addressed in detail, and the court found out that all the actions of the bailiff had in fact been legal and conducted in an appropriate manner.[34]

The courtroom was also the place where the bailiff could instigate other means to exact repayment of tax debts. If, after there had been tax debts for three years or more, and there was no room for negotiation (nor grain, cattle, or money left); then the whole farm could eventually be repossessed. At this point the property rights could be transferred from the tax defaulter to the Crown or nobility in charge of taxation. This touches on a larger social issue that has otherwise not really been discussed in most previous studies,[35] but from the bailiff's perspective it was a simple case that criteria had to be met, and that was that. For Påwal Callia it seemed to be both a procedure that must be carried out, and a threat that could be used as leverage. The transfer of ownership did not necessarily mean being directly cast off the land, but it certainly made this a more obvious possibility, and encouraged people to pay their taxes on time; even if this procedure was carried out in a variety of ways in the different bailiwicks of Sweden.

Bailiffs also had to be alert to the fact that peasants could resist their efforts by making legitimate appeals to the highest echelons of the administration. However, it was more usual that appeals to higher authority would only be allowed after they had first been thoroughly examined in the local court. But this was sometimes enough, as the local courts did not always rule in the bailiff or tax collector's favour. In the early 1620s, for example, the crown bailiff of the 'hundred' of Halikko, Mats Olafsson, approached a member of the nobility who had not collected taxes from one of his subjects and ordered his men arrest both the noble and subject until the tax had been paid; but in court his actions were deemed extortionate, and the bailiff was sentenced to pay fines for disturbing the peace.

In another case, dating from the 1670s, the crown bailiff Kristian Willingshusen of Northern Ostrobothnia was suspended from his duties, after there were complaints to the governor from the locals about his harsh methods of collecting taxes. The local pastor (*kyrkioherde*), Ericus Granberg (1620–1687) helped his parishioners write their complaints. Some time before this, in the 1650s, Crown Bailiff of the hundred of Lohtaja, Jöran Jöransson, ended up losing his title after attempting to repossess some property by force. He had also demanded from those who had not paid enough tax for them to give him a lift on their horses without legitimate grounds. Meanwhile, in Kalajoki, the chief of the rural police, Carl Persson, was suspended from duty after the local court found that he had forced people to let him have a ride on their horse to settle private matters, whilst also demanding payments for military expenditure that were too much. Again, it was the Church (Vicar Josef Mathesius, 1640–1689) who came to the defence of the common people and was behind these accusations.[36]

All tax grievances could also be addressed directly to the diet, but it seems that few were made directly against bailiffs during the seventeenth century. For example in the diet's case registry for Finland, there are only 34 complaints made against bailiffs (*befalningsman, fogde*) during the whole of the seventeenth century, of which some did not relate to the abuse of power. However, of those that did relate to this, most were criticisms of the bailiff's work (such as how he dealt with pleas for tax concessions) rather than accusations of corruption as such.[37] This overview may only give an approximate picture of the moral standards of bailiffs, but it nevertheless suggests that corruption was only rarely encountered within the administration. It of course existed, but it could be countered with different procedures, some of which were even supervised by the common people themselves.

## *The reputation of the bailiff in the community*

The bailiff was not only answerable to his superiors and God. The local community also played a part in his conscience and moral behaviour. In his correspondence, Påwal Callia often referred to the "honest men" as well as God when he was justifying his actions. In other words he meant that he was ready to answer accusations in front of common folk, as he believed the honourable and respectable members of the community would confirm his honesty and integrity if needed.

The state-building process in seventeenth century Sweden differs from its central European counterparts when it comes to how control was established at the local level. It is commonly thought that in Sweden the local elites were not strong enough to challenge the Crown in any significant way. Not only was the nobility weak in the countryside, but the Church was also. The Crown's policy of donating tax incomes to the nobility in the early seventeenth century did create some social tension between commoners and the nobility, but it gradually eased off after the midpoint of the century, at least partly because of the commoners' efforts in the diet. Some of them even benefited from the emergence of the new state. Some of the wealthier peasants became even wealthier as they were able to purchase landed properties that were desolated, while others could now apply for a career in administration or church.[38]

The overall state of affairs in the local scene determined the agency of all local officials. The reference to the honest men of the community in the bailiff's oath suggests however, that this setting could vary greatly. In the absence of local elites, where political and administrative structures would have been the principal channels for resolving social issues, the agency within a local community was regulated instead by unwritten micro-economic dependencies, kinship, and status systems that needed to be taken into account whether or not the bailiff officially had the authority.[39]

A commitment to honesty in front of the people showed how agency was determined by the locality. It suggested that the community itself had an informal way of defining the legitimacy of the bailiff's authority. Ultimately, it was they who defined which people were honourable and worthy of respect among them, and the Crown and the nobility knew this. Schering Rosenhane (1609–1663) went so far as to recommend that the nobility with taxation rights hire their servants from among the local people, in other words from those who were not only familiar to locals but hopefully also respected members of the community. It is easy to read this as a shrewd move to secure the smooth running of administration, but it does also testify to the power of the local community, and the fact that the bailiff required their respect.[40]

How did the bailiff earn this respect and authority among the people with whom he worked? It seems clear that it helped if the official had some roots of his own in the neighbourhood. In this way, the community would feel it had a better understanding of him as a person, but reputation was based on more than just details of a man's character. Knowing someone's reputation meant knowing a person's family history, his relatives, and how successful as farmers they had been; and a member of a wealthy farming family would generally attract more respect.

Personal reputation featured in everyday life too. The bailiffs could seek an assessment from the jurors of the local court for their actions, if they needed a recommendation to clear their name or apply for a new post somewhere else. In the hundred of Lappee, the common people gave a favourable review of their crown bailiff, Hans Johansson, regarding his actions during the war years, when they were under scrutiny in the local court. The locals confirmed that Hans Johansson had "lived a godly and honourable life, conducted himself honestly with the people and had never taken away the last pot or cow from a poor man". In Kaarina, the claims by former crown bailiff Henrik Bähr that he had been a decent official were backed up by the local population in 1691. The jurors declared that he had been an "alert and hard-working" servant, not to mention a sober one too, who had always looked out for the best interests of the people.[41]

The reviews were not spontaneous, nor were they precise in their evaluation though. They had a ceremonial nuance to them, which underlined the important relationship between the common people and the authorities. The people were not just considering whether the official had conducted his duties according to official regulations, but whether the official had been a respectable, honourable man and whether he had treated people with dignity. But it was not just his own reputation that was of importance to his work; knowing about the reputation of others was crucial to getting his job done. If, in Pori County for example, Påwal Callia knew the farmer was a decent person and a hard-working man, he would be more likely to grant him tax reductions in difficult years. If the farmer was a drunk or unreliable however, no reductions were granted.

In fact, Callia verbally attacked many who failed to pay their taxes if he felt it was because their moral character was lacking in some way. In his correspondence and tax records we can see that Callia branded peasants with a wide range of derogatory descriptions: "useless", "crook", "malicious", "restless fellow", "thug", "lazy", "wasteful", "drunk", "drinks as much as he can get". Although Callia may not have used these exact words actually in front of them, he did not hide his contempt, as challenging the personal reputation of your opponents was seen as an important part of a local officials job and the customary law. Tax collection disputes, just like any other conflict within rural communities were conflicts that were solved by the local court in a process where lots of informal factors were taken into account. Basically the reputation was very important. If Callia got into a dispute over taxation with someone, he usually questioned the integrity of the person, while at the same time showing that he was acting according to the law; while they, in turn, questioned the integrity of the bailiff and did everything they could to bolster their reputation and clear their name.[42]

Different kinds of conflicts and disagreements were part and parcel of administrative life in the seventeenth century. Besides the ideal of the righteous and honourable official, there were also other desirable attributes that defined his agency. The crown bailiff instructions of 1688 not only called for the local official to "support" and "advance" the Crown's interests but also, if necessary, to "defend" them from "damage". The presumption that the bailiff would be met with fundamental hostility at the local level meant that he was expected to be persistent, tough and, if necessary, aggressive to be able to defend the rights of the Crown as long as possible. After all, land ownership was a process by which an owner legitimised his possession by not only dictating the rights and limits of his property, but also actively ensuring the land was used properly. Such a system presupposed that the bailiff would act quickly and decisively, and this was also at the root of all other social and administrative activities. Honour, for example, had to be defended with the same decisiveness and vigour too.[43]

The dual nature of the bailiff's existence was such that he needed to be both a good person in the eyes of his fellow men, and at the same time a defender of his master's rights. Whatever actions were taken, it was important for bailiffs to temper their assertiveness and vigour so that they would not cross the line and turn into crimes. Aggressively destroying a recalcitrant taxpayer's reputation could backfire and become defamation; and while it was important to defend the interests of your superiors at every opportunity, it was also essential that a harmonious way was found to conclude the collection of taxes. In various administrational procedures, the phrasing was such that taxes should be paid "benevolently". In other words, there needed to be an overall agreement between the taxpayer and collector as to the legitimacy of the transaction. Ultimately, it was compassion that was expected to prevail inside the patriarchal society.[44]

In the case of Påwal Callia, this balancing act proved to be difficult to follow through. His career ended when he got into a serious conflict with the vicar of Huittinen, Johannes Keckonius (1643–1719), at the same time as his reputation as an office-holder was at stake. Callia and Keckonius first disagreed over whether the vicar was entitled to some concessions or not, but it soon turned into a matter of personal dislike. Both men accused each other of malpractice, but more than anything they attacked each other with verbal defamations and dragging each other's name in the dirt. Ultimately the supporters of Keckonius succeeded in spreading gossip about the bailiff being corrupt; and although Påwal Callia received a vote of confidence from the common people of the local courts for being a fair bailiff, the conflict between him and Keckonius nevertheless took its toll on his reputation among the local elite, and in the records he starts to be referred to as an "old dog".

Påwal Callia was suspended from his duties as bailiff in 1678 and was accused of corruption, but it proved to be difficult to find concrete evidence against him, even after years of investigations. But his case demonstrates that corruption was not always necessary to bring an end to a local official's career. Agency could be dictated by informal factors that were beyond the control of the Crown, because local communities had their own hierarchies and mechanisms for defining authority. It is possible that Påwal Callia's problems with his brother Henrich had damaged his reputation, and when Påwal Callia got into another conflict, he already had a name for himself. There was thus already plenty of dirt for Keckonius to smear Callia with, and as the criticism went on, it began to undermine the position of Callia in the eyes of Countess Bielke too, whose latent suspicions were now given further fuel despite the lack of any concrete evidence of malpractice.

Thus the agency of a local official covered a grey area between following official instructions and commanding respect among the local population, which was dependent on informal factors in everyday life. Ideally, therefore, a bailiff knew the community he was working in, but the ties he had with it were not strong. But everyone knew that this was frequently impossible and the bailiff was usually more inclined one way or the other. The Crown and nobility looked for men who commanded informal authority among locals, and yet at the same time, for those same reasons, they would constantly harbour suspicions about the bailiff's ability to remain loyal to the higher authorities if all of his friend and relatives were living in his jurisdiction. This contradiction may have been the reason behind why many bailiffs' careers were often cut short.

In the sixteenth century, the bailiffs rarely served in the same location for long periods, and this continued on into the seventeenth century. Yrjö Blomstedt's list of crown bailiffs suggests that each held his post for usually a period of only between 1–3 years. In other parts of the country there were a handful of posts that were held by the same official for 5–10 years in the late 1650s and 1660s (and a couple for even longer), but generally speaking it seems that they were an exception. Those bailiffs who worked for nobility in the donations had careers that lasted slightly longer than those who served the Crown, but the variation was not huge. In Jokipii's catalogue, there are more bailiffs serving longer periods under the nobility than the Crown, but there are also those who served only 1–3 years. Again, there were several reasons for the fast turnover. As the cases presented above show, there were not only cases where the abuse of power and corruption could lead to a bailiff's dismissal, but also others where he was either simply unable to collect the taxes, or else moving on to a better assignment.

Biographical studies demonstrate that the position of bailiff was a cornerstone in the careers of many social climbers. For example, Christier Månsson (1595–1659), who worked as a donation bailiff for Counts Magnus Brahe (1564–1633) and Jakob De la Gardie (1583–1652) pursued his own business alongside his bailiff duties, to eventually become an iron forgery industrialist and a merchant. Meanwhile, Nils Börjesson (1580–1655), who was the crown bailiff of Västergötland in the 1610s, went on to become the Mayor of Göteborg and a major private landlord (*arrendator*) there. In 1630, the German merchant Johan Bochmöller moved to Oulu to become a burgher of the town, and went on to become the crown bailiff in a number of bailiwicks from the end of that decade for almost another twenty years.[45] As for Henrik Corte (d. 1680), who was a bailiff in the 1650s and 1660s of the barony of Kajaani donated to Per Brahe (1602–1680), and went on to become a burgher and eventually Mayor of Raahe; he managed to run his own business successfully at the same time as taking care of extensive duties in Brahe's service. Behind his administrative titles, Corte was essentially a client of Count Brahe, and a member of an informal network that served the interests of the count inside the administration. As such, Corte was hardly an exception, and while the significance of patron-client networks cannot be discussed here in any greater detail, suffice it to say, the bargaining skills of a bailiff were also the same skills needed at the heart of those networks.[46]

It seems evident then that bailiffs could in many cases extend their activities without neglecting their basic duties of office. If there was no nearby town for the bailiff to became a burgher of, he could try to focus instead on intensive farming or to address other rural assets. Zacharias Willandh (d. 1667), for instance, who was the crown bailiff of the hundred of Savolax was running a fishery in addition to his administrative duties. On top of this, he acquired land and properties, eventually ending up with one manor and two farms in the parish of Rantasalmi. Meanwhile Daniel Tollet (d. 1699), Crown Bailiff of the hundred of Hattula (1665–1685) became a major farmer, and went on to become Mayor of Hämeenlinna; while Pawal Callia was also a farmer while a bailiff, as was his brother Henrich as Crown Bailiff of the hundred of Lower Satakunta on three separate occasions (1651–1655, 1664–1666, and 1671–1673).[47]

The fact that bailiffs were often able to pursue private interests, and sometimes hold more than one office at the same time as carrying out the duties of the post, is yet further proof that most bailiffs were rising from the grassroots level to a middle ranking office. It was an attractive prospect that there would be other jobs made available for anyone appointed as a bailiff who showed promising bargaining skills which were clearly transferrable elsewhere; and this acted as a positive counterbalance to the all the negative sides of the job (including the fact that they would be ultimately liable for any unpaid taxes).

## *The agency of bailiffs*

In this chapter, the discussion has not been limited to simply crown bailiffs, as by the seventeenth century there were bailiffs of various kinds in Sweden and, although it is debatable as to whether this same title truly connects these officials in any way, they all did share one key element in their duties – acting as the broker between the common people and the authorities. The job of each thus involved using skills in negotiation, mutual exchange and even coercion to collect taxes; but this varied from post to post in terms of what level it happened at. What agency did bailiffs really have then, to allow them to carry out these tasks?

The management of taxation presupposed organisational and logistical skills. The bailiff had to be able to carry out tax collection on schedule and according to established rules by following the orders of the governor and his office. Occasionally, tax collection or the collection of the unpaid taxes would turn into a physical altercation, and so the bailiff and his servants had to be prepared for this. Aggressiveness (or at least assertiveness) was in fact a virtue for a local level official, as it helped them defend the interests of the authorities. The need to fulfil their obligations was thus a major factor in their agency, as if they failed in delivering taxes on time, they could face a personal bankruptcy of their own.

At the same time they were expected to act fairly, and pay attention to the well-being of common people. The collection of taxes was tightly connected to gaining information on the tax-paying abilities of people. However, this was not restricted to a simple inventory of a persons goods and chattels; it also extended to a sensitive analysis of each taxpayer as a person, and this added a certain moral dimension to the agency of bailiffs. To properly evaluate the integrity, honesty and decency of people in cases when they were having difficulties in paying the official rate of tax was thus a task that was prone to meeting with conflict.

Because of this moral dimension, bailiffs were also left exposed to similar moral assessments by the local populace. They not only asked whether the tax collector was fair and reasonable in his judgements, but also whether he was a good and honourable man. A lot of the guidelines used in this task were ultimately biblically derived, and the local clergymen were thus important agents in local affairs too, as they could assess the morality of the official in religious terms. All the bailiff could do was to make sure he followed the unofficial norms of the community in which he worked. The agency of bailiffs was thus simultaneously shaped from below as well as from above.

The research on which this publication is based was funded by the Academy of Finland (grant no. 137741).

## NOTES

1. Mats Hallenberg, *Kungen, fogdarna och riket. Lokalförvaltning och statsbyggande under tidig Vasatid* (Stockholm: Brutus Östlings Bokförlag Symposion, 2001), pp. 19–21, 88–90; Eva Österberg, *Gränsbygd under krig. Ekonomiska, demografiska och administrativa förhållanden i sydvästra Sverige under och efter nordiska sjuårskriget*. Bibliotheca historica Lundensis 26 (Lund: Gleerups, 1971), p. 221; Marie Lennersand, *Rättvisans och allmogens beskyddare. Den absoluta staten, kommissionerna och tjänstemännen, ca 1680–1730*. Studia Historica Upsaliensia 190 (Uppsala: Uppsala universitet Lennersand, 1999), p. 39; Björn Asker, *I konungens stad och ställe. Länsstyrelser i arbete 1635–1735* (Uppsala: Stiftelsen för utgivande av Arkivvetenskapliga studier, 2004), p. 60.
2. Joh. Axel Almquist, *Den civila lokalförvaltningen i Sverige 1523–1630. Första delen* (Stockholm: Norstedt, 1917), pp. 112–134; Pentti Renvall, "Valtiolliset vaiheet ja hallinnollis-oikeudellinen kehitys". In: *Varsinais-Suomen historia V:1* (Turku: 1949), pp. 134–146; Kyösti Kiuasmaa, *Suomen yleis- ja paikallishallinnon toimet ja niiden hoito 1500-luvun jälkipuoliskolla (vv. 1560–1600). Hallinto- ja yhteiskuntahistoriallinen tutkimus*. Historiallisia Tutkimuksia 63 (Helsinki: Finnish Historical Society, 1962), pp. 27–43; Anssi Mäkinen, *Linnaleirit ja vainovalkeat. Viipurin läänin asutus kaksikymmentäviisivuotisen sodan (1570–1595) jaloissa*. Bibliotheca Historica 73 (Helsinki: The Finnish Literature Society, 2002), pp 124–140, 209–211; Österberg, *Gränsbygd under krig*, pp. 220–230.
3. Janne Haikari, *Isännän, Jumalan ja rehellisten miesten edessä. Vallankäyttö ja virkamiesten toimintaympäristöt satakuntalaisessa maaseutuyhteisössä 1600-luvun jälkipuoliskolla*. Bibliotheca Historica 121(Helsinki: The Finnish Literature Society, 2009).
4. The Finnish national biography (*Kansallisbiografia*, http://www.kansallisbiografia.fi/) and the Swedish biograpical database (Svenskt biografiskt lexikon, http://sok.riksarkivet.se/SBL/Start.aspx)
5. Hallenberg, *Kungen, fogdarna och riket*, pp. 218–236.
6. Hallenberg, *Kungen, fogdarna och riket*, pp. 335–337; Levi, Giovanni, *Aineeton perintö. Manaajapappi ja talonpoikaisyhteisö 1600-luvun Italiassa*. Kääntäneet Kaisa Kinnunen, Elina Suolahti. Tutkijaliiton julkaisusarja 73 ([Helsinki]: Tutkijaliitto,

1992), pp. 144-145, 168-170; Almquist, *Den civila lokalförvaltningen*; Kiuasmaa, *Suomen yleis- ja paikallishallinnon toimet*; Mauno Jokipii, "Porin kreivikunta". *Historiallinen Arkisto 54* (Helsinki: Suomen historiallinen seura, 1953); Mauno Jokipii, *Suomen kreivi- ja vapaaherrakunnat I.* Historiallisia Tutkimuksia 58: 1 (Helsinki: Finnish Historical Society, 1956); Mauno Jokipii, *Suomen kreivi- ja vapaaherrakunnat II.* Historiallisia Tutkimuksia 58: 2 (Helsinki: Finnish Historical Society, 1960); Robert Swedlund, *Grev- och friherreskapen i Sverige och Finland. Donationerna och reduktionerna före 1680* (Uppsala: Almqvist & Wiksells, 1936); Pentti Renvall, "Valtiolliset vaiheet" and Pentti Renvall, "Virkakierto Suomen voutien piirissä 1500-luvulla", *Historiallinen Aikakauskirja 1940: 4* studies individual actors inside the administration, but the focus is solely on the sixteenth century.

7   Petri Karonen, *Pohjoinen suurvalta. Ruotsi ja Suomi 1521-1809* (Helsinki: The Finnish Literature Society, 2014), pp. 182-206; Mats Hallenberg, *Statsmakt till salu. Arrendesystemet och privatiseringen av skatteuppbörden i det svenska riket 1618-1635* (Lund: Nordic Academic Press, 2008), pp. 12, 37-39.

8   Samuel Clason, *Till reduktionen förhistoria: gods- och ränteafsöndringarna och de förbudna orterna* (Stockholm: Uppsala, 1895), pp. 87-102; Sven A. Nilsson, *Krona och frälse i Sverige 1523-1594. Rusttjänst, länsväsende, godspolitik* (Lund: Gleerup, 1947), pp. 111-122; Swedlund, *Grev- och friherreskapen*, pp. 207-225; Jokipii, *Suomen kreivi- ja vapaaherrakunnat I*, pp. 95-99; Hallenberg, *Statsmakt till salu*, pp. 209-218; Kimmo Katajala, *Nälkäkapina. Veronvuokraus ja talonpoikainen vastarinta Karjalassa 1683-1697.* Historiallisia Tutkimuksia 185 (Helsinki: Suomen Historiallinen Seura, 1994), pp. 89-101; Kimmo Katajala, *Suomalainen kapina. Talonpoikaislevottomuudet ja poliittisen kulttuurin muutos Ruotsin ajalla (n. 1150-1800).* Historiallisia Tutkimuksia 212 (Helsinki: The Finnish Literature Society, 2002), pp. 213-215; Kasper Kepsu, *Den besvärliga provinsen. Reduktion, skattearrendering och bondeoroligheter i det svenska Ingermanland under slutet av 1600-talet* (Helsingfors: Helsingfors universitet, 2014).

9   Jokipii, *Suomen kreivi- ja vapaaherrakunnat I*, pp. 95-111; Swedlund, *Grev- och friherreskapen*, pp. 196-207; John Gardberg, *Kimito friherreskap. En studie över feodal läns- och godsförvaltning* (Helsingfors, 1935), pp. 15-16; Georg Haggrén, "Louhisaaren kulta-aika – 1600-luvun puolivälin kartanokeskus". In: Lounatvuori, Irma, Knapas, Marja Terttu Knapas (toim.), *Louhisaaren kartano. Suku ja rälssi – säteri ja kirkko.* (Helsinki: Museovirasto, 2005), p. 52; Kepsu, *Den besvärliga provinsen*, pp. 171-179.

10  Jokipii, *Suomen kreivi- ja vapaaherrakunnat*, I, p. 96.

11  Björn Asker, *I konungens stad och ställe*, p. 367; Eino Jutikkala, *Suomen talonpojan historia* (Porvoo: WSOY, 1942), pp. 375-381; Pentti Renvall, "Valtiolliset vaiheet", pp. 171-198; Pentti Renvall, "Murroksen vuosisata – Kustaa Vaasasta Kustaa II Aadolfiin". In: *Suomen kulttuurihistoria II* (Jyväskylä: Gummerus, 1934), pp. 148-156; Hannu Soikkanen, *Kunnallinen itsehallinto, kansanvallan perusta. Maalaiskuntien itsehallinnon perusta* (Helsinki: Maalaiskuntien liitto, 1966), pp. 9-23; Eero Matinolli, "Lääninhallinto". In: *Varsinais-Suomen historia VI, 3* (Turku: Varsinais-Suomen maakuntaliitto, 1971), pp. 15-27.

12  Yrjö Blomstedt, *Suomen kihlakunnanvoudit 1630-1713. Tarkistamaton kihlakunnittainen luettelo* (Helsinki, 1958), pp. 302-307; Päiviö Tommila, *Nurmijärven pitäjän historia. II osa. Itsenäisen Nurmijärven pitäjän vaiheet.* (Nurmijärvi: Nurmijärven kunta, 1975), p. 16; Pentti Virrankoski, "Uskonpuhdistuksesta isoonvihaan". In: *Suur-Kalajoen historia I* (Kalajoki: Suur-Kalajoen historiatoimikunta,1956), p. 253; Erik von Hertzen, "Kiikalan historiallinen aika". In: Sarvas, Anja, von Hertzen, Erik, *Kiikalan historia* (Kiikala: Kiikalan kunta, seurakunta ja manttaalikunta), pp. 124, 204-305; Virmala, Anja, Ruotsalainen, Pirjo, *Lammin pitäjän historia I. Ruotsin vallan loppuun* (Lammi: Lammin kunta,1972), pp. 254–

255; Veli-Matti Syrjö, *Lappeen kihlakunnan historia II. 1620-luvulta 1860-luvulle* (Lappee: Lappeen kihlakunnan historiatoimikunta, 1985), pp. 116–121; Timo Havia, "Ruotsinvallan aika". In: Havia, Timo, Luoto, Jukka, *Piikkiön historia I* (Piikkiö: Piikkiön kunta, 1989), pp. 282–285; Kari Alifrosti, "Historia". In: *Kalannin historia* (Uusikaupunki: Uudenkaupungin kaupunki, 1999), p. 426; Kerttu Innamaa, *Kaarinan pitäjän historia. Osa II* (Kaarina: Kaarinan historiatoimikunta, 1952), pp. 102–103; Eero Matinolli, "Suur-Pyhäjoen historia uuden ajan murroksesta 1860-luvulle". In: *Suur-Pyhäjoen historia vanhimmista ajoista 1860-luvulle.* Eero Matinolli (toim.) (Kokkola: Suur-Pyhäjoen historiatoimikunta, 1969), pp. 335–339; Seppo Tiihonen, Paula Tiihonen, *Suomen hallintohistoria* (Helsinki: Valtion koulutuskeskus, 1984), pp. 77–81; Björn Asker, *I konungens stad och ställe*, pp. 141–145; Björn Asker, *Hur riket styrdes. Förvaltning, politik och arkiv 1520–1920* (Stockholm: Riksarkivet, 2007).

13 Österberg, *Gränsbygd under krig*; Eva Österberg, "Svenska lokalsamhällen i förändring ca 1550–1850. Participation, representation och politisk kultur i den svenska självstyrelsen. Ett angeläget forskningsområde", *Historisk Tidskrift 107 (1987)*; Lennersand, *Rättvisans och allmogens beskyddare*; Peter Ullgren, *Lantadel. Adliga godsägare i Östergötland och Skåne vid 1600-talets slut* (Lund: Sisyfos, 2004); Alexander Jonsson, *De norrländska landshövdingarna och statsbildningen 1634–1769*. Skrifter från institutionen för historiska studier 10 (Umeå: Umeå universitet, 2005); Johan Holm, *Konstruktionen av en stormakt. Kungamakt, skattebönder och statsbildning 1595–1640*. Stockholm Studies in History 90 (Stockholm: Stockholms universitet, 2007).

14 Nils Erik Villstrand, *Anpassning eller protest. Lokalsamhället inför utskrivningarna av fotfolk till den svenska krigsmakten 1620–1679* (Åbo: Åbo Akademi, 1992); Katajala, *Nälkäkapina*; Katajala, *Suomalainen kapina*; Kepsu, *Den besvärliga provinsen*.

15 C. G. Styffe, *Samling af instructioner för högre och lägre tjenstemän vid landtregeringen i Sverige och Finnland* (Stockholm: Hörbergska boktryckeriet, 1852), p. 45.

16 Styffe, *Samling af instructioner*; Gardberg, *Kimito friherreskap*, pp. 16–19; Jokipii, *Suomen kreivi- ja vapaaherrakunnat I*, pp. 95–110.

17 Styffe, *Samling af instructioner*, pp. 42–69.

18 Hallenberg, *Kungen, fogdarna och riket*, pp. 97–101; Asker, *I konungens stad och ställe*, pp. 362–365; Matti Walta, *Virkamiehiä. Lääninhallinnon virkamiehet 1721–1808*. Suomen sukututkimusseuran julkaisuja 56 (Helsinki: Suomen Sukututkimusseura, 2005), p. 17.

19 Styffe, *Samling af instructioner*, pp. 46, 48, 52–54, 56.

20 Kristoffers landslag, Tingamaalabalken, clauses XIX and XXI, http://project2.sol.lu.se/fornsvenska/01_Bitar/B.L1.A–KrL.html, accessed October 15, 2015; Sven A. Nilsson, *De stora krigens tid. Om Sverige som militärstat och bondesamhälle*. Studia Historica Upsaliensia 161 (Uppsala: Uppsala universitet, 1990); Cecilia Ihse, *Präst, stånd och stat. Kung och kyrka i förhandling 1642–1686*. Stockholm Studies in History 78 (Stockholm: Stockholms universitet, 2005), pp. 106–108, 188–189; Anna Maria Forssberg, *Att hålla folket på gott humör. Informationsspridning, krigspropaganda och mobilisering i Sverige 1655–1680* (Stockholm: Almqvist & Wiksell, 2005), pp. 43, 55, 80–87; Bill Widén, *Predikstolen som massmedium i det svenska riket från medeltiden till stormaktstidens slut*. Studia historica ecclesiastica Academiae Aboensis 1 (Åbo: Åbo Akademi, 2002), pp. 57–61, 88–100; Lennersand, *Rättvisans och allmogens beskyddare*, p. 28; Elisabeth Reuterswärd, *Ett massmedium för folket. Studier i de allmänna kungörelsernas funktion i 1700-talets samhälle*. Studia Historica Lundensia 2 (Lund: Lund University Press, 2001); Göran Malmstedt, *Bondetro och kyrkoro. Religiös mentalitet i stormaktstidens Sverige* (Lund: Nordic Academic Press, 2002).

21 Carl-E. Normann, *Prästerskapet och det karolinska enväldet. Studier över det svenska prästerskapets statsuppfattning under stormaktstidens slutskede.* Samlingar och studier till svenska kyrkans historia. 17 (Stockholm: Svenska kyrkans diakonistyrelse, 1948), p. 21; Sven Ingebrand, *Olavus Petris reformatoriska åskadning* (Uppsala: Uppsala universitet, 1964), p. 190.

22 Karonen, *Pohjoinen suurvalta*, pp. 161–163; Petri Karonen, "Johdanto. Moninainen patriarkaalisuus – normien ja käytäntöjen solmukohdat". In: Einonen, Piia, Karonen, Petri (toim.), *Arjen valta. Suomalaisen yhteiskunnan patriarkaalisesta järjestyksestä myöhäiskeskiajalta teollistumisen kynnykselle (v. 1450–1860).* Historiallinen Arkisto 116 (Helsinki: The Finnish Literature Society, 2002), pp. 14–21; Jari Eilola, *Rajapinnoilla. Sallitun ja kielletyn määritteleminen 1600-luvun jälkipuoliskon noituus ja taikuustapauksissa.* Bibliotheca Historica 81 (Helsinki: The Finnish Literature Society, 2003), pp. 189–192; Peter Englund, *Det hotade huset. Adliga föreställningar om samhället under stormaktstiden* (Stockholm: Atlantis, 1989), pp. 92–97, 203.

23 Schering Rosenhane, *Oeconomia.* Utgiven av Torsten Lagerstedt (Uppsala, 1944), pp. 8–10; Per Brahe, *Oeconomia eller Hushållsbok för ungt adelsfolk.* Utgiven med inledning, kommentar och ordförklaringar av John Granlund och Gösta Holm. Nordiska museets handlingar 78 (Lund: Nordiska museet, 1971), pp. 49–53, 78–90, 201–202, 224; Englund, *Det hotade huset*, pp. 94–96.

24 Rosenhane, *Oeconomia*, pp. 22–29; Brahe, *Oeconomia*, pp. 204–205; Eriksson, Bo, *Statstjänare och jordägare. Adelsideologi i Per Brahe den äldres "Oeconomia"* (Stockholm: Dialogos, 2008), pp. 113–135; Runefelt, Leif, *Hushållningens dygder. Affektlära, hushållningslära och ekonomiskt tänkande under svensk stormaktstid.* Stockholm Studies in Economic History 34 (Stockholm: Almqvist & Wiksell International, 2001), pp. 92–104, 122–127.

25 Hallenberg, *Kungen, fogdarna och riket*, pp. 221–236; Österberg, *Gränsbygd under krig*, pp. 227–230.

26 Mirkka Lappalainen, *Jumalan vihan ruoska. Suuri nälänhätä Suomessa 1695–1697* (Helsinki: Siltala, 2012), pp. 11, 230; Ilkka Mäntylä, *Kruunu ja alamaisten nälkä. 1690-luvun katovuosien verotulojen vähennys Pohjanmaalla ja esivallan vastatoimenpiteet.* Scripta Historica 13 (Oulu: Oulun Historiaseura, 1988), pp. 63–70.

27 Haikari, *Isännän, Jumalan ja rehellisten miesten edessä*, pp. 188–189; Blomstedt, *Suomen kihlakunnanvoudit*, p. 7.

28 Lappalainen, *Jumalan vihan ruoska*, pp. 180–189.

29 Haikari, *Isännän, Jumalan ja rehellisten miesten edessä.*

30 Katajala, *Nälkäkapina*, p. 225; Renvall, "Valtiolliset vaiheet", pp. 171–198; Maria Ågren, *Att hävda sin rätt. Synen på jordägandet i 1600-talets Sverige, speglade i institutet urminnes hävd.* Skrifter utgivna av Institutet för rättshistorisk forskning. Serien 1, Rättshistoriskt bibliotek 57 (Stockholm: Institutet för rättshistorisk forskning, 1997), pp. 64, 163.

31 Gardberg, *Kimito friherreskap*, pp. 32–33, 56–58.

32 R. A. Mäntylä, "Raision vaiheet 1600-luvun alusta ison vihan päättymiseen". In: *Raision historia I* (Raisio: Raision historiatoimikunta, 1960), p. 288; Virrankoski, *Suur-Kalajoen historia I*, p. 279.

33 Erkki Lehtinen, *Suur-Ulvilan historia 1* (s.l.: Ulvila, 1967), pp. 242–243.

34 Haikari, *Isännän, Jumalan ja rehellisten miesten edessä*, pp. 154–155.

35 Kurt Ågren, *Adelns bönder och kronans. Skatter och besvär i Uppland 1650–1680.* Studia Historica Upsaliensia 11 (Uppsala: Uppsala universitet, 1964); Eibert Ernby, *Adeln och bondejorden. En studie rörande skattefrälset i Oppunda härad under 1600-talet.* Studia Historica Upsaliensia 64 (Uppsala: Uppsala universitet, 1975).

36 Havia, "Ruotsinvallan aika", pp. 279–280; Armas Luukko, "Suur-Lohtajan historia vuoteen 1809". In: *Suur-Lohtajan historia I. Esihistoriallisesta ajasta Suomen sotaan*

(Kokkola: Suur-Lohtajan historiatoimikunta, 1957), pp. 418–419, 597; Virrankoski, *Suur-Kalajoen historia I*, p. 241.
37 Sakregister till allmogens besvär till år 1720, Riksarkivet (Swedish National Archive, Stockholm).
38 Mirkka Lappalainen, "Regional Elite Group and the Problem of Territorial Integration. The Finnish Nobility and the Formation of the Swedish 'Power State', c. 1570–1620", *Scandinavian Journal of History* 26, 2001, pp. 5–10, 14–17; Ullgren, *Lantadel*, pp. 16, 181–183; Nilsson, *De stora krigens tid*; Villstrand, *Anpassning eller protest*; Katajala, *Nälkäkapina*.
39 Max Gluckman, *Politics, Law and Ritual in Tribal Society* (Oxford: Basil Blackwell, 1984); Fredrik Barth, "Process and form in social life". In: *Selected essays of Fredrik Barth*. Volume I (London, Boston and Henley: Routledge & Kegan Paul, 1981), pp. 16–24; F. G. Bailey, "Gifts and Poison". In: Bailey, F. G. (ed.), *Gifts and Poison. The Politics of Reputation* (Oxford: Basil Blackwell, 1971).
40 Rosenhane, *Oeconomia*, p. 21.
41 Syrjö, *Lappeen kihlakunnan historia II*, pp. 145–147; Innamaa, *Kaarinan pitäjän historia*, p. 108.
42 Eilola, *Rajapinnoilla*, pp. 259–270; Olli Matikainen, *Verenperijät. Väkivalta ja yhteisön murros itäisessä Suomessa 1500–1600-luvulla*. Bibliotheca Historica 78 (Helsinki: The Finnish Literature Society, 2002), pp. 131–143.
43 Styffe, *Samling af instructioner*, pp. 42–45; Ågren, *Att hävda sin rätt*, pp. 49–50, 167, 191.
44 Haikari, *Isännän, Jumalan ja rehellisten miesten edessä*; Hallenberg, *Kungen, fogdarna och riket*, p. 144.
45 B. Boéthius, "Christier Månsson (Christiernin)" (*Svenskt biografiskt lexikon*, 1929); B. Linden, "Nils Börjesson" (*Svenskt biografiskt lexikon*, 1927); Pentti Virrankoski, "Bochmöller, Johan, Oulun pormestari, kruununvouti (K 1682 jälkeen)" (*Kansallisbiografia*, 2000).
46 Marko Hakanen, *Vallan verkostoissa. Per Brahe ja hänen klienttinsä 1600-luvun Ruotsin valtakunnassa*. Jyväskylä Studies in Humanities 157 (Jyväskylä: Jyväskylän yliopisto, 2011), pp. 74–79, passim.; H. Impiwaara, "Henrik Corte" (*Svenskt biografiskt lexikon*, 1931).
47 Veijo Saloheimo, "Willandh, Zacharias Zachariaanpoika, vouti (K 1667)" (*Kansallisbiografia*, 2001); Eero Mäntylä, *Hattulan historia* (Hattula: Hattulan kunta, 1976), pp. 172, 287, 324, 325, 341, 343, 355, 360, 435.

# Sources

## Printed sources

Brahe, Per (1971): *Oeconomia eller Hushållsbok för ungt adelsfolk*. Utgiven med inledning, kommentar och ordförklaringar av John Granlund och Gösta Holm. Nordiska museets handlingar 78. Lund: Nordiska museet.
Rosenhane, Schering (1944): *Oeconomia*. Utgiven av Torsten Lagerstedt. Uppsala.
Sakregister till allmogens besvär till år 1720, Riksarkivet.
Styffe, C. G. (red.) 1852: *Samling af instructioner för högre och lägre tjenstemän vid landt-regeringen i Sverige och Finnland*. Stockholm: Hörbergska boktryckeriet.

## Literature

Alifrosti, Kari 1999: "Historia". In: *Kalannin historia*. Uusikaupunki: Uudenkaupungin kaupunki.
Almquist, Joh. Axel 1917: *Den civila lokalförvaltningen i Sverige 1523–1630*. Vol. 1. Stockholm: Norstedt.
Almquist, Joh. Axel 1919–1922: *Den civila lokalförvaltningen i Sverige 1523–1630*. Vol 2. Stockholm.
Asker, Björn 2004: *I konungens stad och ställe. Länsstyrelser i arbete 1635–1735*. Uppsala: Stiftelsen för utgivande av Arkivvetenskapliga studier.
Asker, Björn 2007: *Hur riket styrdes. Förvaltning, politik och arkiv 1520–1920*. Stockholm: Riksarkivet.
Bailey, F. G. 1971: "Gifts and Poison". In: Bailey, F. G. (ed.), *Gifts and Poison. The Politics of Reputation*. Oxford: Basil Blackwell.
Barth, Fredrik 1981: "Process and form in social life", *Selected essays of Fredrik Barth*. Volume I. London, Boston and Henley: Routledge & Kegan Paul.
Blomstedt, Yrjö 1958: *Suomen kihlakunnanvoudit 1630–1713. Tarkistamaton kihlakunnittainen luettelo*. Helsinki.
Blomstedt, Yrjö 1981: *Asikkalan historia*. Asikkala: Asikkalan kunta.
Boéthius, B. 1929: "Christier Månsson (Christiernin)". *Svenskt biografiskt lexikon*, accessed October 18, 2015.
Clason, Samuel 1895: *Till reduktionen förhistoria. Gods- och ränteafsöndringarna och de förbudna orterna*. Stockholm: Uppsala.
Eilola, Jari 2003: *Rajapinnoilla. Sallitun ja kielletyn määritteleminen 1600-luvun jälkipuoliskon noituus ja taikuustapauksissa*. Bibliotheca Historica 81. Helsinki: The Finnish Literature Society.
Englund, Peter 1989: *Det hotade huset. Adliga föreställningar om samhället under stormaktstiden*. Stockholm: Atlantis.
Eriksson, Bo 2008: *Statstjänare och jordägare. Adelsideologi i Per Brahe den äldres "Oeconomia"*. Stockholm: Dialogos.
Ernby, Eibert 1975: *Adeln och bondejorden. En studie rörande skattefrälset i Oppunda härad under 1600-talet*. Studia Historica Upsaliensia 64. Uppsala: Uppsala universitet.
Forssberg, Anna Maria 2005: *Att hålla folket på gott humör. Informationsspridning, krigspropaganda och mobilisering i Sverige 1655–1680*. Stockholm: Acta Universitatis Stockholmiensis, Almqvist & Wiksell.
Gardberg, John 1935: *Kimito friherreskap. En studie över feodal läns- och godsförvaltning*. Helsingfors.
Gluckman, Max 1984: *Politics, Law and Ritual in Tribal Society*. Oxford: Basil Blackwell.
Haggrén, Georg 2005: "Louhisaaren kulta-aika – 1600-luvun puolivälin kartanokeskus". In: Lounatvuori, Irma, Knapas, Marja Terttu (toim.), *Louhisaaren kartano. Suku ja rälssi – säteri ja kirkko*. Toimittaneet Helsinki: Museovirasto.
Haikari, Janne 2009: *Isännän, Jumalan ja rehellisten miesten edessä. Vallankäyttö ja virkamiesten toimintaympäristöt satakuntalaisessa maaseutuyhteisössä 1600-luvun jälkipuoliskolla*. Bibliotheca Historica 121. Helsinki: The Finnish Literature Society.
Hakanen, Marko 2011: *Vallan verkostoissa. Per Brahe ja hänen klienttinsä 1600-luvun Ruotsin valtakunnassa*. Jyväskylä Studies in Humanities 157. Jyväskylä: Jyväskylän yliopisto.
Hallenberg, Mats 2001: *Kungen, fogdarna och riket. Lokalförvaltning och statsbyggande under tidig Vasatid*. Stockholm: Brutus Östlings Bokförlag Symposion.
Hallenberg, Mats 2008: *Statsmakt till salu. Arrendesystemet och privatiseringen av skatteuppbörden i det svenska riket 1618–1635*. Lund: Nordic Academic Press.

Harnesk, Börje 2002: "Den svenska modellens tidigmoderna rötter?", *Historisk Tidskrift* 122.
Havia, Timo 1989: "Ruotsinvallan aika". In: Havia, Timo, Luoto, Jukka, *Piikkiön historia I*. Piikkiö: Piikkiön kunta.
Hertzen, Erik von 1987: "Kiikalan historiallinen aika". In: Sarvas, Anja, von Hertzen, Erik, *Kiikalan historia*. Kiikala: Kiikalan kunta, seurakunta ja manttaalikunta.
Holm, Johan 2007: *Konstruktionen av en stormakt. Kungamakt, skattebönder och statsbildning 1595–1640*. Stockholm Studies in History 90. Stockholm: Stockholms universitet.
Ihse, Cecilia 2005: *Präst, stånd och stat. Kung och kyrka i förhandling 1642–1686*. Stockholm Studies in History 78. Stockholm: Stockholms universitet.
Impiwaara, H.1931: "Henrik Corte", *Svenskt biografiskt lexikon*, accessed October 18, 2015.
Ingebrand, Sven 1964: *Olavus Petris reformatoriska åskadning*. Uppsala: Uppsala universitet.
Innamaa, Kerttu 1952: *Kaarinan pitäjän historia. Osa II*. Kaarina.
Jokipii, Mauno 1953: "Porin kreivikunta". *Historiallinen arkisto 54*. Helsinki: Finnish Historical Society.
Jokipii, Mauno 1956: *Suomen kreivi- ja vapaaherrakunnat I*. Historiallisia 58: I. Helsinki: Finnish Historical Society.
Jokipii, Mauno 1960: *Suomen kreivi- ja vapaaherrakunnat II*. Historiallisia Tutkimuksia 58: 2. Helsinki: Finnish Historical Society.
Jonsson, Alexander 2005: *De norrländska landshövdingarna och statsbildningen 1634–1769*. Skrifter från institutionen för historiska studier 10. Umeå: Umeå universitet.
Jutikkala, Eino 1934: *Sääksmäen pitäjän historia*. Sääksmäki.
Jutikkala, Eino 1942: *Suomen talonpojan historia*. Porvoo: WSOY.
Karonen, Petri 2002: "Johdanto. Moninainen patriarkaalisuus – normien ja käytäntöjen solmukohdat". In: Einonen, Piia, Karonen, Petri (toim.), *Arjen valta. Suomalaisen yhteiskunnan patriarkaalisesta järjestyksestä myöhäiskeskiajalta teollistumisen kynnykselle (v. 1450–1860)*. Historiallinen Arkisto 116. Helsinki: The Finnish Literature Society.
Karonen, Petri 2014: *Pohjoinen suurvalta. Ruotsi ja Suomi 1521–1809*. Helsinki: The Finnish Literature Society.
Katajala, Kimmo 1994: *Nälkäkapina. Veronvuokraus ja talonpoikainen vastarinta Karjalassa 1683–1697*. Historiallisia Tutkimuksia 185. Helsinki: Finnish Historical Society.
Katajala, Kimmo 2002: *Suomalainen kapina. Talonpoikaislevottomuudet ja poliittisen kulttuurin muutos Ruotsin ajalla (n. 1150–1800)*. Historiallisia Tutkimuksia 212. Helsinki: The Finnish Literature Society.
Kepsu, Kasper 2014: *Den besvärliga provinsen. Reduktion, skattearrendering och bondeoroligheter i det svenska Ingermanland under slutet av 1600-talet*. Helsingfors: Helsingfors universitet.
Kiuasmaa, Kyösti 1962: *Suomen yleis- ja paikallishallinnon toimet ja niiden hoito 1500-luvun jälkipuoliskolla (vv. 1560–1600). Hallinto- ja yhteiskuntahistoriallinen tutkimus*. Historiallisia Tutkimuksia 63. Helsinki: Finnish Historical Society.
Lappalainen, Mirkka 2001: "Regional Elite Group and the Problem of Territorial Integration. The Finnish Nobility and the Formation of the Swedish "Power State", c. 1570–1620", *Scandinavian Journal of History 26*.
Lappalainen, Mirkka 2012: *Jumalan vihan ruoska. Suuri nälänhätä Suomessa 1695–1697*. Helsinki: Siltala.
Lehtinen, Erkki 1961: "Suomen kameraalinen keskushallinto 1600-luvun alkupuolella", *Historiallinen Arkisto 57*. Helsinki: Finnish Historical Society.
Lehtinen, Erkki 1967: *Suur-Ulvilan historia 1*. s.l.: Ulvila.

Lennersand, Marie 1999: *Rättvisans och allmogens beskyddare. Den absoluta staten, kommissionerna och tjänstemännen, ca 1680–1730*. Studia Historica Upsaliensia 190. Uppsala: Uppsala universitet.

Levi, Giovanni 1992: *Aineeton perintö. Manaajapappi ja talonpoikaisyhteisö 1600-luvun Italiassa*. Kääntäneet Kaisa Kinnunen, Elina Suolahti. Tutkijaliiton julkaisusarja 73. [Helsinki]: Tutkijaliitto.

Lindegren, Jan 1980: *Utskrivning och utsugning. Produktion och reproduktion i Bygdeå 1620–1640*. Studia Historica Upsaliensia 117. Uppsala: Uppsala universitet.

Linden, B. 1927: "Nils Börjesson", *Svenskt biografiskt lexikon*, accessed October 18, 2015.

Luukko, Armas 1957: "Suur-Lohtajan historia vuoteen 1809". In: *Suur-Lohtajan historia I. Esihistoriallisesta ajasta Suomen sotaan*. Kokkola: Suur-Lohtajan historiatoimikunta.

Malmstedt, Göran 2002: *Bondetro och kyrkoro. Religiös mentalitet i stormaktstidens Sverige*. Lund: Nordic Academic Press.

Malmström, Joakim 2006: *Herrskapen och den lokala politiken. Eds socken ca 1650–1900*. Studia Historica Upsaliensia 222. Uppsala: Uppsala universitet.

Matikainen, Olli 2002: *Verenperijät. Väkivalta ja yhteisön murros itäisessä Suomessa 1500–1600-luvulla*. Bibliotheca Historica 78. Helsinki: The Finnish Literature Society.

Matinolli, Eero 1969: "Suur-Pyhäjoen historia uuden ajan murroksesta 1860-luvulle". In: Eero Matinolli (toim.), *Suur-Pyhäjoen historia vanhimmista ajoista 1860-luvulle*. Kokkola: Suur-Pyhäjoen historiatoimikunta.

Matinolli, Eero 1976: "Lääninhallinto". In: *Varsinais-Suomen historia VI, 3*. Turku.

Matinolli, Eero 1971: "Paikallinen itsehallinto Varsinais-Suomessa 1600- ja 1700-luvulla". In: *Varsinais-Suomen historia VII, 1*. Turku: Varsinais-Suomen maakuntaliitto.

Mäkinen, Anssi 2002: *Linnaleirit ja vainovalkeat. Viipurin läänin asutus kaksikymmentäviisivuotisen sodan (1570–1595) jaloissa*. Bibliotheca Historica 73. Helsinki: The Finnish Literature Society.

Mäntylä, Eero 1976: *Hattulan historia*. Hattula: Hattulan kunta.

Mäntylä, Ilkka 1988: *Kruunu ja alamaisten nälkä. 1690-luvun katovuosien verotulojen vähennys Pohjanmaalla ja esivallan vastatoimenpiteet*. Scripta Historica 13. Oulu: Oulun Historiaseura.

Mäntylä, R. A. 1960: "Raision vaiheet 1600-luvun alusta ison vihan päättymiseen". In: *Raision historia I*. Raisio: Raision historiatoimikunta.

Nilsson, Sven A. 1947: *Krona och frälse i Sverige 1523–1594. Rusttjänst, länsväsende, godspolitik*. Lund: Gleerup.

Nilsson, Sven A. 1990: *De stora krigens tid. Om Sverige som militärstat och bondesamhälle*. Studia Historica Upsaliensia 161. Uppsala: Uppsala universitet.

Normann, Carl-E. 1948: *Prästerskapet och det karolinska enväldet. Studier över det svenska prästerskapets statsuppfattning under stormaktstidens slutskede*. Samlingar och studier till svenska kyrkans historia. 17. Stockholm: Svenska kyrkans diakonistyrelse.

Renvall, Pentti 1934: "Murroksen vuosisata – Kustaa Vaasasta Kustaa II Aadolfiin". In: *Suomen kulttuurihistoria II*. Jyväskylä: Gummerus.

Renvall, Pentti 1940: Virkakierto Suomen voutien piirissä 1500-luvulla. Historiallinen Aikakauskirja 1940: 4.

Renvall, Pentti 1949: "Valtiolliset vaiheet ja hallinnollis-oikeudellinen kehitys". In: *Varsinais-Suomen historia V:1*. Turku.

Reuterswärd, Elisabeth 2001: *Ett massmedium för folket. Studier i de allmänna kungörelsernas funktion i 1700-talets samhälle*. Studia Historica Lundensia 2. Lund: Lund University Press.

Runefelt, Leif 2001: *Hushållningens dygder. Affektlära, hushållningslära och ekonomiskt tänkande under svensk stormaktstid*. Stockholm Studies in Economic history 34. Stockholm: Almqvist & Wiksell International.

Saloheimo, Veijo 2001: "Willandh, Zacharias Zachariaanpoika, vouti (K 1667)", *Kansallisbiografia*: http://www.kansallisbiografia.fi/kb/artikkeli/4410/, accessed June 1, 2015.

Soikkanen, Hannu 1966: *Kunnallinen itsehallinto, kansanvallan perusta. Maalaiskuntien itsehallinnon perusta.* Helsinki: Maalaiskuntien liitto.

Swedlund Robert 1936: *Grev- och friherreskapen i Sverige och Finland. Donationerna och reduktionerna före 1680.* Uppsala: Almqvist & Wiksells.

Syrjö, Veli-Matti 1985: *Lappeen kihlakunnan historia II. 1620-luvulta 1860-luvulle.* Lappee: Lappeen kihlakunnan historiatoimikunta.

Tiihonen, Seppo, Tiihonen, Paula 1984: *Suomen hallintohistoria.* Helsinki: Valtion koulutuskeskus.

Tommila, Päiviö 1975: *Nurmijärven pitäjän historia. II osa. Itsenäisen Nurmijärven pitäjän vaiheet.* Nurmijärvi: Nurmijärven kunta.

Ullgren, Peter 2004: *Lantadel. Adliga godsägare i Östergötland och Skåne vid 1600-talets slut.* Lund: Sisyfos.

Walta, Matti 2005: *Virkamiehiä. Lääninhallinnon virkamiehet 1721–1808.* Suomen sukututkimusseuran julkaisuja 56. Helsinki: Suomen Sukututkimusseura.

Widén, Bill 2002: *Predikstolen som massmedium i det svenska riket från medeltiden till stormaktstidens slut.* Studia historica ecclesiastica Academiae Aboensis 1. Åbo: Åbo Akademi.

Villstrand, Nils Erik 1992: *Anpassning eller protest. Lokalsamhället inför utskrivningarna av fotfolk till den svenska krigsmakten 1620–1679.* Åbo: Åbo Akademi.

Virmala, Anja, & Ruotsalainen, Pirjo 1972: *Lammin pitäjän historia I. Ruotsin vallan loppuun.* Lammi: Lammin kunta.

Virrankoski, Pentti 1956: "Uskonpuhdistuksesta isoonvihaan". In: *Suur-Kalajoen historia I.* Kalajoki: Suur-Kalajoen historiatoimikunta.

Virrankoski, Pentti 2000: "Bochmöller, Johan, Oulun pormestari, kruununvouti (K 1682 jälkeen)", *Kansallisbiografia*: http://www.kansallisbiografia.fi/kb/artikkeli/5784 (1.6.2015).

Ågren, Kurt 1964: *Adelns bönder och kronans. Skatter och besvär i Uppland 1650–1680.* Studia Historica Upsaliensia 11. Uppsala: Uppsala universitet.

Ågren, Maria 1997: *Att hävda sin rätt. Synen på jordägandet i 1600-talets Sverige, speglade i institutet urminnes hävd.* Skrifter utgivna av Institutet för rättshistorisk forskning. Serien 1, Rättshistoriskt bibliotek 57. Stockholm: Institutet för rättshistorisk forskning.

Österberg, Eva 1971: *Gränsbygd under krig. Ekonomiska, demografiska och administrativa förhållanden i sydvästra Sverige under och efter nordiska sjuårskriget.* Bibliotheca historica Lundensis 26. Lund: Gleerups.

Österberg, Eva 1987: "Svenska lokalsamhällen i förändring ca 1550–1850. Participation, representation och politisk kultur i den svenska självstyrelsen. Ett angeläget forskningsområde", *Historisk Tidskrift 107.*

# Clergy VII

Mikko Hiljanen[1]
http://orcid.org/0000-0003-3441-5354

# Servants of the Crown or Trustees of the People? Personal Agency Among the Local Clergy (1550–1610)

During the early modern era, clerical appointment was neither a simple nor straightforward task in the Realm of Sweden. Any authorities who had the power to influence this process did so – the Crown, nobility, bishops and local parishioners[2] – all of them did their best to intervene. But as if the system of appointments was not already complicated enough, the significance of the appointments themselves was more so. The entire Reformation in Sweden, in fact revolved around the topic of clerical appointments. The Swedish Realm broke off from Rome started because King Gustavus Vasa (1496–1560) wanted to take the right to appoint bishops away from the Pope.[3]

The point of departure for this study lies in the fact that pastors (*kyrkoherde*)[4] had an important, if somewhat complicated, part to play in state-building. This chapter approaches the state-building process in standpoint of clerical appointments. Clerical appointment process is seen as a two-folded procedure where on one hand, the authorities who had a lawful right to appoint pastors, contested with each other for who could use the right. As many previous studies have shown, the Crown held most of the powers to appoint – at least during Gustavus Vasa's reign and in some parishes – even if these laws and norms seemed to be in a constant state of flux during the sixteenth century.[5]

But though the Crown was the winner in this first part of the process (it could appoint pastors independently in at least some of the parishes), it was not the same who was appointed to the post; different pastor-candidates had different attributes and know-how that could benefit the authority on the local level. Thus at the second stage of the negotiating process, there were representatives of the Crown, local parishioners, and the pastor-candidates themselves who figuratively discussed who would eventually be appointed. Here the goal was to decide which of the candidates was most appealing to all the parties assembled.

This chapter concentrates on pastoral appointments at the local level (the second type of negotiating process). It asks what kind of people were eventually appointed pastor and why? The answer to this question shed light on a number of issues. Not only on whether the Crown varied its appointments according to the political times, but also on the kind of pastors local parishioners preferred, as most pastors had worked in the same parish before their appointment (i.e., parishioners already knew them). And what happened in cases where the parishioners' and Crown's preferences differed? Also, did the Reformation change the relationship between parishioners and clergy in any way? By studying these situations up close like this, it is possible to find out how deals were struck to get a pastor that both parties could accept. Answers to these questions may not shed light on the personal agency of clergymen per se, but they certainly render it visible by revealing the boundaries of their actions. By understanding the boundaries of what actions they permitted themselves to carry out, we thereby get an idea of the extent of their personal agency.

The focus area of this study – the diocese of Turku – was spread over five different provinces during the latter part of the sixteenth century: Varsinais-Suomi, Satakunta, Uusimaa, Häme and Pohjanmaa (see map). This area covered both the oldest population centres of Finland (Turku), and areas where the population was growing during the century. In ecclesiastical terms, even though Finland was divided into two separate dioceses in 1554 – Turku in the West and Vyborg (Viborg) in the East – it was the former that was considered the "head-diocese". This was not just because Turku was the oldest of the two dioceses, but also because there were periods when there was no appointed bishop in Vyborg (1563–1568 and 1578–1618), so the ecclesiastical responsibilities for the whole of Finland fell on the shoulders of the Bishop of Turku.[6]

The time frame of this chapter covers the reigns of the kings immediately after Gustavus Vasa: Eric XIV (1560–1568), John III (1568–1592), Sigismund (1592–1599), and Charles IX – both as regent (1599–1604) and king (1604–1611). The time frame is particularly interesting from the state-building point of view. During these years, the hegemony of the Crown was almost constantly being challenged by both nobles and dukes (brothers or uncles of the king). At the same time, the religious turmoil brought on by the Reformation was drawing to a conclusion. By the 1610s, Sweden was a Lutheran country, or the most important clergymen and office-holders were, at least on paper, Lutheran. In addition, due to the harsh war times, the clergy had to take part on the secular matters during the reign of Gustavus Adolphus (1611–1632) too, when pastors were burdened with the tough responsibility for population accounting and tax-collecting (together with bailiffs).[7] Thus, the period studied in this chapter is particularly important in adding knowledge on the building of the Swedish governmental system at the local level on the early years of the era known as the Age of Greatness.

During the Middle Ages and early modern era, there were three types of parish one could be appointed to as a cleric: regal, consistorial, and patronal. In regal parishes, the Crown would appoint the pastor, while in consistorial parishes the job fell to the parishioners and the bishop and chapter of the diocese. Meanwhile, in patronal parishes this responsibility lay with a noble patron.[8] Yet in all these cases, parishioners, or at least the head of each parish had some part to play in nominating the pastor they favoured and this had to be legally taken into account before making an appointment to the post.[9]

During the Middle Ages and first decades of sixteenth century, most parishes were consistorial. In consistorial parishes, parishioners chose and nominated the candidate they wanted, while the bishop's task was to check that the nominated person had the education and knowledge required.[10] However, after the Reformation, King Gustavus Vasa claimed responsibility for all clerical appointments. He also limited the rights of bishops and the chapters of dioceses; and confiscated the land that used to belong to the church and monasteries. All this increased the Crown's influence over clerical appointments. Gustavus Vasa also claimed that any new parishes established should be regal ones.[11]

After the death of Gustavus Vasa, the political struggle between his sons started almost immediately, also clerical appointments in the duchies, especially in Finland, became a flashpoint for conflict. At the same time, the Church tried to get back what it had lost in the Reformation. By the latter part of the sixteenth century, the Realm of Sweden felt the need to improve the way Finland was governed because of the ongoing war with Russia (1570–1595). This meant putting more power in the hands of the governor there, who now had great prerogatives – for example, he could intervene in the clerical appointing process.[12] So by the end of the 1500s, clerical appointments had become one more factor in a complicated ongoing game of power.

Usually the pastor was appointed in the form of a letter (collation).[13] The structure of collations is quite technical and with little other information. It mentions the name of the appointee and the parish to which the pastor is to be posted; and there are instructions for the parishioners and the pastor from the authority that issued the collation. This was normally the King, and it would ask that the parishioners accept the nominated pastor to be their shepherd and that the pastor would promise to practice religion in pure way. It is notable that the form of collation would vary slightly depending on who was giving it. For example, Charles IX's collations underline the purity of the religion, which is understandable considering his religious convictions and the events of the late 1590s in Finland.[14]

## Sources and methods

The results of this study are based on the clergy-database (CDB) that I have created. Information for the database has been collected from various sources. The main source is a compilation called *Turun hiippakunnan paimenmuisto 1554–1721* collected by Kyösti Väänänen.[15] *Paimenmuisto* (*herdaminne* in Swedish, *Pfarrerbuch* in German) contains micro-biographies and registers of the clergy. The information has been collected from official documents, letters from the King to pastors (such as collations), histories of the parishes, and literature on the subject etc. The information contained in *Paimenmuisto* has been de-coded and enriched by adding new information from documents such as bailiffs' accounts[16] that has not been used in *Paimenmuisto*. De-coding the information and constructing the database has helped for example to see the connections between clergies that would have remained in the shadows if one just reads the original documents and information.

Because of the database and the analysis it has involved, the theoretical framework of this chapter leans towards prosopography. However the methods used are not purely prosopographic. Usually in the field prosopography, the database is created in a way that the researcher decides what kind of information he or she brings to it. Normally the information that turns out to be most pertinent, and is thus collected, is the kind of which is known for every person of the group studied (for example, the date and place of birth, name of father and mother, godparents and godchildren etc.).[17]

To offer a wealth of information, I have used a method that goes beyond the boundaries of prosopography: I have collected and used *all* available information from lives of the clergies not just the information that is pertinent to the questions of the chapter. To be more precise, my database includes information, not just about clerical appointments, but on the lives and careers of the clergymen from a broad perspective. As a consequence, I do not have the same kind of data on every clergyman.[18] I believe, however, that this approach is a particularly fertile for this chapter as it sheds more light on the overall extent of personal agency among the clergy. By focusing on all aspects of clerical life, not just the information represented in their appointments per se, a deeper understanding can be gained of the structures and culture that determined the way clergymen lived and what they could and could not do.

The database has been analyzed first of all, to examine how many pastors were appointed and which kind of the authority appointed them to the post. Altogether there were 267 pastors appointed in the diocese of Turku between 1560 and 1611. Of these 267, 46 (roughly 17%) were appointed by the king, 19 (or 7%) by the Bishop of Turku, five (2%) by dukes (John and Charles), and four (1.5%) got their appointments via the nobility.[19] It is these 74 clergymen that form the base-group for the study described in this chapter. It is unknown how the rest of the pastors were chosen and appointed, as in every case, the procedure was somewhat unofficial. Either there were no documents of the appointments in the first place, or they have not been preserved.

However, in the 74 cases where the person who appointed the pastor *is* known, a more detailed analysis has been possible. But this is not due to any further information in the collations themselves. If one wants to find out why a particular clergyman got the post, one has to look elsewhere for the reason, as the collations had scant else but the names of places and people involved in the appointment. This challenge has been met here by analyzing information on the lives and careers of the clergymen in question. By studying their whole life and entire career, it is possible to find out the kind of clergymen that were most appreciated, and those that had a harder time. Within the 74 cases, I have chosen key cases to be presented below. These cases illustrate the different factors that affected clerical appointments. To summarize the main argument, the political and religious situation in the realm affected the clerical appointments. In addition, pastors had to keep in mind the situation at their own parishes where they exercised their duties. Pastors had to balance between the riptides of these two due to the fact that the expectations towards the pastor were different at the central and local level of realm.

As always with case studies, the results of this chapter beg the question about generalization and coverage. Even though this chapter reveals some of the reasons behind clerical appointments, it does not provide fully comprehensive results. Due to the rather limited availability of historical sources on the lives and careers of sixteenth century clergy, the results here are more suggestive than normative. In addition, information on some clergymen is more extensive than on others, and it is fair to say that the key cases I have chosen are the examples where there is more information available. It should also be noted that the cases where the information is richer are for those appointments that were disputed, because these conflicts needed to be investigated and documented, which means more documentation and thus a greater chance of documents surviving to this day. So there is perhaps an inherent bias in the examples studied here against those clerical appointments and careers where all went well (as these would not have been so well documented). However it is impossible to say whether the clergymen who left historical sources behind them were the exceptions, or whether their lives and careers were typical of most.

## Political power and the loyalty of pastors

Swedish history in the second half of sixteenth century was characterized by political turmoil. Later on, in the 1590s, political turmoil focused increasingly on the power struggle between the King Sigismund and his uncle Duke Charles.[20] But at first it centred around the competing claims of Gustavus Vasa's sons. Even though Gustavus's purpose had been to secure the dominant status of the Vasa family by enfeoffing critical parts of the realm to his sons (i.e., making the new king's brothers dukes), the reality proved quite different. The duchies became instead a means to challenge the hegemony of the king and an obstacle to national cohesion.

One aspect of the political struggle between the king and dukes was that dukes now also had the right to appoint people to various offices of political importance. Finnish historian Yrjö Blomstedt has noted, in his study concerning the chief and district judges of Finland, that especially during the 1560s, the rotation of judges accelerated. There were two incidents that caused this – the defeat of Duke John, in 1563, and then the deposition of King Eric five years later[21]. After the defeat of John, the Crown dismissed judges who had been loyal to the duke. In their place, the king appointed judges in whom he could trust[22]. A similar chain of events happened in 1568, but this time the change of judges went the other way. Now that John was king (John III), he replaced the judges in every corner of the eastern part of the realm – especially those judges who had once loyally served him when he was a duke, but had then changed allegiance under Eric.[23]

As the case of the judges illustrates, political events affected the appointment of office-holders. And this applied to the office of clergyman too, as politics and religion were inextricably linked in the early modern era, especially in Sweden.[24] The political struggle was not so much at the individual level, but in terms of opposing networks with either the king or the dukes at the tip of each iceberg. The king and dukes tried to increase their influence by appointing skillful and capable agents to strengthen their power-base at the local level. In return, these local agents – such as pastors – could further their own careers by showing loyalty to the network.[25] In other words there was sufficient supply to meet the demand. As a local authority, pastors offered an important means of support to either the king or duke in their political struggles.

The conflict between Eric and John certainly had repercussions on the life of clergymen in the diocese of Turku.[26] By the end of the 1550s and beginning of the 1560s, Duke John had taken an oath of allegiance from the Finnish clergy in his duchy. Many of the Finnish pastors were fined because of the oath, but more radical action was to come. For example, the Chaplain of Pertteli Nicolaus (lifetime unknown) was executed because he had given information about the king's army to John.[27]

The Pastor of Taivassalo, Matthias Michelis Carpelan (d. c. 1561), was sentenced to death too, but his sentence was never carried out as the parishioners of Taivassalo testified that he had not supported the duke. Due to their appeal, the king pardoned Carpelan and let him return to his old post. In addition to the testimony of the parishioners, there is evidence that Carpelan actually did not support John's policies, and this also helped tip the balance in his favour. This case suggests that the Crown purged persons who were loyal to Duke John, but the enemies of John were friends of new king and they could stay in their post. But this was a double-edged sword, as Carpelan was doomed to lose a major part of his property in 1580 for the very same reason that he did not approve of King John III's liturgy.[28]

Even though the networks were built more or less on a foundation of politics and loyalty, in the case of the clergy, religion was of course a key factor in joining the network. This was particularly the case with the Swedish kings of the late sixteenth century, who often distinguished themselves from each other by their religious conviction. It was perhaps most acute under John III, who inclined towards Catholicism especially during the 1560s and 70s, while other kings (Sigismund is an exception) were more or less reformed Protestants. Religious conviction was particularly prominent in the power struggle between John and his younger brother Charles.[29]

From the point of view of clerical appointments, it was not so much the accession of John III in 1568 that changed matters in Finland,[30] but the Church Ordinance of 1571 that was compiled during his reign and was perhaps the most important legislative reform of the sixteenth century. Even though, on paper, it sought to restore the Church's priority in making appointments, the reality was somewhat the opposite. Especially halfway through the 1570s, when John tried to carry through the liturgical reforms[31] he wanted, he found himself using clerical appointments and discharges as leverage instead.[32]

Pastors who accepted the new liturgy were helped with their careers. For example, Martinus Olai (c. 1510–1585), the Pastor of Rauma and born in the 1510s, had been originally ordained as a Catholic and was a stalwart supporter of the new liturgy. John so favoured him that in 1577, the king appointed him as preacher for the theological school in Stockholm, with a view to him completing the establishment of the new liturgical program. Later in the decade, the King also used Olai's knowledge to negotiate with Rome about restoring the Catholic religion to Sweden.[33]

Within the diocese of Turku, pastors who supported the new liturgy were in the majority. The few clergymen, who did not support it, could expect a difficult career.[34] One of them was the Pastor for the Cathedral Parish of Turku,[35] Henricus Jacobi (d. c. 1582), who was excused from his post via a letter from the king in 1581[36]. In his place, Thomas Laurentii (d. c. 1595) was appointed, who was an enthusiastic supporter of the new liturgy. John also sent him to study in University of Tübingen to learn Greek so that he could be used as a religious negotiator with Constantinople after negotiations with Rome had broken down.[37]

As the cases above suggest, the clergymen's relationship with the Crown was important in many ways. The fact that those clergymen who accepted the new liturgy did well until the end of John's reign, but after his death ran into difficulties would seem to confirm this. In addition, there are cases which show that the clergymen were aware of the political situation in the realm and how they might have to react or adapt to its changes.

In the Uppsala Assembly of 1593, a church policy was announced to replace the one that John had started in 1570s.[38] Understandably, the changes meant problems for the clergymen who had previously enjoyed the favours of King John III. For example, Thomas Laurentii faced accusations in the Uppsala assembly from Karl Henriksson Horn, a supporter of Duke Charles. He was accused of scheming behind the back of the pastor who had preceded him in his post, and had used John's favoured liturgy to have him discharged. Laurentii denied this accusation to begin with, but later was made to apologize his conduct.[39]

Even though Laurentii was allowed to hold on to his post, he only lived for a few more years after the Uppsala assembly. His successor – Gregorius Martinti Teet (c. 1560–1615) – was appointed by Duke Charles. During John III's reign, Teet had supported the red book, but had changed his mind after the king's death. Once he became Pastor of the Cathedral Parish of Turku, Teet avoided Catholic-style ceremonies and he enjoyed Charles' trust. For example, Charles nominated him twice to the bishopric of Turku, but he never got the post.[40] Teet's case not only illustrates both the shift in religious and domestic policy brought on by the death of John III and the Uppsala assembly, but also that pastors could take advantage of these shifts if willing to change their own opinions about religion.

The pastorate of the Cathedral Parish of Turku was not the only post that was contested during the 1590s. Another was the post of Cathedral Dean, which became vacant in 1594 when Henricus Canuti (c. 1520s–1595) resigned due to his old age. Canuti had had the trust of King John during his lifetime, for example, working as a substitute bishop from 1576 to

1583 when the king did not appoint a new bishop to Turku in place of the dead one. Also from 1578 onwards, Canuti was made the Superintendent of Vyborg (Viborg) when Ericus Matthiae Härkäpää (c. 1520s–1578), the Bishop of Vyborg, died; effectively making him in charge of the Church in the entire eastern part of the Swedish Realm.[41] But when the post of Cathedral Dean became vacant, Duke Charles appointed a clergyman called Petrus Henrici Melartopaeus (c. 1550–1610). If the old Cathedral Dean had been John's trusted man, the new one was quite the opposite. Melartopaeus was born in Finland, but after he had finished his studies abroad, he did not return to his home diocese, but instead sought his way to Charles' duchy. During his years in Sweden, he had taken part in meetings of the clergy, which had decided to oppose John's liturgy, pledging themselves instead to the Augsburg Confession and Lutheranism. As Cathedral Dean it was thus perhaps not surprising that Melartopaeus tried to extirpate all Catholic convention from religious services.[42]

With the decline in careers of clergymen that Duke Charles did not approve of – such as Thomas Laurentii, came the rise of those that he did. For example Melartopaeus became the substitute Bishop of Turku when Bishop Ericus Erici Sorolainen was imprisoned and suspended in 1600. And in 1604, when Charles broke down the chapter institution, Melartopaeus moved back to Sweden where he worked as a superintendent in Mariestad. He enjoyed Charles' trust to the end of his life: for example he was one of the clergymen who amended Charles' proposal of the Church Code.[43]

These cases illustrates that, due the fact that the power- and religion politics intermingled, the power struggle of the latter part of sixteenth century affected to the lives of ecclesiastical agents as well. By supporting and sharing the religious ideas of the Crown, clergymen could promote their career. However, this was winning tactic only as far as the Crown lived and reigned. After his death, these kinds of tendencies became burden especially if the successor had different kinds of religious thoughts.[44] It is notable that although politics and religion was still merged in seventeenth century and later, the phenomenon where the religious conviction of the King affected his subjects is strongly tied to the sixteenth century. After the reign of Charles IX the religion played much more insignificant role.[45]

The above examples of the kinds of administrative post that were hotly contested, because by having one of their men in such a post, the king or duke could control the whole diocese.[46] However, the Crown did not only appoint the head of the Church. Another group of clergymen that were appointed by the king because of their relationships with the king were those who had served in the royal court or as a chaplain in army.[47] Appointing them to a post that was more profitable from an economic point of view or more respected professionally was one way for the king to reward the clergymen who had served well.[48] But it was also in the Crown's interest to appoint loyal pastors who were leaders of the parishes and representatives of its authority at the local level[49] as they could secure the support of the entire parish. Clergymen who had got their post this way (as a gift), also owed a debt of gratitude to the person who had appointed them.[50]

Finally, economic reasons and personal material capital affected clerical appointments as well. Clergymen could bribe the Crown for a pastorate. This was particularly usual during the reign of Gustavus Vasa and illustrates the notorious avarice of the King.[51] For example in 1556, the pastor's post of Eura was vacant and two candidates were competing for it. The first was Matthias Henrici Raucka (d. c. 1589), whose election was supported by the Bishop of Turku, Mikael Agricola. However the King neglected the support and appointed his competitor Johannes Jacobi Wenne (1510s–1572) to the post after Wenne had donated estate that he had inherited to the Crown.[52]

After the reign of Gustavus Vasa however, the situation went somewhat the other way. In the latter part of the sixteenth century, rather than asking to be paid for making appointments, those who wanted greater political power actively sought pastoral loyalty by promising economic benefits or relief from taxation to loyal clergymen instead.[53] For example, during the 1590's, Duke Charles promised part of the Crown's fishing profits from the river Lammaistenkoski to the Pastor of Kokemäki (Johannes Michaelis (d. c. 1612)) in return for his loyalty against King Sigismund. And later when Michaelis supplied at least two horsemen to the king's army, Claes Fleming (the royal regent of Finland) granted Michaelis tax-revenue from four farms.[54] This would seem to suggest that during the latter part of the sixteenth century, when the political struggle heated up, the Crown (or Duke Charles) needed the help of pastors more than pastors perhaps needed them. Indeed, they were now willing to pay pastors for their loyalty in the struggle for power.

## *Persons of trust and reputation – a template for future officeholders of the realm?*

Although – as pointed out above – politics, loyalty and religion played a meaningful part in the clerical appointment process, the reason for appointment in most cases was that pastors had worked previously as a chaplain or assistant-pastor; or else the appointee was directly related to the previous pastor of the parish (e.g., his son).[55] In fact, the Reformation made possible that the son of a pastor could inherit his father's old post.[56]

Since we have no way of proving whether these appointments may also have been the Crown attempting to the spread its power networks, because most of them concerned 'normal' parishes (i.e., they were not significant administrational posts in the Church) and occurred at times when there were no significant political upheavals like regime change or liturgical reform – like the cases in former subsection – it is reasonable to look elsewhere for an explanation. One could, for example, look more closely at pastors' relationship with their parishioners to get a better idea of the expertise valued by the authorities that clergymen got earlier in their career as a chaplain or assistant clergy; and to examine what it means in broader, state-building, perspective.

Studies of the sixteenth and seventeenth century clergy emphasize the trust and loyalty that existed between parishioners and pastors. Parishioners clearly valued those pastor-candidates they knew, who lived like everybody else in the parish, and who knew the local area. And although to inherit a pastorate was forbidden by the Church Ordinance of 1571, in practice it was not long after the Reformation that offices began to run in the family. The parishioners, in particular, seemed to encourage the inheritance of posts, usually giving their support to the pastor's sons and sons-in-law, when a new pastor was to be chosen.[57] But this was not always the case. For example, in 1589, the parishioners of Karkku supported a pastor-candidate called Henricus Petri, preferring him over Matthaeus Matthiae (d. c. 1639), the son of the previous incumbent, who had worked as a chaplain under his father.[58] If parishioners usually preferred those candidates they already knew, why was this not the case here?

There were of course other criteria than just familiarity for parishioners' choice. Having a decent reputation was important for the pastor as well. In this case, the previous pastor, Matthias Martini (d. c. 1596), was discharged in 1588 and his relatively large property confiscated. The dismissal probably came down to the liturgical reforms of King John III. The clergymen in the Swedish parts of the realm particularly resisted the reforms and fought it out until the end of the king's reign. But by the end of the 1570s and beginning of the 1580s, the struggle intensified and more extreme methods were used to implement the reforms. One such method was to discharge pastors who did not accept them and to confiscate their property.[59] The case suggests that Matthias Martini not only lost his pastorate and property, but his reputation as well. Since in the early modern era it the reputation of an individual was tied to the reputation of one's kin, this would perhaps explain why Martini's son lost the support of local parishioners.[60]

Reputation was the measure of a pastor's social status and social status helped clergymen into office. So if someone wanted to replace the pastor, he could try to slander the pastor's reputation. There is one example of this from 1599, when Duke Charles and parishioners of Kokemäki accused the pastor, Johannes Michaelis, of being a witch and called for his dismissal.[61] The power of accusations lay in the fact that simply being accused was enough to damage one's reputation. The motives for making such accusations were usually competitive, as this case perfectly illustrates. During the civil war of the 1590s, Michaelis supported the legal ruler (Sigismund) and his companion, and was therefore against Duke Charles, who evidently felt the need to slender his opponent. The accusation seemed to work as, in 1600, Bishop Sorolainen told the Diet (Riksdag) of Linköping that the parishioners of Kokemäki had complained that their shepherd mismanaged his job, and he had been dismissed.[62]

Simply being rich could be enough to ruin a clergyman's reputation as well; especially if it was felt that the wealth had been gained through preying on the weakness of parishioners. Gunnar Suolahti and Esko M. Laine note in their research that during the sixteenth and seventeenth centuries, clergy purchased property by occupying the deserted homesteads that had formerly belonged to those who could no longer afford to pay taxes, and often the issue would end up having to be resolved in court.[63] Material disputes could thus also have been behind the accusations made against

Johannes Michaelis by the parishioners of Kokemäki. He was paying taxes on two houses which suggest that he might well have one of the clergy who had occupied a deserted homestead. To make matters worse for himself, he demanded that if parishioners did not pay their taxes in time, they should settle their debt by doing extra work.[64] This clearly did not make him very popular among the poorer parishioners.

However, personal wealth could also work in a pastor's favour. One example of this comes, funnily enough, from Kokemäki again. Around year 1600 the parishioners of Kokemäki asked the chaplain of Kaarina, Jacobus Erici (d. c. 1603), to become their new pastor. Erici was also a relatively wealthy man, but unlike Michaelis, his material wealth did not anger the parishioners. In hard times, rather than get the poor to repay their debts in kind, he had lent money to the peasants so that they could pay their taxes and, in this way, he actually improved his social status and reputation.[65]

Pastors could of course ruin their reputation quite by themselves as well. For example, they would be directly dismissed for committing a felony[66] (such as adultery or manslaughter), but this also applied to crimes related to their office. For example, if a pastor married a couple for who did not have lawful permission to do so, the punishment could be that he be discharged (at least partially).[67]

Reputation and trust were understandably important qualities for a pastor to have. Kyösti Kiuasmaa has studied office-holding in the central and local government of late sixteenth century Finland. He has noticed that the nature of offices changed somewhat in the 1560s. During the Middle Ages, and the first part of the sixteenth century, secular offices (such as bailiffs and clerks) relied on a system trust and loyalty between the office-holders and people. But from the 1560s onwards this loyalty started to break down and office-holders became more responsible for the legality of their actions. This led to more intensive supervision by the central government, and the increasing professionalization of administrative posts.[68]

The cases above suggest that the relationship between pastors and parishioners remained to be based on trust and reputation while the role of secular office-holders changed. Unlike secular office-holders, they did not simply depend on the goodwill of the king for their post. However, this was not for any lack of trying on the part of the Crown.[69] There were even some cases when the parishioners and the Crown had quite different people in mind for a pastorate.

## Conflicts between parishioners and the authorities over pastoral appointments

The motives behind parishioners' and the authorities' nominations for appointments often differed. In some cases the authorities appointed the person they wanted to the post, irrespective of the parishioners' will. For example, in the case of Matthaeus Matthiae, Bishop Sorolainen appointed him pastor in 1588 anyway, even though parishioners supported another candidate.[70] In other cases, parishioners did not just passively stand by and accept the decision made by authorities.⁷¹ For example, in 1581 the clergyman Martinus Olai⁷² received a collation from the Crown that awarded him the pastorate of Laitila, after the Cathedral Dean of Turku (Henricus Canuti) had recommended him to the post. But even though Olai was the lawful pastor, parishioners would not accept him, and instead gave their support to the clergyman Henricus Petri, who had worked previously as the substitute-pastor of the parish. With the help of the parishioners, Petri eventually chased Olai off even though Olai appealed against this to the chapter of Turku and the secular court. Nevertheless, in spite of the fact that Petri and the parishioners had violated the king's order, Petri stayed in the post.⁷³

So even though pastors were often appointed by central government, they still needed a form of confirmation on the local level from parishioners. This begs at least two further questions:

1. Why did the support that parishioners showed sometimes lead to appointments, while other times it did not?

2. If the pastor had to gain the acceptance of parishioners, even after he had been legally appointed to the post by the authorities, how does this reflect on the state-building process?

Swedish historian Mats Hallenberg has noted that the social networks that pastors had cultivated, played a significant role in deciding the outcome of conflicts on a local level. Their links with parishioners, other local authorities (pastors of neighbouring parishes or the bailiff), and the Crown meant they had to carefully pick which of these three sides to ally themselves with, if a conflict arose, if they were to gain anything from it.⁷⁴ In this way, Hallenberg's notions may provide an answer to our first question regarding clerical appointments. In the examples of Matthiae and Olai, both had powerful local authority supporters – Matthiae was the son of the last pastor and his brother-in-law was the head of Turku castle, while Olai's patron was Cathedral Dean. But whereas Matthiae's network supported him to the very end of the controversy, Olai's diocese deputed his appeal to the secular court which found in favour of Petri.⁷⁵ In this case, the network of parishioners was stronger than the network of local authority, and Olai had chosen the weaker allies.

The second question takes us to a deeper level of local society. Göran Malmstedt has noted in his study on the seventeenth century religious mentality of Swedish peasants and clergy, that pastors were not always undebatable the head of a parish; and that parishioners would in fact often challenge his authority. Pastors had to first earn their authority and respect by interacting on a day-to-day basis with parishioners to gain the right to be the head of the parish.⁷⁶ The cases above support Malmstedt's notions, but suggest further that, not just parishioners and pastor, but all three parties – pastor, parishioners and higher authorities (e.g., the Crown) – were involved in the interaction that determined how the pastor earned his authority. The higher authority provided the official authorization by giving the collation, while parishioners granted the unofficial authorization that was important on a day-to-day basis. It is clear that it was in everybody's interest that the pastor who was appointed was accepted by both the authorities and parishioners. However in reality, persons who fulfilled the requirements of both did hardly always exist. But by negotiating, the demands of all parties were met and a pastor that everyone could accept was chosen. Thus, from the state-building point of view, the clerical appointment process was an important event where the authorities and the people could meet and build the state at the local level.

There is one more case that supports this hypothesis. In year 1562, the Chaplain of Pori, Marcus Gregorii, was awarded the pastorate of Närpiö in a collation from the Crown. The Bishop of Turku and Duke John, however, had not considered Gregorii as a candidate for this post at all. Instead, they had nominated the Chaplain of Mustasaari, Olaus Nicolai, who was also supported by the parishioners. The result was an ongoing dispute between the candidates. In the middle of this, the Crown advised Gregorii to withdraw his candidature and let Nicolai have the post, but this never happened. Nicolai had to eventually return to his old post in Mustasaari.[77] Gregorii's war of attrition seemed to have worked and he remained in the post for the next decade. However, the parishioners had not forgotten, and in 1574 and 1575 they appealed to the Crown that Gregorii had collected too much tax and the tax-goods he had claimed were the kind that he could then sell on at a profit. Even if these accusations might have been exaggerated (it was quite normal for the people to appeal to the Crown about, for example, corrupt bailiffs),[78] he was discharged by the diocese of Turku in 1575.[79] The result suggests that the authorities were also looking for a reason to get rid of him. Furthermore, this suggests that sooner or later the pastor who did not have the support of parishioners or the Crown was discharged.

Appealing to the Crown was not the only way for parishioners to show their dissatisfaction with a pastor. For example, there was also the more radical practice of literally throwing the pastor over the church fence, which was an age-old tradition for removing unwanted clergy. Even though this kind of behaviour was one that the authorities were trying to weed out after the Reformation, there are still examples from the sixteenth century that show the habit had not yet fully died out.[80] Parishioners therefore had more than one way to remove an unwanted pastor.

## Conclusion

Politics and religion intermingled in sixteenth century Sweden and, as we have seen in this chapter, different kings and dukes had different ideas about what constituted the one true religion. This chapter goes on to suggest that the most important posts in the diocese of Turku were appointed on such a political and religious basis. John III favoured those who accepted his liturgy, but after his death, these same people incurred the wrath of especially Duke Charles, who was a steady Lutheran and more inclined towards Calvinism. Later, after the death of John III, Charles was also opposed to the Catholic King Sigismund. When he competed to the throne with Sigismund,

Charles filled the major posts of the diocese of Turku with men he trusted that were stalwart Lutherans. During the reign of John, most of these men had already served Charles in his duchy.

In addition, the authorities – especially the Crown – would reward some of the men who had served in his court or in the army by appointing them to a pastorate, which was normally financially and socially rewarding. In these men, the king got loyal and trustworthy servants, who could promote the king's business at a local level. This kind of help and support was important especially in times when the king was competing, for example, with dukes (who were also trying to spread their networks at the local level).

The second major point this chapter makes is that, even if politics and religion played an important part in clerical appointments, the clergy-database reveals most appointments were made to those who had worked in the same parish beforehand or were relatives to the previous pastor (i.e., parishioners already knew that person and trusted him). As mentioned above, Kyösti Kiuasmaa has pointed out that the nature of office-holding changed in the latter part of the sixteenth century. The fact that trust and loyalty, which had played such a significant part in the relationship between clergy and parishioners since the Middle Ages, were still important, suggests that role of office-holder of the clergy did not change much when the rules of secular office-holders changed.[81] During the studied period, the authorities would appoint those persons they wanted, but the pastors also had to have the trust of people if they wanted to stay in the post. Speaking of clergymen's personal agency, they had to adapt to the new rules and ever-changing environment of the sixteenth century. In this respect, it is important to emphasize that the clergy were not passive players between the authorities and parishioners, but could very much choose whether or not to further their careers by picking the right allies among parishioners, other local authorities, and the Crown.

Because the Swedish state became more centred around the Crown during the sixteenth century, the pastors who supported the Crown were thereby participating in the state-building process. By supporting the king, promoting his cause, and spreading it at the local level, through the channels of ecclesiastical administration, the clergy acted as an important and unique builder of the state – there was no other group of office-holders who could offer the Crown the same kind of local building blocks as the clergy. The point here is that it was not just secular agents of the Crown that helped build the Swedish state, but also pastors with their particular kind of personal agency and privileged position of trust among parishioners.

However, the pastors who gave their loyalty to the other authorities besides the Crown, acted also as builders of the state. By opposing the religious conviction of the Crown and leaning on to other authorities (such as the pastors who seek to the duchy of Charles during the reign of John III did), pastors forced the state to act and to strengthen its capacity to uphold policy and religion. Thus, the question concerns much about whose state it was to be built: was it Crown's or other authorities, such as Dukes'?

The question centers on the personal agency of the clergy. The political and religious upheavals in studied period offered possibilities for the clergy to use their personal agency. In practice pastors could choose to support either the king or his opponents. The choice was a rational one: pastors weighted the situation in the realm and at the local level in their own parishes, took account their personal values, ideals, norms, emotions and opportunities and acted as they thought it was the best. I want to emphasize the fact that the religion was also flexible: in a way, pastors were able to balance between different types of Christian belief (Catholic or Reformed) and could change their opinions with the changing religious environment of the realm and according to their own thoughts about those changes.

In the end, the literature on state-building in sixteenth century Sweden generally emphasizes the importance of those who participated in tax-collecting and were able to read and write for this process (skills also useful in warfare).[82] These were also skills the clergy of the sixteenth and seventeenth centuries possessed. My purpose is not to deny that these skills were important in state-building, but to add that the clergy was, more often than not, trusted by local parishioners and this made him a powerful link for the state. He could not only relay information, but appease local areas. During the sixteenth century, the Crown may have tried to bend the clergy to its will, but did not really succeed, as in most cases the clergy's relationship with parishioners remained based on trust. This cannot have been irrelevant from the state-building point of view. For common people, it was supposedly important that they had a literate person, who was not entirely dependent on the central authority but was also servant of the people as well. All this emphasizes the clergy's key role as arbitrator between the authorities and the people, and in the state-building process as a whole.

The research on which this publication is based was funded by the Academy of Finland (grant no. 137741).

## Notes

1 Acknowledges: The Academy of Finland, Svenska Litteratursällskapet i Finland, The Finnish Cultural Foundation, Jalmari Finne's foundation and Alfred Kordelin foundation had endowed making of this chapter.
2 In this chapter term *authority/authorities* refers to the Crown, bishop and chapter of diocese and nobility (noble office-holders aswell). However, when it is important to show who appointed the pastor, the quarter is named (if it is known). Local parishioners, even they had role in appointment process, are not concluded to the group of authority, but parishioners are seen partly as an opposite to the authority. However, it is noteworthy to remind that the parishioners were not always a uniform group in their decisions and there could have been small interest groups in the parishes or individuals who acted as a spokesman of the whole parish as Lindström points out. Peter Lindström, *Prästval och politisk kultur 1650–1800*. Skrifter från institutionen för historiska studier 4 (Umeå: Umeå universitet, 2003), 112. See also Mats Hallenberg & Johan Holm, *Man ur huse. Hur krig, upplopp och förhandlingar påverkade svensk statsbildning I tidigmodern tid* (Lund: Nordic Academic Press: 2016).
3 Michael Roberts, *The Early Vasas. A History of Sweden, 1521–1611* (London: Cambridge University Press, 1968), p. 64.

4   Pastors were in charge of religious life in parishes. They held services, taught and supervised the parishioners. In addition, among other things, pastors acted as the chairmen of the meeting of the parishes (*sockenstämma*) and held judicial power at some level too. They also worked sometimes also as parish scribes (*sockenskrivare*), and could for example to write petition letters to the King at parishioners request. It is important to notice how the role of the pastors changed after the Reformation and especially at the seventeenth century.

5   Hjalmar Holmquist, *Tillsättningar av gäll i Sverige under reformationsårhundradet*. Historisk tidskrift (1933), pp. 97–100; Tore Heldtander, *Prästtillsättningar i Sverige under stormaktstiden. Tiden före kyrkolagen 1686* (Uppsala: Svenska Kyrkohistoriska föreningen, 1955), pp. 15–16; Martin Sandahl, *Prästval i Sverige mot kulturell och social bakgrund* (Stockholm: Gummesson, 1966), p. 39; Roberts, *The Early*, p. 273; Kauko Pirinen, "Papinvaalilainsäädännön kehitys Suomessa vuoteen 1964". In: Hannu Mustakallio (ed.), *Suomen kirkkohistoriallisen seuran vuosikirja 79* (Helsinki: The Finnish Society of Church History, 1989), p. 34; Tuula Hockman, "Kuninkaan valvonnan alle". In: Lahtinen, Anu, Ijäs, Miia (toim.), *Risti ja lounatuuli. Rauman seurakunnan historia keskiajalta vuoteen 1640* (Helsinki: Suomalaisen kirjallisuuden seura, 2015), p. 105; Cp. Mikko Hiljanen, "Limits of Power: Clerical appointment as part of domestic policy in Sweden after the Reformation, 1560–1611", *Perichoresis*, Vol. 13 (2) (2015), pp. 35–55.

6   For example Jukka Paarma, *Hiippakuntahallinto Suomessa 1554–1604. Hiippakuntahallinto Suomessa 1554–1604*. Suomen kirkkohistoriallisen seuran toimituksia 116 (Helsinki: The Finnish Society of Church History, 1980), pp. 115–138.

7   Roberts, *The Early*; Petri Karonen, *Pohjoinen suurvalta. Ruotsi ja Suomi 1521–1809* (Helsinki: The Finnish Literature Society, 2014); Sven A. Nilsson, *De Stora krigens tid. Om Sverige som militärstat och bondesamhälle*. Studia Historica Upsaliensia 161 (Uppsala: Uppsala universitet, 1990), pp. 64–66; Mats Hallenberg, Johan Holm and Dan Johansson, "Organization, Legitimation, Participation. State formation as a dynamic process. Swedish example, c. 1523–1680", *Scandinavian Journal of History*, 33, 2008, pp. 259.

8   However in Diocese of Turku, the nobles did not take advantage of this privilege. Instead they tried to get the pastor they wanted by sending letters of recommendation. K. A. Appelberg, *Bidrag till belysning af sättet för prästtjänsternas besättande i Finland från reformationen till medlet af 17:de seklet* (Helsingfors, 1896), p. 128.

9   For example Paarma, *Hiippakuntahallinto*, pp. 363–364. The peasantry's role was not only a significant player in ecclesiastical matters, but also in national politics right from the beginning of the Swedish Realm. Hallenberg, Holm and Johansson, "Organization", pp. 253–254.

10  During the Middle Ages some of the posts were appointed by the Pope. Some officials of the Pope's court tried to take advantage of this and get themselves appointed to the pastorates. Sometimes this led to the situation where the Pope nominated some of these sharks to an open post even though the shark had no plans to actually take care of it. These situations then led to conflict between the appointee and chapter of the local diocese, who had planned to appoint some other clergyman. Clerical appointments were the most common kind of disagreement brought before the Pope's tribunal (*Sacra Romana Rota*). Kirsi Salonen, *Kirkollisen oikeuden päälähteillä. Sacra Romana Rotan toiminta ja sen oikeudellinen tausta myöhäiskeskiajalla ja uuden ajan taitteessa*. Suomen kirkkohistoriallisen seuran toimituksia 221 (Helsinki: The Finnish Society of Church History, 2012).

11  For example Appelberg, *Prästtjänsternas*, pp. 2–3, 48–49; Gunnar Suolahti, *Suomen papisto 1600- ja 1700-luvuilla* (Porvoo: WSOY, 1919), pp. 121, 124; Sandahl, *Prästval*, pp. 39–40, 42; Paarma, *Hiippakuntahallinto*, pp. 363–365. Conditions in clerical appointments during the reign of Gustavus Vasa in some sense reminds

later the era of autocracy (1680–1718): The King was, or wanted to be, in charge of the clerical appointments. Lindström, *Prästval*, pp. 65–66.
12 Appelberg, *Prästtjänsternas*, pp. 62–63; Holmquist, *Tillsättningar*, pp. 116–118; Heldtander, *Prästtillsättningar*, p. 20; Paarma, *Hiippakuntahallinto*, pp. 366–379.
13 Especially the collations that the king gave have been preserved fairly well. However there are no collations that have been given by other authority. Nevertheless there are sources that reveal that other authority than the King appointed pastor. For example there is confirmation letters where the King confirms the collation that for example bishop had given. HFKP 1, pp. 88, 67–68; also Paarma, *Hiippakuntahallinto*, p. 389.
14 Example of Charles' collation, for example HFKP 3, pp. 278, 209–210. The form and phrasing of a mandate that the King gave to the bailiffs reminds lot of collations. However the bailiffs' mandate did not changed during sixteenth century. Mats Hallenberg, *Kungen, fogdarna och riket. Lokalförvaltningen och statsbyggande under tidigt Vasatid* (Stockholm: Symposium, 2001), pp. 97–98.
15 Kyösti Väänänen, Turun hiippakunnan paimenmuisto 1554–1721 (electronic publication). Studia Biographica 9. Helsinki: Suomalaisen Kirjallisuuden Seura, 2011. On line at: http://www.finlit.fi/henkilohistoria/paimenmuisto.
16 On bailiff's accounts for instance Petri Karonens and Marko Hakanens article in this anthology.
17 See for example the introduction of this book and chapter of Marko Hakanen and Ulla Koskinen about councillors of the realm. Also Merja Uotila, *Käsityöläinen kyläyhteisönsä jäsenenä. Prosopografinen analyysi Hollolan käsityöläisistä 1810–1840*. Jyväskylä Studies in Humanities 237 (Jyväskylä: University of Jyväskylä, 2014), pp. 31–43.
18 Most extensive is the information about pastors' names and length of their careers; when they started in some post and when they moved to somewhere else (in every case the years are not perfectly known). I have this information from all the persons who worked as a pastor in 1560–1611.
19 CDB 2014. For detailed information about the numbers, see Hiljanen, *Limits*.
20 For example Roberts, *The Early*, pp. 296–300; Karonen, *Pohjoinen suurvalta*, pp. 92–96, 103–106.
21 As soon as King Eric XIV inherited the crown, controversy between him and his younger brother John, the Duke of Finland, began. The conflict came to a conclusion in 1563 when the Diet (the Riksdag, meeting of the estates) doomed John to treachery and his duchy was struck off. With the support of the Diet, the king then marched a huge army to Finland Proper, imprisoned the duke and decapitated men who were loyal to John. In 1568 however, Duke John managed to depose Eric with the help of Councillors of the Realm and his younger brother Duke Charles (of Södermanland). Eric was sentenced to prison and John acceded to the throne. Roberts, *The Early*, pp. 206–211; Karonen, *Pohjoinen suurvalta*, pp. 96–100; Lars Ericson Wolke, *Johan III. En biografi* (Lund: Historiska media, 2006), pp. 75–81.
22 Helge Pohjolan-Pirhonen points out that Eric XIV secured his hegemony in the eastern part of the kingdom by trying to keep Duke John apart from the Finnish nobility. He did this by giving judges' posts as a reward to those who switched sides and became loyal to the Crown. In addition, Eric knighted some people and a few of them became members of the Council of the Realm. These rewards impressed Finnish nobles and many consequently left Duke John to become the servant of the king. Helge Pohjolan-Pirhonen, *Suomen historia 1523–1617* (Porvoo: WSOY, 1960), pp. 255–259.
23 Yrjö Blomstedt, *Laamannin- ja kihlakunnantuomarinvirkojen läänittäminen ja hoito Suomessa 1500- ja 1600-luvuilla (1523–1680). Oikeushistoriallinen tutkimus.*

Historiallisia Tutkimuksia 51 (Helsinki: Finnish Historical Society, 1958), pp. 77–80.

24 Ingun Montgomery, *Värjostånd och lärostånd. Religion och politik i meningsutbytet mellan kungamakt och prästerskap i Sverige 1593–1608*. Studia historico-ecclesiastica Upsaliensia 22 (Uppsala: Uppsala universitet, 1972), pp. 28, 403.

25 From the form of the networks of the early modern period, for example Marko Hakanen, *Vallan verkostoissa. Per Brahe ja hänen klienttinsä 1600-luvun Ruotsin valtakunnassa*. Jyväskylä Studies in Humanities 157 (Jyväskylä: Jyväskylän yliopisto, 2011).

26 Diocese of Turku was the part of John's duchy. The city of Turku was the headquarters of both the bishop and duke.

27 CDB 2014: Nicolaus. Also Paarma, *Hiippakuntahallinto*, pp. 417–419; Hockman, "Kuninkaan", pp. 115–116.

28 CDB 2014: Matthias Michelis Carpelan. Pohjolan-Pirhonen claims that Carpelan was loyal to John and he was pardoned because of the parishioners' appeal (especially those who spoke Finnish). Pohjolan-Pirhonen, *Suomen*, pp. 280–281.

29 Ericson Wolke, *Johan III*, pp. 191–193; Erik Pettersson, *Den skoningslöse. En biografi över Karl IX* (Stockholm: Natur & kultur, 2008), pp. 79–80, 83–86; Lennart Hedberg, *Karl IX. Företagfursten och enväldhärskaren* (Stockholm: Prisma, 2009), pp. 221–222, 228–229.

30 Paarma, *Hiippakuntahallinto*, p. 419.

31 John's liturgical reform began in 1575 when he established the *Nova Ordinantia* (New Ordinance). It was not entirely "Catholic", but differed in two respects from the preceding Lutheran order: firstly the texts of the old church-fathers were recommended as reading, and secondly there was a warning about the polemic of Lutheran reformers. A year later, the new liturgy appeared (commonly known as the Red Book, due the colour of its cover). It was a mixture of the Swedish Protestant service and Catholic Mass. For example, Paarma, *Hiippakuntahallinto*, pp. 224–225; Ericson Wolke, *Johan III*, pp. 196–197.

32 Appelberg, *Prästtjänsternas*, pp. 68, 84–85; Holmquist, *Tillsättningar*, pp. 110–112; Heldtander, *Prästtillsättningar*, p. 18; Roberts, *The Early*, p. 412; Paarma, *Hiippakuntahallinto*, pp. 371–375; Hiljanen *Limits*, pp. 44–46, 51.

33 CDB 2014: Martinus Olai. Also Hockman, "Kuninkaan", pp. 113–115.

34 There were more pastors who did not accept the John's liturgy in the western part of the realm, as they had had to flee or move to Charles' duchy as it was a haven to clergymen who held the Lutheran faith. For example, Ericsson, *Johan III*, p. 201; Hedberg, *Karl IX*, pp. 221–222.

35 The Pastor for the Cathedral Parish was also a member of the diocese administration and was thus a more important clergyman than pastors of "normal" parishes.

36 CDB 2014: Henricus Jacobi.

37 CDB 2014: Thomas Laurentii. Also Appelberg, *Prästtjänsternas*, p. 90; Jussi Nuorteva, *Suomalaisten ulkomainen opinkäynti ennen Turun akatemian perustamista 1640*. Bibliotheca historica 27 (Helsinki: Finnish Historical Society, 1997), pp. 274–275.

38 For example Ericson Wolke, *Johan III*, pp. 210–211.

39 CDB 2014: Thomas Laurentii.

40 CDB 2014: Gregorius Martini Teet.

41 CDB 2014: Henricus Canuti & Ericus Matthiae Härkäpää.

42 CDB 2014: Petrus Henrici Melartopaeus.

43 CDB 2014: Petrus Henrici Melartopaeus. In addition, when Duke Charles occupied Finland in 1599, Bishop Ericus Erici Sorolainen was imprisoned, but Melartopaeus and Teet were not; Paarma, *Hiippakuntahallinto*, p. 432. This illustrates the fact that both were part of Charles' network.

44 Tuula Hockman gives other examples of this same phenomenon by studying several well-educated men from town of Rauma which did not end up in pastoral

career in the diocese of Turku. For this reason, these men are not included in my database. Hockman, "Kuninkaan", pp. 121–122.

45 Nilsson, *De stora*, pp. 64–66; Hallenberg, Holm and Johansson, "Organization", p. 259. During the first part of the seventeenth century, people in Sweden feared that Catholics especially from Poland would try to get administrative posts in secret; which in turn might help Sigismund back to the Swedish throne. After all, he was the lawful heir to the Swedish throne. Mirkka Lappalainen, *Pohjolan leijona. Kustaa II Aadolf ja Suomi 1611–1632* (Helsinki: Siltala, 2014).

46 We have to keep in mind that the chapter of each diocese could also appoint pastors. By taking control of the diocese's administration, Duke Charles could trust that the chapter would appoint only those clergymen who resist John's liturgy, or later, the hegemony of Sigismund.

47 For example, John appointed Andreas Andreae (d. c. 1601), from his own court, to the pastorate of Kemiö in 1587. In addition, Christianus Henrici Winter (d. c. 1586 or 1587), who had served as a chaplain in John's court was appointed the first Pastor of Pori in 1584. CDB 2014: Andreas Andreae & Christianu Henrici Winter.

48 For example Suolahti, *Suomen*, p. 122; Hélène Millet, Peter Morraw, "Clerics in the State". In: Reinhard, Wolfgang (ed.), *Power Elites and State Building*. European Science Foundation, The Origins of the Modern State in Europe, 13th–18th Centuries, Theme D. General Editors: Wim Blockmans & Jean-Philippe Genet (Oxford: Clarendon Press, 1996), p. 187.

49 Roberts, *The Early*, pp. 179–180; Göran Malmstedt, *Bondetro och kyrkoro. Religiös mentalitet i stormaktstiden Sverige* (Lund: Nordic Academic Press, 2002), p. 73; Mats Hallenberg, "Församlingspräst i det Svenska riket under 1500-talet. Traditionell auktoritet under omförhandling". In: Eva-Marie Letzter (ed.), *Auktoritet i förvandling. Omförhandling av fromhet, lojalitet och makt i reformationens Sverige*. Opuscula Historica Upsaliensia 49 (Uppsala: Uppsala universitet, 2012), p. 113.

50 For example, Gustavus Vasa rewarded men who had served in his court during their youth by appointing them later to judge in different districts of the realm. Kaarlo Blomstedt has assumed that these men had become close to the King during their service. Later on they were also usable in situations where the King needed trusted people. Blomstedt, *Laamannin*, p. 76.

51 Holmquist, *Tillsättningar*, p. 96. Hallenberg has noticed that some of the bailiffs that were charged with misconduct when in office during the reigns of Gustavus Vasa and Eric XIV could remain in their post by simply paying the Crown; Hallenberg, *Kungen*, pp. 382–383, 388.

52 CDB 2014: Matthias Henrici Raucka & Johnnes Jacobi Wenne. Also Hockman, "Kuninkaan", pp. 105–107. For more on the value of the goods, chattels and estates that clergymen in general donated to the Crown, Aarre Läntinen, *Kuninkaan "perintöä ja omaa" (arv och eget). Kameraalihistoriallinen tutkimus Kustaa Vaasan maaomaisuudesta Suomessa vuosina 1531–1560* (Jyväskylä: Jyväskylän yliopisto, 1981), pp. 122–126. On clercy's economic situation at the sixteenth century in general Mikko Hiljanen, *Kirkkoherrojen taloudellinen asema ja siinä tapahtuneet muutokset 1500-luvulla* (Helsinki: The Finnish Society of Church History, 2016).

53 For example Appelberg, *Prästtjänsternas*, p. 34; Suolahti, *Suomen*, p. 122.

54 CDB 2014: Johannes Michaelis. On Johannes Michaelis, see the next subchapter.

55 CDB 2014.

56 For example, Lena Huldén points out that the social status of the people where the pastors were recruited changed after the Reformation; for example higher nobility was not interested in the clerical career as much as during the Middle Ages. In addition, the position of female (nobles) changed too, because it was impossible to seek to the monasteries after the Reformation. Lena Huldén, "Maktstrukturer i det tidiga finska 1500-talssamhälle", *Genos*, 1998, pp. 111, 117.

57 For example Suolahti, *Suomen*, pp. 67, 85–86; Eero Matinolli, *Turun hiippakunnan papinvaalit ja papinvirkojen täyttäminen aikakautena 1721–1808. Sosiaalihistoriallinen tutkimus.* Turun yliopiston julkaisuja. Humaniora 51 (Turku: Turun yliopisto, 1955), p. 150; Malmstedt, *Bondetro*, p. 171.

58 CDB 2014: Henricus Petri & Mattheus Matthiae. It is notable that studies have not confirmed that Matthaeus Matthiae was son of Matthias Martini. The only thing that refers to father-son relationship is the patronym of Matthaeus.

59 CDB 201: Matthias Martini. Also Roberts, *The Early*, pp. 281, 290; Paarma, *Hiippakuntahallinto*, pp. 223–237, 374–375; Ericson Wolke, *Johan III*, pp. 206–210.

60 For example Mika Jokiaho, "Miehen kunnia ja maine 1600-luvun pohjalaisessa maalaisyhteisössä". In: Einonen, Piia, Karonen, Petri (toim.), *Arjen valta. Suomalaisen yhteiskunnan patriarkaalisesta järjestyksestä myöhäiskeskiajalta teollistumisen kynnykselle (v. 1450–1860)*. Historiallinen Arkisto 116 (Helsinki: The Finnish Literature Society, 2002), p. 205; Jari Eilola, *Rajapinnoilla. Sallitun ja kielletyn määrittäminen 1600-luvun noituus- ja taikuustapauksissa* (Helsinki: The Finnish Literature Society, 2003), pp. 262–267; Karonen, *Pohjoinen suurvalta*, p. 50.

61 CDB 2014: Johannes Michaelis.

62 CDB 2014: Johannes Michaelis. Olli Matikainen, *Verenperijät. Väkivalta ja yhteisön murros itäisessä Suomessa 1500-1600-luvulla* (Helsinki: The Finnish Literature Society, 2002), pp. 98–101; Eilola, *Rajapinnoilla*, pp. 259–263, 273–275. The Diet of Linköping marked the final stage in the dispute between Duke Charles and the Finnish clergy that had started after the death of John III. In Linköping, Charles accused that the Finnish clergy of supporting Sigismund at the end of the 1590s. In addition, he accused the clergy of not following the resolutions agreed in Uppsala and the Diet of Söderköping. Although the clerical estate investigated this and concluded that the pastors of Finland (in general) did not do anything wrong, the Diet finally decided to fine the Finnish clergy. For example Paarma, *Hiippakuntahallinto*, pp. 433–437.

63 Suolahti, *Suomen*, p. 201; Esko M. Laine, "Papisto ja yhteiskunta Suomessa 1600-luvulla". In: Merja Lahtinen (ed.) *Historiallinen arkisto 105* (Helsinki: Finnish Historical Society, 1995), p. 159.

64 CDB 2014: Johannes Micheallis.

65 CDB 2014: Jacobus Erici.

66 For example, the Pastor of Kemi was dismissed in 1578 because he committed manslaughter. Meanwhile, the Pastor of Liminka (Thomas Ingonis (d. 1574)) was accused by a local trader of stealing the seal of the preceding pastor to get appointed to the post. But this backfired, and Ingonis was accused of having sinful life and sentenced to death. CDB 2014: Jacobus Olai & Thomas Ingonis.

67 Paarma, *Hiippakuntahallinto*, pp. 402–403. These crimes did not only affect the reputations of pastors, but of all office-holders, such as bailiffs. For example Hallenberg, *Kungen*, p. 388; Matikainen, *Verenperijät*, p. 99.

68 Kyösti Kiuasmaa, *Suomen yleis- ja paikallishallinnon toimet ja niiden hoito 1500-luvun jälkipuoliskolla (vv.1560–1600). Hallinto- ja yhteiskuntahistoriallinen tutkimus.* Historiallisia Tutkimuksia 63 (Helsinki: Finnish Historical Society, 1962), pp. 463–465. Also Suolahti, *Suomen*, pp. 53–55. Mats Hallenberg points out in his dissertation that even though bailiffs were first and foremost the trusted men of the king, they lived and worked at the local level, and the Crown could not supervise every office-holder. There were thus some cases where bailiffs could act in their own self-interest, but they could not ignore the local population for long, especially as there was usually an ongoing dispute between the people and bailiff about taxes. In this situation, there was a need to negotiate. Hallenberg, *Kungen*, pp. 399–401, 419.

69 As already mentioned, in the Church Ordinance of 1571 the inheritance of pastorates was restricted. The son of the old pastor could be appointed to the post only if he was the best of available candidates. In practice though, this did not make much difference, but law could be interpreted also as an attempt to break

the loyalty-based relationship between the clergy and parishioners, for example Suolahti, *Suomen*, p. 72.
70 CDB 2014: The appointment of Matthaeus Matthiae suggests that the reputation of the pastor's family was not so important in the eyes of the authorities. In fact, it seems that Matthiaes' father settled his differences with the authorities three years after being discharged, and he got back the property that the Crown had confiscated. CDB 2014: Matthias Martini.
71 Note Hallenberg's (*Kungen*, p. 401) notion about conflicts between bailiffs and local people.
72 This is a different Olai from the one mentioned earlier.
73 CDB 2014: Martinus Olai & Henricus Petri.
74 Hallenberg, *Församlingspräst*, pp. 129–130. For alliances in the Diet from the peasant's perspective, Johan Holm, "Att välja sin fiende. Allmogens konflikter och allianser i riksdagen 1595–1635", *Historisk tidskrift* 123:1, 2002; Johan Holm, *Konstruktionen av en stormakt. Kungamakt, skattebönder och statsbildning 1595–1640*. Stockholm Studies in History 90 (Stockholm: Stockholms universitet, 2007); Joakim Scherp, *De ofrälse och makten. En institutionell studie av riksdagen och de ofrälse ståndens politik i maktdelningsfrågor 1660–1682*. Stockholms Studies in History 96 (Stockholm: Stockholms universitet, 2013). In clergy's perspective, Cecilia Ihse, *Präst, stånd och stat. Kung och kyrka i förhandling 1642–1686*. Stockholm studies in history 78 (Stockholm: Stockholms universitet, 2005).
75 CDB 2014: Matthaeus Matthiae, Martinus Olai & Henricus Petri.
76 Malmstedt, *Bondetro*, pp. 170–172.
77 CDB 2014: Marcus Gregorii & Olaus Nicolai.
78 Kiuasmaa, *Suomen*, pp. 421–428. Kiuasmaa claims that there might have not been much illegality in tax-collecting, but bailiffs might have collected extra-taxes that the Crown had claimed, or back taxes. People might have thought that these kinds of collections were illegal and thus appealed to the Crown. For more on appeals to the Crown during the sixteenth century also Pentti Renvall, "*Kuninkaanmiehiä ja kapinoitsijoita Vaasa kauden Suomessa*" (Helsinki: Tammi, 1949), pp. 143–144; Nilsson, *De stora*, pp. 81–91.
79 CDB 2014: Marcus Gregorii. Dismissal of a pastor was not a common practice during this period and only a dozen cases have been found. Most dismissals were tied to the political struggle or on going liturgical reforms. Only a few pastors lost their post for other reasons, such as committing a felony. CDB 2014.
80 For example, in 1558, the parishioners of Lempäälä threw their pastor Olaus Martini Krook over the church fence before the service. CDB 2014: Olaus Martini Krook. Later in 1596, Claes Fleming, who was the biggest enemy of Duke Charles in Finland, urged those loyal to the Crown in Turku to throw all the clergymen over the church fence who had accepted the decision of Uppsala meeting. Heikki Ylikangas, *Nuijasota* (Helsinki: Otava, 1977), p. 68. For more on the habit of throwing the clergyman over the church fence also Asko Vilkuna, *Tavan takaa. Kansatieteellisiä tutkimuksia tapojemme historiasta*. Etnologian laitoksen tutkimuksia 24 (Jyväskylä: Jyväskylän yliopisto, 1989).
81 According to Peter Lindström (*Prästval*, 191), the pragmatic appointing policy which favoured the local parishes´ will – i.e. authorities (especially the bishops and the head of dioceses) appointed pastors who parishioners wanted – was normal at least until the end of the seventeenth century. Thus it seems that the trust and loyalty remained in the core of clergies´ role at the local societies at least to the end of the seventeenth century.
82 For example: Nilsson, *De stora*; Charles Tilly, *Coercion, Capital and European States, AD 990–1990* (Cambridge: Blackwell, 1990); Jan Glete, *War and the state in early modern Europe. Spain, the Dutch Republic and Sweden as fiscal-military states, 1500–1660* (London: Routledge, 2002); Hallenberg, Holm and Johansson, "Organization".

# Sources

## CLERGY DATABASE 2014 (CDB)

### Sources:

Kyösti Väänänen, Turun hiippakunnan paimenmuisto 1554–1721 -verkkojulkaisu. Studia Biographica 9. Helsinki: Suomalaisen Kirjallisuuden Seura, 2011. http://www.finlit.fi/henkilohistoria/paimenmuisto

HFKP I–II 1892–1907: Handlingar rörande finska kyrkan och presterskapet. Utgifven af K. G. Leinberg. Jyväskylä.

Kansallisarkisto, Helsinki (Finnish National Archive), Bailiffs´ accounts (*fogderäkenskaper*). Used digital archive at http://digi.narc.fi/digi/

### Literature

Appelberg, K. A. 1896: *Bidrag till belysning af sättet för prästtjänsternas besättande i Finland från reformationen till medlet af 17:de seklet.* Helsingfors.

Blomstedt, Yrjö 1958: *Laamannin- ja kihlakunnantuomarinvirkojen läänittäminen ja hoito Suomessa 1500- ja 1600-luvuilla (1523–1680). Oikeushistoriallinen tutkimus.* Historiallisia Tutkimuksia 51. Helsinki: Finnish Historical Society.

Eilola, Jari 2003: *Rajapinnoilla. Sallitun ja kielletyn määritteleminen 1600-luvun jälkipuoliskon noituus ja taikuustapauksissa.* Bibliotheca Historica 81. Helsinki: The Finnish Literature Society.

Ericson Wolke, Lars 2006: *Johan III. En biografi.* Lund: Historiska Media.

Glete, Jan 2002: *War and the state in early modern Europe. Spain, the Dutch Republic and Sweden as fiscal-military states, 1500–1660.* London: Routledge.

Hakanen, Marko 2011: *Vallan verkostoissa. Per Brahe ja hänen klienttinsä 1600-luvun Ruotsin valtakunnassa.* Jyväskylä Studies in Humanities 157. Jyväskylä: Jyväskylän yliopisto.

Hallenberg, Mats 2001: *Kungen, fogdarna och riket. Lokalförvaltning och statsbyggande under tidig Vasatid.* Stockholm: Brutus Östlings Bokförlag Symposion.

Hallenberg, Mats 2012: "Församlingspräst i det Svenska riket under 1500-talet. Traditionell auktoritet under omförhandling". In: Eva-Marie Letzter (red.), *Auktoritet i förvandling. Omförhandling av fromhet, lojalitet och makt i reformationens Sverige.* Opuscula Historica Upsaliensia 49. Uppsala: Uppsala universitet.

Hallenberg, Mats, Holm, Johan, Johansson, Dan 2008: "Organization, Legitimation, Participation. State formation as a dynamic process – The Swedish example, c. 1523–1680", *Scandinavian Journal of History* 33: 3.

Hallenberg, Mats, Holm, Johan 2016: *Man ur huse. Hur krig, upplopp och förhandlingar påverkade svensk statsbildning I tidigmodern tid.* Lund: Nordic Academic Press.

Hedberg Lennart 2009: *Karl IX. Företagarfursten och enväldshärskaren.* Stockholm: Prisma.

Heldtander, Tore 1955: *Prästtillsättningar i Sverige under stormaktstiden. Tiden före kyrkolagen 1686.* Skrifter utgivna av Svenska Kyrkohistoriska föreningen 2. Ny följd 10. Uppsala: Svenska Kyrkohistoriska föreningen.

Hiljanen, Mikko 2015: "Limits of Power. Clerical appointment as part of domestic policy in Sweden after the Reformation, 1560–1611", *Perichoresis* 13(2).

Hiljanen, Mikko 2016: *Kirkkoherrojen taloudellinen asema ja siinä tapahtuneet muutokset 1500-luvulla.* Helsinki: The Finnish Society of Church History.

Hockman, Tuula 2015: "Kuninkaan valvonnan alle". In: Lahtinen, Anu and Ijäs, Miia (toim.), *Risti ja lounatuuli. Rauman seurakunnan historia keskiajalta vuoteen 1640.* Helsinki: The Finnish Literature Society.

Holm, Johan 2003: Att välja sin fiende. Allmogens konflikter och allianser i riksdagen 1595–1635", *Historisk tidskrift* 123(1).

Holm, Johan 2007: *Konstruktionen av en stormakt. Kungamakt, skattebönder och statsbildning 1595–1640.* Stockholm Studies in History 90. Stockholm: Stockholms universitet.

Holmquist, Hjalmar 1933: "Tillsättningar av gäll i Sverige under reformationsårhundradet", *Historisk tidskrift.*

Huldén, Lena 1998: "Maktstrukturer i det tidiga finska 1500-talssamhälle", *Genos*, 1998.

Ihse, Cecilia 2005: *Präst, stånd och stat. Kung och kyrka i förhandling 1642–1686.* Stockholm Studies in History 78. Stockholm: Stockholms universitet.

Jokiaho, Mika 2002: "Miehen kunnia ja maine 1600-luvun pohjalaisessa maalaisyhteisössä". In: Einonen, Piia, Karonen, Petri (toim.), *Arjen valta. Suomalaisen yhteiskunnan patriarkaalisesta järjestyksestä myöhäiskeskiajalta teollistumisen kynnykselle (v. 1450–1860).* Historiallinen Arkisto 116. Helsinki: The Finnish Literature Society.

Karonen, Petri 2014: *Pohjoinen suurvalta. Ruotsi ja Suomi 1521–1809.* Helsinki: The Finnish Literature Society.

Kiuasmaa, Kyösti 1962: *Suomen yleis- ja paikallishallinnon toimet ja niiden hoito 1500-luvun jälkipuoliskolla (vv. 1560–1600). Hallinto- ja yhteiskuntahistoriallinen tutkimus.* Historiallisia Tutkimuksia 63. Helsinki: Finnish Historical Society.

Laine, Esko M. 1995: "Papisto ja yhteiskunta Suomessa 1600-luvulla". In: Merja Lahtinen (ed.) *Historiallinen arkisto 105.* Helsinki: Finnish Historical Society.

Lappalainen, Mirkka 2014: *Pohjolan leijona. Kustaa II Adolf ja Suomi 1611–1632.* Helsinki: Siltala.

Lindström, Peter 2003: *Prästval och politisk kultur 1650–1800.* Skrifter från institutionen för historiska studier 4. Umeå: Umeå universitet.

Läntinen, Aarre 1981: *Kuninkaan "perintöä ja omaa" (arv och eget). Kameraalihistoriallinen tutkimus Kustaa Vaasan maaomaisuudesta Suomessa vuosina 1531–1560.* Studia Historica Jyväskyläensia 21. Jyväskylä: Jyväskylän yliopisto.

Malmstedt, Göran 2002: *Bondetro och kyrkoro. Religiös mentalitet i stormaktstiden Sverige.* Lund: Nordic Academic Press.

Matikainen, Olli 2002: *Verenperijät: väkivalta ja yhteisön murros itäisessä Suomessa 1500–1600-luvulla.* Bibliotheca historica 78. Helsinki: The Finnish Literature Society.

Matinolli, Eero 1955: *Turun hiippakunnan papinvaalit ja papinvirkojen täyttäminen aikakautena 1721–1808. Sosiaalihistoriallinen tutkimus.* Turun yliopiston julkaisuja. Humaniora 51. Turku: Turun yliopisto.

Millet, Hélène and Moraw, Peter 1996: "Clerics in the State". In: Wolfgang Reinhard (ed.), *Power Elites and State Building.* Oxford: Clarendon Press.

Montgomery, Ingun 1972: *Värjostånd och lärostånd. Religion och politik i meningsutbytet mellan kungamakt och prästerskap i Sverige 1593–1608.* Studia historico-ecclesiastica Upsaliensia 22. Uppsala: Uppsala universitet.

Nilsson, Sven A. 1990: *De stora krigens tid. Om Sverige som militärstat och bondesamhälle.* Studia Historica Upsaliensia 161. Uppsala: Uppsala universitet.

Nuorteva, Jussi 1997: *Suomalaisten ulkomainen opinkäynti ennen Turun akatemian perustamista 1640.* Bibliotheca historica 27. Helsinki: Finnish Historical Society.

Paarma, Jukka 1980: *Hiippakuntahallinto Suomessa 1554–1604.* Suomen kirkkohistoriallisen seuran toimituksia 116. Helsinki: The Finnish Society of Church History.

Pohjolan-Pirhonen, Helge 1960: *Suomen historia 1523–1617.* Suomen historia VII. Porvoo: WSOY.

Pettersson, Erik 2008: *Den skoningslöse. En biografi över Karl IX.* Stockholm: Natur & kultur.

Pirinen Kauko 1989: "Papinvaalilainsäädännön kehitys Suomessa vuoteen 1964". In: Hannu Mustakallio (ed.), *Suomen kirkkohistoriallisen seuran vuosikirja 79*. Helsinki: The Finnish Society of Church History.

Renvall, Pentti 1949: *Kuninkaanmiehiä ja kapinoitsijoita Vaasakauden Suomessa*. Helsinki: Tammi.

Roberts, Michael 1968: *The Early Vasas. A History of Sweden, 1525–1611*. Cambridge: Cambridge University Press.

Salonen, Kirsi 2012: *Kirkollisen oikeuden päälähteillä. Sacra Romana Rotan toiminta ja sen oikeudellinen tausta myöhäiskeskiajalla ja uuden ajan alun taitteessa*. Suomen kirkkohistoriallisen seuran Toimituksia 221. Helsinki: The Finnish Society of Church History.

Sandahl, Martin 1966: *Prästval i Sverige mot kulturell och social bakgrund*. Stockholm: Gummesson.

Scherp, Joakim 2013: *De ofrälse och makten. En institutionell studie av riksdagen och de ofrälse ståndens politik i maktdelningsfrågor 1660–1682*. Stockholm Studies in History 96. Stockholm: Stockholms universitet.

Suolahti, Gunnar 1919: *Suomen papisto 1600- ja 1700-luvuilla*. Porvoo: WSOY.

Tilly, Charles 1990: *Coercion, capital and European states, AD 990–1990*. Cambridge: Blackwell.

Uotila, Merja 2014: *Käsityöläinen kyläyhteisönsä jäsenenä. Prosopografinen analyysi Hollolan käsityöläisistä 1810–1840*. Jyväskylä Studies in Humanities 237. Jyväskylä: Jyväskylän yliopisto.

Vilkuna, Asko 1989: *Tavan takaa. Kansatieteellisiä tutkimuksia tapojemme historiasta*. Etnologian laitoksen tutkimuksia 24. Jyväskylä: Jyväskylän yliopisto.

Ylikangas, Heikki 1977: *Nuijasota*. Helsinki: Otava.

# Royal Mayors VIII

Petri Karonen
http://orcid.org/0000-0001-6090-5504

# Royal Mayors (1620–1700): The Bane of the Burghers, the Crown's Scourge, Effective Developers of Urban Government?

Sweden's position as a great European power reached its zenith in the period between the 1640s and the 1660s. However, it is in exactly this period that researchers have discovered the existence of state officials who were indispensable for the proper functioning of the realm but whose competence would seem to have left a lot to be desired: "A weak and insignificant person – a servant of Axel Oxenstierna even after his appointment as mayor" (Västerås, 1640s–1650s);[1] "Despotic and lacking self-control" (Gävle, 1640s);[2] and "The new mayor was an officious and pedantic braggart, who angered the people of Oulu by his autocratic behaviour and his pursuit of his own gain that led to dishonest deeds" (Oulu, 1640s–1660s).[3] Harsh judgments of this kind have made by historians above all about the so-called "royal mayors". But can these judgments be generalized? Do they hold true at all beyond the individual level?

This chapter examines the activities of the royal mayors who were appointed in the period 1620–1720 in the "old towns" of the Kingdom of Sweden.[4] It proceeds from the premise that the personal agency of functionaries – which was constituted by the norms that directed their activities, the implementation of these norms, and the individual's actions – is often of crucial significance in assessing their activities as a whole within the existing relatively strictly state-regulated institutional structures.[5] The appointment of royal mayors in principle involved a significant infringement of the autonomy of the towns, to which the existing legislation accorded a considerable amount of freedom. In this connection, the historico-cultural and historico-political perspectives come to the fore since the interpretations of the activities of royal mayors have naturally been influenced at different times by the chronologically bound views and contexts both of their contemporaries and of later researchers.

The term "royal mayor" is here broadly defined to include both functionaries appointed by a secular authority (the ruler, a governor general (*generalguvernör*) or a county governor (*landshövding / ståthållare*) and officials who were assigned to their posts on the basis of a warrant issued by the holder of a grand fief (a count or a baron). On the other hand, mayors who had received the support of the townsfolk before their selection are not included.[6]

The term "old towns" is here used to refer to towns that were founded before 1632, i.e. before the coming to power of the guardian regency in the early reign of Queen Christina. The justification for this chronological boundary is that in practice for all towns that were founded after 1632 mayors were appointed on the strong recommendation of the ruler or the holder of the fief.[7] By contrast, the appointments of mayors in the territories conquered by Sweden from Denmark in the 1640s and 1650s, that is modern southern Sweden, constituted part of an organized Swedification policy that was implemented in this area particularly at the stage when possession was being taken of the towns. The implementation of this policy was much harsher than the in itself effective policy of integration of the administration that was realised in Finland. The towns of the dominions have also been omitted from this examination.[8]

No particular learning was required of royal mayors in the early seventeenth century, and the ruler often appointed men without any university education at all. The situation changed during the course of the century, which in itself suggests that the educational system was developed to produce enough "academics" to occupy posts in local government, when previously the qualified candidates had all been snatched for central and provincial government duties.[9] On the other hand, the ennoblement of mayors was rare, and when it did happen the mayor usually relinquished his urban administrative duties.[10]

The royal mayors have been the object of study in Sweden and Finland ever since the second half of the nineteenth century. Historians have repeatedly addressed the subject, for example in numerous town histories and doctoral theses. In practice, all Swedish and Finnish town histories deal with the interconnections between the royal mayors and the burghers and on a general level with the work of the town courts, which functioned under the mayors.[11] For example, Gudrun Andersson has analysed the family connections of mayors in her research on elite groups in Arboga and noted the importance of arranged marriages in the integration of royal mayors into the urban community.[12] In addition, a certain amount has been written in biographical reference works like *Svensk biografiskt lexikon* (SBL), *Kansallisbiografia* (KB) and *Biografiskt lexikon för Finland* (BLF), but they contain no analyses of the actions of the mayors or the effects of these.[13]

The basic material for this chapter on the appointment of royal mayors has been gathered from the indices of the Institute of Urban History (*Stadshistoriska institutet*) (SIR), which is located in the National Archives (*Riksarkivet, SRA*) in Stockholm, and it is supplemented with data from the Swedish National Records (*Riksregistratur*) and previous research. This combination of different sources has made it possible to conduct a more profound enquiry into the personal agency of royal mayors.

*The justification and legitimation of mayoral appointments*

In the Early Modern Age, the grip of the state on the towns tightened almost everywhere in Europe.[14] The state authorities in Sweden, particularly in the early years of the seventeenth century, considered that it was indispensable to improve the efficiency of the administration because the state needed ever more financial resources during the on-going protracted period of warfare, and the levying of taxes entailed a viable organization. Thus taxes, particularly in the form of ready cash, were sorely needed to pay for the expenses of war, and it was thought that only the towns would be able to provide these to a sufficient extent. Therefore, the economic level of the towns and their tax-paying capability had to be enhanced. The central administration regarded the towns' own ability and willingness to develop measures of this kind with scepticism, and therefore it sought to take even small towns under its supervision.

In 1619, on the basis of experience obtained in Stockholm, Chancellor Axel Oxenstierna (1583–1654) drew up a directive for the towns (*1619 års stadga om städernas administration*), most of the regulations of which concentrated on enhancing their economic life. Among other things, the directive proposed to increase the number of functionaries, tighten up scrutiny and make the towns' judicial institution into a two-tier establishment, measures that all aimed at making local administration more efficient. Thus, in the course of time, lower instances which passed quick judgments in minor cases were established to operate under the town courts in many towns. The towns tried to implement the directive of 1619, although the regulations often proved difficult to obey immediately.[15] Consequently, the required changes were not put into effect, or matters proceeded too slowly from the point of view of the state authorities, and it became necessary for them to move on from the mere expression of normative wishes to ensuring their practical realisation – from ideas to actions. Finally, therefore, in the 1630s, the central government adopted a new approach, first of all in those towns that it deemed to be important. Men furnished with a royal letter of appointment, royal mayors, were sent to them to act as watchdogs and taskmasters. In the major towns on the Finnish side of the realm, Turku (Åbo) and Vyborg (Viborg), the governors general had already successfully dealt with the recruitment of officers for town courts. Now the same methods began to be applied in Sweden proper, and the influence of the state was extended even to towns that were of minor significance.[16]

However, the government had to be able to justify the appointments of royal mayors to the burghers, who constituted an estate that, while admittedly disunited and politically not so significant, was nevertheless glamorous and economically crucial.[17] How could the government legitimate its actions in planting its own favourites to govern the towns?

With the advent of the royal mayors to control of the towns, which had hitherto possessed a strong degree of formal autonomy, the power over urban administration passed in practice to the Crown, although it is true that even before that the ruler had had some say in the government of the towns: it was a particular feature of Swedish towns that they were politically and also juridically subject to the king.[18] Thus there was not a single city that had simply *come into being*; all of them had been *founded*.[19]

David Beetham defines legitimacy as being "legality, normative justifiability, express consent". In Sweden, the strong role of the state vis-à-vis the towns maintained its legitimacy even in those times when there were offences against the autonomy of the latter, although the quotations cited at the beginning of this chapter might indicate the contrary.[20]

The state obtained strong backing from the regulations of the Instrument of Government of 1634 (*regeringsform*) and the regulations issued to county governors the following year, on the basis of which the latter replaced governors equipped with vague instructions at the head of the reformed county government. The county governor did not personally participate in the administration of law in the towns of the area under his jurisdiction since the supervision of the lower courts had been transferred *in toto* to the courts of appeal. On the other hand, the remit of the head of the county had expanded to such an extent that he could no longer be expected to engage in the previous kind of personal supervision of affairs at the local level. Despite this, the central government naturally considered it important that it should have its "own" representatives in the towns. However, the Burghers had been secured the right in the mediaeval Town Law of King Magnus Eriksson (*stadslag*) to freely elect their own administrative officers, and consequently the government could not in principle interfere in the appointment of mayors, for instance, and thereby influence the administration and dispensation of justice.[21]

In order to preserve the legitimacy of its actions and to maintain a dialogue with the towns, the state temporarily adopted office titles that were unknown in the Town Law: it could if it so desired instate in the towns officials like a "burgrave" (*borggreve*) or a "president" totally without seeking the consent of the townsfolk at all. The new officials ranked above the mayors and the aldermen in the hierarchy of the town's administration.[22] It was above all a temporary measure since the *primus motor* of the policy for the towns, Axel Oxenstierna, stated in the early 1640s that in the future it would be necessary to strengthen the authority of the mayors. The state had to seek cooperation with the burghers, and in this respect the relationship between the state and the towns was reciprocal, although it was the central government that held the upper hand in this asymmetrical relationship. At the same time, the state authorities sought to ensure that the officials sent to the towns would be at least formally competent to perform their duties in their communities – their execution of these duties affected the success of the measure more than institutional limitations.[23]

The state's discreet way of winning over the townsfolk to accept their proposals took the form of concessions to the towns which were typically connected with various excise dues and import duties paid to the town (*tolag*) as well as other taxes that were paid in money. When the Crown offered to pay back some of the dues it had levied to pay for the salaries of the mayor and the aldermen, it at the same time bound the urban government to ensure the efficiency and profitability of its administration. This in turn promoted the growth of the Crown's tax revenues, too. The appointment of mayors was in this respect a most opportune bargaining point, as the case of Hans Prytz ((lifetime unknown), who was appointed Mayor of Nyköping, illustrates. In its letter to the county governor, the central government gave him to understand that the appointment was a sensitive matter on account of the regulations of the Town Law. Therefore it was hoped that he would present the matter discreetly to the town administrative board and to the burghers. In the end, the issue did not raise any problems, a result that was naturally helped by the fact that it was linked to tax concessions.[24]

In the 1630s and particularly the 1640s, the towns applied to the monarch in person for funds to pay the salaries of their officials.[25] They thus nursed the hope that the state would pay for the salaries of local officials generally and in particular for the maintenance of mayors, but in practice just about all the towns were soon disappointed in this hope. Halfway through the century, the government generally required the towns themselves to pay the salaries of their officials.[26] The salary issue was naturally a potential cause of dispute, but the adequate and regular reimbursement of officials was important since among other things it would genuinely help to prevent corruption (the definition of which is admittedly difficult in the context of the seventeenth century) and other supererogatory activities that were detrimental to the organization of the town court.[27]

In any case, in the seventeenth century one finds only a couple of mayoral appointments in connection with which the central authorities enforced their will without hearing the burghers' views at all. Generally, a solution was sought through milder means and by making the town an offer that it could not refuse, although the wording of the monarch's letters in itself was stern: it was nearly always stated that the finances of the city in questions had been poorly handled and the privileges graciously awarded to it by His/Her Majesty neglected. Generally the same phrases were repeated from one letter to the next. That, however, was not the case in Arboga in 1642, to which exceptionally the guardian regency acting for Queen Christina simply appointed two royal mayors simultaneously.[28] The reason for the state's exceptional severity was probably the fact that the town had for years suffered a state of extreme crisis, which was particularly reflected in the weak authority of its administrative and judicial organs.[29]

Thus the forceful implementation of the state's decisions was rare, and even when this did happen, there was no guarantee of its being successful. In Jönköping, in the late 1650s, the county governor tried to forcefully install one Johan Persson, a lawyer of the Göta Court of Appeal (*Göta hovrätt*), as mayor. However, the town administrative board and the burghers unanimously opposed the appointment and demanded that their right of election be adhered to, stating that they would rather give up their status as burghers than accept this person as their mayor. In the end, the county governor withdrew his candidate – the matter had clearly not been prepared and carried out on the level to which the burghers were accustomed.[30]

## Appointments of royal mayors

The state authorities had intervened at an early stage in the appointments of mayors, especially in the largest and most important towns. Certainly from the time of Gustavus Vasa (1496–1560) on, persons who had been approved by the monarch were appointed as mayors of Stockholm, although usually the first royal mayor is considered to have been Olaus Bureus, who was appointed to the post in 1621 and was often referred to as "the Royal Mayor of Stockholm".[31] Moreover, even before the official regulations were issued in the seventeenth century, the governors, the predecessors of the county governors, had addressed defects that they observed in the administration of the towns since at least the most important (frontier) towns had to be properly administered if for no other reason then for the external security of the realm.[32] The monarch issued reminders to the prefects concerning towns where the governor or county governor maintained his residence that they should keep a close eye on events and the legality of activities in the town courts.[33]

In Finland, the appointment of royal mayors from the 1620s to the 1650s was largely the responsibility of the governors general, who enjoyed wide powers. Thereafter, from the mid-century on, the holders of grand fiefs sometimes made appointments in the towns located in areas under their jurisdiction. In a class all of his own was Count Per Brahe (1602–1680), who was twice Governor General of Finland (*generalguvernör*) and at the same time Lord High Chancellor (*drots*) and a nobleman who held grand fiefs both in Sweden and in Finland. He had a considerable influence on official appointments in the Finnish half of the realm right up to the end of the 1670s. Just as in Sweden, persons without offices or posts did not just wait passively at home to be summoned; rather they were active in contacting their patrons, whose recommendation carried great weight in the filling of posts.[34] Similarly, royal letters of appointment were sought in the hope that they would lead to even better positions: for example, the persons chosen as Mayors of Arboga in the years 1644 and 1654 did not take up their posts: one of them opted to go rather to Stockholm and the other to Västerås.[35]

By the mid-century, the majority of the old towns in Sweden (N = 32) and Finland (N= 12) had received at least one royal mayor. The last of the towns in the eastern half of the realm to which a royal mayor was appointed was Borgå (Porvoo) in 1658. On the other hand, on the Swedish side, no royal mayor was appointed in every fourth town, but all of these were provincial towns that were deemed to be of little importance.[36]

The first times when appointments were made naturally do not as such reveal everything about the total number of persons who served as mayors or about the quality of their work in particular. Altogether 162 mayors held office in the old towns of the Finnish side of the realm in the period 1620–1720. About half of them (N = 79) were royal mayors, half of whom served until they died, while 15 of them (about 20% of all royal mayors) were dismissed from their posts. On the Swedish side of the kingdom, corresponding information has been systematically gathered for three different towns: the ecclesiastical and university town of Uppsala, the industrial town and staple port of Norrköping and the medium-sized provincial town of Linköping.[37] On the basis of this information, observations made from research literature and estimates, in all about 800 mayors served in the old towns in the whole realm of Sweden in the period 1620–1720. About 350 of them had royal letters of appointment. In Sweden proper, the dismissal of royal mayors was considerably rarer in relation to

Table 1. The first royal mayors in the period 1621-1679 in the old towns of the Kingdom of Sweden. Sources: Karonen, *"Raastuvassa tavataan"*, Table 1 and the sources mentioned therein; O. Danielsson, "Rättskipning och förvaltning". In: *Mariestad 1583-1933* (Mariestad: Karströms bokhandel 1933), pp. 155-156; Nils Hj. Holmberg, *Lidköpings historia till 1860* ([Lidköping]: [Drätselkammaren] 1946), pp. 86-88; Claes Westling, "Vadstena och centralmakten". In Göran Söderström (red.), *600 år i Vadstena. Vadstenas historia från äldsta tider till år 2000* (Vadstena: Vadstena kommun 2000), p. 290; Petri Karonen, "Borgmästare mellan staten och stadssamhället. Förvaltnings- och rättskulturer i det svenska rikets städer under stormaktstiden". In: Harnesk, Börje, Taussi Sjöberg, Marja (ed.), *Mellan makten och menigheten. Ämbetsmän i det tidigmoderna Sverige*. Institutet för rättshistorisk forskning. Serien III. Rättshistoriska skrifter. Första bandet (Stockholm: Institutet för rättshistorisk forskning 2001b), 134-135; Westling, *Småstadens dynamik*, pp. 124, 177.

| Period | Appointments in Swedish towns | Appointments in Finnish towns |
| --- | --- | --- |
| 1621-1630 | N = 2 (Stockholm, Gothenburg) | N = 3 (Turku; Vyborg; Uusikaupunki, Nystad) |
| 1631-1640 | N = 5 (Sala, Kalmari, Norrköping, Västerås, Nyköping) | N = 4 (Kokkola, Gamlakarleby; Helsinki, Helsingfors; Rauma, Raumo; Tammisaari, Ekenäs) |
| 1641-1650 | N = 25 (Jönköping, Örebro, Strängnäs, Karlstad, Arboga, Uppsala, Köping, Torshälla, Skara, Gävle, Hudiksvall, Härnösand, Växjö, Vadstena, Sundsvall, Söderhamn, Linköping, Torneå, Umeå, Filipstad, Mariefred, Enköping, Hedemora, Söderköping, Skänninge) | N = 5 (Uusikaupunki; Vaasa, Vasa; Oulu, Uleåborg; Naantali, Nådendal; Pori, Björneborg) |
| 1651-1660 | N = 3 (Borås, Lidköping Västervik) | N = 1 (Porvoo, Borgå) |
| 1661-1679 | N = 3 (Falköping, Eksjö, Mariestad) | – |
| Total 1621-1679 | N = 38 (75 % of the old towns, N = 51)) | N = 13 (100 % of the old towns, N = 13)) |

the number of towns than it was in Finland. Assessed on this basis, in the whole kingdom about every tenth royal mayor was forced to quit his post against his will. This number may be considered a low one.[38]

## The operations of the royal mayors and their conflicts with the burghers

When there was a conflict between the townsfolk and the mayor, it was usually connected with various reforms and the increased surveillance of the inhabitants. C. T. Odhner, who studied this subject back in the 1860s, noted that in many towns the burghers were disappointed in their royal superiors because of the strict demands made on them by the latter.[39] Often it was a question of a clash of different administrative cultures: it was the task of the royal mayors to act specifically as instigators of change, an endeavour in which conflicts were difficult to avoid.[40] A solution to the in part only apparent contradiction between the conceptions that have previously been presented and the findings of the present chapter is sought by examining the achievements of the royal mayors. After all, the central authorities did not establish their own candidates in posts just for them to twiddle their thumbs.[41]

In 1641, Jacob Lithman (1611–1674), the son of the Rector of Örebro, was appointed to be the mayor of his home town at the age of 30. His letter of appointment became a veritable model since its contents were repeated word for word in the warrants of at least 25 town mayors over the next 15 years. According to this document, the county governor and the royal bailiff should have participated in the administration of the town, but their other duties prevented them from attending the meetings of the town court. Lithman was thus appointed to be the representative of the king, for which task he was furnished with a set of 13 instructions. The special duties of the mayor were connected with the surveillance and development of justice and administration in accordance with the state's longer-term plans and the supervision of the town's privileges, industries and economy generally. A new addition to the instructions was the supervision of the condition and use of the town's public infrastructure. The list of tasks is focal in judging the personal agency of the mayors. It would appear that other mayors received similar instructions since they, too, most commonly focussed their attention on matters like those mentioned above.[42]

Often the most important task of the royal mayors was connected with supervising the systems of justice and administration and improving their efficiency. Typically, various administrative and juridical reforms were implemented soon after the arrival of a new mayor. In Örebro, the energetic Jacob Lithman followed his instructions and among other things drew up a special set of judicial directions, strictly defined the time and place where business might be conducted, promoted and supervised the activities of artisans and set limits on the lavishness of entertainments at weddings and other parties. These measures were not greeted with joyful acclaim by the burghers or in the town administrative court, but the monarch recognized Lithman's abilities and soon made him Assessor of the Göta Court of Appeal. He later served as an under- and vice-lawspeaker (*lagman* – a district chief judge) in the countryside and he was ennobled for his achievements in 1654.[43]

The presidents, who served as "models" for the royal mayors, were also without exception resolute in developing the towns' systems of administration and justice.[44] Many of the mayors who received royal letters of appointment from the monarch followed suit, and typical among the new ideas they implemented were the division of the town court into departments (*collegium*) and the reorganization of the justice system in the form of the establishment of lower town courts (*kämnerrätt*) to operate under the town courts (*rådshusrätt*).[45] Almost without exception, the quality of the material describing the activities of the town's organ of administration and justice improved after the appointment of a royal mayor. However, it is not possible to make a direct connection between the arrival of a mayor and the dense recording of the minutes of meetings of the town court.[46]

From the 1630s on, considerable attention was paid in Sweden to the drafting of new town plans.[47] The dismantling of the complicated, fire-prone networks of streets, which failed to match the Central European ideal of urban planning, became the main task of many royal mayors. This was the case with Daniel Kempe (1604–1654), a junior lawyer at the Svea court of appeal (*Svea hovrätt*) who was appointed as Royal Mayor of Västerås. It is an indication of Kempe's reputation that the history of the town has been periodized according to his time in office (1641–1654).[48]

The routine official tasks of the royal mayors have not generally been brought out in assessing their work; rather, various "violent disagreements"[49] or other types of conflict situations in which the relations between them and the other members of the town administrative board and/or the burghers became inflamed have been sought. When a mayor was accused of abusing his position or of malfeasance, the Crown usually appointed a commission made up of disinterested parties (*commissorial rätt*) or some other neutral organ to investigate the claims. Such temporary investigatory and judicial organs were needed in the towns strikingly often in the 1650s and 1660s, after which they became rare.[50]

The arguments almost always concerned money in one way or another. The reimbursement of the royal mayors was a constant source of dispute, especially when the burghers found that they would be totally or partly responsible for it. It rarely occurred to them that by paying for the salary of the official they might thereby engage his extended loyalty to the community – on the contrary, they usually suspected that the mayor was serving the interests of the state authorities.[51] However, most commonly the problem was that the salary was felt to be too high, and in some smaller towns the mayors sometimes agreed to accept lower emoluments.[52]

The monarch certainly became interested in the internal affairs of the town if there were complaints about financial wrongdoings. For example, the ruthless implementation of regularization in Västerås gave rise to extensive investigations, as a result of which both the town's "own" mayor and the royal mayor were sentenced to pay reparations amounting to thousands of silver thalers.[53] In Jönköping, problems arose between the royal mayor, Johan Håkansson Reese (also known as Johannes Haquini Rhezelius, d.1666), and the burghers over the renting of the "town cellar" (a restaurant reserved for the burghers). The mayor was dismissed for malfeasance during the years 1661–1664, but he was restored to his post by the monarch at the beginning of 1665.[54]

In Uppsala in the early 1660s, the mayor Jacob Abrahamsson Ruuth (d.1666) was accused of malpractice in the administration of justice and of the illegal usufruct together with other mayors of lands awarded by the Crown to the town. Ruuth was found guilty of grievous malfeasance and neglect of his duties, as a result of which he and several other important members of the town court were suspended from their posts. Eventually Ruuth was dismissed altogether, but in his decision His Royal Majesty stressed the fact that that he had not been stripped of his honour and thereby of opportunities to serve in Crown offices elsewhere than Uppsala.[55]

In a class of their own are cases where the mayor completely lost his self-control and through his colourful language and other inappropriate behaviour caused trouble for himself. There are glaring examples in many towns of mayors abusing and showing downright contempt for their subordinates and the burghers of the towns under their jurisdiction. Many of the royal mayors who got into the worst difficulties were lawyers by training, but even so – or perhaps for that very reason – they used coarse language in the letters and various reports that they sent to the courts of appeal and even to the monarch. Such documents naturally constitute central evidence about the *behaviour* of an official and they illustrate various conflict situations, but one must take a cautious attitude to their use for directly assessing a person's work in the past.[56]

Although some of the problems affecting the royal mayors' execution of their duties have been focused on above, in fact the burghers usually accepted the central authority's choice of candidate and in some cases were even satisfied with the work of their mayors. The burghers would seem above all to have expected the mayor to act in accordance with the requirements of his post; in other words, to be the leader of the town and to bear responsibility for the duties attached to his official position. This was noticed in the 1650s by Casper Eichman (c. 1590–1670), the Mayor of Nystad (Uusikaupunki), who liked to appear as the "boss" (*förman*) of the town and, in accordance with the patriarchal ideal of the age, as the "father" of the townsfolk. He blustered repeatedly about his own authority and honour and was constantly badgering the burghers to give their opinions about the general efficiency of the town's administration and his own work. And time and again the assessment was excellent. In return, the burghers required the "boss" to shoulder his responsibilities, and thus in 1655 they unanimously demanded that he, with all his experience of attending meetings of the estates, should represent the town's interests at the Diet (Riksdag) in Stockholm. Exceptionally, Eichman was not willing to travel: on the agenda there were expected to be certain difficult issues connected with disputes over financial interests, in which Nystad would be opposed by the earldom of Wasaborg, which had originally been granted to Gustaf Gustafsson af Wasaborg (1616–1653), the illegitimate son of King Gustavus Adolphus (1594–1632). Casper Eichman appealed many times to the fact that his situation was an awkward one: he had received his letter of appointment as mayor from the now deceased holder of the earldom but he was the leaseholder of the customs house of Nystad and also the representative of the town. The strict requirement of the townspeople finally silenced Eichman, although "weeping, he begged their pardon and hoped that someone else might take the task upon himself" and, because he feared the reaction of the holder of the fief, was "between two fires". However, the burghers cried out as one man that because he was the leader of the town and the mayor, they could not entrust this matter to anyone else. The mayor's representation of the town at the Diet did, in fact, cause a rift in relations between him and the holder of the earldom, which drove Eichman, who was already in financial straits, to the brink of ruination. His execution of his duties was also encumbered. He was dismissed from his post for the first time in 1663, but he returned briefly to his duties, only to be sacked finally at the end of the decade.[57]

Similarly, Daniel Kröger (d. 1672), who pursued a long albeit disrupted career (1647–1662) in Oulu (Uleåborg), was the object of the aggression of many of the town's burghers. Kröger, the son of the Mayor of Gävle, had studied at university and was a client of Lord High Steward Per Brahe. He was dismissed from his post several times as a result of complaints and the ensuing enquiries, but he was repeatedly reinstated by the Turku Court of Appeal (*Åbo hovrätt*). Kroger's position was certainly not helped by the fact that in the opinion of the townsfolk he had neglected his duties particularly during Charles X Gustav's Russian War (1656–1658). It was rumoured in the town that the mayor had fled to Stockholm out of fear of a Russian attack. Earlier in the same decade, the mayor and the aldermen under him were accused of planning "to get rich with our [the burghers'] money", since Kröger and his accomplices had obtained a monopoly of beer brewing. The mayor was finally sacked in 1662, but like the above mentioned Mayor of Uppsala, Jacob Ruuth, he was allowed to keep his honour and thereby his legal capacity.[58]

## *Leaders in the cross-fire of different demands in changing times*

In the early seventeenth century, Sweden, a mainly agricultural country that was rapidly becoming a great power in Europe, needed towns that could quickly supply the resources required for the protracted wars. Dozens of towns were founded in the course of the century, and experienced men were engaged to be the leaders (mayors) of many of these new urban communities. At the same time, it was also necessary to develop the old towns of Sweden, some of which had been founded 300–400 years earlier. However, it was fairly quickly realised that the autonomy of the towns and the initiative of the burghers alone were not sufficient to ensure that the royal directives were transformed into practical actions. One important solution to the problem took the form installing mayors furnished with royal letters of appointment who were expected to speed up the development and reorganization of the towns.

The appointment of royal mayors was common in the seventeenth century, and there were hundreds of them. As has become apparent above, their appointment usually involved some sort of trade-off between the ruler, or an organ representing him or her, and the town community. Previous research has often emphasized the steamrolling actions of the state authorities in connection with the appointments. However, the example of Arboga briefly described above was exceptional, although admittedly the measures taken by the state especially in the Swedification process of the former Danish territories in what is today southern Sweden were considerably harsher than elsewhere. Even so, if it had so wished, the central government could have imposed its will on the towns since it was the ruler who ultimately decided on their privileges and other benefits and on the salaries of the aldermen.

The autonomy of the towns and its loss as a result of the state's interference in official appointments has been highlighted as a central theme especially in the histories of the towns. However, the intervention in the burghers' right to elect local government officers was partly self-inflicted, for the towns themselves had proposed that the Crown should participate in paying the salaries of functionaries, and it was probably clear to the people of the time that, in a period of continual wars, the Crown would not provide any funding out of the mere kindness of its heart. Indeed, it was precisely because of the straitened situation that the hope of "sharing" the costs of administration had arisen in the towns because the demands of the state authorities on them generally, and particularly the taxes that were levied on them, were simultaneously growing. On the other hand, the person furnished with a royal letter of appointment who appeared in the town court with the task of ensuring the viable and efficient conduct of affairs was usually someone who was already familiar to the townsfolk, for it was very rare for a complete stranger to be assigned to the post. In Finland the most vociferous disputes between the mayors and their local communities arose when the newcomer was a person who was unfamiliar with local ways and strove to change them radically, although admittedly it was precisely leaders who could bring about change that the central authorities wanted.[59]

The personal agency of the royal mayors has often been seen as being characterized by conflicts between them and the townsfolk. Most typically, the unfolding of the drama has been constructed as a struggle of the town's "own" officials and burghers struggled against a mayor who was "a newcomer, an outsider who offended the administrative autonomy of the town". And it is true that the judgment rolls and the minutes of various temporary investigatory bodies do describe conflicts of this kind. For the most part, the disputes resulted from the fact that the mayors were implementing directions issued by the central authority and national regulations. Even so, they were not mere lapdogs of the Crown, and they usually prosecuted the interests of their towns efficiently. Moreover, because of their backgrounds, they were normally extremely well suited to handle the interaction between the central authorities and the local communities. The royal mayors often served as representatives at the Diet, and rarely did the burghers complain that their interests had been poorly or deficiently prosecuted.[60]

As *a group*, the royal mayors handled their thankless duties very well. Especially in small and economically weak towns, the burghers complained about the high salary expenses. Unlike their predecessors, the new mayors rarely engaged in commerce, and they lived off their salaries. In the late seventeenth century, most of the royal mayors had a university education, which on the one hand meant that they had much more theoretical expertise than many of their predecessors and on the other that the persons who were most important for the business life of the towns, the merchants, could concentrate more fully on the activities that were ordained in the fundamental principles of the society of the estates, in other words their business activities carried on within the framework of their estate privileges. In this way, through the royal mayors, the formal level of the judiciary was raised and the division of duties that was crucial for promoting the efficient running of society was increased.

The research on which this publication is based was funded by the Academy of Finland (grant no. 137741).

## Notes

1. Sven Olsson, *Västerås genom tiderna. 4. Burskap och makt: Västerås politiska historia 1613–1862* (Västerås: Västerås kommun, 1988), p. 103.
2. Percy Elfstrand, "Ur förvaltningshistorien". In: *Ur Gävle stads historia*. Utgiven till femhundraårs jubileet (Gävle, 1946), p. 497.
3. A. H. Virkkunen, *Oulun kaupungin historia I* (Oulu: Oulun kaupunki (2nd edition, 1953, originally 1919)), p. 392.
4. In 1723 the burghers received the right to choose three candidates for mayor, and the monarch selected the most suitable and best qualified of these. Nils Herlitz, *Svensk stadsförvaltning på 1830-talet* (Stockholm: Norstedt, 1924), p. 96; Oscar Nikula, "Kaupunkilaitos 1721–1875", *Suomen kaupunkilaitoksen historia 1. Keskiajalta 1870-luvulle* (Vantaa: Suomen kaupunkiliitto, 1981), p. 193; Ilkka Mäntylä, *Valitut, ehdollepannut ja nimitetyt. Pormestarin vaalit 20 kaupungissa 1720–1808*. Historiallisia Tutkimuksia 114 (Helsinki: Finnish Historical Society, 1981), pp. 30–31.
5. For a more detailed treatment, see the chapter by Petri Karonen and Marko Hakanen in the present work.
6. Usually the tasks of the royal mayors included several kinds of missions: in general, he acted as the leader of the town, as a chair of the town court (*rådstuguruätten*) and executed all the instructions given by the central government and county administration (including also orders by the military officials). Thus, royal mayor was in charge concerning the town community as a whole.
7. Many of the towns in the Kingdom of Sweden were small communities of usually fewer than a thousand inhabitants. On population sizes, see for example Sven Lilja, *Städernas folkmängd och tillväxt. Sverige (med Finland) ca 1570-tal till 1810-tal*. Historisk tätortsstatistik utgiven av stads- och kommunhistoriska institutet. Del 2 (Stockholms universitet: Stockholm, 1996); cf. however Claes Westling, *Småstadens dynamik. Skänninges och Vadstenas befolkning och kontaktfält ca 1630–1660*. Linköping Studies in Arts and Science 264 (Linköping: Linköpings universitet, 2002, (http://www.diva-portal.org/smash/get/diva2:20705/FULLTEXT01.pdf)), Ch. 4. In fact the majority of European towns were very small. Antoni Maczak und Christopher Smout (hrsg.), *Gründung und Bedeutung kleinerer Städte im nördlichen Europa der frühen Neuzeit. Wolfenbütteler Forschungen*. Herausgegeben von der Herzog August Bibliotek. Band 47 (Harrassowitz: Wiesbaden, 1991); Peter Clark (ed.), *Small Towns in Early Modern Europe. Themes in International Urban History 3* (Cambridge: Cambridge University Press, 1995).
8. Admittedly Karl Bergman (*Makt, möten, gränser. Skånska kommissionen i Blekinge 1669–70*. Studia Historica Lundensia (Lund: Lunds universitet, 2002); "Erövrade danska provinser. Rum, erfarenhet och identitet". In: Engman Max, Villstrand, Nils Erik (red.), *Maktens mosaik. Enhet, särart och självbild i det svenska riket* (Stockholm: Atlantis, 2008)), for example, questions whether there was any Swedification in the former Danish territories at any rate before 1680. See, however,

Lars Ericson, "Absolutism eller nationalism? Till frågan om försvenskningen av magistraterna i de erövrade Danska städerna under 1600-talet". In: *Karolinska förbundets årsbok 1984* (Stockholm: Karolinska förbundet, 1985); Knud Fabricius, *Skaanes overgang fra Danmark till Sverige. Studier over nationalitetsskiftet i de skaanske landskaber i de naermeste slaegtled efter Brømsebro- og Roskildefredene.* Anden del (1660–1676). Nyt uforandret Optryk (København: Nordisk forlag, 1955); Knud Fabricius, *Skaanes overgang fra Danmark till Sverige. Studier over nationalitetsskiftet i de skaanske landskaber i de naermeste slaegtled efter Brømsebro- og Roskildefredene.* Fjerde del (København: Nordisk forlag, 1958). Antti Räihä "Övergångsprocess, besittningstagande och lokala sedvänjor. Erövrade provinser under den nya överheten i Ryssland och Sverige under 1600- och 1700-talen" (*Scandia* 2011) offers an interesting comparison between the process of possession in what is today southern Sweden and that which was implemented in "Old Finland"; see also Antti Räihä, *Jatkuvuus ja muutosten hallinta. Lappeenranta ja Hamina Ruotsin ja Venäjän alaisuudessa 1720–1760-luvuilla.* Studies in Humanities 183 (Jyväskylä: Jyväskylän yliopisto, 2012). On the Swedish mayors appointed in Estonia, see for example Arnold Soom, "Jacob Fougdt", urn:sbl:14406, *Svenskt biografiskt lexikon* 1964–1966. On the integration policy practised in Finland, see Erkki Lehtinen, *Hallituksen yhtenäistämispolitiikka Suomessa 1600-luvulla (1600– n. 1680).* Historiallisia Tutkimuksia 60 (Helsinki: Finnish Historical Society, 1961).

9   Cf. Eino E. Suolahti, *Opinkäynti ja sen aiheuttama säätykierto Suomen porvariston keskuudessa 1600-luvulla* (Helsinki: WSOY, 1946), pp. 139–152; Lars Ericson, *Borgare och byråkrater. Omvandlingen av Stockholms stadsförvaltning 1599–1637.* Stockholmsmonografier utgivna av Stockholms stad 84 (Stockholm: Stockholms stad, 1988); Kekke Stadin, *Stånd och genus i stormaktstidens Sverige* (Lund: Nordic Academic Press, 2004), pp. 116–117, 247.

10  However, in the seventeenth century, there were ennobled mayors for example in Helsinki in 1653, Arboga in 1654, Vyborg in 1654, Örebro in 1654 and Norrköping in 1663. Stadshistoriska Institutets registersamling (SIR) Kungliga brev, Sakregister 1561–1720 (SIR card index); Carl-Fredrik Corin, *Arboga stads historia. Andra delen. Från 1500-talets mitt till 1718* (Arboga: Arboga kommun, 1978), p. 237; Petri Karonen, *"Raastuvassa tavataan". Suomen kaupunkien hallinto- ja oikeuslaitoksen toimintaa ja virkamiehiä suurvalta-aikana.* Studia Historica Jyväskyläensia 51 (Jyväskylä: Jyväskylän yliopisto, 1995, also www: https://jyx.jyu.fi/dspace/handle/123456789/19532)), pp. 187, 196; it was not common even for the mayors of Stockholm to be ennobled (information supplied by Piia Einonen 8.5.2015).

11  C. T. Odhner, *Bidrag till svenska stadsförfattningens historia* (Uppsala: C. A. Leffler, 1861); C. T. Odhner, *Sveriges inre historia under drottning Christinas förmyndare* (Stockholm: Norstedt, 1865); C. T. Odhner, "Om de svenska städernas kommunala utveckling under 17:de århundradet". In: *Nordisk tidskrift för politik, ekonomi och litteratur november–december* (1867); Aimo Halila, *Suomen kaupunkien kunnallishallinto 1600-luvulla I–II.* Historiallisia Tutkimuksia 58: 1–2 (Helsinki: Finnish Historical Society, 1942); Petri Karonen, *Kämnerinoikeudet Suomen kaupungeissa suurvalta-ajan alkupuolella (noin 1620–1660).* Studia Historica Jyväskyläensia 48 (Jyväskylä: Jyväskylän yliopisto, 1994, also www: file://fileservices.ad.jyu.fi/homes/karonen/Downloads/9789513943615%20(1).pdf); Anders Olsson, *Borgmästare, bastioner och tullbommar. Göteborg och Halmstad under statligt inflytande 1630–1660.* Bibliotheca historica Lundensis 84 (Lund: Lund universitet, 1995).

12  Gudrun Andersson, *Stadens dignitärer. Den lokala elitens status- och maktmanifestation i Arboga 1650–1770* (Stockholm: Atlantis, 2009), for example pp. 59–60.

13  SBL contains the biographies of altogether 14 seventeenth-century mayors, of whom only two mayors of towns in the former Danish territories (Nicolaus Petri

Agrelius (d. 1681) and Jacobus Petri Chronander (d. 1694)) together with the Mayor of Stockholm Olaus Bureus (1578–1655) can be considered royal mayors proper. This subject has aroused considerably more interest in Finland, although the writer of the present chapter is himself partly responsible for this situation. Altogether 13 biographies of mayors can be found in KB (N =12) and SBL, (N = 1), of whom 10 were royal mayors.

14 The amount of Nordic research on the structure of state administration is extensive (see the publications mentioned in Petri Karonen's and Marko Hakanen's chapter in the present work), but the interaction between the central authorities and the towns has rarely been the focus of attention. An interesting point of comparison can be found in James Lee's ("Urban policy and urban political culture: Henry VII and his towns", *Historical Research* 217 (2009) article on the interaction between provincial towns and Henry VII in England and the limits of the towns' autonomy at the turn of the fifteenth and sixteenth centuries. On this subject, see in particular Charles Tilly and Wim Blockmans (Charles Tilly and Wim P. Blockmans (eds), *Cities and the Rise of States in Europe A.D. 1000 to 1800*. Boulder: Westview Press, 1994); see also Charles Tilly, *Coercion, Capital, and European States, AD 990–1990*. Studies in Social Discontinuity (Oxford: Blackwell, 1990); Christopher R. Friedrichs, *The Early Modern City 1450–1750. A History of Urban Society in Europe*. Edited by Robert Tittler (London: Longman, 1995), pp. 44–45, 54–57; Michael J. Braddick, *State Formation in Early Modern England, c. 1550–1700* (Cambridge: Cambridge University Press, 2000). On the development in different parts of Europe, see Christopher Friedrichs, "Urban Politics and Urban Social Structure in Seventeenth-Century Germany", *European History Quarterly* 22 (1992), pp. 193–194; Heinz Schilling, *Die Stadt in der frühen Neuzeit*. Enzyklopädie deutscher Geschichte 24. Herausgegeben von Lothar Gall (München: R. Oldenbourg, 1993), pp. 47, 73–81; S. Annette Finley-Croswhite, *Henry IV and the towns: the pursuit of legitimacy in French urban society, 1589–1610*. Cambridge studies in early modern history (Cambridge: Cambridge University Press, 1999), particularly Ch. 6; Christopher R. Friedrichs, *Urban Politics in Early Modern Europe* (London: Routledge Friedrichs, 2000), pp. 13, 21–22, 66–67; Manon Van Der Heijden, "State Formation and Urban Finances in Sixteenth and Seventeenth-century Holland", *Journal of Urban History* 32 (2006); Robert von Friedeburg, "Urban Riots and the Perspective of "Qualification for Office": The Pecualiarities of Urban Government and the case of the 1672 Disturbances in the Netherlands". In: Jan Hartman, Jaap Nieuwstraten, Michel Reinders, (eds), *Public Offices, Personal Demands: Capability in Governance in the Seventeenth-Century Dutch Republic* (Newcastle upon Tyne: Cambridge Scholars Publication, 2009); Peter Clark, *European cities and towns 400–2000* (Oxford: Oxford University Press, 2009), Ch. 11; Fiona Williamson, "When "Comoners Were Made Slaves by the Magistrates". The 1627 Election and Political Culture in Norwich", *The Journal of Urban History* (2015).

15 Folke Lindberg, "1619 års stadga om städernas administration", *Svenska stadsförbundets tidskrift* 1937; Folke Lindberg, *Fogde, råd och menighet* (Stockholm: Bonnier, 1941); Sven Ljung, *Uppsala under yngre medeltid och Vasatid. Uppsala stads historia II* (Uppsala: Historiekomitté, 1954), pp. 320–328; Ericson, *Borgare och byråkrater*; Robert Sandberg, *I slottets skugga. Stockholm och kronan 1599–1620*. Stockholmsmonografier utgivna av Stockholms stad 105 (Stockholm: Stockholms stad, 1991); Karonen, *"Raastuvassa tavataan"*, Ch. II; Piia Einonen, *Poliittiset areenat ja toimintatavat. Tukholman porvaristo vallan käyttäjänä ja vallankäytön kohteena n. 1592–1644*. Bibliotheca Historica 94 (Helsinki: The Finnish Literature Society, 2005).

16 Lehtinen, *Hallituksen yhtenäistämispolitiikka*; Karonen, *Kämnerinoikeudet*; Karonen, *"Raastuvassa tavataan"*, p. 34.

17 On the debate over the issue, see for example Dag Lindström, "Förhalandets

praktik. En politisk och social strategi i det tidigmoderna Sverige", *Historisk tidskrift* 125: 1 (2005), pp. 5–24; Dag Lindström, "Om konsten att inte säga nej. Kungliga resolutioner på städers besvär under 1680-talet". In: Peter Ericsson, Fredrik Thisner, Patrik Winton och Andreas Åkerlund (ed.), *Allt på ett bräde. Stat, ekonomi och bondeoffer. En vänbok till Jan Lindegren*, Studia Historica Upsaliensia 249 (Uppsala: Uppsala universitet, 2013), pp. 235–245.

18 However, there was another side to this matter, as is well illustrated for example in a comparison with the very independent Dutch towns of the seventeenth century: Jan Hartman, Jaap Nieuwstraten and Michel Reinders (Hartman, Jan, Nieuwstraten, Jaap, Reinders, Michel, "Introduction". In: Jan Hartman, Jaap Nieuwstraten, Michel Reinders (eds), *Public Offices, Personal Demands: Capability in Governance in the Seventeenth-Century Dutch Republic*. Newcastle upon Tyne: Cambridge Scholars Publications, 2009, p. 3) state: "Since there was no monarch, Dutch urban aldermen lacked royal authority that could sanctify and support their rule." Cf. also Tom Scott, *The city-state in Europe, 1000–1600. Hinterland, territory, region* (Oxford: Oxford University Press, 2012).

19 On the state's policy on towns, see in particular Eli F. Heckscher, "Den ekonomiska innebörden av 1500- och 1600-talens svenska stadsgrundningar", *Historisk Tidskrift* 43 (1923); Lars-Arne Norborg, "Krona och stad i Sverige under äldre vasatid. Några synpunkter", *Historisk tidskrift* 83 (1963), pp. 370–371, 374–375; Lennart Hedberg, *Företagarfursten och framväxten av den starka staten. Hertig Karls resursexploatering i Närke 1581–1602* (Örebro studies 11. Örebro högskolan: Örebro, 1995), pp. 6–10; Åke Sandström, *Plöjande borgare och handlande bönder. Mötet mellan den europeiska urbana ekonomin och vasatidens Sverige*. Studier i stads- och kommunhistoria 15 (Stockholm: Stockholms universitet, 1996); from an international perspective, see Tilly & Blockmans (eds), *Cities and the Rise*. On the right granted to the holders of grand fiefs to found towns, see Robert Swedlund, *Grev- och friherreskapen i Sverige och i Finland. Donationerna och reduktionerna före 1680* (Uppsala, 1936), pp. 233–234, 239; Mauno Jokipii, *Suomen kreivi- ja vapaaherrakunnat. I–II*. Historiallisia Tutkimuksia 58: 1–2 (Helsinki: Finnish Historical Society, 1956, 1960).

20 David Beetham's ("Max Weber and the Legitimacy of the Modern State", *Analyse und kritik*. – http://www.analyse-und-kritik.net/1991-1/AK_Beetham_1991.pdf, 1991, pp. 42–43 (quote); David Beetham, *The Legitimation of Power. 2nd Edition. Political Analysis* (Basingstoke: Palgrave Macmillan, 2013) criticism is directed against the conceptual vocabulary of legitimacy developed by Max Weber and above all against the use of Weber's concepts in twentieth-century comparative research. The concepts of authority and legitimacy in a Nordic context have been studied for example by Magnus Perlestam, *Lydnad i karolinernas tid* (Lund: Nordic Academic Press, 2008), e.g. pp. 23–24, 26–31; Mats Hallenberg, "Svenskarna och westfaliska freden – en talande tystnad? Krig och fred i den statliga propagandan från stormaktstid till frihetstid". In: *1648. Den westfaliska freden. Arv, kontext och konsekvenser* (Lund: Nordic Academic Press, 2009), pp. 44–45; cf. Ericson, *Borgare och byråkrater*.

21 A town bailiff (*stadsfogde*) appointed for the purpose by the king (*en stadsfougde af konungen därtill förordnat*) was always to be installed in the town court, and either the county governor or the castellan was henceforth to occupy himself with the activities of the town court (*och hvarken landshöfdingen eller slottshöfvitsmannen härefter hafva med rådstugun till att göra*). Emil Hildebrand (ed.), *Sveriges regeringsformer 1634–1809 samt konungaförsäkringar 1611–1800* (Stockholm, 1891), p. 22 (26§); Olof Sörndal, *Den svenska länsstyrelsen. Uppkomst, organisation och allmänna maktställning* (Lund: Lunds universitet, 1937), pp. 33–46, 53–59; Halila, *Suomen kaupunkien kunnallishallinto*, pp. 37–43, 93–95; Lehtinen, *Hallituksen yhtenäistämispolitiikka*, pp. 140–142; Göran

Rystad, *Jönköping under stormaktstiden*. Jönköpings stads historia. Del II. Från stadens brand till kommunalreformen 1862 (Värnamo, 1965), pp. 154–155; Folke Lindberg, *Linköpings historia. 2. 1567-1862. Näringsliv och förvaltning* (Linköping: Kommittén för Linköpings historia, 1975), pp. 149–166; Ericson, *Borgare och byråkrater*, p. 38; Björn Helmfrid, *Söderköpings historia. 2. Tiden 1568-1690* (Söderköping: S:t Ragnhilds gille, 2001), pp. 147–148; Björn Asker, *I konungens stad och ställe. Länsstyrelser i arbete 1635-1735*. Arkivvetenskapliga studier 7 (Uppsala: Stiftelsen för utgivande av Arkivvetenskapliga studier, 2004); Alexander Jonsson, *De norrländska landshövdingarna och statsbildningen 1634-1769*. Skrifter från institutionen för historiska studier 10 (Umeå: Umeå universitet, 2005).

22  There was a burgrave in Gothenburg and Turku in the 1620s (Lehtinen, *Hallituksen yhtenäistämispolitiikka*, pp. 145–147; Karonen, *Kämnerinoikeudet*, pp. 85–86) and in Rauma (Raumo) and Uusikaupunki (Nystad) a joint lord mayor in the early 1640s (Karonen, "Raastuvassa tavataan", pp. 73–75). The office of president existed in both Kalmar and Norrköping. Odhner, *Sveriges inre historia*, pp. 184–186; Odhner, "Om de svenska", p. 672; Aimo Halila, *Suomen kaupunkien kunnallishallinto*, pp. 92–93; Björn Helmfrid, *Norrköpings stads historia. 2. Tiden 1655-1719* (Stockholm, 1971), pp. 247–248, 265–269; Karonen, "Raastuvassa tavataan", p. 50; the sources mentioned in these works.

23  On the interaction and the relationship between the towns and the enforced measures of the central authorities, see the chapter by Petri Karonen and Marko Hakanen in the present volume and the literature mentioned therein. Odhner, *Sveriges inre historia*, p. 186; Karonen, "Raastuvassa tavataan", p. 50.

24  Riksarkivet, Stockholm (SRA) (Swedish National Archives), Riksregistraturet (RR) (Swedish National Records), 30th of April, 1638: 430v.–431; 29th of January, 1645: 187–188. In Stockholm, taxes and fees and official appointments had previously been linked together. Ericson, *Borgare och byråkrater*, pp. 96–98; see also Rystad, *Jönköping*, p. 156.

25  Odhner, "Om de svenska", p. 672; Folke Lindberg, *Västerviks historia. Tiden 1275-1718* (Västervik: Västerviks stadsfullmäktige, 1933), p. 262; Halila, *Suomen kaupunkien kunnallishallinto*, pp. 92, 118; Elfstrand, "Ur förvaltningshistorien", p. 496; Torsten Petré, *Uppsala stads historia 3. Uppsala under merkantilismens och statskontrollens tidsskede: 1619-1789* (Uppsala: Historiekommission, 1958), pp. 232–233; Rystad, *Jönköping*, pp. 156–157; Karonen, *Kämnerinoikeudet*, p. 85.

26  The only exceptions to this were small towns and towns in the former Danish territories.

27  For example, in 1643, it was specifically stated in the letter of appointment of Elias Mörck (d. 1647) as the Mayor of Uppsala that his salary of 500 silver thalers was to be paid out of the town's funds. Later, in the 1640s, dozens of such specifications were issued. Karonen, "Raastuvassa tavataan", p. 52, as well as notes 52–53 and the *Riksregistratur* (RR) (Swedish National Records) and *Personal stater* material used therein. See also for example Rystad, *Jönköping*, pp. 157–158; Corin, *Arboga*, p. 231. On the relationship between salary payment and corruption, cf. Bo Rothstein, "Anti-corruption: The Indirect 'Big Bang' Approach", *Review of International Political Economy* 18: 2 (2011), pp. 228–250; Anders Sundell, "Understanding Informal Payments in the Public Sector: Theory and Evidence from Nineteenth-century Sweden", *Scandinavian Political Studies* 37: 2 (2014).

28  SRA RR 25th of April, 1642: 507v.–508; SRA RR 30th of June, 1644: 790–790v., 793–794v.; Corin, *Arboga*, pp. 228–229; Karonen "Raastuvassa tavataan", p. 51; Andersson, *Stadens dignitärer*, pp. 59–60.

29  The situation did not begin to improve in this respect until the end of the 1650s. Petri Karonen, "A Life for a Life versus Christian Reconciliation: Violence and the Process of Civilization in the Kingdom of Sweden, 1540-1700". In: Heikki Ylikangas, Petri Karonen, Martti Lehti, *Five Centuries of Violence in Finland and*

*the Baltic Area. With a Foreword by Eric H. Monkkonen*. The History of Crime and Criminal Justice Series (Columbus: Ohio State University Press, 2001a), pp. 81–118.

30 Rystad, *Jönköping*, pp. 159, 161.
31 Ericson, *Borgare och byråkrater*, pp. 112–115, 144, 146; Sandberg, *I slottets skugga*, pp. 224–232.
32 For example, there is a case in Vyborg at the time of the 25-year war with Russia in which the local prefect together with the town burghers dismissed negligent mayors and replaced them with new incumbents. Folke Lindberg (ed.), *Privilegier, resolutioner och förordningar för Sveriges städer. Tredje delen (1560–1592). Första och andra halfbandet* (Stockholm, 1939), no. 146 (30th of July, 1573), p. 270.
33 See for example Folke Sleman *Privilegier, resolutioner och förordningar för Sveriges städer. Femte delen (1611–1620)* (Stockholm, 1964), nr 135 (30th of December 1617), nr 181 (14th of April 1620); Rystad, *Jönköping*, p. 150.
34 According to Marko Hakanen (*Vallan verkostoissa. Per Brahe ja hänen klienttinsä 1600-luvun Ruotsin valtakunnassa*. Jyväskylä Studies in Humanities 157 (Jyväskylä: Jyväskylän yliopisto, 2011, appendix)), Per Brahe's clients included at least 30 or so mayors of Finnish towns and cities. Cf. Svante Norrhem, *Uppkomlingarna. Kanslitjänstemännen i 1600-talets Sverige och Europa*. Umeå Studies in the Humanities 117 (Umeå: Umeå universitet, 1993); Karonen, "*Raastuvassa tavataan*", appendices.
35 Corin, *Arboga*, pp. 230, 237.
36 Royal mayors were appointed to Södertälje and Trosa in the 1690s. On the basis of the SIR material and the town histories that have been consulted, the following towns in Sweden did not have royal mayors at all: Sigtuna, Öregrund, Norrtälje, Bogesund, Hjo, Skövde, Piteå, Luleå, Alingsås, Vimmerby and Östhammar. Odhner, "Om de svenska", p. 673; Raimo Ranta, "Suurvalta-ajan kaupunkilaitos". In: *Suomen kaupunkilaitoksen historia 1. Keskiajalta 1870-luvulle* (Vantaa: Suomen kaupunkiliitto, 1981), p. 103; Karonen, *Kämnerinoikeudet*, pp. 42–43; Karonen, "*Raastuvassa tavataan*", pp. 44–45.
37 Karonen, "*Raastuvassa tavataan*", Ch. 6, Tables 2–7; Björn Helmfrid, *Norrköpings stads historia 1568–1719. 1. Tidsavsnittet 1568–1655* (Stockholm, 1963); Helmfrid, *Norrköpings historia. 2*; K. W. Herdin, *Uppsala på 1600-talet. Bidrag till stadens historia. Rättsväsendet. 2. Livsbilder: av borgmästare och råd m.fl.* (Uppsala, 1927); Lindberg, *Linköpings historia*. On the numbers of mayors, see also Halila, *Suomen kaupunkien kunnallishallinto*; Ranta, "Suurvalta-ajan kaupunkilaitos".
38 Within the spatial and chronological limits of this chapter, there were altogether 64 old towns in the realm of Sweden, of which four fifths were located in Sweden proper and one fifth in Finland.
39 Odhner, "Om de svenska", pp. 674–676. Later, for example David Gaunt (*Utbildning till statens tjänst. En kollektivbiografi av stormaktstidens hovrättsauskultanter*. Studia Historica Upsaliensia 63 (Uppsala: Uppsala universitet, 1975), p. 162) has expressed doubts about the coverage of the examples. On the emphasizing of the conflicts, see in particular Ericson, "Absolutism eller nationalism?", pp. 52–57; Ericson, *Borgare och byråkrater*, pp. 38–41.
40 For a further discussion, see Karonen, "Borgmästare mellan staten", which draws on Fred W. Riggs's "The Theory of Prismatic Society".
41 Karonen, *Kämnerinoikeudet*; see also Gaunt, *Utbildning*, p. 164; cf. for example Ericson, Borgare och byråkrater, pp. 38, 41; Olsson, Västerås genom tiderna, pp. 35, 88–103.
42 However, the set of detailed instructions given to Lithman is the only one of its kind. Karonen, "*Raastuvassa tavataan*", pp. 24–29, 51–52 and the sources mentioned therein.

43 Odhner, "Om de svenska", p. 675; Gustaf Elgenstierna, *Den introducerade svenska adelns ättartavlor. Med tillägg och rättelser* (Stockholm: Norstedt, 1925–1936); Sören Klingnéus, "'Vi flyttar inte även om man skär halsen av oss' – när Nerikes faktori skulle centraliseras till staden Örebro". In: Sören Klingnéus (ed.), *Vasatidens Örebro. En antologi under medverkan av Jan Brunius et. al. Projektet Örebro historia*. Örebro studies 4 (Örebro: Örebro högskola, 1988), pp. 185, 190, see also note 155; Karonen, *"Raastuvassa tavataan"*, p. 54.

44 See for example Helge Almquist, *Göteborgs historia. Grundläggningen och de första hundra åren. Förra delen. Från grundläggningen till enväldet (1619–1680)*. Skrifter utgivna till Göteborgs stads trehundraårsjubileum genom jubileumsutställningens publikationskommitté 1:1 (Göteborg, 1929), pp. 150–151, 341–353; Helmfrid, *Norrköpings stads historia 1*, pp. 598–599, 601, 605.

45 In Uppsala, a doctor of laws called Elias Mörck improved the efficiency of the administration of justice, as did Bengt Joensson Arhusius in Enköping. Herdin, *Uppsala på 1600-talet, 2*, pp. 49, 51–53, 60–66, 78–83; Petré, *Uppsala*, pp. 20, 233, 253; Sven Ljung, *Enköpings stads historia. 1. Tiden till och med 1718* (Enköping: Kommunfullmäktige, 1963), pp. 290–291.

46 On the comprehensive and also the quantitative handling of the material of the town courts and lower town courts, see Karonen, *Kämnerinoikeudet*; Karonen, *"Raastuvassa tavataan"*; Dag Lindström, "Från lokal konfliktlösare till administrativ stab. Råd och kämnärsrätt i Karlstad under 1600-talet", *Scandia* 69: 1 (2003). Cf. also Griet Vermeesch, "Capability, Patrimonialism and Bureaucracy in the Urban Administrations of the Low Countries (c. 1300–1780)". In: Jan Hartman, Jaap Nieuwstraten, Michel Reinders, Michel (eds), *Public Offices, Personal Demands: Capability in Governance in the Seventeenth-Century Dutch Republic* (Newcastle upon Tyne: Cambridge Scholars Publication, 2009), p. 54.

47 See in particular Gerhard Eimer, *Die Stadtplanung im Schwedischen Ostseereich 1600–1715. Mit Beiträgen zur Geschichte der Idealstadt* (Stockholm: Scandinavian university books, 1961); Juhani Kostet, *Cartographia urbium Finnicarum. Suomen kaupunkien kaupunkikartografia 1600luvulla ja 1700luvun alussa*. Monumenta cartographica septentrionalia 1 (Rovaniemi: Pohjois-Suomen historiallinen yhdistys, 1995); Marjut Kirjakka, *The Orthogonal Finnish Town 1620–1860. Its Structure, Components and Dimensions* (Espoo: Helsinki University of Technology, 1995); Nils Ahlberg, *Stadsgrundningar och planförändringar. Svensk stadsplanering 1521–1721*. Acta Universitatis agriculturae Sueciae, 2005: 94 (Uppsala: Swedish University of Agricultural Sciences. http://diss-epsilon.slu.se:8080/archive/00000930/01/avhandling_ahlberg_low_res.pdf 2005(a)); Nils Ahlberg, *Stadsgrundningar och planförändringar. Svensk stadsplanering 1521–1721. Kartor*. Acta Universitatis agriculturae Sueciae 2005:94. Uppsala: Swedish University of Agricultural Sciences: Uppsala. http://diss-epsilon.slu.se:8080/archive/00000930/03/avhandling_ahlberg_kartor_low_res.pdf 2005 (b)).

48 Olsson, *Västerås genom tiderna*, pp. 88–89, 96.

49 Rystad, *Jönköping*, pp. 159, 161; see also for example Lars-Olof Larsson, *Växjö genom 1000 år* (Stockholm: Norstedt, 1991), p. 104. Cf. Karonen, *"Raastuvassa tavataan"* (Ch. 7), in which the negative conceptions attached to a single royal mayor (Jochim Timme) are deconstructed.

50 Temporary investigatory organs and commissions operated in the seventeenth century in the following towns and cities: Gävle 1651 (Elfstrand, "Ur förvaltningshistorien", p. 501); Västerås 1654 (Olsson, *Västerås genom tiderna*, p. 100–101); Oulu 1654 (Virkkunen, *Oulun kaupungin historia*); Söderköping 1660 (Helmfrid, *Söderköpings historia*, p. 154); Uppsala 1664 (Petré, *Uppsala*, p. 28), Uusikaupunki1667 (Karonen, *"Raastuvassa tavataan"*, p. 189; Petri Karonen, "Casper Eichman (ca 1590–ca 1670), Handelsman, borgmästare, riksdagsman". In:

*Biografiskt lexikon för Finland 1. Svenska tiden*. Helsingfors, Stockholm: Svenska litteratursällskapet, Atlantis (also www: http://www.blf.fi/index.php), 2008). On the use of commissions to settle disputes in the new towns, see in particular Carl-Fredrik Corin, *Vänersborgs historia. I. Tiden t. o. m. 1834* (Göteborg, 1944), pp. 133–134, 136–138, 143, 148; generally on the commissions, see Sven A. Nilsson, *De stora krigens tid. Om Sverige som militärstat och bondesamhälle*. Studia Historica Upsaliensia 161 (Uppsala: Uppsala universitet, 1990); Marie Lennersand, *Rättvisans och allmogens beskyddare. Den absoluta staten, kommissionerna och tjänstemännen, ca 1680–1730*. Studia Historica Upsaliensia 190 (Stockholm: Uppsala universitet, 1999); Bergman, *Makt, möten, gränser*.

51 In Arboga in the early 1650s, the townsfolk accused the royal mayor of failing to be sufficiently assiduous in protecting and promoting the interests of the town. Corin, *Arboga*, p. 285.

52 See for example Gösta Bucht, *Härnösands historia. Del I. Tiden 1585–1721* (Härnösand: Härnösand stad, 1935), pp. 81–82; Rystad, *Jönköping*, p. 158; Larsson, *Växjö*, p. 98.

53 Olsson, *Västerås genom tiderna*, p. 101. Cf. Söderköping, where the royal mayor was claimed to have appropriated war taxes for his own use, and Härnösand, where all the other aldermen accused the mayor, Johan Hansson Höijer (d. 1654), of financial malfeasance. Helmfrid, *Söderköpings historia*, p. 154; Bucht, *Härnösands historia*, p. 78.

54 Disputes connected with alcohol were common in many towns. Rystad, *Jönköping*, p. 162; Halila, *Suomen kaupunkien kunnallishallinto*, passim.

55 Petré, *Uppsala*, pp. 24–25, 29, 31, 34; cf. K. W. Herdin, *Uppsala på 1600-talet. Bidrag till stadens historia. Rättsväsendet. 1. Stadsstyrelsens organisation och rättsskipning* (Uppsala, 1926), pp. 181–195.

56 These juicy cases have received considerable attention in previous research: see for example Bucht, *Härnösands historia*, p. 79 (Härnösand); Elfstrand, "Ur förvaltningshistorien", pp. 497–498 (Gävle); Olsson, *Västerås genom tiderna*, pp. 96–99 (Västerås); Larsson, *Växjö*, p. 180 (Växjö); Jonsson, *De norrländska landshövdingarna*, p. 142 (Oulu).

57 Karonen, "Casper Eichman" and the sources quoted therein.

58 At least four other royal mayors in Finland at that time were actively engaged in the beer brewing business. Santeri Ingman, "Eräs vanha pormestari-riita", *Joukahainen. Pohjalais-osakunnan toimittama*. Yhdestoista vihko (Helsinki: Pohjalais-osakunta, 1897), p. 55; Virkkunen, *Oulun kaupungin historia*, pp. 391–414; Karonen, *Kämnerinoikeudet*, appendices; Petri Karonen, *Patruunat ja poliitikot. Yritysjohtajien taloudellinen ja yhteiskunnallinen toiminta Suomessa 1600–1920*. Historiallisia Tutkimuksia 217 (Helsinki: The Finnish Literature Society, 2004), p. 159 (quotation); Jonsson, *De norrländska landshövdingarna*, pp. 140–143.

59 See for example Halila, *Suomen kaupunkien kunnallishallinto* 1942, p. 97; Karonen, *Kämnerinoikeudet*, pp. 157, 171; Karonen, "Borgmästare mellan staten".

60 Karonen, *Patruunat ja poliitikot*, particularly Ch. III; on the representatives at the Diets during the great power era, see Nils Ahnlund (ed.), *Borgarståndets riksdagsprotokoll före frihetstiden* (Stadshistoriska institutet: Uppsala, 1933), pp. 212–218, 221–229, 354–412; for a complete list of the representatives of the Finnish Burgher Estate at the Diets in the seventeenth century, see Carl von Bonsdorff, "De finska städernas representation intill frihetstiden", *HArk XIII* (Helsinki: Finnish Historical Society, 1893).

# Sources

## Archival sources

Riksarkivet, Stockholm (SRA) (Swedish National Archives)
Riksregistratur (RR) (Swedish National Records) 1620-1680.
Stadshistoriska Institutets registersamling (SIR), Kungliga brev, Sakregister 1561-1720.

## Printed sources

BR (1933). *Borgarståndets riksdagsprotokoll före frihetstiden.* Ed. Av Nils Ahnlund. Uppsala: Stadshistoriska institutet.
*Privilegier, resolutioner och förordningar för Sveriges städer. Tredje delen (1560-1592)* (1939): Utgiven av Folke Lindberg. Första och andra halfbandet. Stockholm.
*Privilegier, resolutioner och förordningar för Sveriges städer. Femte delen (1611-1620)* (1964): Utgiven av Folke Sleman. Stockholm 1964.
*Privilegier, resolutioner och förordningar för Sveriges städer. Sjätte delen (1621-1632)* (1985): Utgiven av Carl-Fredrik Corin och Folke Sleman. Stockholm.
Hildebrand, Emil (red.) 1891: *Sveriges regeringsformer 1634-1809 samt konungaförsäkringar 1611-1800.* Utg. av Emil Hildebrand. Stockholm.

## Databases

Biografiskt lexikon för Finland (BLF) [http://www.blf.fi/sok.php], accessed April 2, 2015.
Kansallisbiografia (KB) [http://www.kansallisbiografia.fi/kb/], accessed April 2, 2015.
Svensk biografiskt lexikon (SBL) [http://sok.riksarkivet.se/sbl/Start.aspx], accessed April 2, 2015.

## Literature

Ahlberg, Nils 2005: *Stadsgrundningar och planförändringar. Svensk stadsplanering 1521-1721.* Acta Universitatis agriculturae Sueciae, 2005:94. Uppsala: Swedish University of Agricultural Sciences. [http://diss- epsilon.slu.se:8080/archive/00000930/01/avhandling_ahlberg_low_res.pdf] (a)
Ahlberg, Nils 2005: *Stadsgrundningar och planförändringar. Svensk stadsplanering 1521-1721. Kartor.* Acta Universitatis agriculturae Sueciae 2005:94. Uppsala: Swedish University of Agricultural Sciences. [http://diss-epsilon.slu.se:8080/archive/00000930/03/avhandling_ahlberg_kartor_low_res.pdf] (b)
Almquist, Helge 1929: *Göteborgs historia. Grundläggningen och de första hundra åren. Förra delen. Från grundläggningen till enväldet (1619-1680).* Skrifter utgivna till Göteborgs stads trehundraårsjubileum genom jubileumsutställningens publikationskommitté 1:1. Göteborg.
Andersson, Gudrun 2009: *Stadens dignitärer. Den lokala elitens status- och maktmanifestation i Arboga 1650-1770.* Stockholm: Atlantis.
Asker, Björn 2004: *I konungens stad och ställe. Länsstyrelser i arbete 1635-1735.* Arkivvetenskapliga studier 7. Uppsala: Stiftelsen för utgivande av Arkivvetenskapliga studier.

Beetham, David 1991: "Max Weber and the Legitimacy of the Modern State", *Analyse und kritik*. [http://www.analyse-und-kritik.net/1991-1/AK_Beetham_1991.pdf]
Beetham, David 2013: *The Legitimation of Power*. 2nd Edition. Political Analysis. Basingstoke: Palgrave Macmillan.
Bergman, Karl 2002: *Makt, möten, gränser. Skånska kommissionen i Blekinge 1669–70*. Studia Historica Lundensia. Lund: Lunds universitet.
Bergman, Karl 2008: "Erövrade danska provinser. Rum, erfarenhet och identitet". In: Engman Max, Villstrand, Nils Erik (red.), *Maktens mosaik. Enhet, särart och självbild i det svenska riket*. Stockholm: Atlantis.
Bonsdorff, Carl von 1893: "De finska städernas representation intill frihetstiden", *HArk* XIII. Helsinki: Finnish Historical Society.
Braddick, M. J. 2000: *State Formation in Early Modern England, c. 1550–1700*. Cambridge: Cambridge University Press.
Bucht, Gösta 1935: *Härnösands historia. Del I. Tiden 1585–1721*. Härnösand: Härnösand stad.
Clark, Peter (ed.) 1995: *Small Towns in Early Modern Europe*. Themes in International Urban History 3. Cambridge: Cambridge University Press.
Clark, Peter 2009: *European cities and towns 400–2000*. Oxford: Oxford University Press.
Corin, Carl-Fredrik 1944: *Vänersborgs historia. I. Tiden t. o. m. 1834*. Göteborg.
Corin, Carl-Fredrik 1978: *Arboga stads historia. Andra delen. Från 1500-talets mitt till 1718*. Arboga: Arboga kommun.
Danielsson, O. 1933: "Rättskipning och förvaltning", *Mariestad 1583–1933*. Mariestad: Karströms bokhandel.
Eimer, Gerhard 1961: *Die Stadtplanung im Schwedischen Ostseereich 1600–1715. Mit beiträgen zur Geschichte der Idealstadt*. Stockholm: Scandinavian university books.
Einonen, Piia 2005: *Poliittiset areenat ja toimintatavat. Tukholman porvaristo vallan käyttäjänä ja vallankäytön kohteena n. 1592–1644*. Bibliotheca Historica 94. Helsinki: The Finnish Literature Society.
Elfstrand, Percy 1946: Ur förvaltningshistorien. *Ur Gävle stads historia*. Utgiven till femhundraårs jubileet. Gävle.
Elgenstierna, Gustaf 1925–1936: *Den introducerade svenska adelns ättartavlor. Med tillägg och rättelser*. Stockholm: Norstedt.
Ericson, Lars 1985: "Absolutism eller nationalism? Till frågan om försvenskningen av magistraterna i de erövrade Danska städerna under 1600-talet", *Karolinska förbundets årsbok 1984*. Stockholm: Karolinska förbundet.
Ericson, Lars 1988: *Borgare och byråkrater. Omvandlingen av Stockholms stadsförvaltning 1599–1637*. Stockholmsmonografier utgivna av Stockholms stad 84. Stockholm: Stockholms stad.
Fabricius, Knud 1955: *Skaanes overgang fra Danmark till Sverige. Studier over nationalitetsskiftet i de skaanske landskaber i de naermeste slaegtled efter Brømsebro- og Roskildefredene*. Anden del (1660–1676). Nyt uforandret Optryk. København: Nordisk forlag.
Fabricius, Knud 1958: *Skaanes overgang fra Danmark till Sverige. Studier over nationalitetsskiftet i de skaanske landskaber i de naermeste slaegtled efter Brømsebro- og Roskildefredene*. Fjerde del. København: Nordisk forlag.
Finley-Croswhite, S. Annette 1999: *Henry IV and the towns: the pursuit of legitimacy in French urban society, 1589–1610*. Cambridge studies in early modern history. Cambridge: Cambridge University Press.
Friedeburg, Robert von 2009: "Urban Riots and the Perspective of "Qualification for Office": The Pecualiarities of Urban Government and the case of the 1672 Disturbances in the Netherlands". In: Hartman, Jan, Nieuwstraten, Jaap, Reinders, Michel (eds), *Public Offices, Personal Demands: Capability in Governance in the*

*Seventeenth-Century Dutch Republic.* Newcastle upon Tyne: Cambridge Scholars Publication.

Friedrichs, Christopher R. 1992: "Urban Politics and Urban Social Structure in Seventeenth Century Germany", *European History Quarterly* Vol. 22: 2.

Friedrichs, Christopher R. 1995: *The Early Modern City 1450–1750: A History of Urban Society in Europe.* Edited by Robert Tittler. London: Longman.

Friedrichs, Christopher R. 2000: *Urban Politics in Early Modern Europe.* London: Routledge.

Gaunt, David 1975: *Utbildning till statens tjänst. En kollektivbiografi av stormaktstidens hovrättsauskultanter.* Studia Historica Upsaliensia 63. Uppsala: Uppsala universitet.

Hakanen, Marko 2011: *Vallan verkostoissa. Per Brahe ja hänen klienttinsä 1600-luvun Ruotsin valtakunnassa.* Jyväskylä Studies in Humanities 157. Jyväskylä: Jyväskylän yliopisto.

Halila, Aimo 1942, 1943: *Suomen kaupunkien kunnallishallinto 1600-luvulla I–II.* Historiallisia Tutkimuksia 28: 1–2. Helsinki: Finnish Historical Society.

Hallenberg, Mats 2009: "Svenskarna och westfaliska freden – en talande tystnad? Krig och fred i den statliga propagandan från stormaktstid till frihetstid". In: *1648. Den westfaliska freden. Arv, kontext och konsekvenser.* Lund: Nordic Academic Press.

Hartman, Jan, Nieuwstraten, Jaap, Reinders, Michel 2009: "Introduction". In: Hartman, Jan, Nieuwstraten, Jaap, Reinders, Michel (eds), *Public Offices, Personal Demands: Capability in Governance in the Seventeenth-Century Dutch Republic.* Newcastle upon Tyne: Cambridge Scholars Publications.

Heckscher, Eli F. 1923: "Den ekonomiska innebörden av 1500- och 1600-talens svenska stadsgrundningar", *Historisk Tidskrift* 43.

Hedberg, Lennart 1995: *Företagarfursten och framväxten av den starka staten. Hertig Karls resursexploatering i Närke 1581–1602.* Örebro studies 11. Örebro högskolan: Örebro.

Helmfrid, Björn 1963: *Norrköpings stads historia 1568–1719. 1. Tidsavsnittet 1568–1655.* Stockholm.

Helmfrid, Björn 1971: *Norrköpings stads historia. 2. Tiden 1655–1719.* Stockholm.

Helmfrid, Björn 2001: *Söderköpings historia. 2. Tiden 1568–1690.* Söderköping: S:t Ragnhilds gille.

Herdin, K. W. 1926: *Uppsala på 1600-talet. Bidrag till stadens historia. Rättsväsendet. 1. Stadsstyrelsens organisation och rättsskipning.* Uppsala.

Herdin, K. W. 1927: *Uppsala på 1600-talet. Bidrag till stadens historia. Rättsväsendet. 2. Livsbilder: av borgmästare och råd m.fl.* Uppsala.

Herlitz, Nils 1924: *Svensk stadsförvaltning på 1830-talet.* Stadshistoriska institutet. Stockholm: Norstedt.

Holmberg, Nils Hj. 1946: *Lidköpings historia till 1860.* [Lidköping]: [Drätselkammaren].

Ingman, Santeri 1897: "Eräs vanha pormestari-riita", *Joukahainen. Pohjalais-osakunnan toimittama.* Yhdestoista vihko. Helsinki: Pohjalais-osakunta.

Jokipii, Mauno 1956, 1960: *Suomen kreivi- ja vapaaherrakunnat. I–II.* Historiallisia Tutkimuksia 58:1–2. Helsinki: Finnish Historical Society.

Jonsson, Alexander 2005: *De norrländska landshövdingarna och statsbildningen 1634–1769.* Skrifter från institutionen för historiska studier 10. Umeå: Umeå universitet.

Karonen, Petri 1994: *Kämnerinoikeudet Suomen kaupungeissa suurvalta-ajan alkupuolella (noin 1620–1660).* Studia Historica Jyväskyläensia 48. Jyväskylä: Jyväskylän yliopisto (also www: [file://fileservices.ad.jyu.fi/homes/karonen/Downloads/9789513943615%20(1).pdf].

Karonen, Petri 1995: *"Raastuvassa tavataan". Suomen kaupunkien hallinto- ja oikeuslaitoksen toimintaa ja virkamiehiä suurvalta-aikana.* Studia Historica Jyväskyläensia 51. Jyväskylä: Jyväskylän yliopisto. also [www:https://jyx.jyu.fi/dspace/handle/123456789/19532].

Karonen, Petri 2001a: "A Life for a Life versus Christian Reconciliation: Violence and the Process of Civilization in the Kingdom of Sweden, 1540–1700". In: Ylikangas, Heikki, Karonen, Petri, Lehti, Martti, *Five Centuries of Violence in Finland and the Baltic Area. With a Foreword by Eric H. Monkkonen.* The History of Crime and Criminal Justice Series. Columbus: Ohio State University Press.

Karonen, Petri 2001b: "Borgmästare mellan staten och stadssamhället. Förvaltnings- och rättskulturer i det svenska rikets städer under stormaktstiden". In: Harnesk, Börje, Taussi Sjöberg, Marja (red.), *Mellan makten och menigheten. Ämbetsmän i det tidigmoderna Sverige.* Institutet för rättshistorisk forskning. Serien III. Rättshistoriska skrifter. Första bandet. Stockholm: Institutet för rättshistorisk forskning.

Karonen, Petri 2004: *Patruunat ja poliitikot. Yritysjohtajien taloudellinen ja yhteiskunnallinen toiminta Suomessa 1600–1920.* Historiallisia Tutkimuksia 217. Helsinki: The Finnish Literature Society.

Karonen, Petri 2008: "Casper Eichman (ca 1590–ca 1670), Handelsman, borgmästare, riksdagsman". In: *Biografiskt lexikon för Finland 1. Svenska tiden.* Helsingfors, Stockholm: Svenska litteratursällskapet, Atlantis (also www: http://www.blf.fi/index.php).

Kirjakka, Marjut 1996: *The Orthogonal Finnish Town 1620–1860. Its Structure, Components and Dimensions.* Espoo: Helsinki University of Technology.

Klingnéus, Sören 1988: "'Vi flyttar inte även om man skär halsen av oss' – när Nerikes faktori skulle centraliseras till staden Örebro". In: *Vasatidens Örebro. En antologi under medverkan av Jan Brunius et. al.* Redaktör: Sören Klingnéus. Projektet Örebro historia. Örebro studies 4. Örebro: Örebro högskola.

Kostet, Juhani 1995: *Cartographia urbium Finnicarum. Suomen kaupunkien kaupunkikartografia 1600-luvulla ja 1700-luvun alussa.* Monumenta cartographica septentrionalia 1. Rovaniemi: Pohjois-Suomen historiallinen yhdistys.

Larsson, Lars-Olof 1991: *Växjö genom 1000 år.* Stockholm: Norstedt.

Lee, James 2009: "Urban policy and urban political culture: Henry VII and his towns", *Historical research* 217.

Lehtinen, Erkki 1961: *Hallituksen yhtenäistämispolitiikka Suomessa 1600-luvulla (1600–n. 1680).* Historiallisia Tutkimuksia 60. Helsinki: Finnish Historical Society.

Lennersand, Marie 1999: *Rättvisans och allmogens beskyddare. Den absoluta staten, kommissionerna och tjänstemännen, ca 1680–1730.* Studia Historica Upsaliensia 190. Uppsala: Uppsala universitet.

Lilja, Sven 1996: *Städernas folkmängd och tillväxt. Sverige (med Finland) ca 1570-tal till 1810-tal.* Historisk tätortsstatistik utgiven av stads- och kommunhistoriska institutet. Del 2. Stockholm: Stockholms universitet.

Lindberg, Folke 1933: *Västerviks historia. Tiden 1275–1718.* Västervik: Västerviks stadsfullmäktige.

Lindberg, Folke 1937: "1619 års stadga om städernas administration", *Svenska stadsförbundets tidskrift.*

Lindberg, Folke 1941: *Fogde, råd och menighet.* Stockholm: Bonnier.

Lindberg, Folke 1975: *Linköpings historia. 2. 1567–1862. Näringsliv och förvaltning.* Linköping: Kommittén för Linköpings historia.

Lindström, Dag 2003: "Från lokal konfliktlösare till administrativ stab. Råd och kämnärsrätt i Karlstad under 1600-talet", *Scandia* 69: 1.

Lindström, Dag 2005: "Förhalandets praktik. En politisk och social strategi i det tidigmoderna Sverige", *Historisk tidskrift* 125: 1.

Lindström, Dag 2013: "Om konsten att inte säga nej. Kungliga resolutioner på städers besvär under 1680-talet". In: Ericsson, Peter, Thisner, Fredrik, Winton, Patrik och Åkerlund Andreas (red.), *Allt på ett bräde. Stat, ekonomi och bondeoffer. En vänbok till Jan Lindegren,* Studia Historica Upsaliensia 249. Uppsala: Uppsala universitet.

Ljung, Sven 1954: *Uppsala under yngre medeltid och Vasatid. Uppsala stads historia II.* Uppsala: Historiekomitté.

Ljung, Sven 1963: *Enköpings stads historia. 1. Tiden till och med 1718.* Enköping: Kommunfullmäktige.

Maczak, Antoni und Smout, Christopher (hrsg.) 1991: *Gründung und Bedeutung kleinerer Städte im nördlichen Europa der frühen Neuzeit. Wolfenbütteler Forschungen.* Herausgegeben von der Herzog August Bibliotek. Band 47. Harrassowitz: Wiesbaden.

Mäntylä, Ilkka 1981: *Valitut, ehdollepannut ja nimitetyt. Pormestarin vaalit 20 kaupungissa 1720–1808.* Historiallisia Tutkimuksia 114. Helsinki: Finnish Historical Society.

Nikula, Oscar 1981, "Kaupunkilaitos 1721–1875", *Suomen kaupunkilaitoksen historia 1. Keskiajalta 1870-luvulle.* Vantaa: Suomen kaupunkiliitto.

Nilsson, Sven A. 1990: *De stora krigens tid. Om Sverige som militärstat och bondesamhälle.* Studia Historica Upsaliensia 161. Uppsala: Uppsala universitet.

Norborg, Lars-Arne 1963: "Krona och stad i Sverige under äldre vasatid. Några synpunkter", *Historisk tidskrift*.

Norrhem, Svante 1993: *Uppkomlingarna. Kanslitjänstemännen i 1600-talets Sverige och Europa.* Umeå Studies in the Humanities 117. Umeå: Umeå universitet.

Näsmark, Johan 1923: *Sala stad. Bidrag till dess historia.* Sala.

Odhner, Clas Theodor 1860: *Bidrag till svenska städernas och borgarståndets historia före 1633.* Uppsala: Edquist.

Odhner, C. T. 1861: *Bidrag till svenska stadsförfattningens historia.* Uppsala: C. A. Leffler.

Odhner, C. T. 1865: *Sveriges inre historia under drottning Christinas förmyndare.* Stockholm: Norstedt.

Odhner, C. T. 1867: "Om de svenska städernas kommunala utveckling under 17:de århundradet", *Nordisk tidskrift för politik, ekonomi och litteratur november–december*.

Olsson, Sven 1988: *Västerås genom tiderna. 4. Burskap och makt: Västerås politiska historia 1613–1862.* Västerås: Västerås kommun.

Olsson, Anders 1995: *Borgmästare, bastioner och tullbommar. Göteborg och Halmstad under statligt inflytande 1630–1660.* Bibliotheca historica Lundensis 84. Lund: Lund universitet.

Perlestam, Magnus 2008: *Lydnad i karolinernas tid.* Lund: Nordic Academic Press.

Petré, Torsten 1958: *Uppsala stads historia 3. Uppsala under merkantilismens och statskontrollens tidsskede: 1619–1789.* Uppsala: Historiekomm.

Ranta, Raimo 1981: "Suurvalta-ajan kaupunkilaitos". *Suomen kaupunkilaitoksen historia 1. Keskiajalta 1870-luvulle.* Vantaa: Suomen kaupunkiliitto.

Riggs, Fred W. 1964: *Administration in Developing Countries. The Theory of Prismatic Society.* Boston: Houghton Milfflin Company.

Rothstein, Bo 2011: "Anti-corruption: The Indirect 'Big Bang' Approach", *Review of International Political Economy* 18: 2.

Rystad, Göran 1965: *Jönköping under stormaktstiden.* Jönköpings stads historia. Del II. Från stadens brand till kommunalreformen 1862. Värnamo 1965.

Räihä, Antti 2011: "Övergångsprocess, besittningstagande och lokala sedvänjor. Erövrade provinser under den nya överheten i Ryssland och Sverige under 1600- och 1700-talen", *Scandia* 77.

Räihä, Antti 2012: *Jatkuvuus ja muutosten hallinta. Lappeenranta ja Hamina Ruotsin ja Venäjän alaisuudessa 1720–1760-luvuilla.* Studies in Humanities 183. Jyväskylä: Jyväskylän yliopisto.

Sandberg, Robert 1991: *I slottets skugga. Stockholm och kronan 1599–1620.* Stockholmsmonografier utgivna av Stockholms stad 105. Stockholm: Stockholms stad.

Sandström, Åke 1996: *Plöjande borgare och handlande bönder. Mötet mellan den europeiska urbana ekonomin och vasatidens Sverige*. Studier i stads- och kommunhistoria 15. Stockholm: Stockholms universitet.

Schilling, Heinz 1993: *Die Stadt in der frühen Neuzeit*. Enzyklopädie deutscher Geschichte 24. Herausgegeben von Lothar Gall. München: R. Oldenbourg.

Scott, Tom 2012: *The city-state in Europe, 1000–1600. Hinterland, territory, region*. Oxford: Oxford University Press.

Soom, Arnold 1964–1966: "Jacob Fougdt". In: *Svenskt biografiskt lexikon*.

Stadin, Kekke 2004: *Stånd och genus i stormaktstidens Sverige*. Lund: Nordic Academic Press.

Strömberg, John 1996: *Studenter, nationer och universitet. Studenternas härkomst och levnadsbanor vid akademin i Åbo 1640–1808*. Skrifter utgivna av svenska litteratursällskapet i Finland 601. Helsingfors: The Society of Swedish Literature in Finland.

Sundell, Anders 2014: "Understanding Informal Payments in the Public Sector: Theory and Evidence from Nineteenth-century Sweden", *Scandinavian Political Studies* 37: 2.

Suolahti, Eino E. 1946: *Opinkäynti ja sen aiheuttama säätykierto Suomen porvariston keskuudessa 1600-luvulla*. Helsinki: WSOY.

Swedlund, Robert 1936: *Grev- och friherreskapen i Sverige och i Finland. Donationerna och reduktionerna före 1680*. Uppsala.

Sörndal, Olof 1937: *Den svenska länsstyrelsen. Uppkomst, organisation och allmänna maktställning*. Lund: Sundqvist & Emond.

Tilly, Charles 1990: *Coercion, Capital, and European States, AD 990–1990*. Studies in Social Discontinuity. Oxford: Blackwell.

Tilly, Charles and Wim P. Blockmans (eds) 1994: *Cities and the Rise of States in Europe A.D. 1000 to 1800*. Boulder: Westview Press.

Van Der Heijden, Manon 2006: "State Formation and Urban Finances in Sixteenth and Seventeenth-century Holland", *Journal of Urban History* 32: 3.

Vermeesch, Griet 2009: "Capability, Patrimonialism and Bureaucracy in the Urban Administrations of the Low Countries (c. 1300–1780)". In: Hartman, Jan, Nieuwstraten, Jaap, Reinders, Michel (eds), *Public Offices, Personal Demands: Capability in Governance in the Seventeenth- Century Dutch Republic*. Newcastle upon Tyne: Cambridge Scholars Publication.

Westling, Claes 2000: "Vadstena och centralmakten". In: 600 år i Vadstena. Vadstenas historia från äldsta tider till år 2000. Red. Göran Söderström. Vadstena: Vadstena kommun.

Westling, Claes 2002: *Småstadens dynamik. Skänninges och Vadstenas befolkning och kontaktfält ca 1630–1660*. Linköping Studies in Arts and Science 264. Linköping: Linköpings universitet [http://www.diva-portal.org/smash/get/diva2:20705/FULLTEXT01.pdf].

Williamson, Fiona 2015: "When "Comoners Were Made Slaves by the Magistrates". The 1627 Election and Political Culture in Norwich", *The Journal of Urban History 42*.

Virkkunen, A. H. 1953: *Oulun kaupungin historia I*. Oulu: Oulun kaupunki (2nd edition, originally 1919).

# Burgomasters IX

Piia Einonen
ⓘ http://orcid.org/0000-0003-4931-2657

# Burgomasters of Stockholm as Agents of the Crown and Self-Interest (1590–1640)

During the late sixteenth and the first decades of the seventeenth century, Sweden's urban administration was in turmoil. Appointments were – especially in Stockholm – under constant surveillance and the agency of office-holders was tied to the Crown in ways it had never been before. Not only were candidates assessed in novel ways, but some of them were also given powers that exceeded the traditional roles and scope of agency. Political circumstances had always been a crucial factor in determining urban administration, but this was especially so during this period, which was witnessing administrative, political and economic reforms that aimed not only to tighten the royal grip on authority but also to cement Sweden's status as a great power.[1]

The highest governmental and judicial administrative body in Stockholm was the magistrates' court (or magistrates' council) (*rådstugurätt*).[2] Traditionally, burgomasters (*borgmästare*) and magistrates (*rådmän*) represented bourgeois values and had similar interests to the burghers of the town. However, from the 1620s on, the royal mayors increasingly directed the magistrates' court to assume the governance of the town and emphasised the Burghers' subservience to them. The burgomasters and magistrates began to emphasise their own paternalistic rule in the belief that they knew what was best for the townsfolk.[3] This chapter sets out to study to what extent this is reflected in the changing agency of office-holders between 1590 and 1640, as this is the period in which the most significant changes in urban administration occurred. As the roles within it became gradually more formalised and bureaucratic, it also became more common for burgomasters and magistrates to be professionally trained for their duties[4].

However, these changes did not just happen by themselves; they were instigated by individuals, the context of whose agency exists in a certain political, economic and cultural space. In any prevailing social culture – now and in the past – there is a cultural model with a shared system of meanings that provides individuals with the means to act within society. As a part of their continuous interaction with their surroundings, individuals interpret and modify their conception of the real world so as to be able to better control their life and environment. Both individual and communal experiences of this interaction are organised within a shared culture that creates a foundation for meaningful action.[5] In terms of the agency of early modern office-holders, this means that individuals and communities had their own sense of commonly accepted administrative behaviour based on their own and their ancestors' experiences. Transforming social and organizational structures showed the functional limits of this agency and whether new modes of action could be practised within them or not.

This chapter deals with early modern office-holding in Stockholm. It concentrates on the official ethos that guided this administrative and judicial work as well as the practical duties and responsibilities of the office-holders. I use "ethos" not so much in its rhetorical sense but more generally to refer to the ethical and moral stance of the office-holders – two aspects that are closely connected. For example, what kind of ethical principles, values and norms guided burgomasters, and how did this affect their agency during this period? It is self-evident that a modern understanding of office as a kind of 'job' (with a salary and norms and regulations determining one's agency) cannot be applied to the early modern era. The office-holders in question here must be interpreted within their own temporal and spatial context.

Many answers to these questions can be found in the extensive court record books of Stockholm.[6] I also use the sporadically preserved correspondence between the Stockholm magistrates and the Crown. These sources, with ethos and morality as methodological key concepts, will be analysed in detail to see what more we can learn about the agency of office-holders. Another source will be Stockholm's register of office-holders,[7] which, as a database, will allow me not only to create a wider picture of the burgomasters as a group but to also make comparisons. It is quite obvious that the educated office-holders of the seventeenth century were creating a new practice of office-holding at the local level. This database contains the basic personal information about both burgomasters and scribes and details of their careers and responsibilities,[8] though the focus will be mainly on burgomasters as their agency is more visible than that of magistrates or scribes.

Burgomasters were essentially the leaders of the town, even though royal mayors came to constitute a further, higher, level in the urban hierarchy. Even if most of the agency of office-holders happened behind the scenes and cannot be traced via the sources, there were some striking conflicts that highlight the generally accepted norms of agency for these offices. One burgomaster who stretched his agency to the limits was an innkeeper called Hans Nilsson Benick (–1639), who was appointed a royal mayor in 1624[9]. He was either an exception among Stockholm office-holders – in unscrupulously exploiting his position and connections with the Crown – or else he was just unlucky to have his deeds revealed. Either way, he presents us with a unique perspective on early modern agency and so is often used as an example in this chapter.

Stockholm's history has been studied in detail ever since the 19th century, not only because of its central role in Swedish history as the capital city but also because of its rich and well-preserved source material. In particular, studies by Lars Ericson, Robert Sandberg, Åke Sandström, Arne

Jansson in the "Stockholm blir huvudstad" (Stockholm becomes a capital) project, and later by Marko Lamberg, give us a varied and thorough picture of the town and its administration during the Middle Ages and the early modern period.[10] However, there are few researchers who refer to office-holding in this context with an emphasis on ethics and morality.[11] This is surprising when one considers that during the formalization of these institutions and organizations, there was plenty of room for individual agency. The normative framework was too general to specifically guide the conduct of office-holders, so actors had a crucial role in interpreting and redefining political and administrative values and the arguments and modes of action that were based on these values. An administration is rarely just a faceless organization – it gets its specific form from the actual behaviour of individuals and groups.[12]

Another point is that the practical problems of the state-building process have remained largely unstudied, with most researchers focusing on the visible structures and legislation of emerging nation states.[13] In this chapter, I understand state-building not so much as a straightforward and systematic process but rather as the Crown's general effort to establish organizations and mechanisms that were more goal-oriented than those of previous times. It was in the Crown's interest to institutionalise the state as a political and social construction, and there were certain political conventions that guided the work. Different towns and other local communities had their own political cultures, and in this sense state-building meant also unifying different opinions on jurisdiction, administration and the role and status of office-holders.

The urban administrators and the burghers were acting under pressure from the growing authority of an emerging centralised nation state. This process began during the reign of Gustavus Vasa in the sixteenth century and reached completion in the first half of the seventeenth. Its central architects were King Gustavus Adolphus (1594–1632) and his chancellor Axel Oxenstierna (1583–1654).[14] To function properly, the new state needed a centralised administration, and Stockholm became increasingly important as many of the new organisations the state required were based in the capital. Because of the city's physical proximity to the organs of central power, it enabled close communication between the city and state authorities on both formal and informal levels, which meant that Stockholm differed from other towns in the realm as its administration and jurisdiction could be more directly influenced by the central government and personal interaction with its officers.[15]

Stockholm proved to be the test bed for administrative reforms, and those that worked there were then adopted in other cities in Sweden. The gradual bureaucratization of governmental and judicial processes had already begun at the start of the seventeenth century. Lars Ericson has – according to Max Weber – named five characteristics of bureaucratization: a hierarchy of offices, a written culture of administration, full-time employment, clearly outlined fields of operation, and regulations guiding agency. Bureaucratization is regarded as including professionalization, in which education and training are emphasized.[16]

The beginning of the seventeenth century was exceptional in many ways, and the 1620s and 1630s were especially turbulent. The growing burden of taxation arising from the mounting expenses of Gustavus Adolphus's various wars were duly felt by the realm's subjects, and growing discontent was channelled into various kinds of resistance. The year 1623 was particularly unsettled due to riots and their aftermath, but also because it alerted the burghers to fact that control and authority in Stockholm were about to shift to the Crown and its local representatives for good.[17]

## Bureaucratization and agency in urban context

In the bourgeois tradition of administration, the urban office-holders – the burgomasters and magistrates – were the representatives of the burghers regardless of how they had been elected. For this reason, the interaction between the town administration and the burghers was tantamount to a discourse between equals. Whereas experience in trade and local government had previously been valued in choosing new magistrates, a gradual process of bureaucratization starting in the 1620s brought changes to this relationship as office-holders increasingly became elected on the basis of their academic merits. The Crown had always taken an interest in Stockholm's burgomaster elections, and now the strengthening central power created an opportunity for a more systematic control of the realm's most important town with the creation of the new office of royal mayors.[18]

At the same time as royal mayors were appearing in the courthouse, two other trends were discernible: the endeavour of both the Crown and the magistrates' courts to emphasise the administrative hierarchy and their joint efforts to discipline the burghers into obedient subjects. These ideas were not novel, but they were formalised and made more explicit in the 1620s and 1630s. As a result, the political importance of the burghers notably decreased. The whole of Stockholm became, in effect, like the central government's sixth collegial body, run along strict lines by the royal mayors and then, from 1634, by Governor General (*överståthållare*) of Stockholm Claes Fleming (1592–1644). At the local level, the central government's efforts to increase the efficiency of government led to a redefinition of traditional power relations as the new office-holders – the royal mayors and the Governor General – fractured the traditional hierarchies of power in Stockholm. For the burghers, this meant that political activity now had to be channelled into the paths defined by the authorities, and this led to a diminution of possibilities for interaction between the authorities and their subjects and even less influence for the burghers.[19]

In fact, the burgomasters and magistrates, too, witnessed a shrinking in their room for agency, as the Crown's grip on urban administration and the magistrates' court grew tighter during this period. In spite of these changes, however, the burgomasters and magistrates still took care of their everyday practical duties in traditional ways. The administrative system, in which the duties and responsibilities of office holders were not regulated and were largely undefined, meant that they had to assume numerous different roles: they were judges and administrators, negotiators and tax authorities, spokesmen and arbitrators. All of these roles included different kinds of tasks involving different abilities and skills for interaction. The urban administrators mainly worked in collaboration and quite often also under pressure from both the representatives of the Crown and the burghers, which set limits to their agency.

As the variety of roles suggests, the agency of burgomasters and magistrates was shaped by several factors. Generally in early modern society, an individual's origin and estate was important in defining his scope for action, and this also applied to office-holders. Individual agency did not consist in some kind of unchangeable condition but was the result of a continuous process created in interaction with other agents. An individual's past influenced the construction of his agency as his background and origin were valued differently in different roles. A person's social, political and economic networks and his urban status as a burgher thus had an effect on agency, but these are rarely visible in the source material. Probably the way in which he was elected and status of his office in the urban hierarchy were also significant in defining the possibilities for an individual's agency.

## Urban office-holding and agency in the whirlpool of politics

In spite of the centralizing reforms, the practices of administration and jurisdiction remained largely the same during this period. However, the authority of the magistrates' court was determined by those elected to office. Burgomasters and magistrates had traditionally been chosen to take care of administrative and judicial duties on behalf of the bourgeoisie, their office more a position of trust than a full-time occupation, as the compensation they received for the time spent administrating and judging was not sufficient to provide them with a living. In practice, this meant that only the wealthier burghers could afford the time for such a position. For craftsmen, for example, it would have been inconceivable for them to spend days in the courthouse.[20] Perhaps for this reason, only two burgomasters, Matthias Trost (1582–1648) and Jakob Grundell (1590–1663), were originally craftsmen, but evidently they were both exceptionally wealthy. Only one craftsman was appointed a magistrate, but he resigned the office after two years because he could not afford to execute it. Although from the 1620s on more burgomasters came to be appointed for their academic merits and experience in the service of the Crown, the majority of magistrates were still merchants. They were not necessarily the richest ones but those who represented the group directly below them in the social hierarchy.[21]

Although state-building is often portrayed as a carefully thought-out process, in reality the practical decisions like recruiting office-holders for central government were often ad hoc and made according to the current situation. Recruiting competent officers for the central government was a challenging task since at the same time Stockholm's local government also needed men of the same ilk. As a result, many office-holders (especially burgomasters) had worked for the Crown before serving Stockholm or were promoted to such offices after their urban administrative careers.[22]

Thus urban office-holding was largely manned by an urban elite; this could create an ethical and moral problem since King Magnus Eriksson's (1316–1374) medieval Town Law stipulated that every group of residents be represented in Stockholm's administration.[23] There was also a clause against nepotism in the code, but there were no exact regulations defining which familial relationships were too close in this respect.[24] As there is no evidence of specific problems connected with family relationships among the office-holders or complaints about the somewhat elitist nature of the administration, it would seem that the people of the time were content with the situation.

The practical agency of office-holders was also restricted and guided by an oath of office that they were required to swear before assuming their posts. The Swedish oath formula was defined in the Town Law of King Magnus Eriksson. In their oath, burgomasters and magistrates pledged to treat everybody fairly and impartially and to be loyal to the Crown. So, if the fairness or honour of a burgomaster or magistrate was questioned, it basically meant that he was being accused of breaking his oath.[25] In early modern society, oaths were crucial in defining power relations, loyalties and responsibilities, and thus they were also a significant factor in determining agency.

Urban office-holders had to work within a complex network of political, social and economic circumstances that often determined how they could act. This was especially the case during the 1590s, when both aspirants to the throne (Sigismund III of Poland (1566–1632) and Duke Charles (1550–1611)) were trying to use Stockholm's administrators as pawns in their struggle for succession. One of the key administrative positions was the office of town scribe, and the fluctuating status of its incumbents seems to reflect the on-going turbulent power struggles, but for the period in focus the source material reveals surprisingly little about the agency of these office-holders. When a scribe called Lars Henriksson died in 1592, for instance, he was succeeded by a magistrate, Berent Jönsson (d. 1597), for only a few months before the latter was replaced by Hans Hansson Bilefelt. Bilefelt was then arrested for being a supporter of Sigismund in 1598. He spent 31 weeks in jail, and afterwards he left Sweden, taking with him the city's court records and account books, which are still missing to this day. He had tried to resign in 1596 but was asked to stay on.[26] He gave no reason for his desire to resign, but we can suppose that it was to do with the ongoing political turmoil. On the other hand, it is obvious that as a former law-reader with experience of working in the Council of the Realm, he could not be replaced easily. However, Duke Charles did not see replacing him as a problem.

Hans Hansson Bilefelt lived in Poland after leaving Sweden, as did the scribe Sven Jönsson, who ran off in 1617 after only two years in office, leaving the city archives in disarray behind him.[27] His predecessor, Karl Månsson Bure, had been ordered to resign in the spring of 1615 as he had been negligent in his duties.²⁸ This shows that there were certain duties that scribes were required to perform, but it is not known exactly what derelictions incurred dismissal. Minor lapses were almost certainly overlooked, but not if they continued for a longer period. Scribes of this period had no formal education, but they evidently had good opportunities for advancement. Out of six ordinary scribes of this period, one later became a magistrate and two were appointed burgomasters, while the other three gained important positions of trust as representatives of both the burghers and the Crown.²⁹ Even though the above mentioned malpractices suggest that scribes sometimes might not meet the requirements of their office, as happened in other towns of the realm as well,³⁰ many of Stockholm's scribes, in particular, eventually made successful careers for themselves, which testifies to their competence as administrators. In an unofficial ordinance of 1619, the administrative duties of the scribe were further emphasised especially in Stockholm, and it is clear from these new guidelines that some education was required of them.³¹ But what eventually happened to the majority of these scribes suggests that it was not so much their competence, education or agency but their political loyalty that was crucial in determining their careers.

The office of scribe was highly esteemed and its demanding nature recognised. In a petition to the Crown in 1616, the burghers of Stockholm complained about the town's scribe's low "maintenance". They stated that he was paid only what his predecessors had received – "*så wääl som hans antesessores*", which was not much, and they petitioned that he might also receive a maintenance allowance like other scribes before him. They argued that the office was arduous, and without decent remuneration no scribe would stay in Stockholm, and they referred to the Crown's previous practice of the paying the scribe an extra tithe allowance.³² This suggests that the agency of scribes was prominent in the wider urban context and the office seen as a labour-intensive one. Whereas burgomasters and magistrates had offices that were traditionally considered to be positions of trust, scribes had a job that was very much full-time. It seems that administrative offices were not regarded as altogether a separate sphere of urban life: rather, the agency of burgomasters, magistrates and scribes was visibly present in the everyday life of the city. Probably one reason for this was that many office-holders were native burghers: local merchants or perhaps craftsmen. However, this period witnessed a significant change in that office-holders were increasingly recruited from outside the urban community, and administrative organs were developed into a machinery extending from the Council of the Realm to local courts.

A former scribe, Olof Pedersson Humbla (1572–1621), was the first academically qualified burgomaster in the period we are looking at. Later on, the first royal mayor, Olaus Bureus (1578–1655), was a doctor of medicine, but otherwise few burgomasters had academic qualifications. However, education became more important as the bureaucratization of urban administration increased, and for example Erik Eriksson Tranevardius (1587–1657, appointed as burgomaster in 1630 and subsequently ennobled as Geete) and Peter Gavelius (1601–1645, appointed in 1637) had academic backgrounds.³³ It seems that it was an academic education in itself that was valued rather than the discipline it involved: it seems hard to imagine how a medical training would benefit an urban administrator in his duties – even though Bureus did also have some expertise in town planning. This indicates the undefined nature of administrative offices: there were no specific guidelines for functioning in an office, and hence there was no training that would meet the requirements of urban administration. Certainly, judicial expertise was useful, but there were numerous other duties that needed to be performed.³⁴ Olaus Bureus was later appointed to the Court of Appeal in Turku, so his administrative experience and activities must had been decisive factors in furthering his career. The fact that he was by training a doctor but made his career in urban administration indicates a lack of bureaucratization in the town's administration rather than an increase in professionalization.

During this period, and especially after 1608, the career path of burgomasters was clearly changing. Over the decades new burgomasters had acquired administrative experience mainly by following a traditional urban career path in which they started as treasurers and worked later as magistrates before being appointed burgomasters. This pattern was broken in the early seventeenth century, when a growing number of the new burgomasters had no previous experience of urban administration.³⁵ The most extreme examples of this were royal mayors who came from outside the urban society and had no practical experience of administration even though they had often served with merit as judges. A certain degree of 'outsiderness' was common among royal mayors in general and was one of the reasons for their unpopularity.³⁶ It is clear that their appointment was seen to break with the tradition of self-governing urban societies, even though burgomaster appointments in Stockholm had been controlled by the Crown ever since the reign of Gustavus Vasa. Royal mayors were thus an example of professionalization and bureaucratization, although for the burghers these developments only led to the alienation of the administrators.

Burgomasters were on average in their 40s when they were appointed, and they would be in office for an average of ten years. So from their age alone we can speculate that they were experienced administrators, as a 60-year-old man was already considered old – with only a few witnessing their seventieth birthday, and even fewer their eightieth, as Olof Nilsson (1570–1650) did. Some of them held other subsequent offices, some died during their period in office, and some also just retired because of old age and/or infirmity.³⁷ Unlike the scribes, there are no references suggesting that burgomasters were negligent in their duties, or at least none were found to be so. On the other hand, there are some remarks which show that not everyone was satisfied with the prevailing practices. However, these remarks concern only formal administrative details. Otherwise there is no evidence of criticism of the actual administrators themselves or their agency – either among the burghers or other members of the administration. The only exception, which I will examine more closely in the next section, seems to have been burgomaster Hans Nilsson Benick.

## Challenging tradition – the new royal mayors

The Crown intended to extend the state-building process into the urban sphere by replacing burgomasters, who represented mainly the Burgher estate, with candidates who had an academic background or men who had proven their skills serving the Crown elsewhere.[38] Their task was to oversee the development of their respective towns. However, while they succeeded in this, implementing a number of new administrative reforms and increasing efficiency, their high-handed approach gave rise to difficulties in their relations both with other officials and with the burghers. And although their actions, judging from historical research on the matter, suggest little reason why they should have acquired quite such a bad reputation as they did, it seems that in Stockholm, at least, they created conflict with the burghers and in the magistrates' court.[39]

The first royal mayor in the realm was Olaus Bureus, who was appointed in 1621 as a kind of chief burgomaster (*överborgmästare*) to reorganise the administration of Stockholm, with which the Crown was not satisfied.[40] According to the court records, he tried to regularise the duties of office-holders, by checking on the presence and absence of burgomasters and magistrates. This was a clear step in the direction of making the system more bureaucratic and professionalised, but its efficacy is questionable as office-holders did not adhere to these tighter regulations. It cannot have helped either that Bureus could not take criticism very well. He would sometimes go straight from the city court to the Council of the Realm in the nearby royal castle to lodge a complaint against burgomasters and magistrates who were not complying with his wishes.[41] He seems to have been well aware of his task as a reformer and also of the fact that the royal mandate was the basis for his status and thus his agency. It is also interesting that Bureus' role in bringing in reforms to urban administration is emphasised in the court records, although not described in detail. He was an active agent in the courthouse, but there is little surviving evidence of his achievements.

In 1624, a couple of years after Bureus, Hans Nilsson Benick received his royal mandate. Benick can be regarded as a typical royal mayor, who acquired his position probably as a reward for his work in the royal customs house and as a tax-renter of small duties. He did not hesitate to blatantly exploit his position and contacts with the Crown, and his agency was particularly characterised by high-handedness.[42] He also become known as the man who had introduced the hated tax on consumables.[43]

Before his career as a burgomaster, Hans Nilsson Benick had been, at least in the opinion of the burghers, a key figure in the imposition of a new tax on different kinds of consumables. This tax was especially hated because it meant extra costs for the burghers and restricted their freedom for manoeuvre as Stockholm, like other towns in the realm from the 1620s on, was surrounded by a tax fence. Because Benick was the one who announced the introduction of the tax, he personified it for the burghers. According to witnesses, he also acted in an offensive and challenging manner when making the proclamation by standing in front of and above the burgomasters. Agency was tightly connected to hierarchies of power and their spatial performance, and therefore such behaviour was considered insulting[44]. The result of the ensuing protests against the new tax and its 'representative' was a riot in which furious burghers attacked and kidnapped Benick. The situation calmed down gradually, and eventually Hans Nilsson Benick was released uninjured, but the hatred towards him continued to grow. His arrogant behaviour was also explicitly mentioned in letters to the King from Governor Gabriel Gustafsson Oxenstierna, and it was thought to be one of the main reasons for the riot.[45]

The archives reveal that the Crown was aware of just how much the Burghers hated Benick, which indicates the ambivalent nature of some office-holders' agency. Benick was probably given the job as a scapegoat so that the King could escape blame. In letters, the King was several times assured that he need not fear a conspiracy as the reasons for the unrest were purely due to Hans Nilsson Benick's behaviour.[46] Perhaps his appointment as a burgomaster was thus a reward for taking the flak for this unpopular tax, or maybe his expertise in tax collection was actually needed in the administration of the town. Whatever the reason was, it is still somewhat puzzling why he was appointed; not only did he have no experience of everyday administration, but his brother, Valentin Nilsson (–1638), was already a magistrate, and thus it was suspicious both should be members of the magistrate's court since his appointment could easily have been construed as nepotism, the prescription of which was one of the few legal regulations concerning office-holding. Probably it was not a problem as he was a burgomaster and his brother a magistrate, but as if to compound matters, the Council of the Realm then suggested, in 1633, that Valentin Nilsson should be appointed a burgomaster. Olaus Bureus reminded the Council that Hans Nilsson Benick was already a burgomaster, but this was not seen as a problem.[47] This concentration of power in the hands of a single family was presumably yet another reason for Benick's unpopularity among the burghers.

Thus, while Hans Nilsson Benick's background was unusual for a royal mayor, it would have been unusual even for a burgomaster representing the burghers since he was not qualified for the latter position: he had not followed the traditional path of being a magistrate before gaining burgomaster status. On the other hand, another important prerequisite for becoming a burgomaster was to have held a position of trust – and this Benick had done. Not only had he been elected one of the 48 Elders, like some other burgomasters, but he had also been Keeper of the Town Keys.[48] Although there is no evidence of the exact motives for the Crown appointing him burgomaster, holding these positions must have certainly worked in his favour.

Hans Nilsson Benick fits the general picture of royal mayors because his merits were in line with the Crown's project of state-building. From the perspective of traditional town administrators and burghers, however, his achievements were viewed as a discredit to him, since he was associated with unpopular and burdensome taxes, small duties and excises. Nonetheless, his appointment strengthened the Crown's control in Stockholm.

## Agency in collision with ethical and moral norms?

Hans Nilsson Benick's period in office was filled with suspicion and disputes. From the Burghers' point of view, he lacked the proper competence for the post, and his twofold role – as an appointed burgomaster and an agent of the Crown – was not a good starting point for a new office-holder as he obviously continued to be a renter of small duties. In his position he was supposed to administer the town and be a father of the local community, but at the same time he continued his activities as a tax farmer collecting taxes and customs duties. Benick's unpopularity among the burghers was possibly due to his role as a tax-farmer. This new system of collecting payments for the Crown by renting out the whole collection system to individual agents was introduced in the 1620s, and it was criticised by the burghers – as well as by other subjects throughout the realm. All kinds of payments both in money and in kind (in the form of lodgings and provisions for example) were seen as a burden, and both tax collectors and tax-farmers were unpopular, and often the discontent with these dues was targeted on them. In Stockholm, Benick, together with Christian Welshuisen, played a key role in implementing this system, and this inevitably affected his agency as a burgomaster.[49]

The early 1620s were anyway an economically burdensome time as payments for the ongoing wars and military remittances increased. Moreover, there were rumours of a Polish invasion, disorderly soldiers lodging in Stockholm, and the plague was rampant in the town. This overall restlessness combined with economic distress led the burghers to protest, and Benick was an easy and visible target.[50] Unlike Benick, Bureus was clearly more involved with the Crown and that side of the administration than with the burghers.[51] In this respect, being a complete outsider with no known past perhaps stood him in better stead and offered him wider options for agency. Benick, on the other hand, despite his achievements could not avoid being known for his previous 'mistakes', and they followed him everywhere in his career and had an effect on his agency.

This was amply shown when the situation about the imposition of small duties flared up again in November 1625 after an altercation between a burgher and a tax-collector on the quayside. The situation appeared to be getting increasingly menacing as the crowd got louder and more restless. The incident resulted in complaints in the courthouse about tax-collectors attacking burghers and vice versa.[52] The magistrate, Anders Henriksson (–1651), warned the burghers against such behaviour, but at the same time he also demanded that Benick put an end to the tax-collectors' violent conduct and chastise them. According to the magistrate, tax collectors should not cause revolt or unrest (*tumult och perlemente*), and Hans Nilsson Benick should punish his employees rather than condone their illegal measures. After hearing these reprimands, Benick answered, "God help the King home; but a thousand devils will plague you, Anders Henriksson!"[53] The burghers reacted noisily to this, at which then they were threatened with being thrown out of the courthouse into the market place, but then the situation seemed to calm down, and no further disciplinary actions were taken.[54]

During this incident, Hans Nilsson Benick was not officially appearing in the courthouse in his role as royal mayor as the Council of the Realm had (just three days previously) exempted him from all duties in the magistrates' court until the King's return. This was warranted by his connection with the unpopular small duties and taxes,[55] but it was probably also prompted by the Burghers' growing discontent with the situation – for which Hans Nilsson Benick was still the perfect scapegoat.[56] Perhaps it was the threat of a riot breaking out that compelled the Crown to adopt this solution. Benick's reply to Henriksson in the court may have been a reference to the Kings' absence, but it was also a boastful allusion to his close contacts with the Crown.

Benick was also criticised by his colleagues. In 1634 the magistrate Anders Henriksson again spoke against him, telling the courthouse how he had been reprimanded by the Council of the Realm for the poor management of buildings and fire-fighting equipment in Stockholm since this was supposed to be Benick's responsibility as Inspector of Buildings. According to Henriksson, Benick was a man who was paid to be a burgomaster but was not doing his job.[57] As office-holding was not yet properly formalised, it was difficult for magistrates and burgomasters to vindicate themselves, and so to prevent further troubles urban office-holders would often ask the magistrates' court to document everything – as Anders Henriksson did in 1625.[58]

One way to regain lost trust was to resign. In 1628, Hans Nilsson Benick complained that not only the burghers but also his colleagues were indolent.[59] He found that anything he did with the assent of a few burgomasters or magistrates was rejected by the others if they were not involved in the decision *(the inthet få wara med i rådh)*. This indicates the existence not only of internal quarrels in the magistrates' court but also of a pre-existing understanding of what a "representative" decision meant, i.e. as binding only on those who had been involved in making that decision. Benick reacted to this obvious lack of confidence in him by offering his resignation.[60] This was a traditional course of action in urban political culture at the time; it was understood as merely a rhetorical ploy to regain trust, not as an actual desire to resign. At this point, the office-holder's colleagues were supposed to persuade him to remain and assure him of their loyalty and obedience. As the authority of the office-holders was created mainly through the office itself together with the honour and social prestige that surrounded it, rebuilding it required these ritual resignations and responsive assurances.[61]

However, according to the court record book, Benick did not receive the usual rhetorical phrases of support he was hoping for. He had obviously offered his resignation merely as a means to confirm his status although in reality he felt no responsibility for the legality of his actions, and his time in office continued to be characterised by various accusations of malpractice and arrogant behaviour. At the local level he was an exception among the office-holders of Stockholm. On the other hand, it is also possible that he may have been the only burgomaster whose illegal actions came to light. Nevertheless, the sources would seem to indicate that it is more likely that other burgomasters and magistrates played more regularly by the rules – or their malpractice was not so patent. Evidently, it was clear that office-holding was taking on a new shape that was in line with the aims of state-building, and the foremost representative of this was Olaus Bureus, whose attitude towards office-holding was characterised by excessive legality, formality, and high moral standards. Unlike Benick, who might not even bother to follow the royal orders, he emphasised the importance of formal procedures. For instance, Benick gave permission for a Catholic woman to be buried in the city in 1629 even though this was prohibited and caused a disturbance.[62] Whether Benick really did not know about the regulation, or whether he was wilfully ignoring it, the incident nevertheless shows his confidence in his own power as an agent. It also bears witness to a certain flexibility, which from the administrative viewpoint was more likely to be seen as arbitrary behaviour and an agency that exceeded normative limits.

Some other examples suggest that even though urban administration was managed collectively, single burgomasters could act independently on some questions. Olaus Bureus, for example, could speak for the whole magistrates' court when in 1624 he promised that Stockholm would pay its share of contributions in kind to the Crown. Only afterwards did he ask for approval from the magistrates and the Council of the Elders. He said that he had personally acted correctly and done what he could to deal with the issue, and that he feared that others might well do nothing.[63] This case demonstrates that at least some burgomasters had broader possibilities for agency than others – or, as in the case of Benick – they considered themselves free to act as they wished. Bureus' comment regarding his personal activities was significant in the sense that he was calling into question the whole collective system of administration. This kind of behaviour would not have been possible for other members of the magistrates' court.

The next thorny issue for office-holders to confront the burghers with, after the trouble with small duties and new taxes, concerned the ship company established in the late 1620s to build the royal fleet. Stockholm and Norra Förstaden were obliged to raise the money for four ships, and this brought protests from the burghers. The directors of the company complained to the magistrates' court about defaults on payments. The one office-holder who again was on the tip of everyone's tongues was Hans Nilsson Benick. It seemed he had overstepped the limits of his agency again by playing a major role in the imposition of this burden and had thereby caused bad blood in Norra Förstaden. The main argument was that he had no authorization to act as he had done in the negotiations with the King. Norra Förstaden's representative stated that Benick was not their superior, and they would not consider him "good" (competent) as such and even less competent to assess their property for payments. According to Burgomaster Mattias Trost, Stockholm's representatives and Hans Nilsson Benick had betrayed the burghers of Norra Förstaden shamefully for "a favour".[64] This is not explained in detail but probably the favour referred to Benick seeking the good graces of the King at any cost. Certainly, Hans Nilsson Benick may have acted in a way that he thought was in the best interests of Stockholm, but again his agency was interpreted as high-handed and obstinate.

The imposition of taxes to finance the ship company was also criticised. Benick had already been charged for malpractice during his period as chief of the customs station on the island of Vaxholm in the Stockholm archipelago.[65] Even though this could not be proved, his later practices during his time in office suggest that he had probably been acting in a similar manner earlier as well. A burgher called Wellam Lehusen (1599–1667/1674, Wilhelm Leuhusen), later a magistrate and burgomaster, accused Benick of abusing his position by imposing taxes and taxing himself as little as he wished. However, taxation was usually carried out under the surveillance of the city court and the Elders, who were supposed to be responsible for these matters, and thus it is hard to believe that he had been able to behave in this way. Nevertheless, there were probably some shady elements in Benick's tax levying, and the burghers were trying to nail him for this.[66] Benick was under constant surveillance, which confirms the view that legality and equality were key values in the agency of office-holders, as they were in political culture generally.[67]

The urban reality was not as egalitarian as the political arguments would have us believe. Even if burghers nominally shared the same status, in practice their economic and social standing varied significantly. Craftsmen were usually the lowest group in the social and economic hierarchy with merchants above them and the wealthiest merchants on top. The latter dominated foreign trade and were often treated with special consideration because of their economic importance and networks. For instance, in 1635 Hans Nilsson Benick warned his brother Valentin Nilsson that a case concerning a merchant who had taken two ships from him could end up harming the town as such accusations offended the wealthiest merchants.[68] Benick was concerned for the city's best interests, or at least used this politically acceptable formulation to mask his own interests. Whatever the real motivation, it is clear that office-holders had to constantly interact with the burghers, and this constrained their agency.

Benick's agency was probably also influenced by the deeds of his employees. His scribe was indicted for stealing a tankard in 1623, and a little later his maid was accused of stealing from another (deceased) maid of his and from Benick himself. As she gave everything back, there is no mention of any punishment, and she was released. However, she was probably dismissed from her job as she was referred to as a former maid in connection with another theft only a few weeks later.[69] The early modern household was a unity consisting of both family and servants, and thus the misdeeds of every member harmed its reputation and impaired its social and economic reliability. As the master was responsible for his household, accusations of crime questioned his ability to control the members of his household.[70] It could be asked whether such man could take care of wider responsibilities and govern the town? Again these cases could be also interpreted as proof of the intense scrutiny that Benick and his household were under.

Despite his unpopularity among his colleagues and the burghers, Hans Nilsson Benick was Stockholm's representative in the Riksdag. Traditionally, the burgomaster representing Stockholm was a central figure as he was also the leader of the whole Burgher estate. In 1632, when Benick was appointed, we know that the Burghers were asked who they wanted to represent them. Obviously they could only exert any influence on the nomination of the representative of their own estate, namely Casper Norten. The other two representatives, chosen by the magistrates' court, were the magistrate Mickel Abrahamsson (–1655) and burgomaster Hans Nilsson Benick. As leading figures of the urban community, burgomasters were often evident choices for the Riksdag as they were well informed and represented the urban community as a whole. Benick's eventual appointment by the members of the court strongly suggests that he was favoured by the King, but he may also have been seen as an influential candidate who could represent Stockholm in other ways too.[71] Benick's good relationship with the Crown is revealed in a couple of letters, which also uncover administrative practices behind the scenes. In 1626 Benick was in Uppsala trying to get an audience with the King, and he reported his diligent pursuit to the Magistrates' Court of Stockholm. As he could not get a royal audience, he had discussed matters concerning Stockholm with the Chancellor, and they had agreed that he would write down the relevant issues and the Chancellor would then discuss these with the King at the latest on their journey back to Stockholm. The town would then receive a response from the King. While Benick was in Uppsala, he was also charged with finding a new treasurer from among the students of the university. He reported that he had discussed this with one possible candidate, but he also reminded the other members of the magistrates courts that Jacob Grundell had wanted to be a treasurer and that he should be consulted first.[72] This shows that, in spite of his faults, Benick had influence, ability and trust in his colleagues, and was prepared to balance traditional forms of appointment with efforts to get better educated office-holders. It also shows that the true extent of agency was often revealed in informal interaction and that burgomasters were active agents behind the scenes.

Perhaps it was only after his retirement in 1636 due to his advanced age and senility (he died three years later) that a clearer picture of Benick's years as an office-holder emerges.[73] This might have been because, as a burgomaster, he had wielded a certain power that made him practically untouchable; but this ended upon retirement and the termination of his royal mandate. Only two days after his announcement of retirement, Wellam Lehusen was demanding that Benick should take an oath – which was the traditional way of purging oneself against accusations – and that he should hand over the customs records. Other activities connected with Benick's discharge of his duties were taken under scrutiny, and he was accused of having abused his position for years and, for instance, of trading plots of land owned by the town as if they were his own. This was an especially severe accusation as Benick had been Inspector of Buildings from 1631 to 1633. He was accused of buying up land on the cheap and selling it on at a substantial profit. Additionally, the court record books in 1628 already refer to some ambiguities connected with customs records, and these were brought up again after his retirement. While Benick's malpractice was being investigated he delayed matters by staying in his country home, arguing that he was too frail to make the journey to court, and so the magistrates failed to charge him.[74] Owing to his incapacity, and because other members of the magistracy were involved in the case, it was decided in 1636 that the accusations against Benick should be investigated in another court of justice.[75]

When Hans Nilsson Benick did finally present himself in court, he was asked to give evidence that he had lawfully acquired the town's plots that he had sold on, but he could not convince others with the document he produced. Though the seal was authentic, the scribe had not actually checked inside because Benick had told him it had been approved by the magistrates' court. Benick had also taken the original documents from the town archives – even though he had then returned them immediately – which was suspicious. As a compromise solution, the court ordered Benick to give back the extra plots he still possessed as he was too old to build on them. Then the dispute was referred to the Svea Court of Appeal. The buyers of the plots were given the legal deeds only if they had paid a price deemed reasonable by the court. The other purchasers were instructed to ask for restitution from Benick (or his inheritors as he died in 1639) of the payments they had earlier made. Benick's widow was also given some reimbursement as some plot transactions were reversed.[76] Since the buyers were forced to pay for the plots again, the city had evidently taken them back and contested Benick's ownership.

It seems that accusations of malpractice did not harm the reputation of Benick's household as his son, Gustaf Hansson (–1674), actually succeeded in his career and was later ennobled.[77] Hans Nilsson Benick's position as the Crown's confidant was strong enough to carry him through the conflicts. It seems that the Crown maintained its trust in him, and in fact he might well have been acting precisely as the King would have wished him to. Moreover, his discharge would have been a major setback for the system of royal mayors in general, which needed both reliability and legitimacy. To ensure these, a persevering appointments policy was required.

## *Reforming administration – forming agency*

Early modern office-holding was not a particularly formalised sphere of life – it was more the case that personal, informal and formal power and agency were all closely intertwined. Even if the medieval Town Law and unwritten norms guided their scope for action, and to some degree their duties (however slightly), the agency of office-holders was defined and redefined through an interaction between the magistrates' court, the Crown and the city's burghers. The pressure from below was palpable, even though the burghers' opportunities for criticizing malpractice were in reality quite limited. Evidently the town court itself watched over – or at least tried to do so – the actions and morality of its members, albeit not especially eagerly. This lack of normative guidelines emphasises the role of morality and ethics that constrained the agency of office-holders.

Traditional power relations were redefined when new office-holders, such as royal mayors and the Governor General, fractured the traditional hierarchies of power in Stockholm. Even though, from the 1520s on, the Crown had been involved in the appointment of burgomasters in Stockholm, royal mayors like Benick were a new phenomenon in the 1620s and, as the title implies, they were clearly servants of the king. It was intended that the introduction of royal mayors would gradually replace most of the burgomasters of burgher backgrounds with men who possessed academic qualifications. Their task in this period was to regenerate the administration of the towns, but their high-handed behaviour and new practices often overshadowed their achievements in local government.

Benick was serving in a high local office during a period when the bureaucratization of Stockholm was only just beginning, and office-holders still had almost unlimited scope for acting independently. It is obvious that he was not considered a competent burgomaster by the Burghers, having started originally as an unschooled innkeeper with no governmental experience. Usually burgomasters started their career as judges in a treasurer's court followed by a period as a magistrate. Only educated men or those with some other qualifications could be exempted from these requirements. In this respect, Benick was an upstart who did not fit into the traditional pattern. This was certainly one of the reasons why the burghers did not see him as a suitable candidate for royal mayor. The scant evidence of interaction between the urban administration and the Crown suggests that Benick was closely connected with the King, and possibly his previous experience and career as an unpopular customs official qualified him as the reformer that the latter needed.

It seems that Benick's activities in office were often were often self-seeking and exceeded all moral considerations and responsibilities. He used his agency to stretch rules and interpret orders for his own benefit, and he neglected his official duties. The bureaucratization and professionalization of administration was taking its first steps in Stockholm during this period, and so there was still plenty of room for individual agency before these processes were eventually duly formalised. It might be possible to interpret the repeated accusations of malpractice as a result of the central administration tightening its grip, but this cannot be verified as there are no other cases that Benick's career can really be compared with. It is clear, however, that office-holders' agency was gradually constrained as urban bureaucratization increased. This narrowing happened (internally) as a result of the office-holders' growing sense of the ethos required for the position, and (externally) through the strengthening grip of the central government. Benick's career was seen to be in such stark contrast to the accepted notions of justice and 'bourgeois equality' of his time that it would have been unacceptable in anyone but particularly in an administrator, who it was thought should set a moral example for others. Perhaps his career is an example of the Crown's endeavour to impose increased centralization in that he was able to challenge the accepted notions of agency for his position and yet remain in office practically up to the day he died.

The research on which this publication is based was funded by the Academy of Finland (grant no. 137741).

## Notes

1. See for example Petri Karonen, *Pohjoinen suurvalta. Ruotsi ja Suomi 1521–1809* (Helsinki: The Finnish Literature Society, 2014), pp. 262–267; Piia Einonen, *Poliittiset areenat ja toimintatavat. Tukholman porvaristo vallan käyttäjänä ja vallankäytön kohteena n. 1592–1644*. Bibliotheca Historica 94 (Helsinki: The Finnish Literature Society, 2005), p. 46, and passim.
2. The magistrates' court (or magistrates' council) refers to the Swedish urban administrative body which took care of both administration and judicature. The treasurers' court (*kämnärsrätt*) was a lower court where petty crimes were handled. For more on this, see Petri Karonen, *Kämnerinoikeudet Suomen kaupungeissa suurvalta-ajan alkupuolella (noin 1620–1660)*. Studia Historica Jyväskyläensia 48 (Jyväskylä: University of Jyväskylä, 1994); Einonen, *Poliittiset areenat ja toimintatavat*, p. 58.
3. Einonen, *Poliittiset areenat ja toimintatavat*, pp. 61–75, 88–92.
4. See Lars Ericson, *Borgare och byråkrater. Omvandlingen av Stockholms stadsförvaltning 1599–1637*. Stockholmsmonografier utgivna av Stockholms stad 84 (Stockholm: Town of Stockholm, 1988), pp. 140–141, 151–156; Einonen, *Poliittiset areenat ja toimintatavat*, pp. 61–65, 68.
5. Einonen, *Poliittiset areenat ja toimintatavat*, pp. 9–10, 271, 300; see also Margaret S. Archer, *Structure, Agency and the Internal Conversation* (Cambridge: Cambridge University Press, 2003), pp. 3, 14–15.
6. Both printed versions and original documents have been used. These are specified in the footnotes and bibliography. Generally STb refers to printed court record books.
7. *Stockholms rådhus och råd. Festskrift utgiven till minne af nya rådhusets invigning hösten 1915. Del II. Matrikel öfver borgmästare och rådmän samt stads- och magistratssekreterare i Stockholms stad och Norra förstaden.* Af Frans de Brun, Gustaf Elgenstierna, Ivar Simonsson, Nils Östman (Stockholm, 1915–1918) (hereafter *Matrikel 1915–1918*).
8. The database was compiled by Lauri Karvonen and revised by Henri Kaunismäki. Magistrates were eventually left out as they were a more heterogeneous group and less is known about their office-holding activities. Often they are presented as a somewhat faceless group. On Stockholm's burgomasters in the period studied, of see *Svenskt biografiskt lexikon*: notes, where only Olaus Bureus (Olof Bure) is mentioned. For more, see E. Vennberg, "Olof Bure", *Svenskt biografiskt lexikon* (SBL) http://sok.riksarkivet.se/sbl/artikel/17159 (accessed April 10, 2015).
9. Ericson, *Borgare och byråkrater*, p. 117; Einonen, *Poliittiset areenat ja toimintatavat*, p. 63. See also Petri Karonen's chapter on royal mayors in this volume.
10. Ericson, *Borgare och byråkrater*; Åke Sandström, *Mellan Torneå och Amsterdam. En undersökning av Stockholms roll som förmedlare av varor i regional- och utrikeshandel 1600–1650*. Stockholmsmonografier utgivna av Stockholms stad 102 (Stockholm: Town of Stockholm, 1990); Arne Jansson, *Bördor och bärkraft: borgare och kronotjänare i Stockholm 1644–1672*. Stockholmsmonografier utgivna av Stockholms stad 103 (Stockholm: Town of Stockholm, 1991); Robert Sandberg, *I slottets skugga. Stockholm och kronan 1599–1620*. Stockholmsmonografier utgivna av Stockholms stad 105 (Stockholm: Town of Stockholm, 1991); Marko Lamberg, *Dannemännen i stadens råd. Rådmanskretsen i nordiska köpstäder under senmedeltiden*. Monografier utgivna av Stockholms stad 155 (Stockholm: Town of Stockholm, 2001). Einonen (in *Poliittiset areenat ja toimintatavat*) deals with

Stockholm's administration in terms of political culture and concentrates mainly on the interaction between the burghers and the urban administration.

11 See for example Lamberg, *Dannemännen i stadens råd*, pp. 237–244; Marie Lennersand, *Rättvisans och allmogens beskyddare. Den absoluta staten, kommissionerna och tjänstemännen, ca 1680–1730*. Studia Historica Upsaliensia 190 (Uppsala: University of Uppsala, 1999), pp. 41–42; Mats Hallenberg, *Kungen, fogdarna och riket. Lokalförvaltningen och statbyggande under tidigt Vasatid* (Stockholm: Symposium, 2001), pp. 351–401. Hallenberg discusses similar questions but does not explicitly address ethics or morality. Niklas Ericsson for his part deals with the criminal cases brought to the courthouse; see Niklas Ericsson, *Rätt eller fel? Moraluppfattningar i Stockholm under medeltid och vasatid*. Stockholm studies in history 68 (Stockholm: Almqvist & Wiksell International, 2003).

12 Einonen, *Poliittiset areenat ja toimintatavat*, pp. 14, 28, 59, 69–72.

13 R. W. Scribner, "Police and the Territorial State in the Sixteenth-century Württemberg". In: Kouri, E. I., Scott, Tom (ed.), *Politics and Society in Reformation Europe* (Basingstoke: Macmillan, 1987), p. 103.

14 See for example Harald Gustafsson, *Gamla riken, nya stater. Statsbildning, politisk kultur och identiteter under Kalmarunionens upplösningsskede 1512–1541* (Stockholm: Atlantis, 2000), pp. 21–31; Hallenberg, *Kungen, fogdarna och riket*, pp. 35–36; Einonen, *Poliittiset areenat ja toimintatavat*, pp. 13, 19–20; Karonen, *Pohjoinen suurvalta*, pp. 47, 182–186.

15 Stockholm was the largest city in the realm, and it was growing fast in spite of constant recurring plagues. In the late 1620s the population was about 14,000 and steadily increasing. The privileges of the estate society defined the burghers as the ordinary residents of Stockholm and as the only group that had the right to act as merchants or craftsmen – trade was only permitted in towns. There were also numerous other groups below and above the burghers in the urban social hierarchy, like servants, nobles, clergy and officials of the Crown. Ericson, *Borgare och byråkrater*, p. 43; Einonen, *Poliittiset areenat ja toimintatavat*, pp. 40, 72, 273, 302.

16 Petri Karonen, "Raastuvassa tavataan". *Suomen kaupunkien hallinto- ja oikeuslaitoksen toimintaa ja virkamiehiä suurvalta-aikana*. Studia Historica Jyväskyläensia 51 (Jyväskylä: University of Jyväskylä, 1995), pp. 61, 126; Ericson, *Borgare och byråkrater*, pp. 53–54; Einonen, *Poliittiset areenat ja toimintatavat*, pp. 61, 69–72; cf. Carl-Fredrik Corin, "Överståthållaren Klas Fleming och Stockholms expansion 1634–1644". In: Staf, Nils (red.), *Studier och handlingar rörande Stockholms historia III* (Stockholm: Stockholms stadsarkiv, 1966), p. 74. See also Aimo Halila, *Suomen kaupunkien kunnallishallinto 1600-luvulla I*. Historiallisia tutkimuksia 28, 1 (Helsinki: Finnish Historical Society, 1942), pp. 136–138.

17 Einonen, *Poliittiset areenat ja toimintatavat*, pp. 166–270. See also Jansson, *Bördor och bärkraft* on later protests.

18 Ericson, *Borgare och byråkrater*, pp. 111–116. During the succession struggle in the 1590s, both King Sigismund and Duke Charles – later Charles IX – tried to dominate Stockholm by manipulating the nominations for offices and discharging members of the urban administration from their duties (see Ericson, *Borgare och byråkrater*, pp. 112–114; Lars Ericson, "Mellan två eldar. Stockholms borgmästare och råd i kampen mellan Sigismund och hertig Karl, 1594–1599". In: *Studier och handlingar rörande Stockholms historia VII* (Stockholm: Stockholms stadsarkiv, 1994), passim.).

19 Einonen, *Poliittiset areenat ja toimintatavat*, pp. 72, 88–92.

20 Ericson, *Borgare och byråkrater*, pp. 121–140, 156–161; Einonen, *Poliittiset areenat ja toimintatavat*, pp. 59–60; Karonen, "Raastuvassa tavataan", pp. 38–39.

21 Ericson, *Borgare och byråkrater*, pp. 122–123; see also Nils Östman, "Stockholms

magistrat och rådhusrätt. Kortfattad öfversikt". In: *Stockholms rådhus och råd I. Festskrift utgifven till minne af nya rådhusets invigning hösten 1915* (Stockholm, 1915), p. 38. Impecunity was a basic argument used widely in early modern discourse, see Einonen, *Poliittiset areenat ja toimintatavat*, for example pp. 146-147.

22 Database; Östman, "Stockholms magistrat och rådhusrätt", p. 37.

23 Ericson, *Borgare och byråkrater*, p. 111. Originally it was stipulated that half of the office-holders be Swedish and the other half German, but from 1471 on offices were allocated to Swedes only. Another requirement was that a burgomaster or magistrate should be a holder of real estate in Stockholm.

24 Ericson, *Borgare och byråkrater*, p. 134. Cf. the case of Hans Nilsson Benick and Valentin Nilsson later in this chapter.

25 Lamberg, *Dannemännen i stadens råd*, pp. 218-219; Einonen, *Poliittiset areenat ja toimintatavat*, p. 59.

26 STb, magistrates' court, fair copy 10$^{th}$ of May, 1596, p. 36; Database; Ericson, *Borgare och byråkrater*, p. 112; Ericson, "Mellan två eldar", p. 50.

27 Database.

28 Database. There is no further evidence of this in the court record books. The records themselves have been preserved only incidentally during the period 1605-1615 and are exiguous compared with the preceding and succeeding periods; see Einonen, *Poliittiset areenat ja toimintatavat*, p. 32.

29 As far as we know, Tileman Abraham (d. before 1591), who served as a scribe in the 1570s and 1580s, had studied in Wittenberg, but according to the sources, the next academically educated scribe was Nils Skunck (d. 1676), appointed in 1645. Olof Pedersson Humbla, later a burgomaster, was also enrolled as a student at Wittenberg University. Database: *Matrikel 1915-1918*, 27-28; see also Sandberg, *I slottets skugga*, pp. 237-238.

30 See Karonen, *"Raastuvassa tavataan"*, pp. 86-87.

31 For more on the ordinance of 1619, see Karonen, *"Raastuvassa tavataan"*, pp. 23-37, 174-179.

32 SSA (Stockholm City Archives), BRA, vol. 65, 19$^{th}$ of June, 1616 supplication to the King, in which it was mentioned that the burghers had complained to the magistrates' court and asked it to pass their message to the King. Obviously this process could have been initiated by the office-holders themselves, but not without the consent of the burghers. Sandberg, *I slottets skugga*, p. 238; see also Halila, *Suomen kaupunkien kunnallishallinto*, pp. 148-149.

33 Olaus Bureus (ennobled in 1621 as Bure) had been a personal physician to Duke Johan (1537-1592) and later to King Gustavus Adolphus. He had some previous experience of town planning but none of administration. Database; *Matrikel 1915-1918*, pp. 31-32; Vennberg, "Olof Bure"; Sandberg, *I slottets skugga*, p. 237; Einonen, *Poliittiset areenat ja toimintatavat*, p. 64.

34 Database; *Matrikel 1915-1918*, pp. 31-32; Vennberg, "Olof Bure". See also Östman, "Stockholms magistrat och rådhusrätt", p. 37.

35 Some of the new burgomasters had previously served as royal scribes or had some experience of working in other town administrations, like Olof Andersson (1576-1627) in Köping and Mattias Trost (1582-1648) in Norra Förstaden (which was reunited with Stockholm in 1635). Database; Ericson, *Borgare och byråkrater*, pp. 143-145; Einonen, *Poliittiset areenat ja toimintatavat*, p. 63-67.

36 Karonen, *"Raastuvassa tavataan"*, pp. 40-41, 57-61.

37 Hans Henriksson (−1638), who resigned in 1630, was granted a yearly allowance of 300 dalers for his maintenance. This seems to be an exception, however, since normally burgomasters were supposed to support themselves. Hans Henriksson had problems with his eyesight, and he was possibly unable to provide for himself, which would explain the payment. Database; *Matrikel 1915-1918*, p. 33. As a result

of the scanty source material, it is difficult to estimate the average life expectancy of burgomasters, but there were surprisingly many, like Jakob Grundell (1590-1663) and Olaus Bureus, who died in their 70s. See Database; for more on age, see Kustaa H. J. Vilkuna, *Katse menneisyyden ihmiseen. Valta ja aineettomat elinolot 1500-1850*. Historiallisia tutkimuksia 253 (Helsinki: The Finnish Literature Society, 2010), pp. 37-59.

38 STb, magistrates' court, fair copy 23rd of July 1621, p. 169; *Matrikel 1915-1918*, pp. 24-28, 31-33; Ericson, *Borgare och byråkrater*, pp. 112-116, 144-146; Sandberg, *I slottets skugga*, pp. 20, 224-232; cf. Karonen, "*Raastuvassa tavataan*", pp. 41-42. There is no evidence of Benick's letter of appointment in the *Riksregistratur* (Swedish National Records), and thus it is not possible to ascertain how his role was defined.

39 Karonen, "*Raastuvassa tavataan*", pp. 40-41, 57-61; Einonen, *Poliittiset areenat ja toimintatavat*, pp. 64-70.

40 See for example Riksarkivet (SRA) (Swedish National Archive), SSA, vol. 2, undated letter (probably from the mid-1620s) from Olaus Bureus possibly to the Council of the Realm; Einonen, *Poliittiset areenat ja toimintatavat*, p. 64. In the letter Bureus stated explicitly that, on the King's orders, he and Benick had tried to organise Stockholm and implement some of the reforms, but many other office-holders considered that they were not empowered to do so. Even when they declared they were acting on behalf of the Crown, the others demanded to see a direct edict signed by the King. This shows how agency was becoming increasingly influenced by written documents.

41 See for example SRA SSA, BRA, A, vol. 51, magistrates' court, draft transcript 15th of August, 1629; SSA, BRA, A, vol. 52, magistrates' court, draft transcript 23rd of June, 1630; *Matrikel 1915-1918*, pp. 166, 171; Einonen, *Poliittiset areenat ja toimintatavat*, pp. 64-65.

42 Petri Karonen (*"Raastuvassa tavataan"*, pp. 60-83) describes a similar example in Finland.

43 These taxes were introduced in 1623 and included excises (*accis*) for baking, brewing and slaughter. Small duties (*lilla tullen*), collected for provisions and consumer goods brought into town, were imposed by the Riksdag in 1622, but probably only collected after 1623. See Sandström, *Mellan Torneå och Amsterdam*, pp. 75, 105.

44 For more on spatial order and perceptions, see Piia Einonen, "Roopet mäst hörtt wordett vthi alle huus kring om Torget". Stadsrummet som protesternas scen vid sekelskiftet 1600". In: Hallenberg, Mats, Linnarsson, Magnus (ed.), *Politiska rum. Kontroll, konflikt och rörelse i det förmoderna Sverige 1300-1850* (Lund: Nordic Academic Press, 2014), pp. 39-58.

45 SRA 1133.07, vol. 20, 14th of February, 1623 and 18th of February, 1623 dated letters from Gabriel Gustafsson Oxenstierna to King Gustavus Adolphus; Einonen, *Poliittiset areenat ja toimintatavat*, pp. 262-266.

46 SRA 1133.07, vol. 20, 14th of February, 1623, 18th of February, 1623 and 21st of February, 1623 dated letters from Gabriel Gustafsson Oxenstierna to King Gustavus Adolphus.

47 Ericson, *Borgare och byråkrater*, p. 134. There was a similar case in Helsinki on the Finnish side of the Swedish realm, but there this was a necessity as the town was so small, and there were only a few suitable candidates for offices (see Sylvi Möller, *Suomen tapulikaupunkien valtaporvaristo ja sen kaupankäyntimenetelmät 1600-luvun alkupuolella*. Historiallisia tutkimuksia 42 (Helsinki: Finnish Historical Society, 1954), p. 73). Together with his brother Valentin, Hans Nilsson Benick ran an inn called *Solen* (the Sun) in central Stockholm. Among others, they lodged foreign guests of the Crown and envoys. See Database; *Matrikel 1915-1918*, p. 32; Ericson, *Borgare och byråkrater*, p. 274.

48 *Matrikel 1915–1918*, p. 32; Ericson, *Borgare och byråkrater*, p. 143. During this period, the Elders did not constitute a representative body as such but rather a tool that the town administration could use to consult the sentiments of the burghers. For aspirants to offices it was a way of acquiring administrative experience and merits. For more on the 48 Elders, see Einonen, *Poliittiset areenat ja toimintatavat*, pp. 145, 225–226, 268–269.
49 For more on tax farming and opposition to it, see Veikko Kerkkonen, *Etelä-Suomen kaupunkien kruununverot 1614–1650*. Historiallisia tutkimuksia 30 (Helsinki: Finnish Historical Society, 1945), pp. 38, 170–174, 189–191; Kimmo Katajala, "The changing face of peasant unrest in early modern Finland". In: Katajala, Kimmo (ed.), *Northern Revolts. Medieval and Early Modern Peasant Unrest in the Nordic Countries* (Helsinki: Finnish Literature Society, 2004), pp. 162, 178–181; Mats Hallenberg, *Statsmakt till salu. Arrendesystemet och privatiseringen av skatteuppbörden i det svenska riket 1618–1635* (Lund: Nordic Academic Press, 2008), passim. On Welshuisen see pp. 101–102.
50 Einonen, *Poliittiset areenat ja toimintatavat*, pp. 266–267; for more on rumours, see Piia Einonen "The politics of talk. Rumour and gossip in Stockholm during the struggle for succession (c. 1592–1607)". *Scandia*, 80 (2014), pp. 9–28.
51 Einonen, *Poliittiset areenat ja toimintatavat*, pp. 64–72.
52 STb, magistrates' court, fair copy 12th of November, 1625, p. 418, see also pp. 524–525 (note 318).
53 "*Gudh hielpe H. K. M:t heem, du Anders Hend. schall få ett tusend dieflar.*" (STb, magistrates' court, draft transcript 12th of November 1625, pp. 419–420 (citation on page 419); STb, magistrates' court, fair copy 7th of November, 1625, pp. 524–526).
54 STb magistrates' court, fair copy 7th of November, 1625, pp. 524–526.
55 *Privilegier, resolutioner och förordningar för Sveriges städer VI (1621–1632)*, (Stockholm: Norstedts, 1985), p. 620, 9th of November 1625 letter from the Council of the Realm (only mentioned here, the original document is in the register of the realm).
56 See for example STb, magistrates' court, draft transcript 12th of November 1625, pp. 417–418.
57 SSA, BRA, A, vol. 54, magistrates' court, draft transcript 8th of January 1634. This referred to Benick's period as inspector of the town's buildings in 1631–1633 (*Matrikel 1915–1918*, p. 32).
58 See for example STb, magistrates' court, fair copy 7th of November 1625, pp. 524–526.
59 This probably refers to burghers who were not implementing proposals that the court had agreed on *(...han förnimer, at de saker som på stadsenns wägna ähre proponerade, inthet giörs till.)*. STb, magistrates' court, draft transcript 26th of June 1628, p. 71.
60 Einonen, *Poliittiset areenat ja toimintatavat*, p. 247.
61 See Einonen, *Poliittiset areenat ja toimintatavat*, pp. 135–136.
62 SSA, BRA, A, vol. 52, magistrates' court, draft transcript 8th of January 1630.
63 "*..huadh icke något till saken giörss så protesterer doctaren att han för sin pärsson haffuer giordt huadh han kundhe, och huar må see sigh före, huru han kan och will beståå.*" SSA, SKA, A1B, vol. 1, treasurers' court 30th of April 1624.
64 "*...borgerschapet på Nårremallm* [sic] *äre schäntligenn bedragne af stadsenns utschickade och i sönderheet af Hanns Nillßonn, som för gunst schulld utlofuar det som omöijeligit är dem at efterkomma.*" SSA, BRA, A, vol. 51, magistrates' court, draft transcript 28th of February 1629. See more on the ship company and forms of protests in Per Göran Norenstedt, *Bildandet av det första seglande kompaniet. Skeppskompaniet 1629–1637* (unpublished thesis, University of Stockholm: 1984), passim.; Einonen, *Poliittiset areenat ja toimintatavat*, pp. 169, 241–249; Ericson, *Borgare och byråkrater*, pp. 216–218.

65 Sandström, *Mellan Torneå och Amsterdam*, pp. 105–106. See also for example SSA, SKA, A1B, vol. 1, treasurers' court, draft transcript 14th of April 1623, 20 May 1623, 16 November 1623.
66 SSA, BRA, A, vol. 51, magistrates' court, draft transcript 12th of October 1629. "*J lijka måtto Hanns Nillßonn: hann skrifuer på sigh huru myki than will, och andre skole bära th[et] up.*" It is indicative that this episode is entered only in the minutes but not in the fair copy version, and there is no evidence of any further measures taken. The case of Benick is not unique; the burgomaster Nils Eriksson was accused in the early seventeenth century both of imposing new payments on the burghers and also of levying too much tax. Eriksson supported Duke Charles in the ongoing struggle for succession, and this was probably the main reason for discontent among the burghers. Einonen, *Poliittiset areenat ja toimintatavat*, pp. 132–134. Wellam Lehusen was appointed magistrate in 1635 and trade burgomaster in 1663 (Database; *Matrikel 1915–1918*, pp. 41–42).
67 Einonen, *Poliittiset areenat ja toimintatavat*, pp. 193–201.
68 SSA, BRA, A, vol. 55, magistrates' court, draft transcript 3rd of October 1635.
69 SSA, BRA, A1B, vol. 1, treasurers' court, draft transcript 9th of September 1623, 20th of October 1623, 13th of November 1623.
70 See for example Lamberg, *Dannemännen i stadens råd*, pp. 132–134, 242–244; Einonen, "The politics of talk", p. 14.
71 SSA, BRA, A, vol. 43, magistrates' court, fair copy 6th of February 1632; Clas Theodor Odhner, *Bidrag till svenska städernas och borgarståndets historia före 1633* (Uppsala: Edquist, 1860), pp. 81–82; Östman, "Stockholms magistrat och rådhusrätt", pp. 27–28; Möller, *Suomen tapulikaupunkien valtaporvaristo*, pp. 77–80; Karonen, *Pohjoinen suurvalta*, p. 208. The process of nominating representatives is only vaguely described in the court record books, with just the names of the nominees and sometimes the burghers' consent to these. See for example SSA, SMRA, A1a, vol. 3, magistrates' court, fair copy 10th of January 1638. Other court record books are similarly lacking in further information on these matters (see for example Folke Lindberg, *Västerviks historia 1275–1718* (Stockholm, 1933), p. 327).
72 SSA, BRA, F, vol. 78, two letters from Hans Nilsson Benick to the magistrates' court dated the 2nd and 5th days of Easter, 1626. Grundell had been a treasurer since 1622, and was appointed a magistrate the following year. Later he followed in Benick's footsteps to become a burgomaster. See Database; *Matrikel 1915–1918*, p. 35.
73 It is worth noting that Benick was already maintaining in 1633 that he was too old and sick to take care of his duties as Inspector of Buildings, and he was understandably released from these duties in 1634, when Jöns Henriksson (d. 1665) took over the post. See SSA, BRA, A, vol. 54, magistrates' court, draft transcript 1st of June, 1633; Database; *Matrikel 1915–1918*, pp. 32, 34. The system of collegiums was only introduced in the urban administration in 1636, but documents show that similar arrangements already existed in the 1620s. The Building Collegium would later take care of buildings owned by the town and rents and protect the interests of the whole city with regard to street regulations and private building. See Östman, "Stockholms magistrat och rådhusrätt", pp. 46–47; Ericson, *Borgare och byråkrater*, pp. 181–187, 195. The former post of inspector of buildings was probably similar, and Benick would have also taken care of Stockholm's land property as well.
74 See for example SSA, BRA, A, vol. 52, magistrates' court, draft transcript 19th of April 1630, 28th of April 1630; SSA, BRA, A, vol. 55, magistrates' court, draft transcript 16th of May 1636; SSA, SMRA, A1a, vol. 1, magistrates' court, fair copy 16th of May 1636, 18th of May 1636, 21st of May 1636, 23rd of May 1636, 17th of May 1636, 15th of October 1636, 19th of November 1636; see also SSA SMRA, A9, vol. 1, 3rd of November, 1637; *Matrikel 1915–1918*, p. 32; Ericson, *Borgare och byråkrater*, pp. 225–228. "*Efter Hanns Nilson haf. köpt tåmpten af staden för en ringa pening och nu sålldtt tompten för dubbellt.*" SSA, BRA, A, vol. 54, magistrates' court, draft

transcript 3rd of November 1634. For example in 1637 (SSA, SMRA, A1a, vol. 2, magistrates' court, fair copy 30th of October 1637) Jakob Allertz represented Benick in the magistrates' court and produced a document concerning five plots that Benick had bought from the town and sold on. Allertz asked that these deals be confirmed, but there was apparently no evidence of such a document in the record books, and Benick was summoned to the court to explain how he had obtained the document.

75 SSA, SMRA, A1a, vol. 1, magistrates' court, fair copy 24th of October 1636.

76 SSA, SMRA, A1a, vol. 3, magistrates' court, fair copy 25th of August 1638, 27th of August 1638; SSA, SMRA, A1a, vol. 4, magistrates' court, fair copy 6th of March 1639, 11th of May 1640; SSA, SMRA, A1a, vol. 5, magistrates' court, fair copy 13th of March 1641. There is no evidence of this dispute in the records of the Svea Court of Appeal, but it had been involved in the customs dispute in 1629, when Benick was asked to explain if he had increased the size of duties. He explained that he was forgetful, but he may have temporarily raised the duty because of the increased value of money. According to the minutes, the burghers had then complained to the Council of the Realm, and it was declared that everybody who had paid too much would be compensated. See SRA, Svea hovrätts arkiv, AIa1, vol. 2, Svea Court of Appeal 29th of April 1629. Benick's inheritors were subjected to confiscation as late as 1641 (if they refused to pay), so the case was still not solved five years later. See SSA, SKA, A1A, vol. 1, treasurers' court, fair copy 17th of April 1641.

77 Valentin Nilsson managed to marry above his class in the social hierarchy, and his son was ennobled. *Matrikel 1915–1918*, pp. 32, 167; Ericson, *Borgare och byråkrater*, p. 124.

# Sources

## Archival sources

Riksarkivet (SRA) (Swedish National Archives), Stockholm
    Stockholms stads acta (SSA), vol. 2, administration
    RA, Skrivelser till konungen, 1103.06, Gustav II Adolf, vol. 20
    RA, Svea hovrätts arkiv (SHA), Huvudarkivet AIa1, vol. 2
Stockholms stadsarkiv (SSA) (Stockholm City Archives), Borgmästare och råds arkiv före 1636 (BRA), Serie A, Tänkeböcker i koncept, vol. 51–52, 54–55
    SSA, Borgmästare och råds arkiv före 1636 (BRA), Serie A, Tänkeböcker i renskrift, vol. 43
    SSA, Borgmästare och råds arkiv före 1636 (BRA), Serie B, Utgångna skrivelser, vol. 65
    SSA, Borgmästare och råds arkiv före 1636 (BRA), Serie F, Handlingar till tänkeböckerna, vol. 78
    SSA, Stockholms magistrats och rådhusrätts arkiv (SMRA), Serie A1a, Tänkeböcker, huvudserie, vol. 1–5
    SSA, Stockholms magistrats och rådhusrätts arkiv (SMRA), Serie A1b, Tänkeböcker, koncept, vol. 1
    SSA, Stockholms magistrats och rådhusrätts arkiv (SMRA), Serie A9, Stadens protokoll i enskilda ärenden, vol. 1
    SSA, Stadens kämnärsrätts arkiv (SKA), Serie A1A, Protokoll i civil- och kriminalmål, huvudserie, vol. 1
    SSA, Stadens kämnärsrätts arkiv (SKA), Serie A1B, Protokoll i civil- och kriminalmål, koncept, vol. 1

## Printed sources

Stockholms tänkeböcker från år 1592 (STb). Utgivna av Stockholms stadsarkiv. Del II, 1596–1599, red. av Daniel Almqvist (Stockholm: Stockholms Stadsarkiv, 1951).

Stockholms tänkeböcker från år 1592 (STb). Utgivna av Stockholms stadsarkiv. Del XII, 1620–1621, red. av Sven Olsson and Naemi Särnqvist (Stockholm: Stockholms Stadsarkiv, 1976).

Stockholms tänkeböcker från år 1592 (STb). Utgivna av Stockholms stadsarkiv. Del XIV, 1624–1625, red. av Sven Olsson and Naemi Särnqvist (Stockholm: Stockholms Stadsarkiv, 1979).

Stockholms tänkeböcker från år 1592 (STb). Utgivna av Stockholms stadsarkiv. Del XVII, 1628, red. av Jan Gejrot (Stockholm: Stockholms Stadsarkiv, 1998).

Privilegier, resolutioner och förordningar för Sveriges städer VI (1621–1632) (PRFSS), ed. by Carl-Fredrik Corin and Folke Sleman (Stockholm: Norstedts Tryckeri, 1985).

## Literature

Archer, Margaret S. 2003: *Structure, Agency and the Internal Conversation.* Cambridge: Cambridge University Press.

Corin, Carl-Fredrik 1966: "Överståthållaren Klas Fleming och Stockholms expansion 1634–1644". In: Staf, Nils (red.), *Studier och handlingar rörande Stockholms historia III.* Stockholm: Stockholms stadsarkiv.

Einonen, Piia 2005: *Poliittiset areenat ja toimintatavat. Tukholman porvaristo vallan käyttäjänä ja vallankäytön kohteena n. 1592–1644.* Bibliotheca Historica 94. Helsinki: The Finnish Literature Society.

Einonen, Piia 2014: "'Roopet mäst hörtt wordett vthi alle huus kring om Torget'. Stadsrummet som protesternas scen vid sekelskiftet 1600". In: Hallenberg, Mats, Linnarsson, Magnus (red.), *Politiska rum. Kontroll, konflikt och rörelse i det förmoderna Sverige 1300–1850.* Lund: Nordic Academic Press.

Einonen, Piia 2014: "The politics of talk. Rumour and gossip in Stockholm during the struggle for succession (c. 1592–1607)", *Scandia* 80.

Ericson, Lars 1988: *Borgare och byråkrater. Omvandlingen av Stockholms stadsförvaltning 1599–1637.* Stockholmsmonografier utgivna av Stockholms stad 84. Stockholm: Town of Stockholm.

Ericson, Lars 1994: "Mellan två eldar. Stockholms borgmästare och råd i kampen mellan Sigismund och hertig Karl, 1594–1599", *Studier och handlingar rörande Stockholms historia VII*, ed. Lars Wikström. Stockholm: Stockholms stadsarkiv.

Ericsson, Niklas 2003: *Rätt eller fel? Moraluppfattningar i Stockholm under medeltid och vasatid.* Stockholm: Almqvist & Wiksell International.

Gustafsson, Harald 2000: *Gamla riken, nya stater. Statsbildning, politisk kultur och identiteter under Kalmarunionens upplösningsskede 1512–1541.* Stockholm: Atlantis.

Halila, Aimo 1942: *Suomen kaupunkien kunnallishallinto 1600-luvulla I.* Historiallisia tutkimuksia 28, 1. Helsinki: Finnish Historical Society.

Hallenberg, Mats 2001: *Kungen, fogdarna och riket. Lokalförvaltning och statsbyggande under tidig Vasatid.* Stockholm: Brutus Östlings Bokförlag Symposion.

Hallenberg, Mats 2008: *Statsmakt till salu. Arrendesystemet och privatiseringen av skatteuppbörden i det svenska riket 1618–1635.* Lund: Nordic Academic Press.

Jansson, Arne 1991: *Bördor och bärkraft: borgare och kronotjänare i Stockholm 1644–1672.* Stockholmsmonografier utgivna av Stockholms stad 103. Stockholm: Town of Stockholm.

Karonen, Petri 1994: *Kämnerinoikeudet Suomen kaupungeissa suurvalta-ajan alkupuolella (noin 1620–1660)*. Studia Historica Jyväskyläensia 48. Jyväskylä: Jyväskylän yliopisto.

Karonen, Petri 1995: "*Raastuvassa tavataan*". *Suomen kaupunkien hallinto- ja oikeuslaitoksen toimintaa ja virkamiehiä suurvalta-aikana*. Jyväskylä: Jyväskylän yliopisto.

Karonen, Petri 2014: *Pohjoinen suurvalta. Ruotsi ja Suomi 1521–1809*. Helsinki: The Finnish Literature Society.

Katajala, Kimmo 2004: "The changing face of peasant unrest in early modern Finland". In: Katajala, Kimmo (ed.), *Northern Revolts. Medieval and Early Modern Peasant Unrest in the Nordic Countries*. Helsinki: Finnish Literature Society.

Kerkkonen, Veikko 1945: *Etelä-Suomen kaupunkien kruununverot 1614–1650*. Helsinki: Finnish Historical Society.

Lamberg, Marko 2001: *Dannemännen i stadens råd. Rådmanskretsen i nordiska köpstäder under senmedeltiden*. Monografier utgivna av Stockholms stad 155. Stockholm: Stockholmiaförlag.

Lennersand, Marie 1999: *Rättvisans och allmogens beskyddare. Den absoluta staten, kommissionerna och tjänstemännen, ca 1680–1730*. Studia Historica Upsaliensia 190. Uppsala: Uppsala universitet.

Lindberg, Folke 1933: *Västerviks historia 1275–1718*. Stockholm.

Möller, Sylvi 1954: *Suomen tapulikaupunkien valtaporvaristo ja sen kaupankäyntimenetelmät 1600-luvun alkupuolella*. Historiallisia tutkimuksia 42. Helsinki: Finnish Historical Society.

Norenstedt, Per Göran 1984: *Bildandet av det första seglande kompaniet. Skeppskompaniet 1629–1637* (unpublished thesis, University of Stockholm).

Odhner, Clas Theodor 1860: *Bidrag till svenska städernas och borgarståndets historia före 1633*. Uppsala: Edquist.

Sandberg, Robert 1991: *I slottets skugga. Stockholm och kronan 1599–1620*. Stockholmsmonografier utgivna av Stockholms stad 105. Stockholm: Town of Stockholm.

Sandström, Åke 1990: *Mellan Torneå och Amsterdam. En undersökning av Stockholms roll som förmedlare av varor i regional- och utrikeshandel 1600–1650*. Stockholmsmonografier utgivna av Stockholms stad 102. Stockholm: Town of Stockholm.

Scribner, R. W. 1987: "Police and the Territorial State in the Sixteenth-century Württemberg". In: Kouri, E. I., Scott Tom (ed.), *Politics and Society in Reformation Europe*. Basingstoke: Macmillan.

Stockholms rådhus och råd. Festskrift utgiven till minne af nya rådhusets invigning hösten 1915. Del II. Metrikel öfver borgmästare och rådmän samt stads- och magistratssekreterare i Stockholms stad och Norra förstaden. Af Frans de Brun, Gustaf Elgenstierna, Ivar Simonsson, Nils Östman (Stockholm, 1915–1918).

Vennberg, E.: "Olof Bure", *Svenskt biografiskt lexikon* (SBL). http://sok.riksarkivet.se/sbl/artikel/17159.

Vilkuna, Kustaa H. J. 2010: *Katse menneisyyden ihmiseen. Valta ja aineettomat elinolot 1500–1850*. Historiallisia tutkimuksia 253. Helsinki: The Finnish Literature Society.

Östman, Nils 1915: "Stockholms magistrat och rådhusrätt. Kortfattad öfversikt", *Stockholms rådhus och råd I. Festskrift utgifven till minne af nya rådhusets invigning hösten 1915*. Stockholm.

# Students X

Kustaa H. J. Vilkuna

# Study Abroad, the State and Personal Agency (1640–1700)
The study trips of Turku students to foreign universities: background factors, the return and careers of the travellers

In the seventeenth century the state invested in the development of the university institution and academic education in Finland when it was realised that the level of expertise of functionaries was downright execrable. It seemed that the officials of the lay administration could hardly write their own names. Certainly, the state could be run by men with modest academic abilities, but the upkeep of the whole administrative machinery required educated professionals. In the course of time there evolved a new and growing group of state officials who had received an academic education, and this group in turn attracted young men who as individual agents planned their future careers in the service of the state.

The development of the University of Uppsala and the foundation of the Universities of Tartu, Turku (Åbo) and Lund were the tools used by the authorities to educate and train the civil service. This required considerable financial investments and the precise allocation of available resources. If the Crown did henceforth have to sponsor training, the investments were appreciably lower than they would have been if civil servants had to be trained abroad. Moreover, the state might expect some return on its investments and, holding the purse strings, would be able to control the training that was given. The expansion and improvement of the university institution served the power state and its administration. The reform of the administration, the diplomacy of the power state and the bureaucratisation and supervision of the realm required a competent, flexible and versatile corps of functionaries. The Crown considered that a civil servant should not pursue a career in only one office; rather every official should be able to change over to any other field at any time.

The Crown participated in the financing of the university institution, and consequently it expected that its ideas would be listened to. And if they were not, then the state laid down the law. King Gustavus Adolphus (1594–1632) and Chancellor Axel Oxenstierna (1583–1654) issued directions to the universities concerning the training of civil servants, emphasising the competence required of a functionary and the role of knowledge and a general education. The king and the chancellor had a clear view about what a modern civil servant of a power state should be like. Thus they pointed out that a functionary should possess a classical education, a familiarity with political theory and law, impeccable manners and the ability to handle practical affairs in state offices. Training in the last-mentioned requirement took place in administrative offices.[1]

The professional civil service qualifications obtained at university simultaneously served the ends of the Crown and made it possible for an individual to pursue a career in the service of the power state. Now it was no longer necessary to obtain such qualifications abroad. The development of the Swedish university institution and the decline of German universities, which had previously been favoured in Sweden, during the Thirty Years War initially led to decreased interest in studying abroad. But soon after the war ended and the German universities began to revive, students again set off for these and other seats of learning in Europe – indeed with an enthusiasm that was not paralleled in either the previous or indeed the following century.[2] The situation became absurd. The question thus arises: What purpose did the study abroad of a whole group of students serve? What did it mean for the state, and what did it offer the individuals concerned?

In my chapter, I address precisely these questions: the students as personal agents, the ideology that influenced their activity, the speeches of the leaders of the universities and the later agency of those who studied abroad in the service of the state or elsewhere. All these levels are in a way representative of personal agency.

I shall focus on young men who studied at the Academy of Turku (Åbo) before setting off to study abroad. This delimitation is justified for four reasons: First, a massive electronic database of the student registers of the Academy of Turku (*Ylioppilasmatrikkeli 1640–1852 – Studentmatrikel 1640–1852*) supplemented with numerous source references has been compiled.[3] It allows one to follow closely the social origins, the academic progress and the events in the lives of individual persons, and it offers one the opportunity to assess the social significance of their studies. Second, by examining the move abroad of a young man who had already undertaken studies, what happened to him in his time there and his possible return to Sweden, one can assess the increased value that accrued from studying abroad to both the individual and the state, for both of whom study in a domestic university would have been sufficient with regard to the person's career. Third, an examination of the lives of students who studied in a "provincial university" (in the sense of the German *Landesuniversität*) within the Swedish realm shows whether the study had only provincial significance or whether it served national unity. Fourth, the precision of the electronic database and the delimitation of the population studied do not leave the same kind of gaps that can be found in previous summarising studies, in which a quarter or even as much as a half of the objects of study have had to be placed in the category "no information". In such cases, the identified data lose considerable significance.

The research population comprises approximately 128 persons, of whom I have compiled a separate database (Database of persons studying abroad 1640–1700). They constituted only a fraction (under two percent) of those citizens of the kingdom who undertook study trips abroad.[4]

## The Academy of Turku and the politico-cultural purpose of study abroad

Turku offered a noteworthy alternative: it provided a possibility for a more extensive group of young men to undertake academic studies, and it attracted students from Sweden proper. In the period 1595–1639, 67 Finns studied abroad and about 220 in the domestic universities of Uppsala and Tartu. The number is so small that one can well understand the efforts of both the local and the state authorities; such a small group would not be able to cope with the expanding bureaucracy. Later, in the years 1640–1700, there were over 4500 young men studying at the Academy of Turku. It was possible there to obtain the practical training that was essential for a career in the civil service, and legal training in Turku Court of Appeal was popular. Of the presidents of Turku Court of Appeal (*Åbo hovrätt*), Jöns Kurck (1590–1652) in particular supported the university, and planned and outlined a training programme.[5] The needs of the Swedish state in Finland were focussed on Turku Court of Appeal and the lower instances under its jurisdiction together with the county administrations. The intense process of bureaucratisation that took place in the seventeenth century demanded more professional personnel, increased the need for training and aroused hopes for professionally oriented studies.

The persons who drew up the general lines of educational policy supported domestic universities and looked askance at foreign ones. In their opinion, travelling to study in Europe was useless if society did not benefit from it. In fact, the attitude to foreign study at the Academy of Turku during the first years of its existence was downright adverse. Here the university was following the views pronounced by Axel Oxenstierna at the Diet of 1634. According to him, Swedes who travelled abroad might be inculcated with altogether noxious notions. Patently, his goal was to promote the realm's own universities. In the seventeenth century, Swedish universities recruited professors from western Europe in order to augment both the level of their scholarship and the prestige of the realm. And in fact they succeeded in attracting some of the best known scholars of the age, such as Hugo Grotius (1583–1645) and Samuel Pufendorf (1632–1694). Therefore, it was not necessary to go far afield to seek learning, and moreover the state was able to supervise what was taught. All in all, the result was that the universities in the realm of Sweden and the education they offered fulfilled the social task allotted to them. Consequently, foreign study took on a new significance, which domestic studies also prepared the students for.[6] From the point of view of the individual agent, the student, this meant that domestic studies provided a sufficient amount of knowledge to equip him for work in the civil service, but it was thought that foreign studies would open the door more rapidly to higher and better positions.

It was not worth sending anyone to study the obscenities offered by the German universities, which had fallen into decay in the Thirty Years War, to witness the destruction of a civilised cultural heritage and observe the wretched state of learning and piety there, as Mikael Wexionius (1609–1670, ennobled with the name Gyldenstolpe in 1650), the Deacon of the

Faculty of Philosophy of the Academy of Turku, put it in his speech at the inauguration of the university. Enevald Svenonius (1627–1688), a student who was a protégé of Wexionius, went even further in *Oratio delineationem magnanimitatis exhibens*, a eulogy of his mentor published in 1643. In it he stated that he was disgusted by the adulation of foreign universities. The assumption of their superior quality was based on rumour since few persons in Turku had any proper experience of travelling abroad. He further claimed that this uninhibited adulation led to laziness and that participation in foreign studies was inspired not by the desire to learn but by the evil of idolisation.[7]

The aims of study abroad changed when the Academy of Turku was founded. Study trips abroad, especially to universities, served the ends of the power state of the great power of Sweden. This was not directly recorded anywhere, but it was apparent in the thinking of the decision-makers and those who funded the trips. It is significant that the nature of these journeys to study abroad was serious: the frivolities of Italy, exotic locations and pleasure were willingly rejected.[8]

A student's social position governed the nature, location and goals of his foreign study. Those for whom a position on the higher rungs of the social ladder had in principal been reserved by the system of privileges travelled differently from those whose careers were directly promoted by travelling abroad. The division was clear: the nobles and the others. The attitude to members of the nobility became extremely liberal, whereas the authorities looked askance at the travel of students of theology, for example, to heretical environments.[9] For instance, the father of Johan Gezelius the elder (1615–1690) urged his son to leave the doctrinally suspect University of Cambridge, although the young man had observed that the teachers there favoured Lutherans and opposed Calvinists.[10] Times and ideas changed, however, and even non-nobles came to be accorded some licence. For example, in the early 1680s, Lars (d. 1686), Magnus (d. 1711) and Nils Sierman (d. 1712), the sons of a clergyman from Småland, who had been students at the Academy of Turku, travelled in Europe. The personal ambitions and agency of the young men differed from one another, and in the case of Magnus also from the immediate goals set by the ideologists. Lars travelled to England, Nils studied as an MA student in Wittenberg, while Magnus made two study trips abroad. On the second of these, he spent a long time in Rome, working as the private secretary *(sekreterare)* of Queen Christina (1626–1689). He was enlightened, accumulated an extensive library and avoided erring into Catholicism.[11]

Usually, the travels of those who did not belong to the nobility were centrally prompted by endeavours to reinforce the intellectual foundation of Sweden as a great power and the exigencies of the power state. Study abroad was regarded as a way of safeguarding Sweden from the Counter-Reformation, and consequently the travellers were advised in advance to protect themselves from possible advances by Counter-Reformists. Admittedly, the religious control was selective: not everyone was suspected of being susceptible to heretical doctrines, whereas others even had to undergo examinations to ascertain the strength of their religious conviction.¹² This factor was taken into consideration in the local system of awarding stipends. For example, it was a condition of a stipend awarded by Bishop Isak Rothovius (1572–1652) in 1649 that the studies must take place in doctrinally orthodox universities.¹³

The funding of the studies was naturally an important question – both for the individual and for society. The more indigent a student was, the more important it was to obtain a stipend. Only 50–70 of those students of the Academy of Turku who travelled abroad to study went directly from that university – or at least without enrolling in some other Swedish university. The majority went abroad after first moving from Turku to Uppsala, Tartu or Lund.¹⁴ There were not many stipends on offer, and in Turku none apart from that granted by Bishop Rothovius, and his stipend went to a promising M.A. student called Johan Ketarmannus (d. 1653), who used his foreign study stipend while studying in the domestic University of Uppsala.¹⁵ Those who wished to obtain a stipend had to travel to the heart of the realm and prove their strong Lutheran convictions. Johan Gezelius the younger (1647–1718) received royal stipend for study abroad after pursuing further studies at the University of Uppsala.¹⁶ Likewise Nils Bergius (1658–1706) obtained a stipend in 1682 after studying at Uppsala, as did Isak Laurbecchius (1677–1716) around 1700 after already getting to Germany using a bursary from the Diocese of Vyborg (Viborg) for indigent school students ¹⁷

Other significant stipends required a sojourn in Uppsala or Stockholm. After studying and completing his master's degree with a pro gradu thesis under the tutorship of Gyldenstolpe at the Academy of Turku in the 1650s, Daniel Rosander, the son of a clergyman from Småland, obtained a post as a teacher at Växjö School. He was dismissed for drunkenness in 1667, after which he abandoned his family and moved to Stockholm. There he received a stipend from Count Tott, which would permit him to study at Königsberg. He did get there, but he did not enrol in the university, but rather continued his unruly way of life in Vyborg and Porvoo in Finland.¹⁸ This stipend brought no benefit to the state, and it did not further Rosander's career. By contrast, the career of Enevald Svenonius, an early mentor of Gezelius and a critic of travels abroad, was facilitated by a stipend that he received. At the end of his career, Svenonius was appointed Bishop of Lund and Vice-Chancellor of the university there. The bulk of his life's work was carried out at the Academy of Turku, but during the time he was completing his master's degree and immediately thereafter he migrated between Turku, Stockholm and Uppsala in an attempt to convince as many financial patrons as possible of his talents and to earn a living by tutoring able young noblemen and maintaining a private theological college. He succeeded in his most important goal and received the significant Gyllenhielm stipend. His personal agency ensured him a living and turned his activities in a new direction. The stipend enabled him to undertake independent work and thus to study abroad. However, after receiving his master's degree, he did not enrol again at the University of Uppsala, which would anyway have been futile after he had been appointed as an assistant teacher in theology.¹⁹

Foreign seats of learning did their best to attract young men from Sweden to study there. The seduction also embodied political ends, as is illustrated by the relationship between the 24-year-old Gabriel Kurck (1630–1712), the son of Jöns Kurck, the President of Turku Court of Appeal, and some professors at Oxford. Kurck was scarcely aware what was going on around him one day when the glib Oxford professors made him out to be a distinguished and learned master.[20] No doubt, the English academics though that the young baron was an important individual agent who would not only promote travel to study at Oxford when he got back to his own country but also as a future influential figure in the state administration would otherwise, too, regard the English with favour.

## *The destinations and durations of the travels*

In the sixteenth century, because of the Reformation and general unrest, the foreign studies of Swedish students became concentrated in the Baltic region. The most popular universities were those of Wittenberg, Greifswald and Rostock, and these still maintained their position in the seventeenth century, despite the fact that Swedish students were pouring into Dutch universities like Leiden. At least 800 young men travelled from Sweden to Holland to study mathematics, law, philology, and medicine. There they could also learn about trade and diplomacy, but for matters like courtly manners and other accomplishments pertaining to the life of the nobility they preferred to go elsewhere, mainly to England and France. In the mid-seventeenth century, young Swedish noblemen rushed to Paris, where they learned practical skills like fencing, dancing, singing, games and languages.[21]

The view of Turku was expressed in Professor Mikael Wexionius' speech at the inauguration of the Academy of Turku in 1640, when he proposed that the Academy of Turku should attain the scholarly position and esteem that the old European universities enjoyed. In connection with this, he referred to the leading prestigious seats of learning in the disciplines of theology (Wittenberg, Helmstedt, Rostock), law (Marburg, Altdorf, Leipzig, Jena) and medicine (Padua, Freiburg, Strassburg, Paris).[22] After the Thirty Years War, popular destinations were Helmstedt, Strassburg and Altdorf.

Wexionius' information was not matched by reality: for theological reasons, the Swedes had favoured the Universities of Wittenberg, Rostock, Greifswald (both on the Baltic coast), Jena, and Helmstedt. Hardly anyone went to Leipzig, while there was a rush to the Netherlands, which became the most important destination of these peregrinations at the beginning of the century. That country and its universities could be accepted as reformed, and its political, economic and doctrinal development were regarded as hitherto unparalleled. Leiden was particularly important because learning in the fields of mathematics, jurisprudence (natural law was an admirably suitable subject for future servants of the state), political science and medicine was of a high level in the university. Moreover, it was easy to combine theory with practice there (for example mathematics with fortification technology).[23]

Swedish students thus favoured Leiden, Greifswald, Wittenberg and Rostock, and two thirds of those who went abroad to study in the seventeenth century made their way to these universities. The next most popular group

Table 1: Nobles (A) and commoners (B) who had studied at the Academy of Turku and pursued their studies at foreign universities between 1641 and 1700.

| University | 1641–1660 A | B | 1661–1680 A | B | 1681–1700 A | B | Total A | B | A & B |
|---|---|---|---|---|---|---|---|---|---|
| Greifswald | 9 | 1 | 5 | - | 8 | - | 22 | - | 22 |
| Leiden | 7 | 4 | 4 | 2 | 5 | - | 16 | 6 | 22 |
| Wittenberg | 3 | - | 6 | - | 12 | - | 21 | - | 21 |
| Rostock | 7 | - | 2 | - | 6 | - | 15 | - | 15 |
| Jena | 2 | - | 4 | 1 | 6 | - | 12 | 1 | 13 |
| Oxford | 5 | 1 | 2 | 1 | 3 | - | 10 | 2 | 12 |
| Giessen | - | - | 1 | 2 | 3 | - | 4 | 2 | 6 |
| Leipzig | 3 | - | 1 | - | 1 | - | 5 | - | 5 |
| Strassburg | 1 | 1 | 2 | - | 1 | - | 4 | 1 | 5 |
| Helmstedt | 1 | - | 3 | - | - | - | 4 | - | 4 |
| Halle | - | - | - | - | 3 | 1 | 3 | 1 | 4 |
| Paris | - | 2 | 1 | 1 | - | - | 1 | 3 | 4 |
| Königsberg | 1 | - | - | - | 2 | - | 3 | - | 3 |
| Tübingen | - | - | 1 | 1 | 1 | - | 2 | 1 | 3 |
| Heidelberg | - | - | - | 3 | - | - | - | 3 | 3 |
| Altdorf | - | - | 1 | - | 1 | - | 2 | - | 2 |
| Basel | - | - | 1 | - | - | - | 1 | - | 1 |
| Cambridge | - | - | - | - | 1 | - | 1 | - | 1 |
| Kiel | - | - | - | - | 1 | - | 1 | - | 1 |
| Utrecht | - | 1 | - | - | - | - | - | 1 | 1 |
| Marburg | - | - | - | 1 | - | - | - | 1 | 1 |
| Total | 39 | 10 | 34 | 12 | 51 | 1 | 127 | 22 | 149 |

Source: Database of persons studying abroad 1640–1700 (University of Jyväskylä, Department of History and Ethnology).

consisted of the Universities of Helmstedt, Jena and Leipzig, although the popularity of the last mentioned seat of learning declined at the end of the Thirty Years War.[24] About 80 students (55 percent of the total population) who had studied at the Academy of Turku enrolled at the Universities of Leiden, Greifswald, Wittenberg and Rostock and 25 (17 percent) at Helmstedt, Jena and Leipzig (see Table 1).

More interesting appears to be the distribution of the degrees obtained abroad. A little under 40 bachelor's and master's degrees, licentiates and doctorates were awarded to students who had previously studied at the Academy of Turku. In other words, every fourth student from there who went abroad obtained a degree. Of these cases, four are very uncertain assumptions based on mentions that the person in question had obtained a master's degree "abroad" or "in Germany".[25] For example, there is no information about exactly where or when Johan Wanzonius (d. 1717), who had studied at the Academy of Turku for a long time, received a licentiate in medicine, but the degree itself is mentioned in a dedication in a dissertation written at the University of Lund in 1695.[26] Most of the information is probably valid, although in a few other connections a reference to studies

281

abroad suggests a fraudulent attempt to promote a person's career. All in all, the number of master's degrees awarded by foreign universities to young men who had started their studies at the Academy of Turku is significant, since, according to Lars H. Niléhn, in the period between 1640 and 1699 this degree was awarded to only 179 students (including those from Turku) at the most important seats of learning: the Universities of Wittenberg, Leiden and Greifswald.[27]

Of the prestigious seats of learning mentioned by professor Mikael Wexionius, really only Wittenberg was popular. Six young men from Turku obtained M.A. degrees from there.[28] In addition, Petter Carstenius (1647–1712) obtained a master's degree in 1674 at the University of Rostock, which was described as "theologically excellent". Most commonly, a master's degree was obtained at the University of Greifswald after a few months' or even days' study; the students had already been written their theses when they enrolled at Greifswald! The university remained a favourite into the 1670s.[29] A few master's degrees were awarded to men from Turku at the Universities of Basel, Oxford, Königsberg and Giessen. Isak Laurbecchius' licentiate in theology was awarded at the University of Altdorf in 1699 and his doctorate at the same university in 1707.[30] There were no degrees in law at Marburg, Altdorf or Leipzig, but Mikael Wisius (1624–1679), who as a protégé of Wexionius had obtained a master's degree at Turku in 1647, enrolled first at Rostock and then at Jena, where he studied from 1652 to 1656. There he was twice president at the defence of doctoral dissertations before he was made Doctor of Roman and Canon Law in 1656. Others became doctors of law and of Roman and canon law at Oxford and Rostock.[31] The students who went abroad to take degrees in medicine went to Leiden rather than Padua, Freiburg, Strassburg or Paris. The degree of Doctor of Medicine was conferred on Johan Munkthelius (1618–1674) in 1649, Olof Figrelius (1629–1671) in 1663 and Erik Tillands (1640–1693) in 1670.[32]

However the real purpose behind these peregrinations was not so much to obtain degrees as to enrol at the universities. The students kept travel albums (*albae amicorum*) and journals and maintained contact with their sponsors. The travel albums and journals comprised accounts of daily events, poems and messages of congratulations and good wishes. These together with the autographs of important university authorities afforded evidence of a European network of connections and complemented the *curricula vitae* in the albums.[33] On return, the owner of the album could use these to further his career and personal agency.

The study trip of Johan Gezelius the younger took in the universities and scholarly communities of Copenhagen, Kiel, Hamburg, Groningen, Amsterdam, Utrecht, Leiden, Oxford, Cambridge, London, Paris, Lyon, Geneva, Savoy, Basel, Strassburg, Cologne, Frankfurt, Erfurt, Jena, Leipzig, Wittenberg and Berlin. It is obvious that in many of these places he only had time to fill in his journal and his travel album. However, he stayed longer, sometimes months, in the most important places (Hamburg, Cambridge, Paris and Leipzig). The principal object of the whole journey was to study and become acquainted with the languages and literature of the Orient and the Bible. In addition to these, he studied modern languages like English,

French and Spanish.³⁴ Paris offered a theologian an opportunity to study and do research on Hebrew and Rabbinical literature, but for the young nobleman it was a place where he could acquaint himself with court manners and the language of diplomacy.³⁵ Sophisticated manners and modern languages paved the way for his personal activities.

The students, who have been well prepared intellectually and spiritually, had no trepidations about becoming acquainted with Calvinist or Catholic universities and their teachers or participating in the instruction that these institutions offered. Such seats of leaning included the Calvinist-controlled Universities of Frankfurt an der Oder, Utrecht and Groningen.

The afore-mentioned Enevald Svenonius used his foreign study effectively. As a young student, he had ranted against study abroad and the adulation of foreign universities, but on receipt of a stipend he spent over three years at Wittenberg. In addition, in the course of less than half a year in 1654 he travelled around Bohemia, Hungary, Austria and Holland mainly on foot, calling in at 24 universities including those of Prague, Erfurt, Jena, Leipzig, Altdorf, Strassburg, Freiburg im Breisgau, Giessen, Marburg, Cologne, Leiden, Amsterdam and Utrecht.³⁶

## The travels and careers of noblemen

The peregrinations of young noblemen (*Kavalierstour*, *Grand Tour*) clearly changed in the course of the seventeenth century along with changes in the noble ideal of *l'honnête homme*. At the beginning of the century, the goal of noblemen studying abroad was to obtain a strong and varied scholarly grounding in the humanities. Towards the end of the century, the objectives became more practical and thus directly served the goals of the administration, the army and the judiciary and thereby the maintenance of Sweden as a great power in Europe. In his study travels, a young nobleman was expected to acquaint himself not only with the ways of thinking of different peoples but also with economic matters (trade), governance and administration (politics), diplomacy, jurisprudence, oratory, history and mathematics (applied, for example, in fortification technology).³⁷ The young nobles were 16–20 years of age when they set off on their travels.³⁸ It was a venture that allowed them to reassert their position in society and as office-holders to distinguish themselves from other civil servants. Study in domestic universities brought merit, but foreign study brought more. In this respect, it was irrelevant whether their eventual careers were in the military or in the civil administration.³⁹

Few of the young noblemen who studied at the Academy of Turku enrolled at foreign universities (Table 1). They certainly made educational trips, but they were not interested in studying on a regular basis. Not all the young nobles who attended the Academy of Turku were even entered in the student registers of that university. One of the original objectives of study at the university was to provide an aristocratic education and hence a grounding in the humanities. The nobility, in particular, being assured of their economic and cultural mission, believed that sophisticated manners, virtues and industriousness would be passed down to the common people through their chivalrous example.[40] Of course this conception was directly connected with the social ideal of the age, which emphasised the position of the nobility, but in the case of Turku the implementation of this idea seemed ridiculous. The nobility in Finland was small in number: 250–300 young noblemen were registered as students at the Academy of Turku or attended the university privately. The process was furthered by an unofficial "collegium for noblemen" composed of language and other tutors employed to mentor the young noblemen.[41] Of these noble students, only 21 went abroad and enrolled at some seat of learning (and in a few cases at two). Between 1641 and 1660, four enrolled at the University of Leiden, two at the University of Paris and one each at the Universities of Greifswald, Strassburg, Utrecht and Oxford, which was turning from being a training establishment for clergymen into one for functionaries. In the years 1661–1680, three enrolled at Heidelberg, two at Leiden and Giessen and one at Oxford, Jena, Tübingen and Marburg. The "Great Reduction" (*den stora reduktionen*, the recuperation of fiefs by the Crown from the high nobility) brought an end to the peregrinations of the nobles. In the last two decades of the century, only one young nobleman travelled abroad to study, and he sought out the security of Halle. The young nobles were raised to be *honnêtes hommes* without any experience of foreign lands and their seats of learning.

The Gyldenstolpes offer a good example of the Turku noblemen who travelled abroad in the seventeenth century. They exuded the noble ideal, which their father, Mikael Wexionius, Professor of Practical Philosophy and Jurisprudence at the Academy of Turku, who was ennobled in 1650 with the name Gyldenstolpe, adapted into a maxim to suit local conditions. Of Mikael Gyldenstolpe's sons, Gabriel (1640–1666) enrolled at the Academy of Turku when he was nine years old, Nils (1642–1709) when he was seven and Daniel (1645–1691) when he was four. They were followed in 1660 by Samuel (1649–1692), who enrolled as a student when he was 11 years of age, and then by Karl (d. 1710) and Gustaf in 1665. Each one of the sons received a stipend at some stage in his studies, but only Daniel and Samuel travelled abroad to study. Nils made a successful career in the state administration and as an ambassador. The high points in his career, sitting as Lord Marshall (*Lantmarskalk*) at the Diet and culminating as Chancery President *(kanslipresident)*, would not have required study abroad, although it must be noted that he had become acquainted with the customs of other peoples in connection with his ambassadorial duties. The military careers of Gabriel, Karl and Gustaf did not presuppose foreign studies.[42]

Daniel Gyldenstolpe defended a thesis in 1660, studied for five more years at Turku, and then set off to study abroad, travelling to Germany, France, Italy, Spain and Holland. The trip covered everything a young man that might be expected to acquaint himself with, and the information accumulated in the course of it could be regarded as being of benefit to the state. On returning from it in 1667, Daniel Gyldenstolpe obtained a post as secretary to Count Per Brahe, after which he was appointed assistant judge of the Noble Class (*assessor i adelsklassen*) at Turku Court of Appeal when his father died and made a judge of a rural district court *(häradshövding)* in 1675. There was little use for his familiarity with foreign peoples in these offices.⁴³ Mikael Gyldenstolpe undertook a four-year study trip in the 1630s after taking a master's degree at the University of Uppsala. In the course of his travels he visited the Universities of Wittenberg, Marburg, Groningen and Leiden. While it did not directly set an example, it benefited in a significant way the Academy of Turku, where he was a leading professor before his career in the judiciary.⁴⁴ The study trip of Daniel Gyldenstolpe rather corresponded with the two made by Per Brahe, but in a more practical form.⁴⁵ The journeys were ideal and of benefit to the state, the nobility and also for example to arrangements for protégés, such as members of the Gyldenstolpe family.⁴⁶ One might say that through his example Per Brahe (1602–1680) created the guidelines for how members of the nobility should plan their journeys. These principles Mikael Gyldenstolpe then passed on to the Academy of Turku, from which it was not possible to compete for royal stipends in the same way as it was in Uppsala.

One example of this is Samuel Gyldenstolpe, who studied for a long time at Turku but only managed to produce two orations. The subject of one was imposing: in *De illustrissima Braheorum prosopia etc.* (published in 1671) Samuel praised the illustrious Brahe family, which had been prominent ever since pagan times and eminent for its long history and its exemplary exploits, as indeed it continued to be. The orations, particularly the one mentioned above, sufficed to bring Samuel a professorship in practical philosophy in 1671, when he had reached the age of 22. He led an unruly and immoral life and did no research or tutoring. And the fact that as a nobleman he had not travelled abroad was also noticed. However, this deficiency was corrected in 1676. Thereafter he continued to hold his professorial chair, though he was suspended for a while for fornication. The university got rid of him in 1681, when he was appointed as a district judge.⁴⁷

Typically, a young nobleman was accompanied on his travels by an older mentor (*præceptor*) or a valet, who took care of his purse, advised and guided him, and naturally, being himself without means, profited from the journey by being able to tour round Europe. The study trip of Henning Johan Grass (1649–1713), the son of Gustaf Grass (d. 1694), the Vice-President of Turku Court of Appeal, and his travel companion, Erik Falander (1640–1697), who was the son of a pastor, is interesting. The journey lasted two years and took in Holland and Germany, where both were enrolled as students in the registers of the University of Giessen. When they set off, Henning Johan Grass was 19 years old and Erik Falander 28. In this respect, they constituted an ideal pair. On his return, Grass rode on his father's reputation and served for a while as a judge. He was eventually made a baron, again thanks to paternal influence.⁴⁸ Erik Falander's path was different, as we shall soon see.

## *The studies and careers of commoners*

The social composition of those who went abroad to study directly from Turku or via another university (Table 2) corresponded proportionally better with that of all those who studied at the university than was perhaps the case in other universities, since out of those whose home backgrounds are known, 37 had fathers who were members of the Clergy, 12 belonged to the Burghers' estate (tradesmen and craftsmen), 19 were functionaries and non-noble military officers and five were peasants. Only 12 had fathers who were members of the nobility.

Table 2. The social backgrounds of persons studying abroad 1640–1700.

|  | Nobles | Clergy | Burghers | Functionaries | Peasants | Total |
|---|---|---|---|---|---|---|
| Departing directly from Turku | 5 | 16 | 10 | 10 | 5 | 46 |
| Departing from elsewhere in Sweden | 7 | 21 | 2 | 9 | 3 | 42 |
| Total | 12 | 37 | 12 | 19 | 8 | 88 |

Source: Database of persons studying abroad 1640–1700.

There were almost the same proportions of all students at the Academy of Turku, although there were more sons of clergymen and fewer of burghers and functionaries.[49]

After their studies, 42 pursued careers as clergymen, professors or teachers, 42 ended up in the judiciary, 24 in the civil service and six in the military, 16 pursued no career at all while for one reason or another. A few failed to return to their native country and a few died before entering on a professional career. Successful high-ranking careers were rare, and thus the returns on the financial investments were often poor.

Table 3. The later careers of persons who studied abroad 1641–1700.

|  | Clergy | Judiciary | Civil service | Military | No career[50] | Total |
|---|---|---|---|---|---|---|
| Departing directly from Turku | 19 | 13 | 4 | 3 | 9 | 48 |
| Departing from elsewhere in Sweden | 23 | 11 | 14 | 3 | 7 | 58 |
| Total | 42 | 24 | 18 | 6 | 16 | 106 |

Source: Database of persons studying abroad 1640–1700.

Most of the Turku students ended up in the clergy, and only a fraction in the judiciary and civil service. Thus their studies abroad did benefit them: they made it possible for them to pursue a professional career and in a few rare cases led to ennoblement for their services as servants of the state.[51] One interesting feature is the fact that those Turku students who went abroad to study via the University of Uppsala tended to follow their fathers in their careers. There was little social mobility, but within the different social ranks, the careers of those who studied abroad appear to have been better.

Erik Falander benefited from his journey in a significant way. When he set off, he was a bachelor of philosophy and a junior lawyer at Turku Court of Appeal. When he returned, he appointed as an assistant teacher in the Faculty of Philosophy, a junior *lagman* (lawspeaker) and soon thereafter Professor of Hebrew and Greek. In 1682 he obtained the vacant professorship of jurisprudence, was appointed as an assistant judge at the Court of Appeal and, after being ennobled, Assistant Judge of the Noble Class. Erik Falander-Tigerstedt even served for some time in the 1690s as the acting county governor.[52]

Although several students took degrees at foreign universities and even did scholarly research at them, the results served other purposes that were set by the state. Enevald Svenonius, who studied for a long time at Wittenberg, defended several theses on subjects dealing with heresy.[53] Of those who had studied at Turku, Bengt and Gustaf Queckfeldt (1628–1712), the sons of the country treasurer Gustaf Queckfeldt, had commenced their studies at Uppsala, defended theses on law at Turku under the supervision of Gyldenstolpe and went to Oxford in 1655, considerably earlier than the Swedish nobles, who rushed there in the 1660s. At Oxford, they became doctors of law in 1656. The elder of the brothers was then appointed as an assistant judge at Tartu Court of Appeal, while the younger continued his studies at Helmstedt before being recruited as a secretary in the Royal Chancery (*kungliga kansli*) in 1659. He was made an assistant judge at Göta Court of Appeal in 1662, was ennobled in 1675 and became the court counsellor of Queen Christina and commissiary general (*överintendent*) in Norrköping in the 1680s.[54]

Ambrosius Nidulius-Nidelberg (d. 1689), the son of the Treasurer (*kammererare*) of the County of Visingsborg, who enrolled at the Academy of Turku in 1658 and received a stipend for six years (which is not surprising in view of the fact that his family had served the Chancellor of the Academy Per Brahe in Visingsborg) pursued a career that corresponded with the hopes of his sponsors. He studied for a while in 1660 at Jena, which was regarded as an advanced seat of learning in the discipline of jurisprudence, then returned to Turku, defended a thesis (*Judex brevi oratione laudatus*) in 1661, underwent court training at Göta Court of Appeal, wrote a thesis on the preservation of the state and the monarchy in particular (*De conservatione reipublicae et praesertim monarchiae*, printed in 1665) under the supervision of Svenonius and Axel Kempe (1623–1682), which brought him a bachelorship in philosophy in 1664, and was made an assistant judge in 1684. All in all, he was regarded as a man with a thorough academic grounding who had published in numerous different fields.[55] In addition, while in the service of Count Brahe, he translated important political and economic work, thereby promoting the social aspirations of the high aristocracy and the economic goals of the great state.[56]

One exciting character who clearly broke the class barriers between the estates should be mentioned: Daniel Sarcovius (1661–1704), the son of a caretaker (*vaktmästare*) of the Academy of Turku, enrolled in the university at the age of 16 in 1677. He delivered a eulogy in 1679 and was in receipt of a stipend for several years. He defended several theses before setting out to study abroad in the years 1684–1687 in Holland, England and Germany. Thereafter he wrote several other theses, one of which was on the subject of the oath. On finishing his studies, he became headmaster of Tallinn School and then Professor of Logic and Theoretical Physics at the University of Tartu.[57]

## *The tools yielded by foreign study in battling against heresy and defending a united realm*

The travels to study abroad may be regarded as mirroring the social development that took place in the seventeenth century. During that century, the administration and economy of Sweden developed rapidly. Both of these areas required a good educational system and the formation of experts. It is precisely these social requirements and the tradition of a pan-European culture that obligated those who belonged to particular social groups to travel abroad and visit foreign universities that Lars H. Niléhn regards as being the major background factors behind this development.[58] That is certainly true, but a more exact analysis reveals something else.

The yield of the study trips abroad lay essentially in the fact that it enabled the professors and bishops to declaim and battle against heresy and to defend what constituted the intellectual core of the great state: an orthodox Lutheran doctrine. There would have been great fear in both Sweden and Finland of a Catholic Counter-Reformation, of syncretic notions, Calvinism, radical Pietism and Cartesianism.[59] Those who set off to study abroad were inoculated against heresy, and they mainly adhered to the same convictions when they returned. The greatest battle against heretics was waged in the universities. There the weapons of orthodoxy obtained while studying abroad were also used against the arms of heresy acquired on these travels.

This picture is corroborated by the enrolments in foreign universities. The commoners went to study at Lutheran universities that were characteristically centres for the training of clergy and theological research, although in the course of their travels they sometimes dropped in at Catholic seats of learning but did not enrol in them. The nobles, by contrast, were unconcerned with confessional questions.[60]

It is illustrative that Enevald Svenonius, who as a student at Turku, had ranted fiercely against foreign universities and study abroad, wrote his first thesis in 1641 under the supervision of Mikael Wexionius on the subject of the wisdom required by legislators and statesmen, in 1646 defended a thesis in Uppsala on the virtues of the hero, and supervised three theses in the 1640s dealing with the legal calling to state office, moral corruption and natural knowledge, became extremely enthusiastic when he was offered the opportunity to travel abroad to study. At Wittenberg, he carried out precisely the kind of research that would serve religious and Swedish Lutheran unity. By contrast, the dissertation (*Ohole Apdno sive jubiles Antichristi Romani*, *ipsus exitium*) written by Johan Gezelius the younger after his study abroad dealt with the festivals and destruction of the Roman Antichrist. It exuded the learning and spirit of combat that he had acquired on his travels.[61]

Of course, the subject can also be examined from a different point of view. The task of the universities was to impart knowledge of God and nature and direct young people towards sensible and decent behaviour. This was an important political mission that served social morality and obedience to authority. Thus the studies were used to provide the kind of notions that supported whatever administration happened to be in power, and on the basis of these ideas academic research studies were written about subjects like the significance of politics, administration, the form of government and virtue. In the 1640s and 1650s, there was an emphasis on the sharing of power, while in the latter half of the seventeenth century autocracy was emphasised; all in all, university studies prepared young men for their future activities in society.[62]

The state, the Crown and the church got what they wanted. However, from the point of view of personal agency, foreign studies would not seem to have played a very significant role. It probably did speed up and facilitate advancement in the students' careers since it enabled them to demonstrate that they possessed skills and networks of connections that those who had only studied at Turku lacked. This conclusion is also supported by the fact that nearly all those who went abroad returned to seek posts. Those who did not return, fell by the wayside on their travels.[63]

Foreign study did not really advance social mobility between the estates. Other values than those that were publically proclaimed were cherished within the society of the estates. Career advancement required money, supporters, patrons and family connections. In this sense, the system was thoroughly corrupt and nepotistic; the posts in the civil service and the judiciary were filled according to other criteria than educational merits. One's family and a patron counted for more in one's curriculum vitae than academic studies.

The research on which this publication is based was funded by the Academy of Finland (grant no. 137741).

## Notes

1 Seppo J. Salminen, *Enevaldus Svenonius I*. Suomen kirkkohistoriallisen seuran toimituksia 106 (Helsinki: The Finnish Society of Church History, 1978), p. 44; Simo Heininen, Jussi Nuorteva, "Finland". In: Jokipii, Mauno, Nummela, Ilkka (eds), *Ur nordisk kulturhistoria. Universitetsbesöken i utlandet före 1660*. Studia historica Jyväskyläensia 22,1 (Jyväskylä: Jyväskylän yliopisto, 1981), pp. 67–118; Lars Niléhn, "Sverige". In: Jokipii, Mauno, Nummela, Ilkka (eds), *Ur nordisk kulturhistoria. Universitetsbesöken i utlandet före 1660*. Studia historica Jyväskyläensia 22,1 (Jyväskylä: Jyväskylän yliopisto, 1981), pp. 167–208; Lars H. Niléhn, *Peregrinatio academica. Det svenska samhället och de utrikes studieresorna under 1600-talet*. Bibliotheca historica Lundensis 54 (Lund: Liber/Gleerup, 1983), pp. 86–89, 154–155; Matti Klinge, "Perustaminen ja tarkoitus". In: *Helsingin yliopisto 1640–1990*

1. *Kuninkaallinen Turun akatemia* (Helsinki: Helsingin yliopisto, Otava, 1987), p. 74; Petri Karonen, "Oxenstierna, Axel (1583–1654) valtakunnankansleri, Kemiön vapaaherra, kreivi". In: *Suomen kansallisbiografia 7*. Studia Biographica 3:7 (Helsinki: The Finnish Literature Society, 2006), pp. 386–389.
2. Jussi Nuorteva, *Suomalaisten ulkomainen opinkäynti ennen Turun akatemian perustamista 1640*. Bibliotheca historica 27 (Helsinki: Finnish Historical Society, 1997), pp. 360–361, 373.
3. http://www.helsinki.fi/ylioppilasmatrikkeli/. Hereafter: Kotivuori, Ylioppilasmatrikkeli. Lars H. Niléhn (*Peregrinatio*, pp. 35, 157) addressed the same kind of questions in his doctoral dissertation but paid scant attention to the broader questions examined here.
4. The majority consists of those who went directly abroad from Turku. However, I also examine a second group of students who first moved from Turku to another Swedish university and from there to a foreign one. In this sense, the distinction does not reflect the actuality of the age, because the realm was a single unit and movement within its confines was therefore considerable. The basis for the division into two groups, however, lies in personal agency: the channels of funding differed greatly in different parts of the kingdom. The proportion of those who studied at Turku out of all Swedes who went abroad to study in the period 1640–1700 was small. This continued a centuries-old tradition. In the period from the 1610s to the 1630s, over 900 young men from Sweden studied at German universities, of whom only a small percentage were Finns. Kustavi Grotenfelt, "Suomalaiset ylioppilaat ulkomaan yliopistoissa ennen v. 1640. 1". In: *Historiallinen Arkisto 13* (Helsinki: Finnish Historical Society, 1893), pp. 92–125; Kustavi Grotenfelt, "Suomalaiset ylioppilaat ulkomaan yliopistoissa ennen v. 1640. 2". In: *Historiallinen Arkisto 17* (Helsinki: Finnish Historical Society, 1901–1902), pp. 277–322; Lars Niléhn, "Universiteten efter reformationen". In: Jokipii, Mauno, Nummela, Ilkka (eds), *Ur nordisk kulturhistoria. Universitetsbesöken i utlandet före 1660*. Studia historica Jyväskyläensia 22,1 (Jyväskylä: Jyväskylän yliopisto, 1981), pp. 15–25; Niléhn, *Peregrinatio*, p. 245; John Strömberg, *Studenter, nationer och universitet. Studenternas härkomst och levnadsbanor vid Akademin i Åbo 1640–1808*. Skrifter utgivna av Svenska litteratursällskapet i Finland 601. (Helsingfors: Svenska litteratursällskapet i Finland, 1996), pp. 54–56, 59–60; Nuorteva, *Suomalaisten opinkäynti*, p. 375.
5. Klinge, "Perustaminen ja tarkoitus", p. 73; Nuorteva, *Suomalaisten opinkäynti*, pp. 359–360; Kotivuori, Ylioppilasmatrikkeli.
6. Niléhn, *Peregratinatio*, pp. 137, 149, 154; Jakob Christensson, "Studieresorna". In: Christensson, Jakob (ed.), *Signums svenska kulturhistoria. Stormaktstiden* (Lund: Signum, 2005), p. 171.
7. Klinge, "Perustaminen ja tarkoitus", pp. 67, 90–91; Raija Sarasti-Wilenius, "De peregrinatione – Näkökulmia ulkomaan matkailuun Suomen latinankielisissä lähteissä". In: *Tieteessä tapahtuu 16:1*, pp. 16–22; Raija Sarasti-Wilenius, *Dear Brother, Cracious Maecenas. Latin Letters of the Gyldenstolpe Brothers (1661–1680)*. Annales Academiae Scientiarum Fennicæ, humaniora 374. (Helsinki: FASL, 2015), pp. 14–15.
8. Nuorteva, *Suomalaisten opinkäynti*, pp. 419–434; Christensson, "Studieresorna", p. 172; Pentti Laasonen, *Vanhan ja uuden rajamaastossa. Johan Gezelius vanhempi ja kulttuurivaikuttajana*. Historiallisia Tutkimuksia 245 (Helsinki: The Finnish Literature Society, 2009), pp. 46–47, 72. In fact, it was so clear that the policy is known to have changed in the course of seventeenth century.
9. Sven Göransson, *De svenska studieresorna och religiösa kontrollen från reformationstiden till frihetstiden*. Uppsala universitets årsskrift 1951:8 (Uppsala, 1951), pp. 84–99; Niléhn, *Peregrinatio*, pp. 90–102, 126, 154–155.
10. Laasonen, *Vanhan ja uuden rajamaastossa*, pp. 62–63.

11 Kotivuori, Ylioppilasmatrikkeli: Lars Sierman, Magnus Sierman, Nils Sierman.
12 Christensson, "Studieresorna", p. 191.
13 Salminen, *Enevaldus Svenonius I*, p. 136. This practice was also in use in other dioceses, for example in Arboga in the 1630s. Niléhn, *Peregrinatio*, p. 153.
14 Database of persons who studied abroad 1640–1700 (University of Jyväskylä, Department of History and Ethnology). See also Niléhn, *Peregrinatio*, p. 245; Jussi Nuorteva, "Lang, Jakob (1648–1716) Linköpingin piispa, Tallinnan piispa, Narvan superintendentti, teologian tohtori". In: *Suomen kansallisbiografia 5*. Studia Biographica 3:5 (Helsinki: The Finnish Literature Society, 2005), pp. 724–726; Iiro Kajanto, "Lund, David (1657–1729) Viipurin piispa, Växjön piispa, pyhien kielten professori, teologian professori". In: *Suomen kansallisbiografia 6*. Studia Biographica 3:6 (Helsinki: The Finnish Literature Society, 2005), pp. 317–315.
15 Johan Jakob Tengström, *Chronologiska Förteckningar och Anteckningar öfver Finska universitetets fordna procancellerer samt öfver faculteternas medlemmar och adjuncter, från universitetets stiftelse inemot dess andra sekularår* (Helsingfors: G. O. Wasenius, 1836), pp. 25–26; Kotivuori, Ylioppilasmatrikkeli: Johan Ketarmannus.
16 It is illustrative that one of the most distinguished Bishops of Turku and Vice-Chancellors of the Academy of Turku, Johan Gezelius the younger, the son of Johan Gezelius the elder, a bishop and vice-chancellor, followed in the footsteps of his father. He enrolled at the University of Uppsala in 1661, when his father received his doctorate there. Johan the younger was entered into the student registers of the Academy of Turku in 1665. There he defended two theses before returning to Uppsala, where he again defended two theses. In Uppsala, he received a royal stipend for a study trip to Germany, Holland, Oxford, France and Switzerland. Thanks to this, he was able to study abroad for nearly four years. On returning to Turku, he was appointed to the post of Professor of Theology, and he defended a doctoral dissertation on that subject. He became Bishop of Turku and Vice-Chancellor of the Academy of Turku after the death of his father in 1690. A. A. Stiernman, *Aboa literata [1719]. Turun akatemian kirjallisuus*. Suomennos Reijo Pitkäranta. Suomalaisen Kirjallisuuden Seuran Toimituksia 518 (Helsinki: The Finnish Literature Society, 1990), pp. 93–94; Niléhn, *Peregrinatio*, p. 54; Kotivuori, Ylioppilasmatrikkeli: Johan Gezelius nuorempi; Laasonen, *Vanhan ja uuden rajamaastossa*, pp. 28–82.
17 Kotivuori, Ylioppilasmatrikkeli: Nils Bergius, Isak Laurbecchius; Esko M. Laine, "Laurbecchius, Isaacus (noin 1677–1716) pietistiteologi, teologian tohtori". In: *Suomen kansallisbiografia 5*. Studia Biographica 3:5 (Helsinki: The Finnish Literature Society, 2005), pp. 765–766; Nils Bergius used his royal stipend to travel to Berlin, Wittenberg, Leipzig, Dresden, Prague, Vienna, Frankfurt am Main, Giessen, central Germany, Holland, England, Paris, Greifswald, Holstein and Denmark between 1682 and 1687. The most intense period of his official studies was in 1684. In that year, he first enrolled as a student at Giessen, where he obtained a master's degree with his pro gradu thesis. Later in the same year, he went to Leiden, Oxford and Cambridge, in each of which he enrolled as a student.
18 Kotivuori, Ylioppilasmatrikkeli: Daniel Rosander.
19 Salminen, *Enevald Svenonius I*, p. 57; Kotivuori, Ylioppilasmatrikkeli: Enevald Svenonius.
20 For example Kotivuori, Ylioppilasmatrikkeli: Gabriel Kurck; Liisa Lagerstam, *A Noble Life: the Cultural Biography of Gabriel Kurck (1630–1712)*. Suomalaisen tiedeakatemia toimituksia, Humaniora 349 (Helsinki: Finnish Academy of Science and Letters, 2007).
21 Niléhn, *Peregrinatio*, pp. 97–102; Nuorteva, *Suomalaisten opinkäynti*, p. 373; Christensson, "Studieresorna", pp. 172–173, 185–186. The transference of Greifswald under the administration of Sweden in 1637 supposedly led to the decline of the university. Klinge, "Perustaminen ja tarkoitus", p. 68; Christian

Callmer, *Svenska studenter i Wittenberg*. Skrifter utgivna av Personhistoriska samfundet 17. (Stockholm: Personhistoriska samfundet, 1976); Christian Callmer, *Svenska studenter i Rostock 1419-1828*. Ed. Maj Callmer. Skrifter utgivna av Personhistoriska samfundet 21. (Stockholm: Personhistoriska samfundet, 1988)
22  Klinge, "Perustaminen ja tarkoitus", p. 91.
23  Niléhn, *Peregrinatio*, pp. 79, 97-102, 121, 161-163; Nuorteva, *Suomalaisten opinkäynti*, pp. 386-408; Simo Heininen, "Tammelin, Lars (1669-1733) Turun piispa, Turun akatemian varakansleri, matematiikan professori". In: *Suomen kansallisbiografia 9*. Studia Biographica 3:9 (Helsinki: The Finnish Literature Society, 2007), pp. 617-618.
24  Niléhn, *Peregrinatio*, pp. 161-163.
25  Kotivuori, Ylioppilasmatrikkeli: Knut Becchius, Johan Törning, Olof Roselius, Johan Tzander, Jonas Emzenius.
26  Kotivuori, Ylioppilasmatrikkeli: Johan Wanzonius.
27  See Niléhn, *Peregrinatio*, p. 251.
28  Israel Starbecchius 1673, Joakim Wittstock 1682, Daniel Unger 1685, Nils Grip 1692, Anders Grip 1692, Anders Lundinus 1692.
29  Johan Klingius 1649, Magnus Klingius 1649, Arvid Grundelius 1650, Erik Halmenius 1652, Israel Krokius 1664, Måns Baaz 1666, Isak Browallius 1675.
30  A master's degree was obtained at Basel University by Jakob Wellinus in 1665, at Oxford by Johan Pontelius (1653) and Gabriel Kurck (1654), at Königsberg by Peter Ungius (1643), at Giessen by Nils Bergius (1684) and at Wittenberg by Samuel Florinus (1695).
31  Doctorates were conferred on Bengt and Gustaf Queckfeldt at Oxford in 1656, and a bachelor's degree was awarded to Georg Mikael Bapzihn at Rostock in 1696.
32  See Eeva Ruoff, "Til-Landz, Elias (1640-1693) lääketieteen professori." In: *Suomen kansallisbiografia 6*. Studia Biographica 3:6 (Helsinki: The Finnish Literature Society, 2005), pp. 817-819.
33  See Salminen, *Enevaldus Svenonius I*, pp. 136-137; Laasonen, *Vanhan ja uuden rajamaastossa*, p. 83.
34  Laasonen, *Vanhan ja uuden rajamaastossa*, pp. 49-82.
35  Nuorteva, *Suomalaisten opinkäynti*, pp. 417-419.
36  Stiernman, *Aboa literata*, p. 25; Tengström, Chornologiska Förteckningar och Anteckningar, p. 134; Salminen, *Enevaldus Svenonius I*, pp. 158-161.
37  Niléhn, *Peregrinatio*, pp. 90-102; Peter Englund, *Det hotade huset. Adliga föreställningar om samhället under stormaktstiden* (Stockholm: Atlantis, 1989); Peter Englund, *Suuren sodan vuodet*. Suom. Timo Hämäläinen (Helsinki: WSOY, 1996); Christensson, "Studieresorna", p. 176.
38  Nuorteva, *Suomalaisten opinkäynti*, p. 364.
39  Nuorteva, *Suomalaisten opinkäynti*, p. 383; Bo Eriksson, "Oeconomia. En lära om social ordning och sammanhållning. En diskussion kring greve Per Brahe d ä:s Oeconomia eller Hushållbok för ungt adelsfolk". In: Dahl, Gunnar, Österberg. Eva (red.), *Renässansens eliter. Maktmänniskor i Italien och Norden* (Lund: Nordic Academic Press, 2000), p. 154; Marko Hakanen, *Vallan verkostoissa. Per Brahe ja hänen klienttinsä 1600-luvun Ruotsin valtakunnassa*. Jyväskylä studies in humanities 157 (Jyväskylä: Jyväskylän yliopisto, 2011), pp. 127-128; Liisa Lagerstam, Jessica Parland-von Essen, "Aatelin kasvatus". In: Hanska, Jussi, Vainio-Korhonen, Kirsi (toim.), Suomen koulutuksen historia 1. Huoneentaulun maailma. Kasvatus ja koulutus Suomessa keskiajalta 1860-luvulle. Suomalaisen Kirjallisuuden Seuran Toimituksia 1266:1. (Helsinki: The Finnish Literature Society, 2010), pp. 197, 200-202. Cf. Niléhn, *Peregrinatio*, pp. 193-199, 267; David Gaunt, *Utbildning till statens tjänst. En kollektivbiografi av stormaktstidens hovrättsauskultanter*. Studia historica Upsaliensia 63. (Uppsala: Uppsala universitet, 1975); Svante

Norrhem, *Uppkomlingarna. Kanslitjänstemännen i 1600-talets Sverige och Europa.* Acta Universitatis Umensis, Umeå Studies in the Humanities 117. (Stockholm: Almqvist & Wiksell; 1993).
40 Niléhn, *Peregrinatio*, pp. 90–96, 143; Klinge, "Perustaminen ja tarkoitus", pp. 66–67.
41 John Strömberg, "Ylioppilaat". In: *Helsingin yliopisto 1640–1990 I. Kuninkaallinen Turun akatemia* (Helsinki: Helsingin yliopisto, Otava, 1987), pp. 322; Strömberg, *Studenter, nationer och universitet*, pp. 159–161.
42 Kotivuori, Ylioppilasmatrikkeli: Nils Gyldenstolpe, Karl Gyldenstolpe, Gustaf Gyldenstolpe; Hakanen, *Vallan verkostoissa*, pp. 107–108; Sarasti-Wilenius, *Dear Brother, Cracious Maecenas*, pp. 16–23.
43 Kotivuori, Ylioppilasmatrikkeli: Daniel Gyldenstolpe; Kustaa H. J. Vilkuna, *Neljä ruumista* (Helsinki: Teos, 2009), p. 191.
44 Kotivuori, Ylioppilasmatrikkeli: Mikael Wexionius-Gyldenstolpe.
45 Per Brahe visited Denmark, Germany, England, Italy, Saxony, Holland and Austria and the major cities in them on his travels. He studied languages at Giessen and other subjects at Padua and Bologna, and he learned to ride and fence in Strassburg. Kotivuori, Ylioppilasmatrikkeli: Per Brahe.
46 See for example Hakanen, *Vallan verkostoissa*, pp. 107–108.
47 Stiernman, *Aboa literata*, p. 102; Tengström, Chronologiska Förteckningar och Anteckningar, p. 140; Kotivuori, Ylioppilasmatrikkeli: Samuel Gyldenstolpe; Vilkuna, *Neljä ruumista*, pp. 221–223. It should be noted that Gyldenstolpe was the president of the defence of Petrus Hahn's dissertation *De majestate ejusque juribus, eccelestiasticis et politicis* in 1679.
48 Lagus, *Åbo hofrätts historia I*, pp. 249–255; Kotivuori, Ylioppilasmatrikkeli: Erik Falander-Tigerstedt, Henning Johan Grass; Vilkuna, *Neljä ruumista*, pp. 246, 286–287.
49 Strömberg, Ylioppilaat, p. 322; Strömberg, *Studenter, nationer och universitet*, pp. 161–165.
50 Died or disappeared during or shortly after the trip.
51 Of those who went abroad directly from Turku, Tigerstedt and Queckfeldt were ennobled, and of those who went by way of Uppsala, Jakob Sneckenberg (c. 1666–1702), Teofil Mellin (ennobled as Ehrenstierna) (1639–1689), Robert Kinninmundt (1647–1720), Lars Brommius (ennobled as Brommenstedt) (c. 1663–1723) and Sven Dimberg (ennobled as Dimborg) (c. 1661–1731). Database; Strömberg, "Ylioppilaat", p. 322; Strömberg, *Studenter, nationer och universitet*, pp. 171–179.
52 Lagus, *Åbo hofrätts historia I*, pp. 249–255; Kotivuori, Ylioppilasmatrikkeli: Erik Falander-Tigerstedt, Henning Johan Grass; Hannu Tapani Klami, "Tigerstedt, Ericus (1640–1697) hovioikeuden asessori, lainopin professori, pyhien kielten professori". In: *Suomen kansallisbiografia 9*. Studia Biographica 3:9 (Helsinki: The Finnish Literature Society, 2007), p. 787; Vilkuna, *Neljä ruumista*, pp. 246, 286–287.
53 Salminen, *Enevaldus Svenonius I*, p. 149.
54 Kotivuori, Ylioppilasmatrikkeli: Bengt Queckfeldt, Gustaf Queckfeldt.
55 Stiernman, *Aboa literata*, p. 73; Vilhelm Gabriel Lagus, *Åbo hofrätts historia I. Biographiska anteckningar om Åbo hofrätts presidenter och ledamöter; jemte förteckning öfver secreterare och advocat-fiscaler därstedes intill den 12. nov. 1823 då Hofrätten firade sin andra secular-fest* (Helsingfors: J. C. Frenckell & Son, 1832), pp. 247–249; Kotivuori, Ylioppilasmatrikkeli: Ambrosius Nidulius-Nidelberg; Vilkuna, *Neljä ruumista*, p. 286.
56 The works of Martinus Martin, Joost Schouten and Michael Hemmersamin (*Historia om thet Tartariske Krijget uthi Konunggarijket Sina, sampt theras seder, Sanfärdig Beskrijffning om Konungarijket Siam ja Kort berättelse om Wäst Indien eller America; som ellies kallas Nya werlden*) were published in Swedish in 1675 in Visingsborg.

57 Stiernman, *Aboa literata*, pp. 115–116; Friedrich Konrad Gadebusch, *Livländische Bibliothek nach alphabetischer Ordnung. Dritter Theil* (Riga: Hartknoch, 1777), pp. 84–86; Kotivuori, Ylioppilasmatrikkeli: Daniel Sarcovius.
58 Niléhn, *Peregrinatio*, pp. 193–199, 259–267, 297. See also Norrhem, *Uppkomlingarna. Kanslitjänstemännen i 1600-talets Sverige och Europa*.
59 For example Seppo J. Salminen, *Enevaldus Svenonius II (1664–1688)*. Suomen kirkkohistoriallisen seuran toimituksia 134 (Helsinki: The Finnish Society of Church History, 1985); Laasonen, *Vanhan ja uuden rajamaastossa*, pp. 103 ff.
60 On the universities, see Niléhn, *Peregrinatio*, pp. 118–131.
61 Stiernman, *Aboa literata*, p. 24; Salminen, *Enevaldus Svenonius I*, p. 43; Salminen, *Enevaldus Svenonius II*; Laasonen, *Vanhan ja uuden rajamaastossa*, pp. 84–95.
62 Stiernman, *Aboa literata*, pp. 73, 115–116; J. Vallinkoski, *Turun akatemian väitöskirjat I*. Helsingin yliopiston kirjaston julkaisuja 30 (Helsinki: Helsingin yliopisto, 1962–1966); Klinge, "Perustaminen ja tarkoitus", pp. 98–101.
63 Gaunt, *Utbildning till statens tjänst. En kollektivbiografi av stormaktstidens hovrättsauskultanter*; Norrhem, *Uppkomlingarna. Kanslitjänstemännen i 1600-talets Sverige och Europa*, pp. 36–39, 80–83, 120–121.

# Sources

Database of persons studying abroad 1640–1700: Kotivuori, Yrjö 2005: *Ylioppilasmatrikkeli 1640–1852*. [http://www.helsinki.fi/ylioppilasmatrikkeli]

## Literature

Callmer, Christian 1976: *Svenska studenter i Wittenberg*. Skrifter utgivna av Personhistoriska samfundet 17. Stockholm: Personhistoriska samfundet.
Callmer, Christian 1988: *Svenska studenter i Rostock 1419–1828*. Ed. Maj Callmer. Skrifter utgivna av Personhistoriska samfundet 21. Stockholm: Personhistoriska samfundet.
Christensson, Jakob 2005: "Studieresorna". In: Christensson, Jakob (red.), *Signums svenska kulturhistoria. Stormaktstiden*. Lund: Signum.
Englund, Peter 1989: *Det hotade huset. Adliga föreställningar om samhället under stormaktstiden*. Stockholm: Atlantis.
Englund, Peter 1996: *Suuren sodan vuodet*. Suom. Timo Hämäläinen. Helsinki: WSOY.
Eriksson, Bo 2000: "Oeconomia. En lära om social ordning och sammanhållning. En diskussion kring greve Per Brahe d ä:s Oeconomia eller Hushållbok för ungt adelsfolk". In: Red. Dahl, Gunnar, Österberg, Eva (red.), *Renässansens eliter. Maktmänniskor i Italien och Norden*. Lund: Nordic Academic Press.
Gadebusch, Friedrich Konrad 1777: *Livländische Bibliothek nach alphabetischer Ordnung. Dritter Theil*. Riga: Hartknoch.
Gaunt, David 1975: *Utbildning till statens tjänst. En kollektivbiografi av stormaktstidens hovrättsauskultanter*. Studia historica Upsaliensia 63. Uppsala: Uppsala universitet.
Grotenfelt, Kustavi 1893: "Suomalaiset ylioppilaat ulkomaan yliopistoissa ennen v. 1640. 1", *Historiallinen Arkisto 13*. Helsinki: Finnish Historical Society.
Grotenfelt, Kustavi 1901–1902: "Suomalaiset ylioppilaat ulkomaan yliopistoissa ennen v. 1640. 2", *Historiallinen Arkisto 17*. Helsinki: Finnish Historical Society.
Göransson, Sven 1951: *De svenska studieresorna och religiösa kontrollen från reformationstiden till frihetstiden*. Uppsala universitets årsskrift 1951:8. Uppsala: Uppsala universitet.

Hakanen, Marko 2011: *Vallan verkostoissa. Per Brahe ja hänen klienttinsä 1600-luvun Ruotsin valtakunnassa.* Jyväskylä studies in humanities 157. Jyväskylä: Jyväskylän yliopisto.

Heininen, Simo 2007: "Tammelin, Lars (1669–1733) Turun piispa, Turun akatemian varakansleri, matematiikan professori", *Suomen kansallisbiografia 9.* Studia Biographica 3:9. Helsinki: The Finnish Literature Society.

Heininen, Simo, Nuorteva, Jussi 1981: "Finland". In: Jokipii, Mauno, Nummela, Ilkka (eds), *Ur nordisk kulturhistoria. Universitetsbesöken i utlandet före 1660.* Studia historica Jyväskyläensia 22,1. Jyväskylä: Jyväskylän yliopisto.

Kajanto, Iiro 2005: "Lund, David (1657–1729) Viipurin piispa, Växjön piispa, pyhien kielten professori, teologian professori", *Suomen kansallisbiografia 6.* Studia Biographica 3:6. Helsinki: The Finnish Literature Society.

Karonen, Petri 2006: "Oxenstierna, Axel (1583–1654) valtakunnankansleri, Kemiön vapaaherra, kreivi", *Suomen kansallisbiografia 7.* Studia Biographica 3:7. Helsinki: The Finnish Literature Society, pp. 386–389.

Klami, Hannu Tapani 2007: "Tigerstedt, Ericus (1640–1697) hovioikeuden asessori, lainopin professori, pyhien kielten professori", *Suomen kansallisbiografia 9.* Studia Biographica 3:9. Helsinki: The Finnish Literature Society, p. 787.

Klinge, Matti 1987: "Perustaminen ja tarkoitus", *Helsingin yliopisto 1640–1990 I. Kuninkaallinen Turun akatemia.* Helsinki: Helsingin yliopisto, Otava.

Laasonen, Pentti 2009: *Vanhan ja uuden rajamaastossa. Johan Gezelius vanhempi ja kulttuurivaikuttajana.* Historiallisia Tutkimuksia 245. Helsinki: The Finnish Literature Society.

Lagerstam, Liisa 2007: *A Noble Life: the Cultural Biography of Gabriel Kurck (1630–1712).* Suomalaisen tiedeakatemia toimituksia, Humaniora 349. Helsinki: Finnish Academy of Science and Letters.

Lagerstam, Liisa, Parland-von Essen, Jessica 2010: "Aatelin kasvatus". In: Hanska, Jussi, Vainio-Korhonen, Kirsi (ed.), *Suomen koulutuksen historia 1. Huoneentaulun maailma. Kasvatus ja koulutus Suomessa keskiajalta 1860-luvulle.* Suomalaisen Kirjallisuuden Seuran Toimituksia 1266:1. Helsinki: Suomalaisen Kirjallisuuden Seura.

Lagus, Vilhelm Gabriel 1832: *Åbo hofrätts historia I. Biographiska anteckningar om Åbo hofrätts presidenter och ledamöter; jemte förteckning öfver secreterare och advocatfiscaler därstedes intill den 12. nov. 1823 då Hofrätten firade sin andra secular-fest.* Helsingfors: J. C. Frenckell & Son.

Laine, Esko M. 2005: "Laurbecchius, Isaacus (noin 1677–1716) pietistiteologi, teologian tohtori", *Suomen kansallisbiografia 5.* Studia Biographica 3:5. Helsinki: The Finnish Literature Society, pp. 765–766.

Niléhn, Lars 1981: "Sverige". In: Jokipii, Mauno, Nummela, Ilkka (eds), *Ur nordisk kulturhistoria. Universitetsbesöken i utlandet före 1660.* Studia historica Jyväskyläensia 22,1. Jyväskylä: Jyväskylän yliopisto.

Niléhn, Lars 1981: "Universiteten efter reformationen". In: Jokipii, Mauno, Nummela, Ilkka (eds), *Ur nordisk kulturhistoria. Universitetsbesöken i utlandet före 1660.* Studia historica Jyväskyläensia 22,1. Jyväskylä: Jyväskylän yliopisto.

Niléhn, Lars H. 1983: *Peregrinatio academica. Det svenska samhället och de utrikes studieresorna under 1600-talet.* Bibliotheca historica Lundensis 54. Lund: Liber/ Gleerup.

Norrhem, Svante 1993: *Uppkomlingarna. Kanslitjänstemännen i 1600-talets Sverige och Europa.* Acta Universitatis Umensis, Umeå Studies in the Humanities 117. Stockholm: Almqvist & Wiksell.

Nuorteva, Jussi 1997: *Suomalaisten ulkomainen opinkäynti ennen Turun akatemian perustamista 1640.* Bibliotheca historica 27. Helsinki: Finnish Historical Society.

Nuorteva, Jussi 2005: "Lang, Jakob (1648–1716) Linköpingin piispa, Tallinnan piispa, Narvan superintendentti, teologian tohtori", *Suomen kansallisbiografia 5*. Studia Biographica 3:5. Helsinki: The Finnish Literature Society.

Ruoff, Eeva 2005: "Til-Landz, Elias (1640–1693) lääketieteen professori", *Suomen kansallisbiografia 6*. Studia Biographica 3:6. Helsinki: The Finnish Literature Society.

Salminen, Seppo J. 1978: *Enevaldus Svenonius I*. Suomen kirkkohistoriallisen seuran toimituksia 106. Helsinki: The Finnish Society of Church History.

Salminen, Seppo J. 1985: *Enevaldus Svenonius II (1664–1688)*. Suomen kirkkohistoriallisen seuran toimituksia 134. Helsinki: The Finnish Society of Church History.

Sarasti-Wilenius, Raija 1998: "De peregrinatione – Näkökulmia ulkomaan matkailuun Suomen latinankielisissä lähteissä", *Tieteessä tapahtuu* 16:1.

Sarasti-Wilenius, Raija 2015: *Dear Brother, Cracious Maecenas. Latin Letters of the Gyldenstolpe Brothers (1661–1680)*. Annales Academiae Scientiarum Fennicæ, humaniora 374. Helsinki: Finnish Academy of Science and Letters,

Stiernman, A. A. 1990 (1719): *Aboa literata. Turun akatemian kirjallisuus*. Suomennos Reijo Pitkäranta. Suomalaisen Kirjallisuuden Seuran Toimituksia 518. Helsinki: The Finnish Literature Society.

Strömberg, John 1987: "Ylioppilaat", *Helsingin yliopisto 1640–1990 I. Kuninkaallinen Turun akatemia*. Helsinki: Helsingin yliopisto & Otava.

Strömberg, John 1996: *Studenter, nationer och universitet. Studenternas härkomst och levnadsbanor vid Akademin i Åbo 1640–1808*. Skrifter utgivna av Svenska litteratursällskapet i Finland 601. Helsingfors: Svenska litteratursällskapet i Finland.

Tengström, Johan Jakob 1836: *Chronologiska Förteckningar och Anteckningar öfver Finska universitetets fordna procancellerer samt öfver faculteternas medlemmar och adjuncter, från universitetets stiftelse inemot dess andra sekularår*. Helsingfors: G. O. Wasenius.

Vallinkoski, J. 1962–1966: *Turun akatemian väitöskirjat I*. Helsingin yliopiston kirjaston julkaisuja 30. Helsinki: Helsingin yliopisto.

Vilkuna, Kustaa H. J. 2009: *Neljä ruumista*. Helsinki: Teos.

# List of Contributors

PIIA EINONEN, (http://orcid.org/0000-0003-4931-2657) Adjunct Professor of Finnish History, Department of History and Ethnology, University of Jyväskylä, Finland

JANNE HAIKARI, Research Fellow of Finnish History, Department of History and Ethnology, University of Jyväskylä, Finland

MARKO HAKANEN, (http://orcid.org/0000-0002-4214-960X) Research Fellow of Finnish History, Department of History and Ethnology, University of Jyväskylä, Finland

MIKKO HILJANEN, (http://orcid.org/0000-0003-3441-5354) Master of Arts of Finnish History, Department of History and Ethnology, University of Jyväskylä, Finland

PETRI KARONEN, (http://orcid.org/0000-0001-6090-5504) Professor of Finnish History, Department of History and Ethnology, University of Jyväskylä, Finland

ULLA KOSKINEN, (http://orcid.org/0000-0002-3430-9810) Research Fellow of Finnish History, School of Social Sciences and Humanities, University of Tampere, Finland and University of Jyväskylä, Finland

MIRKKA LAPPALAINEN, (0000-0002-5674-3597) Adjunct Professor of Finnish and Nordic History, University lecturer of Finnish and Nordic history, Department of Philosophy, History, Culture and Art Studies, University of Helsinki, Finland

OLLI MATIKAINEN, Adjunct Professor of Finnish History, Department of History and Ethnology, University of Jyväskylä, Finland

KUSTAA H. J. VILKUNA, Professor of Finnish History, Department of History and Ethnology, University of Jyväskylä, Finland

# Abstract

## Personal Agency at the Swedish Age of Greatness 1560–1720

Edited by Petri Karonen and Marko Hakanen

Internationally, the case of early modern Sweden is noteworthy because the state building process transformed a locally dispersed and sparsely populated area into a strongly centralized absolute monarchy and European empire at the beginning of the 17th century. This anthology provides fresh insights into the state-building process in Sweden. During this transitional period, many far-reaching administrative reforms were carried out, and the Swedish state developed into a prime example of the early modern 'power-state'.

The contributors approach Sweden's rise to greatness from the point of view of personal agency. In early modern studies, agency has long remained in the shadow of the study of structures and institutions. This novel approach enables us to expose the difficulties, setbacks and false steps that the administration had to deal with. State building was a more diversified and personalized process than has previously been assumed. Numerous individuals were also crucially important actors in the process, and that development itself was not straightforward progression at the macro-level but was intertwined with lower-level actors.

Each chapter in this volume employs partially different methods depending on the source material and subject. This means that both qualitative and quantitative material is combined, different ways of making sense of it (i.e. research traditions) are brought together and a multi-method design is used in analyzing source material. One of the central methods is the systematic use of previous biographical research. We want to give the individuals and their actions under discussion a background that reflects the contemporary structures of individual life cycles. With the existing biographical research, it is possible to create a comprehensive set of data that provides the general outlines of individual lives or the career tracks of various estates or social groups, and even to construct collective biographies of certain groups.

# Index of Names

Agrelius, Nicolaus Petri 232
Agricola, Mikael 93, 201
Allertz, Jakob 270
Anders Henriksson 257–258
Anders Pedersson 175
Andersson, Gudrun 220
Andreas Andreae 211
Arhusius, Bengt Joensson 237
Arvid Matsson 154–155
Asker, Björn 35, 38, 67, 115, 128, 148

Baaz, Måns 292
Banér, Axelsson 55
Banér, Gustav 57
Banér, Per 62–63, 98
Banér, Sten 57–58
Banér, Svante 74
Bapzihn, Georg Mikael 292
Barnes, Barry S. 19, 36
Becchius, Knut 292
Beetham, David 221, 234
Benick, Hans Nilsson 248, 254–263, 267–270
Berent Jönsson 252
Bergius, Nils 279, 291–292
Berndes, Johan 91
Bielke, Gunilla 55
Bielke, Hogenskild 55, 57–59, 91
Bielke, Johan Axelsson 55
Bielke, Nils 119
Bielke, Sigrid 197, 170, 173, 175
Bielke, Svante 59–60, 102
Bielke, Ture 55, 58
Bilefelt, Hans Hansson 252
Blomstedt, Yrjö 144–145, 147–151, 180, 197
Bochmöller, Johan 180
Bock, Knut 149, 153, 155
Boëthius, B. 91
Boije, Göran 59
Boije, Margareta 150
Bonde, Krister 124
Bonney, Richard 48, 54
Brahe, Abraham 60, 63
Brahe, Magnus 60, 63
Brahe, Per the elder 22, 53, 55, 57, 60, 62
Brahe, Per the younger 22, 26, 98–100, 105, 124, 126, 148, 150, 155
Bris, Erik Eriksson 94

Brommius, Lars (ennobled as Brommenstedt) 292
Browallius, Isak 292
Bure, Karl Månsson 252
Bureus, Olaus (Bure, Olof) 224, 233, 253–257, 259, 264, 266–267
Bååt, Erland 63
Bähr, Henrik 178
Böcke, Herman 147–148, 152

Caine, Barbara 22–23, 37
Carl Persson 176
Carpelan, Matthias Michelis 198, 210
Carstenius, Petter 282
Callia, Henrich 170
Callia, Påwal 167, 169, 170, 173–176, 178–179
Carpelan, Matthias Michelis 198, 210
Charles IX (Duke Charles) 8, 198, 210
Charles X Gustav 9, 64, 96, 229
Charles XI 9, 22, 64, 169
Chesnecopherus, Nils 59
Chronander, Jacobus Petri 233
Christier Månsson 180
Christian II of Denmark 50
Christina 9, 22, 47, 64, 66, 72, 220, 223, 278, 287
Cicero 49
Collins, James B. 85
Corte, Henrik 180
Creutz, Ernst Johan 129–130, 132, 137, 150
Creutz, Lorentz 124
Cromwell, Thomas 85
Curnovius, Johan 148

Dawson, John P. 144
De la Gardie, Axel Julius 172
De la Gardie, Jacob 63, 180
De la Gardie, Johan 117–119
De la Gardie, Magnus Gabriel 124
De la Gardie, Pontus 55–56
Dimberg, Sven (ennobled as Dimborg) 293
Duwall, Jacob 124, 126–129

Edén, Nils 54
Ehrensteen, Edvard 95
Eichman, Casper 228–229

Einonen, Piia 27, 115, 297
Emzenius, Jonas 292
Eric XIV 8, 22, 74, 53, 65, 70, 85, 88–92, 103, 194, 209, 211
Ericson(Wolke), Lars 54
Erik Hansson 104, 153–155
Erik Matsson 88–92
Eskilsson, Grels 172

Falander, Erik (ennobled as Tigerstedt) 285, 287
Figrelius, Olof 282
Fincke, Gustav 147, 152
Fincke, Gödik 147
Fleming, Claes (1592–1644) 62–63, 99, 250
Fleming, Claes (Eriksson) (1535–1597) 56, 95, 116, 201
Fleming, Claes Hermansson (d. 1616) 150
Fleming, Herman 149–150
Fleming, Lars 124
Florinus, Samuel 292
Forbus, Sofia Juliana 172
Fuchs, Stephan 19

Gabriel Påhlsson 152
Gavelius, Peter 253
Gezelius, Johan the elder 278, 291
Gezelius, Johan the younger 279, 282, 289, 291
Glete, Jan 32, 34, 55
Grip, Anders 292
Grip, Nils 292
Gode, Hans Hansson 167, 169–170, 173–174
Graan, Johan 122, 128, 135–137
Granberg, Ericus 176
Grass, Gustaf 285
Grass, Henning Johan 285
Grotius, Hugo 277
Grundelius, Arvid 292
Grundell, Jakob 251, 261, 267, 269
Gustaf Gustafsson af Wasaborg 228
Gustaf Hansson (Benick) 262
Gustavus Adolphus 8, 9, 16, 22, 60–64, 66, 116–120, 125, 150, 228, 249–250, 266, 275
Gustavus Vasa 8, 14, 15, 22, 47, 50–54, 56, 65, 85, 88–90, 92, 115, 131, 146–147, 165, 193–195, 197, 201, 208, 211, 223, 249, 254
Gyllenhielm, Carl 63
Gyllenstierna, Erik (1602–1657) 154

Gyllenstierna, Jöran 60
Gyllenstierna, Nils 58
Gyllenstierna, Nils (Göransson) 56
Gyldenstolpe, Daniel 284–285
Gyldenstolpe, Gabriel 284
Gyldenstolpe, Gustaf 284
Gyldenstolpe, Karl 284
Gyldenstolpe, Nils 284
Gyldenstolpe, Samuel 284–285

Hallenberg, Mats 34, 166, 204, 211–213
Halmenius, Erik 292
Hans Henriksson 266
Hans Johansson 178
Hemmersamin, Michael 293
Henricus Canuti 199–200, 204
Henricus Jacobi 199
Henricus Petri 202, 204
Henrik Isaksson 174
Hildebrand, Emil 52
Hockman, Tuula 210
Horn, Arvid 59, 124
Horn, Claes 63, 75
Horn, Gustaf 74, 167, 175
Horn, Henrik Claesson 95
Horn, Karl Henriksson 75, 199
Huldén, Lena 211
Humbla, Olof Pedersson 253, 266
Härkäpää, Ericus Matthiae 200
Höijer, Johan Hansson 238

Jacobus Erici 203
Jansson, Arne 248–249
Johan Henriksson 85, 92
Johan Persson 223
Johannes Michaelis 201–203
John III 8, 16, 22, 47, 51, 54–57, 68, 65, 70, 85, 88–92, 94–95, 103, 194, 197–199, 202, 205–206, 212
Jokipii, Mauno 180
Jonsson, Alexander 115, 118, 128
Jöns Henriksson 269
Jöran Jöransson 176
Jöran Thomasson 174

Karvonen, Lauri 264
Kauer, Ludbert 58, 60
Kaunismäki, Henri 264
Keckonius, Johannes 179
Kempe, Axel 287
Kempe, Daniel 227
Ketarmannus, Johan 279
Kinninmundt, Robert 293
Kiser, Edgar 19, 35–36

*Index of Names*

Kiuasmaa, Kyösti 203, 206, 212–213
Klingius, Johan 292
Klingius, Magnus 292
Kouvo, Markus Matsson 175
Kranck, Hans Eriksson 88, 93–95
Krister Simonsson 153
Krokius, Israel 292
Krook, Olaus Martini 213
Kruus, Mats 60
Kröger, Daniel 229
Kurck, Gabriel 280
Kurck, Jöns 277, 280
Kurck, Knut 124

Laine, Esko M. 202
Lamberg, Marko 249
Lars Henriksson 252
Laurbecchius, Isak 279, 282
Lehusen, Wellam (Wilhelm Leuhusen) 260, 261, 269
Leijonhufvud, Axel 57, 116
Leijonhufvud, Mauritz 59
Leijonhufvud, Sten Eriksson 53
Leppänen, Matti 174
Letto-Vanamo, Pia 149
Lilliecrona, Gustaf 124
Lithman, Jacob 226, 236
Lindberg, Folke 115–116, 269
Lindström, Peter 207, 213
Ludvigsson, Rasmus 89
Lundinus, Anders 292
Lytthraeus, Anders 152, 155

McLaren, John 143, 150
Magnus Eriksson (King) 49, 222, 252
Malmstedt, Göran 204
Marcus Gregorii 205, 213
Martinus Martin 293
Martinus Olai 199, 204
Matthaeus Matthiae 202–204, 212–213
Mathesius, Josef 176
Matthias Martini 202, 212–213
Mats Olafsson 176
Melartopaeus, Petrus Henrici 200
Mellin, Teofil (ennobled as Ehrenstierna) 293
Metstake, Reinhold 152
Michael I of Russia 99
Michel Olofsson 94
Mickel Abrahamsson 261
Munkthelius, Johan 282
Mörck, Elias 235, 237

Nils Börjesson 180
Nils Eriksson 269
Nicolaus, the Chaplain of Pertteli 198
Nidulius-Nidelberg, Ambrosius 287
Niléhn, Lars H. 282, 288, 290
Nilsson, Olof 254
Nilsson, Sven A. 34, 54–55
Norten, Casper 261

Odhner, C. T. 225–226
Olaus Nicolai 205
Olaus Petri 144
Oliveblad, Clemet Hansson 89
Olof Andersson 89
Olof Sverkersson 92, 94
Oxe, Harald 170
Oxenstierna, Axel 9, 22, 61–63, 66, 86–87, 94, 114, 117–118, 120, 143–144, 174, 219, 221–222, 249, 275, 277
Oxenstierna, Carl 74, 98
Oxenstierna, Gabriel Bengtsson 63–64
Oxenstierna, Gabriel Gustafsson 256
Oxenstierna, Johan 58, 60

Palmbaum, Ambrosius 89
Palmbaum, Zacharias 148
Persson, Jöran 85, 92–93
Persson, Ture 149
Petrellius, Nikolaus 149
Piper, Henrik 152
Pontelius, Johan 292
Posse, Göran Knutsson 57
Prytz, Hans 222
Pufendorf, Samuel 277

Queckfeldt, Bengt 287, 292
Queckfeldt, Gustaf (the elder) 287
Queckfeldt, Gustaf (the younger) 287, 292–293

Raam, Peder Nilsson 152
Raucka, Matthias Henrici 201
Reese, Johan Håkansson (Johannes Haquini Rhezelius) 227
Renvall, Pentti 55, 115–116
Ribbing, Bo 63
Ribbing, Erik 56–60
Ribbing, Peder 60
Ribbing, Seved 58–60
Riitta Matintytär of Halikko 154
Roberts, Michael 32, 54, 89–90
Roos, John E. 55
Rosander, Daniel 279

Roselius, Olof 292
Rosencrantz, Krister Nilsson 150–151
Rosenhane, Johan 151
Rosenhane, Schering 177
Rothovius, Isak 279
Ruuskanen, Jaakko 151
Ruuth, Jacob Abrahamsson 227
Ryning, Axel 59–60
Rålamb, Bror Andersson 126
Rålambsstierna, Magnus 154

Salakka, Antti 153
Samuelson, Jan 52, 58, 67
Sandberg, Robert 248
Sandström, Åke 248
Sansovino, Francesco 85
Sarcovius, Daniel 287
Saringius, Jacob 172
Scheiding, Filip 63
Schouten, Joost 293
Sierman, Lars 278
Sierman, Magnus 278
Sierman, Nils 278
Sigismund 8, 56, 59–61, 65, 86, 92, 94, 103, 116–117, 121, 124, 194, 197–198, 201–202, 205, 207–208, 252, 265
Sjödell, Ulf 67, 91
Skunck, Nils 266
Skytte (Schroderus), Johan Bengtsson 63–64, 85
Sneckenberg, Jakob 293
Sorolainen, Ericus Erici 200, 202–203, 210
Soop, Gustav 124
Soop, Matthias 74, 147–148
Sparre, Carl 127
Sparre, Erik 56–58, 103
Sparre, Erik Larsson 55
Sparre, Johan 74
Starbecchius, Israel 292
Sten Henriksson 146
Stenbock, Erik 57
Stenbock, Gustaf 63
Stenbock, Gustaf Olsson 54, 115
Stiernskiöld, Nils 63
Stiernsköld, Jöran 59–60
Strömberg-Back, Kerstin 57
Strömfelt, Johan Fagraeus 96
Sture, Svante 70
Suolahti, Gunnar 202
Svalenius, Ivan 84, 90, 103
Sven Elofsson 92
Sven Jönsson 252

Svenonius, Enevald 278–279, 283, 287–288
Sörndal, Olof 115

Taube, Bernhard 153–154
Tawast, Arvid Henriksson 93–95
Teet, Gregorius Martinti 99, 210
Tegel, Erik Jöransson 85
Thomas Ingonis 212
Thomas Laurentii 199–200
Tileman Abraham 266
Tillands, Erik 282
Tilly, Charles 17–18
Timme, Jochim 278
Tollet, Daniel 181
Tott, Claes Åkesson 56
Tranevardius, Erik Eriksson (Geete) 253–254
Trost, Matthias 251, 259, 266
Tulppo, Sipi 174–175
Tungel, Lars 97
Tungel, Nils 97–100
Tzander, Johan 292
Törning, Johan 292
Törnsköld, Jacob 127

Ulfsparre, Jöran 60
Unger, Daniel 292
Ungius, Peter 292
Utriainen, Pekka 146

Valentin Nilsson (Benick) 256, 260, 267, 270
Wanzonius, Johan 281
Weber, Max 19, 35–36, 144, 234, 249
Wellinus, Jakob 292
Welshuisen, Christian 257
Wenne, Johannes Jacobi 201
Wexionius, Mikael (ennobled as Gyldenstolpe) 277–278, 280, 282, 284, 288
Wildeman, Arvid Tönneson 117
Willandh, Zacharias 181
Willingshusen, Kristian 176
Winter, Christianus Henrici 211
Wisius, Mikael 282
Wittstock, Joakim 292
von Falkenberg, Melchior 129–130
Von Pyhy, Conrad 51, 85
Wrangel, Herman 116–117
Väänänen, Kyösti 195

Österberg, Eva 34, 155

# Index of Subjects

Administrative cultures 119–120, 225–226
Agency 19–20, passim.
Appointments
 – after studying abroad 279, 284–285, 287, 291
 Burgomasters (see also royal mayors) 251–254, 255–256, 247–270 (passim.)
 Clergy 15–16, 27, 193–213 (passim.)
 Councillors, secretaries, chancellors 48–49, 51–52, 58–60, 62–64, 86–87, 97–100
 Governors, governor generals, stewards 116–117, 119, 123–125
 Law-readers, judges 145–146
 Royal mayors (see also burgomasters) 27, 223–225, 219–238 (passim.)
Aristocracy 48–58, 65–66, 83, 86, 88–93, 100–101, 121, 125, 129, 145–150, 287

Bailiff 27, 29, 50, 125–126, 128–129, 131, 144, 149–152, 154, 165–186 (passim.), 194, 195, 203– 205, 226, 234
Biography 23–24, 48, 84–85
Bureaucracy 16, 83–84, 86–87, 90, 125, 165, 169, 250–251, 262–263, 277
Burgher 90, 153, 180–181, 219–238 (passim.), 247–270 (passim.), 285–286
Burgomaster, see also Royal Mayor 25, 27–28, 247–270 (passim.)

Centralization 13–16, 26, 55–56, 113, 118–125, 130–133, 144, 251, 298
Chancellor (of the Kingdom of Sweden) 22, 29, 59, 85, 87, 88, 120, 143, 221, 261, 275
Chaplain 198, 200–203, 205, 211
Clergy 14–16, 193–213 (passim.)
 Sons of clergymen studying abroad 285–286
Collective biography 23, 48, 84–85
Corruption 94–95, 173, 176, 179, 180, 223
Councillors of the Realm 26, 47–75 (passim.), 85–87, 88, 92, 96, 99–100
Court of Appeal 9, 17, 29, 31, 129, 145, 148–149, 149–154, 154–155, 222, 277, 287

Diplomacy 64, 90, 275, 280, 283
Donations 148, 167, 171

Estates 15, 17, 18, 21, 29, 67, 90, 122, 148, 171, 228, 230–231, 287–289

Fiefdom 47, 99
Friendship 50, 93

Government 14–17, 29, 53–54, 56, 61, 65–67, 85–88, 95–98, 100–101, 123–127, 130–131, 220–223, 247, 249–252, 263
Governor, county governor 25–26, 29, 113–137 (passim.), 147, 149–154, 170, 176, 181, 195, 219, 222–224, 226, 256, 287
Governor General 115–116, 119, 126, 219, 221, 224, 250, 262
Governor General (överståthållare, in Stockholm) 62–63, 115, 250
G-reat Reduction 9, 148, 167, 172, 284

Household 170–171, 260
House of Nobility 48

Information 15, 22–24, 50, 60, 83–85, 95–96, 98–99, 122–123, 131–133, 171, 173–174, 181
Interaction 17–23, 34, 65, 91, 145, 154, 156, 165–166, 168, 170–171, 175, 204–205, 230, 247–249, 250–251, 261, 262–263
Interregnum 62, 64

Judge 26–27, 29, 57, 59–60, 120, 122, 130–131, 143–158 (passim.), 197–198, 209, 254, 263

Kinship 50, 177

Law of King Christopher 50
Law-reader 143–144 (definition), 143–158 (passim.),
Legislation 47, 50, 219, 249
Legitimacy 150–151, 155, 169, 177, 179, 221–222, 234, 262
Lord High Chancellor 26, 86–87, 97–98, 102, 149, 224
Lutheranism 169, 200

303

Loyalty
  Councilors 49, 54, 57
  King´s secretaries 91, 100
  Stewards and Governors 116–117, 121, 123, 126–127, 131
  Pastors 197–201, 203, 206, 213
  Mayors and Burgomasters 227, 253, 258

Mayor 130, 180–181, see also "Royal Mayor".
Meritocracy 95

Network 17–19, 25–26, 60, 64–65, 83–85, 89, 91, 92–95, 95–101, 113, 117, 128, 180, 198, 201, 204, 251–252, 260, 282, 289
Nobility 16–17, 47–48, 50, 53–58, 58–64, 66–67, 86–87, 90–101, 125, 128, 132, 167, 170–177, 180, 211, 278, 283–286

Office-holders 17, 25, 55–56, 194, 198, 203, 206, 212, 247–270 (passim.), 283

Parish 16, 29, 146, 165–168, 173–176, 193–213 (passim.)
Pastor 169–170, 176, 193–213 (passim.)
Patriarchality 170–171, 228, 148
Patronage 84–87, 95–101, 148
Privileges
  Nobility 47, 54, 57, 62, 86, 90–91, 96–97
  Cities, towns 223, 226
Privy Council, also the Council of the Realm 15, 26, 29, 47, 49–50, 47–75 (passim.), 89–87, 88–90, 95–99, 143, 255–256, 258
Profession 16–17, 33, 65–67, 85, 144–145, 148, 154–155, 166–167, 247, 262–263, 276–277
Prosopography 23, 48, 196

Rational choice theory 19–20, 36
Reciprocity 49, 91, 93–95, 100, 144, 222
Reformation 15–16, 27, 51–52, 90, 100, 144, 193–195, 201–202, 208
  counter-reformation 278, 288
Reforms 86–88, 100–101, 118–120, 143–145, 166, 202, 225–226, 249–250, 255, 260–263, 275
Royal Mayor, see also burgomaster 27, 219–220 (definition), 219–238 (passim.), 255–256, 247–270 (passim.)
Rural police chief (länsman) 168, 174

Secretaries 25–26, 50, 53–54, 58, 64, 50, 64, 83–106 (passim.)
Social network 25–26, 64–65, 83–85, 92–95, 98–100, 204
State building 13–14, 17–23, 25, 74, 66, 90, 113, 130–133, 169–170, 177, 193, 204–207, 249, 255–256
Steward, see also governor 25–26, 29, 52, 115–118 (the steward system), 113–137 (passim.)
Student 275–294 (passim.)

Taxes 118–119, 121, 131, 167–170, 178–181, 202–203, 213, 220–223, 230, 257–260, 267
  Collecting process 171–176
Tax collectors 167, 171–176, 182, 257
The Riksdag (The Diet) 202, 209, 228, 260–261
The Instrument of Government 9, 16–17, 75, 121, 222
The Royal Chancellery 85–87, 97–100
Town law 222–223, 252, 262

Vicar 151, 176, 179

## Studia Fennica Ethnologica

**Memories of My Town**
*The Identities of Town Dwellers and Their Places in Three Finnish Towns*
Edited by Anna-Maria Åström, Pirjo Korkiakangas & Pia Olsson
Studia Fennica Ethnologica 8
2004

**Passages Westward**
Edited by Maria Lähteenmäki & Hanna Snellman
Studia Fennica Ethnologica 9
2006

**Defining Self**
*Essays on emergent identities in Russia Seventeenth to Nineteenth Centuries*
Edited by Michael Branch
Studia Fennica Ethnologica 10
2009

**Touching Things**
*Ethnological Aspects of Modern Material Culture*
Edited by Pirjo Korkiakangas, Tiina-Riitta Lappi & Heli Niskanen
Studia Fennica Ethnologica 11
2008

**Gendered Rural Spaces**
Edited by Pia Olsson & Helena Ruotsala
Studia Fennica Ethnologica 12
2009

Laura Stark
**The Limits of Patriarchy**
*How Female Networks of Pilfering and Gossip Sparked the First Debates on Rural Gender Rights in the 19th-century Finnish-Language Press*
Studia Fennica Ethnologica 13
2011

**Where is the Field?**
*The Experience of Migration Viewed through the Prism of Ethnographic Fieldwork*
Edited by Laura Hirvi & Hanna Snellman
Studia Fennica Ethnologica 14
2012

Laura Hirvi
**Identities in Practice**
*A Trans-Atlantic Ethnography of Sikh Immigrants in Finland and in California*
Studia Fennica Ethnologica 15
2013

Eerika Koskinen-Koivisto
**Her Own Worth**
*Negotiations of Subjectivity in the Life Narrative of a Female Labourer*
Studia Fennica Ethnologica 16
2014

## Studia Fennica Folkloristica

**Narrating, Doing, Experiencing**
*Nordic Folkloristic Perspectives*
Edited by Annikki Kaivola-Bregenhøj, Barbro Klein & Ulf Palmenfelt
Studia Fennica Folkloristica 16
2006

Mícheál Briody
**The Irish Folklore Commission 1935–1970**
*History, ideology, methodology*
Studia Fennica Folkloristica 17
2008

Venla Sykäri
**Words as Events**
*Cretan Mantinádes in Performance and Composition*
Studia Fennica Folkloristica 18
2011

**Hidden Rituals and Public Performances**
*Traditions and Belonging among the Post-Soviet Khanty, Komi and Udmurts*
Edited by Anna-Leena Siikala & Oleg Ulyashev
Studia Fennica Folkloristica 19
2011

**Mythic Discourses**
*Studies in Uralic Traditions*
Edited by Frog, Anna-Leena Siikala & Eila Stepanova
Studia Fennica Folkloristica 20
2012

Cornelius Hasselblatt
**Kalevipoeg Studies**
*The Creation and Reception of an Epic*
Studia Fennica Folkloristica 21
2016

**Genre – Text – Interpretation**
*Multidisciplinary Perspectives on Folklore and Beyond*
Edited by Kaarina Koski, Frog & Ulla Savolainen
Studia Fennica Folkloristica 22
2016

## Studia Fennica Historica

**Modernisation in Russia since 1900**
Edited by Markku Kangaspuro & Jeremy Smith
Studia Fennica Historica 12
2006

SEIJA-RIITTA LAAKSO
**Across the Oceans**
*Development of Overseas Business Information Transmission 1815–1875*
Studia Fennica Historica 13
2007

**Industry and Modernism**
*Companies, Architecture and Identity in the Nordic and Baltic Countries during the High-Industrial Period*
Edited by Anja Kervanto Nevanlinna
Studia Fennica Historica 14
2007

CHARLOTTA WOLFF
**Noble conceptions of politics in eighteenth-century Sweden (ca 1740–1790)**
Studia Fennica Historica 15
2008

**Sport, Recreation and Green Space in the European City**
Edited by Peter Clark, Marjaana Niemi & Jari Niemelä
Studia Fennica Historica 16
2009

**Rhetorics of Nordic Democracy**
Edited by Jussi Kurunmäki & Johan Strang
Studia Fennica Historica 17
2010

**Fibula, Fabula, Fact**
*The Viking Age in Finland*
Edited by Joonas Ahola & Frog with Clive Tolley
Studia Fennica Historica 18
2014

**Novels, Histories, Novel Nations**
*Historical Fiction and Cultural Memory in Finland and Estonia*
Edited by Linda Kaljundi, Eneken Laanes & Ilona Pikkanen
Studia Fennica Historica 19
2015

JUKKA GRONOW & SERGEY ZHURAVLEV
**Fashion Meets Socialism**
*Fashion industry in the Soviet Union after the Second World War*
Studia Fennica Historica 20
2015

SOFIA KOTILAINEN
**Literacy Skills as Local Intangible Capital**
*The History of a Rural Lending Library c. 1860–1920*
Studia Fennica Historica 21
2016

**Continued Violence and Troublesome Pasts**
*Post-war Europe between the Victors after the Second World War*
Edited by Ville Kivimäki and Petri Karonen
Studia Fennica Historica 22
2017

**Personal Agency at the Swedish Age of Greatness 1560-1720**
Edited by Petri Karonen & Marko Hakanen
Studia Fennica Historica 23
2017

PASI IHALAINEN
**The Springs of Democracy**
*National and Transnational Debates on Constitutional Reform in the British, German, Swedish and Finnish Parliaments, 1917–19*
Studia Fennica Historica 24
2017

## Studia Fennica Anthropologica

**On Foreign Ground**
*Moving between Countries and Categories*
Edited by Marie-Louise Karttunen & Minna Ruckenstein
Studia Fennica Anthropologica 1
2007

**Beyond the Horizon**
*Essays on Myth, History, Travel and Society*
Edited by Clifford Sather & Timo Kaartinen
Studia Fennica Anthropologica 2
2008

TIMO KALLINEN
**Divine Rulers in a Secular State**
Studia Fennica Anthropologica 3
2016

## Studia Fennica Linguistica

**Minimal reference**
*The use of pronouns in Finnish and Estonian discourse*
Edited by Ritva Laury
Studia Fennica Linguistica 12
2005

Antti Leino
**On Toponymic Constructions as an Alternative to Naming Patterns in Describing Finnish Lake Names**
Studia Fennica Linguistica 13
2007

**Talk in interaction**
*Comparative dimensions*
Edited by Markku Haakana, Minna Laakso & Jan Lindström
Studia Fennica Linguistica 14
2009

**Planning a new standard language**
*Finnic minority languages meet the new millennium*
Edited by Helena Sulkala & Harri Mantila
Studia Fennica Linguistica 15
2010

Lotta Weckström
**Representations of Finnishness in Sweden**
Studia Fennica Linguistica 16
2011

Terhi Ainiala, Minna Saarelma & Paula Sjöblom
**Names in Focus**
*An Introduction to Finnish Onomastics*
Studia Fennica Linguistica 17
2012

**Registers of Communication**
Edited by Asif Agha & Frog
Studia Fennica Linguistica 18
2015

Kaisa Häkkinen
**Spreading the Written Word**
*Mikael Agricola and the Birth of Literary Finnish*
Studia Fennica Linguistica 19
2015

**Linking Clauses and Actions in Social Interaction**
Edited by Ritva Laury, Marja Etelämäki, Elizabeth Couper-Kuhlen
Studia Fennica Linquistica 20
2017

## Studia Fennica Litteraria

**Aino Kallas**
*Negotiations with Modernity*
Edited by Leena Kurvet-Käosaar & Lea Rojola
Studia Fennica Litteraria 4
2011

**The Emergence of Finnish Book and Reading Culture in the 1700s**
Edited by Cecilia af Forselles & Tuija Laine
Studia Fennica Litteraria 5
2011

**Nodes of Contemporary Finnish Literature**
Edited by Leena Kirstinä
Studia Fennica Litteraria 6
2012

**White Field, Black Seeds**
*Nordic Literacy Practices in the Long Nineteenth Century*
Edited by Anna Kuismin & M. J. Driscoll
Studia Fennica Litteraria 7
2013

Lieven Ameel
**Helsinki in Early Twentieth-Century Literature**
*Urban Experiences in Finnish Prose Fiction 1890–1940*
Studia Fennica Litteraria 8
2014

**Novel Districts**
*Critical Readings of Monika Fagerholm*
Edited by Kristina Malmio & Mia Österlund
Studia Fennica Litteraria 9
2016

Elise Nykänen
**Mysterious Minds**
*The Making of Private and Collective Consciousness in Marja-Liisa Vartio's Novels*
Studia Fennica Litteraria 10
2017

www.ingramcontent.com/pod-product-compliance
Lightning Source LLC
Chambersburg PA
CBHW080800300426
44114CB00020B/2781